Oil and Gas M&A

A Practical Handbook, Second Edition

Consulting Editors **Marc Hammerson** and **John C LaMaster**

Consulting editors
Marc Hammerson and John C LaMaster, Akin Gump Strauss Hauer & Feld LLP

Managing director
Sian O'Neill

Oil and Gas M&A, A Practical Handbook, Second Edition
is published by

Globe Law and Business Ltd
3 Mylor Close
Horsell
Woking
Surrey GU21 4DD
United Kingdom
Tel: +44 20 3745 4770
www.globelawandbusiness.com

Oil and Gas M&A, A Practical Handbook, Second Edition

ISBN 9781787421486
EPUB ISBN 9781787421493
Adobe PDF ISBN 9781787421509
Mobi ISBN 9781787421516

FSC
www.fsc.org
MIX
Paper from responsible sources
FSC® C013604

Table of contents

Introduction

Paul Bannister
Mark W Llamas
GMP FirstEnergy

The global M&A and acquisition and divestment (A&D) market has, over the last 10 years, moved through a number of phases which have been influenced by multiple factors, including:

- the availability of capital;
- the growth of unconventional resource exploitation;
- the reaction to the Macondo oil spill in the Gulf of Mexico;
- social and political unrest in key producing regions;
- the acquisition strategy of Asian national oil companies; and
- the strategy and behaviour of the Organisation of the Petroleum Exporting Countries.

However, the key factor affecting both the appetite to transact and the ability to do so, and hence influencing absolute deal flow, is commodity pricing and in particular price volatility. Rapid price spikes and dramatic falls can lead to divergent price expectations between buyers and sellers, thereby presenting a fundamental barrier to agreement on deal value.

1. Impact of 2014 commodity price shock

The commodity price shock in mid-2014, when supply growth outpaced demand, has had a profound and long-lasting impact on global M&A and A&D markets. Unlike in previous downturns, commodity prices failed to bounce and recover quickly into long-term consensus ranges and buyers remained cautious, such that a significant gap developed between the price expectation of sellers and the prices being offered by buyers. In common with previous periods of price volatility, rather than transacting outside long-term consensus price ranges, market participants selected, where possible, to defer activity. The extended and well-documented downturn led to many stalled transactions and frustrated the typical portfolio management initiatives of E&P players which depend upon industry transactions to pursue growth and diversification, manage risk and capital exposure, attract specific expertise to particular projects, seek liquidity/exit strategies for shareholders or simply manage large portfolios to focus human and capital resources. For many, deferring transactions for an extended period ceased to be a viable option and buyers and sellers had to explore creative commercial solutions to bridge the valuation gap and stimulate activity. Despite the recent improvement in commodity prices, ongoing price uncertainty persists and current backwardation in the market has resulted in buyers and sellers continuing to adopt more creative solutions within traditional deal structures.

Figure 1. Brent crude and forward curves

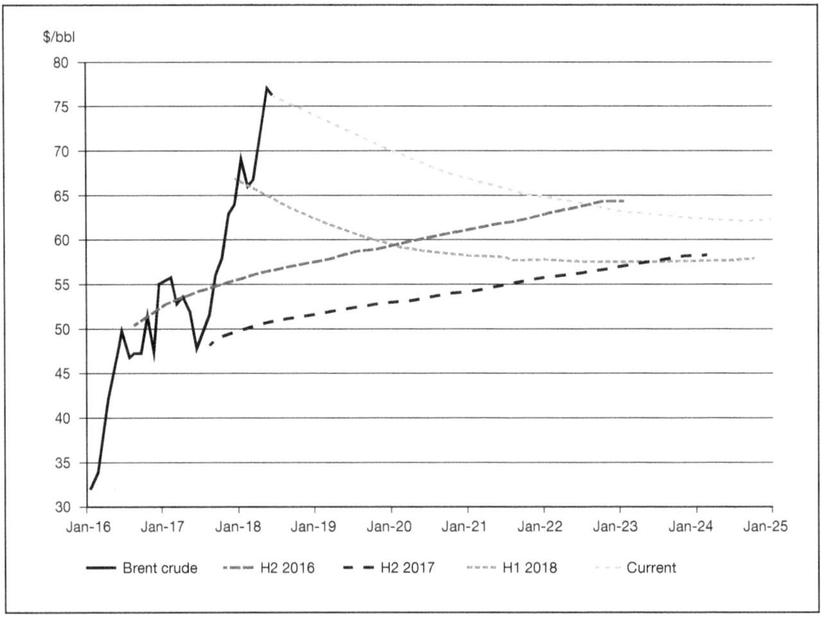

2. Current trends

As we write this introduction, Brent oil price is once again trading above $70/bbl (its highest level since the 2014 downturn) and there is evidence of a reawakening in the global M&A and A&D markets, with encouraging levels of activity continuing into 2018.

Calculated implied long-term price assumptions from recent disclosed deals also indicate some confidence returning to the markets and it is clear that many feel prices will not return, in the near term, to the low levels seen in the current cycle. The acceptance of a 'lower for longer' cycle has seen the sector make profound adjustments to spending levels, but has also seen the implementation of positive cost and operational efficiencies. While the sector has had to adapt quickly to the new commodity price environment, there is also some relief that the alternate 'lower forever' scenarios predicted by some were overly pessimistic.

The recent recovery in commodity pricing has led to improved sentiment in the debt and equity capital markets. During the downturn, private equity moved quickly to exploit the funding gap in the market although its focus was limited to a small number of regions outside North America. The North Sea (dominated by the UK and Norwegian sectors) has been a particular focus area and in 2017 the proportion of global M&A and A&D occurring in the North Sea increased from historic levels of 2% to 3% to some 15%.

Figure 2. Transaction market by region

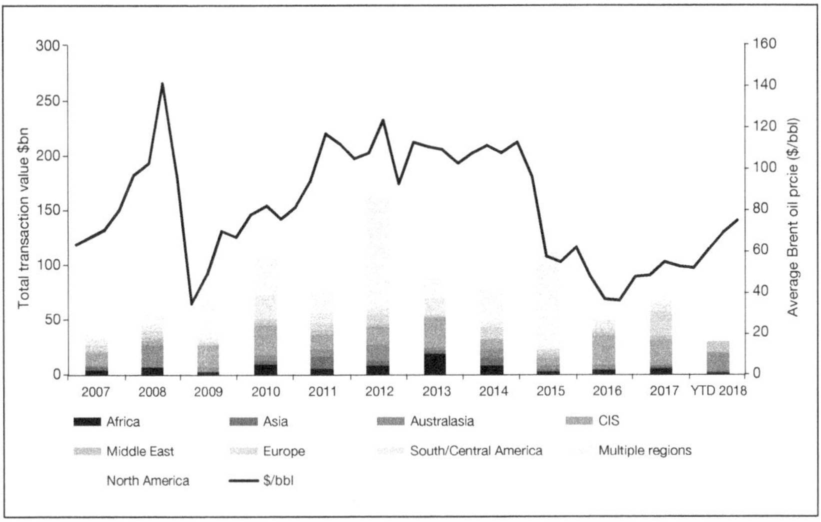

Source: IHS Markit

Figure 3. Transaction market, regional change

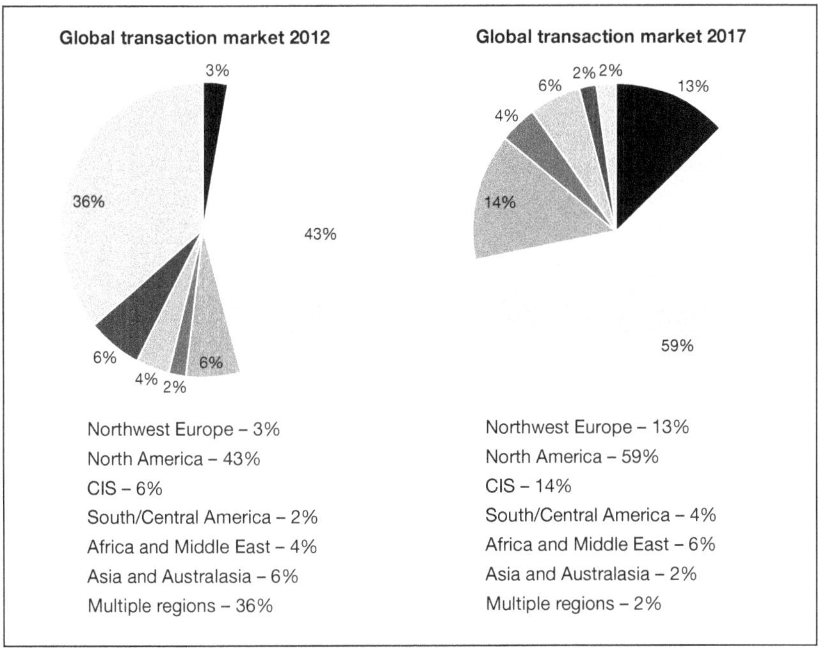

Source: IHS Markit

Following a dramatic reduction in interest from the equity capital markets in late 2014/early 2015, the appetite to deploy capital has gathered momentum. At this stage, capital appears to be flowing back to the sector on a selective basis, initially supporting lower-risk opportunities. The availability of more diverse sources of capital is helping to fuel increased transaction activity.

Figure 4. AIM exploration and production financing – past 5 years

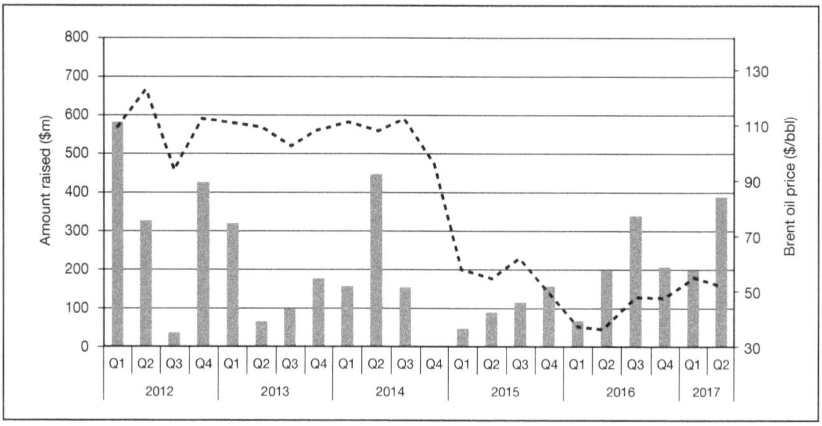

Source: GMP FirstEnergy/ LSE

3. Contrasting downturn cycles and their impact on global M&A and A&D

The downturn in M&A and A&D activity associated with the global financial crisis in 2008 actually started some months earlier, when the crude oil price spiked to a peak of $147/bbl. Buyer and seller negotiations were hampered by this volatility in crude pricing and further complicated by the precipitous fall to levels below $35/bbl by the end of the year, at which point deal flow had almost ground to a halt. From this low point, however, prices bounced sharply, recovering much of the lost ground within six to nine months and continuing to rise steadily to levels in excess of $100/bbl. The recovery allowed companies to reconsider transactions and the initial increase in activity was dominated by corporate transactions (some hostile in nature), as companies with stronger balance sheets targeted those weakened in the aftermath of the financial crisis. By 2010, crude prices had returned to consensus ranges and the proportion of asset deals increased and total deal flow exceeded historic levels. Active buyers during this period included Asian buyers, European gas utilities, majors and large independents. Majors took advantage of the more robust markets to rationalise portfolios by selling more mature assets and reinvesting in high-impact exploration, large-scale liquefied natural gas and unconventional resources.

The 2008 cycle mirrored previous downturns and many anticipated that the 2014 cycle would follow a similar pattern. Following an initial recovery, however, prices hit a ceiling fluctuating in the mid-$40/bbl to mid $50/bbl range as concerns over a global production glut persisted. Without exploring the fundamentals behind the current cycle, the key factor in terms of deal flow has been the longer wave

Figure 5. Transaction market by deal type

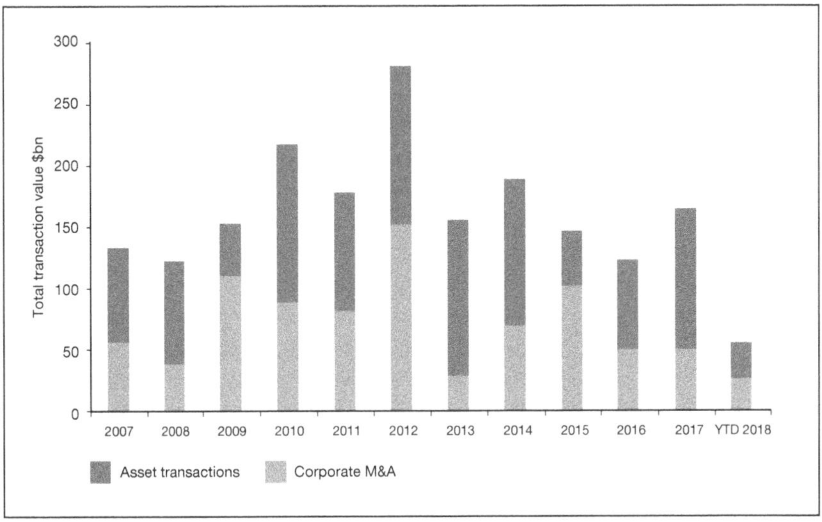

Source: IHS Markit

length and the lack of confidence in price direction. In order to kick-start deal flow, buyers and sellers have therefore had to take a more creative approach to deal structure, adopting new commercial and legal structures.

4. How more creative deals are being structured and the additional complexity and importance of legal and commercial documentation

As described previously, seller price expectations have been governed by anticipation and hope that price levels will recover, but are also tied to some degree to internal valuations. Given that valuations were established during a more favourable commodity environment, sellers have had to consider the impact of associated writedowns. Buyers, by contrast, have had to factor in the risk that prices will remain 'lower for longer' and/or the impact of cost inflation should commodity prices recover. Buyers have therefore had limited ability to align their commodity price forecasts with sellers and justify a mutually acceptable valuation for both their investors and the seller.

Rather than sell in to a low value deal, sellers have sought to reduce costs, re-negotiate contract terms and 'hold out' for improved conditions – all of which has led to an increase in stalled deals and a general slowdown in transaction activity. In the absence of more traditional sources of finance, M&A and A&D initiatives became one of the only ways of effectively funding projects and, under the challenging conditions, led to some opportunistic bidding by buyers seeking to exploit perceived seller weakness.

In the past, smaller and mid-sized companies have been able to more easily access equity and debt via the capital markets; however, in the post-2014 period this supply of capital was severely restricted. As a result, alternative sources of finance have had to be pursued, including private equity, trader pre-payment contracts, service company and vendor finance. The differing nature, risk profile, return requirements and demands from these 'alternative' sources of finance have contributed to the recent evolution of deal structures, causing a shift of risk between buyer and seller in the form of an increase in deferred and contingent elements and decommissioning liability retention.

The increased adoption and acceptance of deferred and contingent elements have enabled sellers to realise and report an acceptable headline consideration in line with internal holding values, and in some cases continued exposure to an asset's cash flow or 'upside potential', while also allowing buyers a means to justify utilisation of more aggressive assumptions related to factors including forward price and operational risk. We have seen a range of payment mechanisms implemented to this effect with contingent elements consisting of performance and/or operational milestones, commodity price kickers, royalty and revenue streams, conditions that introduce carry repayments, excess expenditure recovery via disproportionate profit share and options to acquire additional interests, as well as more straightforward deferred payments, with the transaction consideration paid in time-specified tranches.

Transaction markets in more mature basins have over the past two years seen a marked shift in decommissioning liability retention among some of the larger incumbent players. While this can perhaps partly be attributed to changes in legislation, there also appears to have been a recognition among sellers that there are mutual benefits in allowing niche players to invest in these assets, leveraging their contrasting capital allocation criteria and their ability to deploy specific expertise, operate on a lower-cost basis or bring more focus and resources to particular assets. This has led to more flexibility in this area of deal structuring and an increase in vendor retention of decommissioning liabilities (albeit with liabilities in most cases capped at a pre-determined estimate).

We have also observed an increased number of transactions executed via service company vendor finance, with these groups seeking to deploy assets and resources (eg, drilling rigs, well management, chemical provision and subsea infrastructure) and proving willing to accept the increased risk incurred with deferred and contingent payments linked to asset performance, or by effectively taking a direct interest in projects in return for these services.

5. Summary

Having previously mentioned 'lower for longer' and 'lower forever', we should now reference the third and final buzzword from the current cycle: the 'new normal' is a term which is increasingly used to describe some of the behaviours and strategies emerging as companies adapt to the new price and cost environment. With new commercial and legal strategies being deployed in the sector, we think that the publication of a second edition of the *Oil and Gas M&A Practical Handbook* is therefore very timely, and we trust that readers will benefit from the excellent insights and best practices described in the following chapters.

Valuation

Christopher R K Moore
Moyes & Co, Inc

1. Introduction

The upstream oil and gas industry operates in an environment of significant technical risks and uncertainties. An individual exploration well may have a probability of success as low as 10% or even less, with the complementary chance of failure 90% or more. Estimates of the size of the accumulation to be discovered may differ by two or even three orders of magnitude between realistic downside and upside estimates. These risks and uncertainties are reduced through the lifecycle of an asset (discovery, appraisal, development and production). Nevertheless an accurate account of the economic performance of an asset is not available until it is abandoned.

The challenge in determining the fair market value (FMV) of individual assets or portfolios of assets is twofold. First, the various risks and uncertainties must be evaluated rigorously using all of the available data. Second, investors are risk averse, and the value must be reduced from a technical risk-weighted value to a certain equivalent amount, to take into account risk aversion.

The risk aversion shown by investors is not just about the possibility of failure (a total loss), but more generally about uncertainty. The term 'risk' can be used for the probability of success or failure (like an on-off switch), to distinguish it from 'uncertainty', meaning the range of any variable (like a volume control). Such variables can be characterised using a probability distribution, from which representative points can be taken. Important characteristics of such distributions are their shapes and widths.

A further characteristic of oil and gas assets is that production from any particular asset inevitably declines through time. No amount of man-made intervention can do more than delay the inevitable decline from the peak production rate. Thus, valuation approaches used in the manufacturing sector based on continuous or growing production are generally inappropriate for valuing firms in the upstream sector.

2. Reserves and resource classifications

In order to capture appropriately the risks and uncertainties in the performance of upstream assets, it is useful to start with a resource classification system. The most recent, comprehensive and most widely used classification system is the petroleum resources management system promulgated by the Society of Petroleum Engineers (SPE), the American Association of Petroleum Geologists, the World Petroleum

Council and the Society of Petroleum Evaluation Engineers (SPEE).[1] The framework is shown in Figure 1.

Figure 1. Petroleum resources management system – a resources classification framework

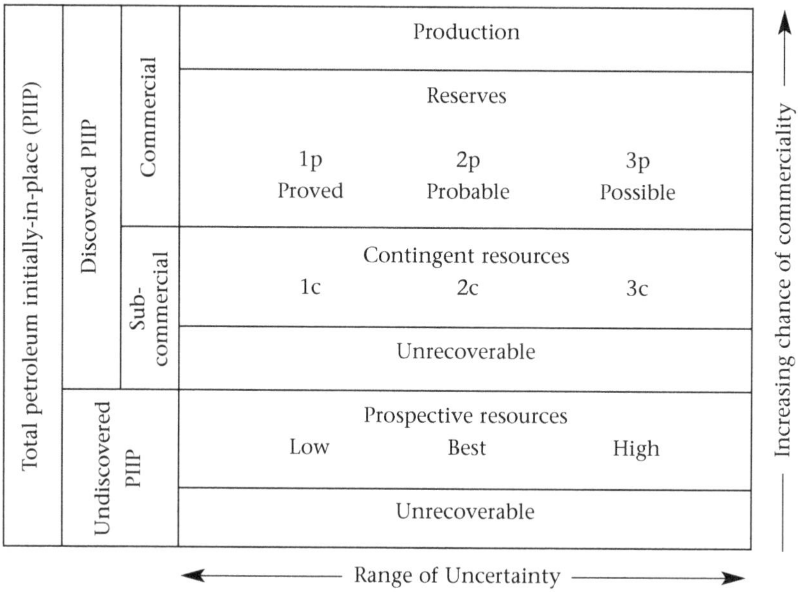

Note that the quantitative uncertainty is captured using three points: a measure of central tendency plus high and low estimates. Both statistical and deterministic treatments are acceptable, with the low estimate being represented by the 90th percentile, denoted P90, and the high estimate being represented by the 10th percentile, P10. Sometimes, especially in the context of exploration in the oil industry, this convention used to be, and occasionally still is, reversed. However, it is usually apparent from the context if the P90 quoted is the value exceeded only 10% of the time, rather than being exceeded 90% of the time. A further convention is that the central estimate quoted is usually the median, denoted P50, rather than the mean. Since the probability distributions of resources or reserves tend to be skewed (and are frequently treated as lognormal), the mean is larger than the P50. In evaluating exploration opportunities the mean value is often quoted rather than the P50.

The other terms in widespread use arise from the fortuitous alliteration of the adjectives used to indicate different degrees of certainty. Thus 1P or 'proved' is used for the low estimate which is reasonably certain to be exceeded. 2P, or 'proved' plus

1 Petroleum resources management system, approved by the SPE Board in March 2007, available free at www.spe.org. A useful companion, Guidelines for Application of the Petroleum Resources Management System, released in November 2011, is also available.

'probable', is the term used for the central estimate. 3P, or 'proved' plus 'probable' plus 'possible', is the term used for the high estimate, which, by analogy, is reasonably certain not to be exceeded. A further convention of note is the use of P1, P2 and P3 for, respectively, the individual proved, probable and possible increments. When the category of contingent resources was added, the same concepts were used with the substitution of the letter C for the letter P (eg, the high estimate is denoted 3C, equal to the sum C1+C2+C3). 'Contingent resources' are resources that have at least one contingency that must be satisfied or removed before they can be regarded as reserves. Associated with contingent resources is a probability that the contingency will go away, although a value for this probability is not always provided. The likelihood that the contingency will be resolved may be very high – for example, merely formal approval of the submitted development plan by the host government. However, it may also be much lower where there are technical or commercial obstacles to be overcome (its complement therefore being a significant chance of the asset never being developed).

Undiscovered, or prospective, resources are frequently estimated using probabilistic techniques. Thus, although the formal classifications refer to low, best and high estimates, pre-drill estimates are often quoted using the usual percentiles, P10, P50 and P90. Note that the SPE convention requires the median to be used as the 'best estimate' although some (including this author) do not like this term to be applied to the median estimate. Prospective resources, like contingent resources, have an associated probability of being developed. Moreover, one should distinguish between the probability of making a discovery regardless of size, and the probability of making a discovery of sufficient size to be commercial. The distinction becomes important where there is a significant likelihood of there being a sub-commercial accumulation. There is no standard terminology for chances of success, and it is not always clear from the context. The notation Ps or P_S can be used for either. One sometimes sees 'geological chance factor' and 'economic chance factor' for, respectively, the probabilities of a discovery regardless of size and a discovery larger than the minimum size that justifies development, but this usage is not universal.

Not included in the basic petroleum resources management system classification, but important to valuation methodology, is the status of reserves within each category. Each reserve category (P1, P2 and P3) may be further subdivided into developed and undeveloped reserves. 'Proved developed producing' (PDP) reserves are, as the name implies, proved reserves that are producible from wells which have already been drilled and are already producing. 'Proved undeveloped' (PUD) reserves are proved reserves for which the wells have not yet been drilled. Two more sub-categories, usually of much less importance in terms of the volumes in the category, are 'proved shut-in' (capable of production but artificially prevented from so doing) and 'proved behind pipe' (in a zone that is not yet completed to allow production, but from an existing wellbore). These two categories may be combined as 'proved developed not producing' (PDNP). By analogy, similar categories may be evaluated for probable and possible reserves (P2DP, P3DP, etc.).

3. Background issues

Before discussing valuation methods in more detail, two important observations may provide useful background. First, FMVs depend on how participants in the market value assets; that is, they depend on industry practice, regardless of whether that practice is theoretically sound. A useful source of information about industry practice is an annual survey by the SPEE.[2] Second, there are systematic differences between US practice and practice elsewhere in the world. These differences arise primarily from three factors: the organisation of the industry, historical stock exchange reporting requirements and tax treatment.

Private ownership of minerals rights in the United States is not in itself the cause of differences in valuation approach. However, private ownership allows for the existence of relatively small leases, frequently smaller than the areal extent of an individual oil or gas field. In contrast, contract areas outside the United States are usually larger than typical field sizes. Moreover, under most host government instruments there is compulsory unitisation of fields that cross contract area boundaries, and consent to produce oil and gas typically requires government approval of a development plan for the entire field. Valuations of non-US assets therefore typically involve the evaluation of interests in fields, carried out at the level of the whole field. In contrast, US valuations typically involve the separate evaluation of interests in individual wells. Although one might expect the two approaches to yield the same results, in practice there can be differences due to at least two effects. First, there may be particular reporting rules or conventions relating to well spacing that may limit the number of wells that may be regarded as PUDs even if there are reasonably certain reserves in additional well locations beyond those allowed. Second, there is a statistical issue called aggregation. For example, the sum of the proved reserves estimates for each of a number of separate wells is less than the proved reserves estimate for the wells in aggregate (unless they are totally dependent, which is unlikely). Although petroleum resources management system guidelines allow statistical aggregation at the field, property or project level, in practice:

- this is not always done; and
- if reported separately because ownership is different, the sum of individual wells in a field will not equal the field total, implying an understatement of each participant's share.

The potential effect of stock exchange reporting requirements is more insidious. In the United States, the rules of the Securities and Exchange Commission prohibited, prior to 2010, disclosure of unproved reserves. Although modern industry decision analysis practice has long been to base investment decisions and the like on central estimates of future performance, considerable time and effort were necessarily spent reporting according to the Securities and Exchange Commission

2 SPEE, Thirty-Second Annual Survey of Parameters Used in Property Evaluation, June 2013. The survey was responded to by 119 professionals, 94% of whom were members of SPEE. The scope of the respondents' experience may be judged from the following statistics: 59% of respondents each had, in the preceding year, valued properties with a total value exceeding $250 million, and 34% had each valued properties with a total value exceeding $1 billion.

rules. In other jurisdictions which allowed or encouraged reporting 2P reserves, the same time and effort were directed at the central estimates, with the results scaled back to get to the more conservative 1P result. There is anecdotal evidence, for example, that the same best fit extrapolation of an individual well's production decline curve would be used either to determine the proved reserves or to determine the 2P reserves, depending on the reporting requirements. Moreover, performance comparisons of US listed oil companies relied upon proved reserves alone. The combined effect of the methodology and performance reporting differences was, at least in this author's opinion, sufficient to result in an over-statement of proved reserves, and particularly PUDs. To compensate, as is discussed later, the value of PUDs in the United States has tended to be discounted much more than their 'reasonably certain' status would suggest is appropriate.

The final difference between US practice and practice elsewhere in the world is that US evaluations frequently ignore US corporate income tax. This important difference is discussed in more detail in a subsequent section.

4. Evaluation basics

The most widely used and preferred method for valuing oil and gas interests is discounted cash-flow analysis. This form of analysis was the method preferred by 92% of respondents in the most recent SPEE survey. Discounted cash-flow analysis involves forecasting the future costs and revenues to which the interest holder is entitled. Each future year's cash flow is reduced by a discount factor to account for the time value of money. The sum of these discounted annual cash flows over the life of the project is called the net present value (NPV). The forecast cash flows are typically obtained from a spreadsheet model or a software package with a model built in. Input to this model consists of a discount rate, forecasts of oil and gas production schedules, product prices, inflation, exploration and development costs and schedules, operating costs and other costs. All of these forecasts are uncertain, even for producing fields with a long history.

Similar techniques are used for both producing properties and exploration rights. The approach used to value exploration properties is to carry out discounted cash-flow analysis of one or more defined prospects. Representative but hypothetical outcomes are modelled, based on the technical assessment of the likely size of the accumulations. The results of these analyses are combined to give the value of the success 'leg'. The discounted cost of an unsuccessful programme, the 'failure leg', is also estimated. The expected present value (EPV) for an exploration prospect is calculated by multiplying the success leg NPV by the probability that a commercial field will be discovered, and subtracting the discounted cost of failure multiplied by the probability of failure.

Note that the term 'NPV' is used not only for individual cash-flow analyses, but also mean values of distributions of present values before incorporating exploration risk. The term 'EPV' is generally restricted to values that incorporate exploration risk. For much of the discussion here, 'EPV' may be taken to mean the risk-weighted present value regardless of whether there is exploration risk (unless the context dictates otherwise).

5. Discount rate

If discounted cash-flow analysis provides the ubiquitous starting point for valuing upstream assets, the choice of discount rate is critical. A particularly important question is whether the discount rate should be increased to account for risk, and in particular whether it should be varied for different projects (or even particular categories of reserves) to reflect different levels of risk.

There is conflicting evidence on the use of discount rates to account for resource uncertainty. The SPEE survey distinguishes two forms of adjustment for risk:

- one that includes an increased discount rate called the risk adjusted discount rate (RADR) with or without reserve adjustment factors; and
- one that does not, relying solely on reserve adjustment factors used with cash flows discounted at what the survey calls the unrisked discount rate.

The two methods are used about equally. 'Reserve adjustment factors' are fractional multipliers applied to different categories of reserves, which are discussed at length in section 8 below. Note that the effect of reserve adjustment factors is independent of the discount rate assumption.

A relatively small number of SPEE respondents take into account the uncertainty in reserves not by increasing the discount rate used throughout the evaluation, but by applying different discount rates to different reserves categories. Taken at face value, the RADRs reported in evaluations of acquisitions and divestitures (ie, not in financing considerations)[3] averaged 13% for PDPs, 29% for PUDs, 45% for probables and 48% for possibles. However, contributing to the high rates for unproved reserves were rates that exceeded the maximum range of RADR used, which was a prior survey question. Analytical arguments for the use of such high rates are absent from the literature.

Surprisingly, the preamble to the SPEE survey question states that the RADR "should include a consideration for the 'cost of capital', a profit or expected rate of return for the buyer and any risk/uncertainty that the evaluator may choose to impute to the asset".[4] This author finds the inclusion of an expected rate of return inappropriate. A more useful approach is to determine the intrinsic value at the appropriate discount rate, and then determine what discount or premium is necessary to arrive at a purchase price that yields acceptable transaction metrics, including an expected rate of return.

In practice, only 35% of respondents using RADRs said that the profit element affected the RADR, the more frequent elements being reserves risk (90%), price uncertainty (69%), expense uncertainty (44%), mechanical risk (58%), and political/regulatory uncertainty (31%). Interestingly, 35% of respondents said that the RADR also took into account "unidentified reserves potential". Presumably this bonus (it can only provide upside) reduced the RADR used by these respondents from what it otherwise would have been. In 2013, respondents using RADRs typically used

---

3 Strictly, the distinction is by employment sector (exploration and production (E&P) companies and consultants versus banks) rather than application.

4 SPEEs, Thirty-Second Annual Survey, note 2 above.

rates between 12% and 16% (this range representing 50% of respondents), with a median of 15% and an average of 15.8%.

There seems to be an unfortunate clash of terminologies here. Most authorities regard the weighted average cost of capital (WACC) in the capital asset pricing model as a risk-adjusted rate, as the cost of equity term includes an equity risk premium over the risk-free rate. It seems clear from the SPEE survey that the unrisked discount rate in the survey is intended to be the cost of capital, with the RADR being the cost of capital further adjusted for additional risks, as discussed above.

Of the risk elements mentioned by respondents as contributing to their RADR, reserves and mechanical risks are diversifiable and should not therefore be included in the required return and thus discount rate. Price and cost uncertainty are not diversifiable, and should be incorporated into the WACC. Political and regulatory uncertainty is assumed to be synonymous with 'country risk', although this author prefers the term 'surface risk' to recognise that surface risk may vary by location in any particular country. This surface risk element was not here taken to indicate a risk premium for overseas locations, but rather for domestic surface risk.

Figure 2 shows the variation of WACC over the last 15 years for two groups of companies, integrated companies with downstream assets, and producing (upstream) companies.[5] The data set includes foreign companies with American depositary receipts, and not just US companies, although the variables (betas, equity risk premium and risk-free rate) are measured with respect to US markets. The averages are 8.4% and 8.1% for integrated companies and producers, respectively.

Figure 2. WACC for integrated and upstream companies

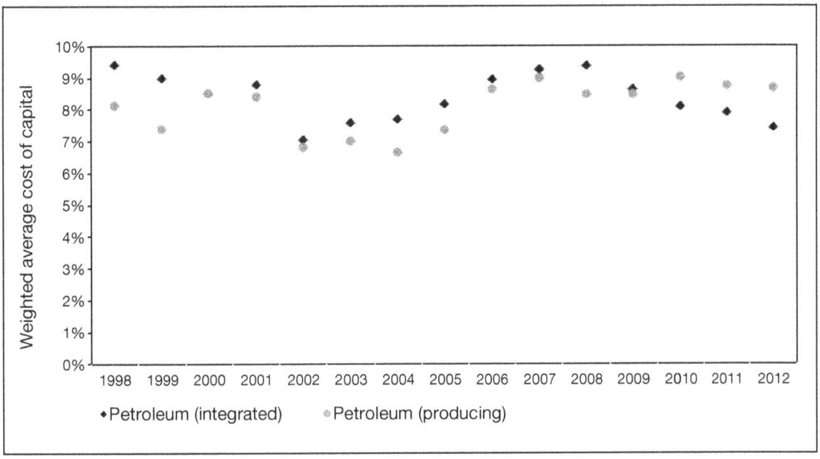

Source: Data from http://pages.stern.nyu.edu/~adamodar.

The precise WACC of the owner is not relevant in the determination of FMV.

5 Data from Damodaran Online, the website of Professor Aswath Damodaran, Professor of Finance at the Stern School of Business at New York University: http://pages.stern.nyu.edu/~adamodar.

What matters is the discount rate used by the market. This will be either the discount rate used by the highest bidder (the lowest discount rate in the market, other things being equal) or some generally accepted discount rate used throughout the industry.

A consensus industry standard is appropriate. The SPEE survey results showed that 51% of respondents used a cost-of-capital (unrisked) discount rate of exactly 10%, with 77% of respondents using a rate in the range 8% to 12% inclusive. It appears that 10% is the rate most frequently quoted since:

- US companies are required to report Standardized Measures of Oil and Gas values to the Securities and Exchange Commission using a discount rate of 10%; and
- it approximates to US companies' after federal income tax WACC (although over recent years this has been a slight over-estimate, as Figure 2 shows).

The SPEE survey results showed that 62% of the respondents arrived at their reported unrisked discount rate based on cost of equity or cost of capital considerations.

Although the absolute number of individual evaluations covered by the SPEE survey is dominated by those in the United States (86%), 40% of respondents indicated that their evaluations included properties outside the United States. As noted earlier, there is no evidence that respondents used a different discount rate to account for overseas surface risk (as opposed to political or regulatory risk which is assumed to have included domestic US issues). It seems likely that this would have appeared as a separate risk component (probably even called 'country risk') if it were common.

Professor Aswath Damodaran provides a useful synthesis of the arguments surrounding country risk premiums.[6] However, his discussion relates mainly to investing in the local stock market, and not in an upstream oil and gas project. Damodaran does argue that multinational companies, particularly suppliers of products to retail markets, are exposed to additional risks when operating in emerging markets. He argues for the use of an additional cost of equity component equal to the country risk premium for that country multiplied by the relative proportion of earnings from that country. This implies that the value of the local operating company or asset should be at the higher discount rate that includes the country's risk premium.

This argument for increasing discount rates beyond the firm's cost of capital is usually seen in damages claims at arbitration, usually argued by academics or damages experts rather than industry professionals.[7] Although the arguments may appear compelling to arbitration panels, there is no evidence that upstream firms apply different discount rates to different projects according to their locations (despite this author's public pleas to be informed of examples of the practice). It is assumed that the principal argument for not applying a country risk premium is that

---

6 A Damodaran, "Measuring Company Exposure to Country Risk: Theory and Practice", September 2003. Available at Damodaran Online, see note 5).

7 See, for example, the dissenting arbitrator's argument in the *Bridas SAPIC v Government of Turkmenistan* arbitration, discussed in TCC Childs, "Update on *Lex Petrolea*: The continuing development of customary law relating to international oil and gas exploration and production", *Journal of World Energy Law and Business* Volume 4, pp214–259 (2011).

the industry is not subject to the same risks that make investing in the local stock market or participating in local markets riskier than participating in more developed economies. The industry's principal product (crude oil) is fungible and priced in US dollars. Its costs are predominantly priced in US dollars and the cost of its labour force, relative to the value of its products, is tiny. It frequently operates in areas remote from the general population. It has a history of continuing to operate during political or economic crises in the host country and even occasionally through civil wars. Surface risk issues may cause projects in emerging markets to be less efficient (costlier or slower) than those in highly developed industrial centres such as the United States. However, these changes are predictable and can be accommodated in the cash-flow projections, and do not require additional compensation through a higher return. Catastrophic surface risk (expropriation or similar) not only is relatively unlikely, but generally results in compensation through contract provisions and/or bilateral investment treaty protections.

Alternatively, firms' reluctance to adjust discount rates upwards for surface risk reflects a perception that market prices are set by firms with the lowest WACC, and upward adjustments would make them even less competitive. It can also be argued that there has been a change in perception of surface risk, with the emergence of buyers, sometimes indigenous, from emerging markets, for which traditional perceived surface risk does not apply. For whatever reason, analysis of transactions between 2009 and 2012 in countries such as Iraq (Kurdistan Region), Pakistan, Syria and Egypt suggests that no additional discount was applied to values to compensate for surface risk.

6. Prices, costs and inflation

A second critical component in valuing upstream assets is the price forecast to be used. There does not appear to be a consensus on incorporating price uncertainty into valuations. In contrast to the statistical techniques used to manage subsurface uncertainty, price uncertainty is frequently treated by preparing arbitrary 'upside' and 'downside' sensitivities. While apparently useful to those making investment decisions, these sensitivities cannot be incorporated into the valuation unless they are associated with some probability. If the mean price case is used, the result will be the mean NPV. However, the variance of the result will be understated if price uncertainty is not quantified.

From a theoretical point of view, there are several reasons why the mean value might be lower than the value obtained using a base-price forecast. There may be strong asymmetry in the distribution of future prices about the base case, with less perceived upside than downside. The fiscal regime may be price sensitive. If the fiscal regime is not price sensitive, there will be pressure to increase host country take at higher prices by negotiation or unilateral action. However, it does not appear that these factors are taken into account quantitatively in valuing projects, possibly because the effect is small compared to technical and product price uncertainties. Despite this, companies spend a lot of effort attempting to incorporate fiscal stability into their host government instruments. It may be assumed that stabilised contracts are more valuable than those that are not stabilised, but evidence for the resulting value premium is lacking.

Much has been written about the poor track record of price forecasts, from the 'hockey sticks' of the early 1980s to sub-$20 flat-real-for-ever in the early 2000s. It is important to note that for market value purposes, it does not matter whether these predictions are ultimately correct or woefully short-sighted. What matters is the consensus in the market as this determines market values.

Over a decade ago, there was a trend of companies moving from arbitrary corporate planning forecasts to the use of forward price strips such as the New York Mercantile Exchange (NYMEX) Sweet Light Crude forward contracts based on West Texas Intermediate (WTI) crude oil. Hedging had become more common, such that companies were often realising strip prices. There appeared to be consensus about long-term prices, as the end of the forward strip tended to regress towards a mean.

Figure 3: Daily spot WTI with NYMEX Sweet Light Crude forward contract strips at the start of each quarter, January 1996 to December 2002, all expressed in US dollars per stock tank barrel

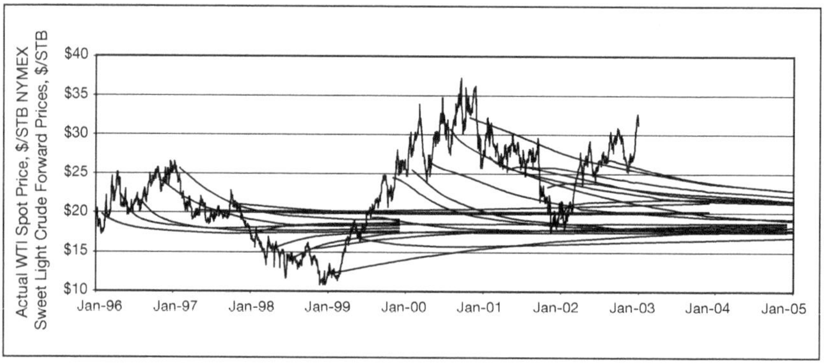

In Figure 3, the thicker spiky line shows the WTI spot price. The thin lines show the NYMEX forward strip for the first day of each quarter. Note the tendency of NYMEX futures curves to be rising when the spot price is low, and falling when the spot price is high. The longest dated NYMEX prices were confined to a relatively narrow band. The consistency of the longest dated futures prices until 2003 is shown in Figure 4.

More recent history has demonstrated that there is no longer the same stability in the futures strip, as illustrated by Figure 4. A gradual rise in the long-term price started in 2003, and accelerated in 2005. The longest dated futures have more recently mirrored the volatility in spot prices. It is argued that the volatility in long-term price outlook is real and is accompanied therefore by real volatility in asset values.

Beyond the strip, it is argued that a neutral and justifiable approach is to maintain prices flat in real terms. Thus prices beyond the strip are escalated at an assumed US dollar inflation rate. As an aside, despite record oil prices in 2008, for the most part the NYMEX strip continued to show declining nominal oil prices for the duration of the strip. This backwardation is counter-intuitive if the cause of the record prices was fear of future demand significantly outstripping supply. Indeed with the exception of a period from late 2008 to 2010, the longest dated futures contract has consistently implied falling real prices since mid-1999. Despite the shape of the futures curve, there

Figure 4. Daily spot WTI compared to the longest dated NYMEX futures prices for the first business day of each month. 'Real' $ are deflated using 2% annual inflation for the period to the longest date[8]

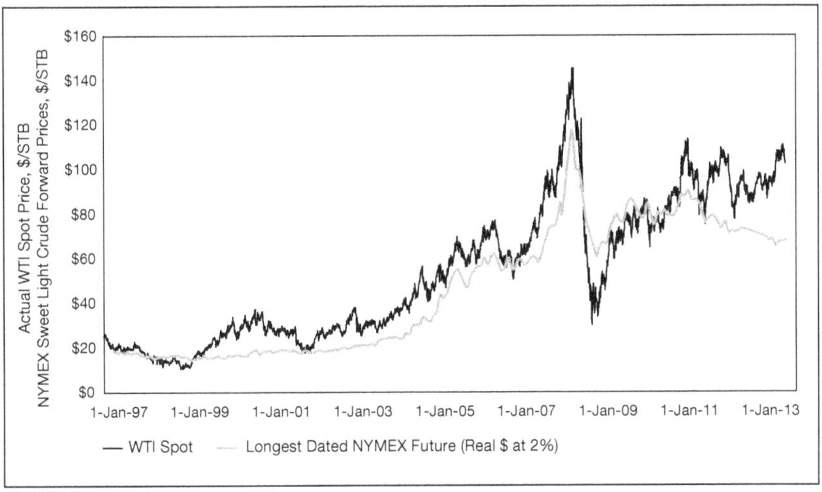

are still evaluators that use forecasts with constant product prices increasing in line with inflation (so-called 'flat real' assumptions). It is tempting to think of this as even-handed, but it should also be noted that SPEE survey results show that evaluators' average escalation rates for drilling and operating costs are higher than their forecasts for the consumer prices index by about 15%.

The particular price for any product at any location is determined by adjusting a suitable regional benchmark price for transportation and quality, usually using historical comparisons of actuals and benchmarks. Care needs to be taken in doing so. The adjustment may be a cost that only varies with inflation (for transportation or perhaps removal of an impurity). However, the adjustment may reflect different product yields, and thus be more appropriately treated as a fraction of the benchmark price. A $2 per barrel transportation cost and a 10% quality discount have the same effect at a $20 per barrel price, but have very different effects at $100 per barrel.

7. Taxation issues

One of the most significant differences in evaluation practice between the United States and the rest of the world is in the treatment of local taxes. According to the SPEE survey, an overwhelming majority of US evaluations are carried out before federal income tax, whereas the majority of non-US properties are valued after corporate taxes.

Several explanations have been suggested, although most are unsatisfactory. First, the existence of carried forward operating losses, the immediate expenses of

8 The longest dated contract is always for December, resulting in a reduction through the year from about seven years out to about six years out for the longest date. Two additional years were added in 2007, so the latest quotes go out about nine years reducing to about eight years.

intangible drilling costs and the 'accelerated' allowances for other capital costs mean that frequently US domestic producers have limited or no short-term tax liability. Moreover, losses and allowances from non-producing fields under development may be used immediately against profits in other assets as there are no 'ring-fences' to limit this. However, this is no different from practice in many other countries, a large number of which have faster depreciation schedules than the United States and a similar lack of ring-fencing. Discounted cash-flow analysis properly accounts for the timing of tax liabilities. Second, tax allowances such as depletion allowance for small producers or the domestic production allowance exacerbate the differences between individual firms' tax positions and therefore the value to them of any asset. Again, differences between the values seen by different valuers are real and should not simply be ignored. The value in the marketplace will be determined by the potential buyer's position. Indeed it may be argued that FMV will be determined by buyers able to take advantage of tax efficiencies, since they will offer the most, other things being equal.

A more plausible argument for valuing US assets before tax is that the value to the purchaser varies with the purchase price. This is because the post-acquisition depreciation base for corporate income tax is the purchase price, rather than the remaining undepreciated capital costs as it is in most jurisdictions. Again, it is argued that this is merely a complication and not an excuse to ignore corporate taxes.

It is possible that FMVs have US federal income tax factored in, making the statement that domestic valuations are determined pre-tax misleading. A more accurate statement would then be that US taxes are not explicitly calculated in domestic valuations. However, this seems surprising in view of the results shown in Figures 3 and 4, which, according to the SPEE survey, were applied to pre-tax values by an overwhelming 95% of respondents. Thus, these plots show the FMV to be a substantial premium to the post-tax 2P NPV.

An alternative view is that firms use a higher 'grossed-up' discount rate to compensate for omitting the effect of US taxes. However, this would introduce a mathematical error since using a different 'before tax' discount rate to compensate for the impact of taxes produces a very different result compared to calculating the taxes and discounting at the after tax' rate. More importantly, if taxes provided the reason for using a higher discount rate, it would surely have been mentioned in the SPEE survey results.

8. Accounting for resource uncertainty: reserve adjustment factors

Cash-flow analyses can be carried out for different categories of reserves and so determining the FMV requires selections from, or combinations of, NPVs for different categories. In some areas of the world, particularly outside the United States, valuations are simply based on the NPV of the 2P reserves. This may be adjusted with the application of a discount for risk aversion and/or surface risk, and occasionally, in competitive situations, a 'strategic premium' (the term here being a euphemism for an amount added in an attempt to ensure a bid is competitive, without there being an appropriate evaluation basis for the increased amount).

A more common approach to account for reserves' uncertainty, according to the SPEE survey, is to use reserve adjustment factors.[9] These are fractional multipliers for

Figure 5. Fair market values. Values (expressed as proportion of 2P NPV) resulting from applying reserve adjustment factors for developed producing reserves across a range of reserves' uncertainty (expressed as the proportion of 2P reserves that are proved for lognormally distributed reserves)

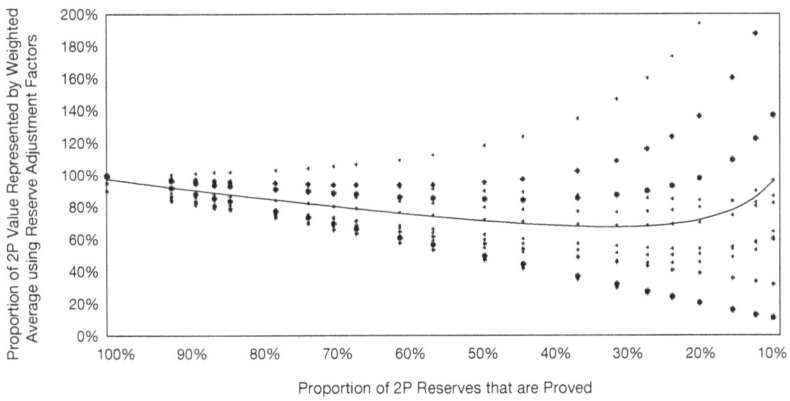

Source: Data from individual SPEE survey responses. Circle size indicates number of identical responses. Thin line is average of all respondents.

each separate category of reserves. In detail, alternative applications are reported. It appears the majority apply the reserve adjustment factors uniformly to the annual net cash flows. However, some apply reserve adjustment factors only to production or revenues, leaving the costs unchanged, and some distort the cash flows by maintaining the same initial rate but increasing the decline rate to obtain the reduced reserve volume. For this discussion, only the results of the majority approach are reviewed. The discussion is also limited to the survey results used in acquisitions evaluations (ie, to determine FMV) rather than evaluating loans.

The reserve adjustment factors are presumably intended to provide a method for accounting for risk aversion. It is instructive to compare results if the reserves follow a lognormal distribution with the proved, 2P and 3P volumes corresponding to P90, P50 and P10 cases (noting that this is not a requirement of the current guidelines). Figure 5 shows the value, expressed as a proportion of the 2P value, resulting from the application of the 22 available sets of reserve adjustment factors for developed producing reserves. The values are plotted against the proportion of 2P reserves that are proved. Moving from left to right, the proportion drops from 100% (no uncertainty) as the uncertainty increases. For 21 of the 22 sets of reserve adjustment factors the value initially decreases as the uncertainty increases, but for many sets the value reaches a minimum and then starts to increase. This occurs because at large

9 SPEE, Thirty-Second Annual Survey, note 2 above. In the survey, 62% of respondents report using reserve adjustment factors, 48% as the sole method for accounting for reserves' uncertainty and 14% in conjunction with discount rate adjustments, discussed earlier.

Figure 6. Fair market values (expressed as proportion of 2P NPV) resulting from applying reserve adjustment factors across a range of reserves' uncertainty (expressed as the proportion of 2P reserves that are proved for lognormally distributed reserves) for different proportions of developed and undeveloped reserves. Data averaged from individual SPEE survey responses

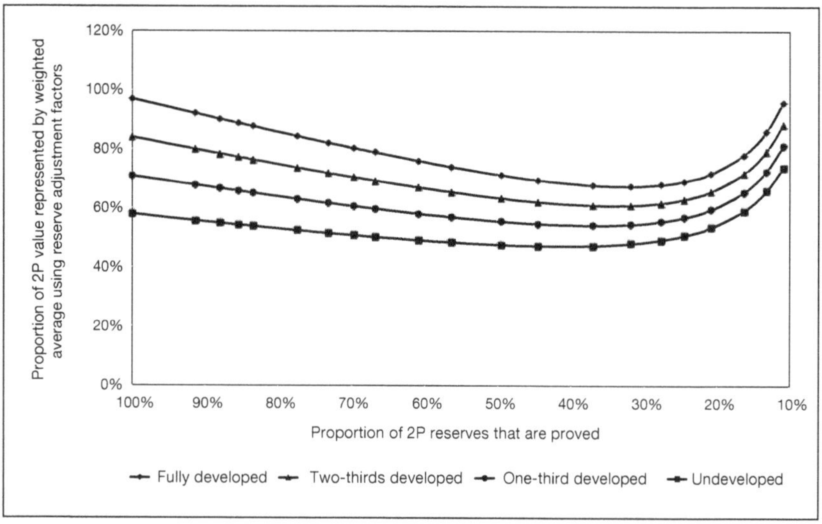

uncertainties the value is enhanced by large volumes of possible reserves, even though their unit value has been substantially reduced. The average reserve adjustment factors (97% for proved, 32% for probable and 7% for possible developed producing reserves) yield values on the line shown in Figure 2, with the minimum value about 67% of the 2P value when the proved reserves comprise about 30% of the 2P. Note, however, that there is a very wide range of values between respondents. For example, when 50% of 2P reserves are proved, the average value is 71% of the 2P value, but the 80% confidence range for all respondents' values brackets a range from 50% to 95% of the 2P value. There is even an outlier, the uppermost line of data on Figure 5, whose reserve adjustment factors yield a substantial premium to the 2P value (117% of it). Interestingly, there does not appear to be significant correlation between self-assessed acquisition success rates and reserve adjustment factors, suggesting any valuation bias is offset by variations in the other underlying evaluation parameters (eg, reserves, costs and prices).

To simplify further analysis, non-producing developed reserves are ignored and the effect of adding undeveloped reserves alone is reviewed. One notable feature of the reserve adjustment factors surveyed is the substantial discount applied to undeveloped as opposed to developed producing reserves. Compared to developed producing reserves, the average reserve adjustment factors for undeveloped reserves drop from 97% to 60% for proved, 32% to 27% for probables and 7% to 5% for possibles. This reflects the US evaluators' distain for PUDs in particular, mentioned earlier. This must reflect two problems: first a belief that these volumes are typically not as reasonably certain to

Figure 7. Fair market values (expressed as proportion of 2P NPV) resulting from applying reserve adjustment factors across a range of reserves' uncertainty (expressed as the proportion of 2P reserves that are proved for lognormally distributed reserves) for different proportions of developed and undeveloped reserves. Most frequently reported value by category from individual SPEE survey responses

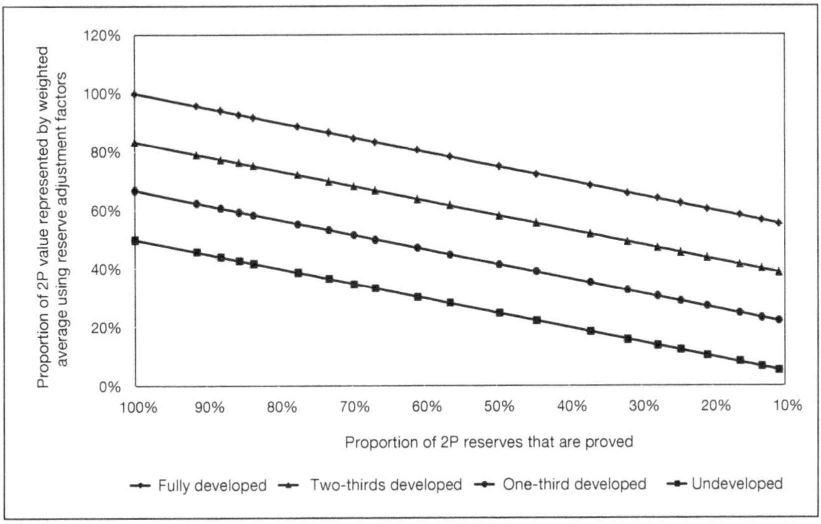

be recovered as they should be (ie, some of them should be probables), and second that their development is not as likely to occur in the short term (although the Securities and Exchange Commission guidelines have been tightened in this regard). Figure 6 shows the average results for the same set of respondents for a range from undeveloped to partly developed then fully developed reserves. Note that undeveloped reserves will already have a lower unit value compared to developed reserves, reflecting the cost of development and the forecast delay until production starts.

This discussion was intended to describe valuation methods rather than prescribe or recommend particular approaches, but it should be pointed out that the shapes of the curves at the right-hand ends of both Figures 5 and 6 are disturbing. If the value contribution of the possible reserves is ignored, as it is in the most frequently used reserve adjustment factors, the problem disappears. The results for these (100% for PDPs, 50% for PUDs and P2DPs, and 0% for P2UDs and P3s) have been plotted on Figure 7. There is now a straightforward continuous slope to the curves, although the disdain for undeveloped reserves remains. If the discount for undeveloped reserves is removed, all reserves would plot on the top curve. Interestingly, this would correspond to a measure that was popular with Canadian evaluators, 100% of proved plus 50% of probable, which this author refers to as 1.5P.

There were no survey questions dealing with contingent resources. A possible approach is simply to use the same approach as for reserves, and then multiply by the probability that the resource will be developed. A more sophisticated approach would recognise that the probability of development taking place is an on-off switch similar to the chance of making a commercial discovery for an exploration asset. That suggests an additional discount to account for risk aversion, but there is no readily available data to quantify the additional discount.

9. Exploration assets

The preceding sections discussed accounting for resource uncertainty for discovered reserves. A further consideration for exploration assets (prospective resources) is the probability of success or failure.

Any valuation system must be able to account for observed behaviour. A particular characteristic of oil and gas company behaviour is the frequency with which companies deliberately limit their working interest to less than 100%. This is true even when there are no capital constraints. Note that the desire to maximise value predicts taking the maximum working interest. Moreover, this remains true even if the valuation method produces a reduced value using a fractional multiplier (eg, a reserve adjustment factor) or a higher discount rate (eg, an RADR). The desire to take a reduced working interest can be explained by risk aversion. An intuitively acceptable technique that explains these behaviours is available from preference theory. Risk-adjusted values (RAV), derived from present value calculations using an exponential utility function, provide a value system that incorporates risk aversion.[10] The method also predicts a working interest that maximises value.[11] This is frequently, but not always, less than 100%. The calculation of RAV requires an additional parameter, the firm's risk tolerance.

Figure 8 illustrates some of the intuitively appealing aspects of RAV. This value equals EPV only at infinite risk tolerance, where firms are truly indifferent to a total loss. In contrast, a firm with zero risk tolerance will value assets based solely on the potential loss, however likely. In between, the optimum working interest, the interest at which RAV is a maximum, increases with increasing risk tolerance up to the practical limit at 100% working interest. Note the straight-line relationship between RAV at optimum working interest. The gross RAV of the project is therefore identical to all participants holding their respective optimum working interest. Of course, this presupposes the firms' evaluations are identical, which would be unusual, but the property is nevertheless important. Partnerships would be unstable if partners' values differed significantly.

A feature of early work on applying RAV to oil and gas interests focused on defining the firm's risk tolerance, which proved to be difficult or at least inconsistent.

---

10 The original application to the oil and gas industry appears to be that of JM Cozzolino, 'A Simplified Utility Framework for the Analysis of Financial Risk', SPE 6359, in Proceedings SPE Hydrocarbon Economics and Evaluation Symposium, Dallas, 21–22 February 1977. For a mathematical overview of current applications see CRK Moore, CP Moyes and PD Patterson, 'The Use of Risk Adjusted Values in Exploration Portfolio Management', SPE 94586, presented at SPE Hydrocarbon Economics and Evaluation Symposium, Dallas, 3–5 April 2005. For a more thorough review, including a suggestion for a modification to the Cozzolino approach, see I Lerche and JA MacKay, *Economic Risk in Hydrocarbon Exploration*, 1999, San Diego: Academic Press.

11 See JA Mackay, 'Utilizing Risk Tolerance To Optimize Working Interest', SPE 30043, in Proceedings SPE Hydrocarbon Economics and Evaluation Symposium, Dallas, 26–28 March 1995, pp103–109. See also Moore, Moyes and Patterson, 'The Use of Risk Adjusted Values', note 10 above.

Figure 8. Risk adjusted value (RAV) versus working interest (WI) for a variety of risk tolerances (RT)

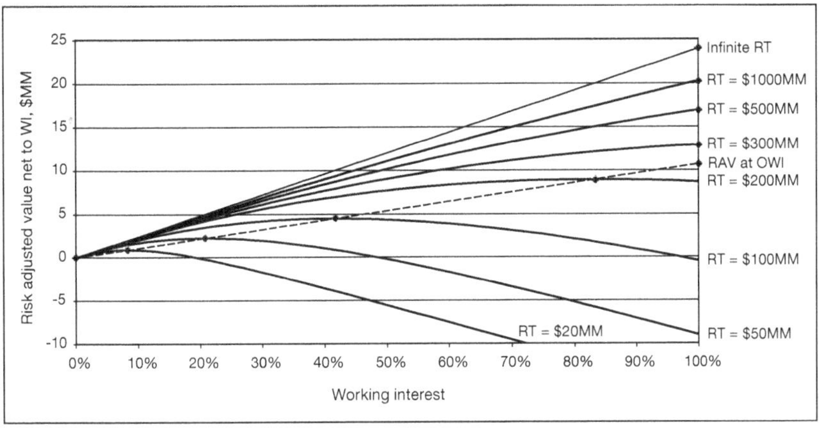

This is, with hindsight, intuitive. Firms have different levels of enthusiasm for different types of projects independent of any particular project EPV. This is reflected in substantial variation in risk tolerance depending on the nature of the project and its location.[12] This is partly to compensate for surface risk, and partly to reflect the firm's strategic focus (preferred types and locations of projects). It explains why large firms will totally ignore small opportunities that would clearly be attractive if the only consideration were the firm's financial risk tolerance. By setting rigorous strategic requirements to concentrate on specific core areas or core activities, the firm is setting a much higher risk tolerance for those activities. Conversely, the behaviour of some large firms in some theatres is consistent with an extremely low risk tolerance.

A powerful feature of the method is that if it is assumed that the firm's working interest is at optimum level, both risk tolerance and RAV may be determined. It may be argued that firms that do not fine tune their working interests and factors beyond their control contribute to the initial working interest level. That is true, but the error in the assumption is believed to be within the accuracy of value determinations generally. When working interests become significantly different from the optimum, firms acquire or divest interests. Indeed the corollary is that acquisitions and divestments of interests are driven entirely by changes in optimum working interest (as EPV evolves or following a change in strategic direction and thus risk tolerance).

A valid criticism of using RAV as a proxy for FMV is that the method is not in widespread use. Instead firms rely on the experience of the decision makers to determine the preferred working interest and the appropriate discount to EPV. This author's experience has been that these decisions and valuations are nevertheless consistent with calculated RAV, in line with other research in this area.[13]

12 See Moore, Moyes and Patterson, "The Use of Risk Adjusted Values", note 10 above.

13 See Moore, Moyes and Patterson, "The Use of Risk Adjusted Values", note 10 above for a more general discussion of research on this subject.

10. Portfolio effect

A further benefit of the RAV approach is that it can be used to calculate the value of a portfolio. The EPV of a portfolio is the sum of the EPV of its constituent projects. However, the RAV of a portfolio is greater than the RAV of the constituents. This is because the value is dominated by the product of the chance of failure and the cost of failure. The overall chance of total failure of the portfolio is much less than the chance of failure of each component, while the overall cost of failure remains constant.

The method is approximate because it requires a single overall risk tolerance. The example shown in Figure 9 uses the average risk tolerance for all portfolio members. It can be argued that the value of an individual project should be calculated as the difference between the portfolio with the project less the portfolio without the project, rather than the standalone project RAV. However, the difference may not be significant when compared with the uncertainty in the underlying analysis.

Figure 9. Cumulative risk adjusted value (RAV) of a portfolio of prospects. Grey area indicates additional value above the sum of the individual prospects

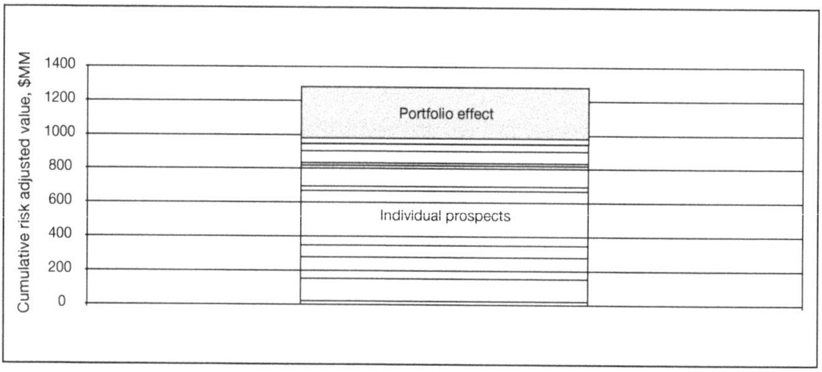

11. Transaction metrics and other valuation methods

The details of transactions involving oil and gas assets are frequently made public. This is especially true of relatively small public companies whose stock exchanges require them to disclose the details of material transactions. Where transactions include reserves, companies are often required to file third-party reserves reports compiled under either standardised or explicit and transparent assumptions. Actual purchase prices may be compared to these evaluation results.

It is tempting to use these as comparable sales in valuing other interests. However, extreme caution is required in defining a 'comparable' interest. A checklist for determining what is comparable is daunting (eg, date, location, contractual terms, lifecycle stage, geologic risk, reserves and contingent or prospective resources). Indeed, it may be argued that the only truly comparable interest is another working interest in the same petroleum right, provided that there have been no material economic or technical changes since the prior transaction (and there are no differences in the working interests' rights – for example, both are non-operators).

One only has to look at the difference in bids for adjacent tracts in the US Gulf of Mexico lease sales to see that values vary significantly over short distances.

Despite this limited applicability in determining absolute value, analysis of comparable transactions provides market information to assist in determining FMV. Normalised metrics (value per acre or value per unit of reserves or unit of production) are frequently quoted and are useful, both as a reality check on values determined analytically and in determining the relationship between FMV and EPV.

For exploration assets, industry transactions are typically structured as farm-in agreements where the purchaser (farmee) earns an interest by paying a disproportionate share of future costs, to include all or part of the seller's (farmor's) future costs through an agreed work programme. Such transactions may be reduced to cash-equivalent terms by observing that the purchase price is equal to the amount of the farmor's future carried costs, rather than the total programme costs paid by the farmee, since the latter includes the farmee's costs paid for its own account. A promise, for example, to fund 100% of a $120 million exploration programme to earn a 75% working interest does not mean that the interest is valued at $120 million. In this case $90 million of the programme is for the account of the company farming in. The result would be identical if the company farming in paid $30 million in cash to the company farming out. Both companies then pay their own working interest shares of the future programme. The cash transaction is thus $30 million to purchase a 75% interest, valuing 100% working interest at $40 million. The confusion arises because typical terms for a farm-in on an attractive project are two for one (paying 100% to earn 50%), which does result in the value of 100% working interest being equal to the gross programme cost. Typically, such calculations ignore the time value of money unless the time over which the work will be carried out is protracted.

This approach may be expanded to estimating likely farm-out terms as an alternative method for valuing exploration acreage. This is particularly useful where prospective resources have yet to be identified or evaluated (although one would usually expect the premium to be lower reflecting that). Other methods for valuing undeveloped acreage include determining the value per acre from entry fees for acreage with comparable prospectivity, based on leasing costs or signature bonuses.

This chapter remains the same as published in the previous edition.

Structuring the transaction

Jubilee Easo
Eversheds Sutherland
Joanna Kay
Orrick, Herrington & Sutcliffe (UK) LLP

1. Introduction

The transfer of an upstream interest typically includes the direct or indirect transfer of the rights acquired under a petroleum exploration and/or production concession, a joint operating or venture agreement and other ancillary agreements – for example, petroleum processing, transportation and sale agreements. At the outset of any such transaction, there will be a number of factors which ultimately determine the structure by which the transfer is effected. This chapter examines the key considerations influencing the choice of sale structure, the sales process and the key elements of the sale and purchase agreement.

2. Takeovers

Where a transaction involves a public takeover, the structure of the transaction will likely need to comply with certain regulatory requirements. A 'public takeover' is the acquisition of control of a company which is listed on a regulated market. It involves the takeover of a company that is the direct or indirect owner of the assets, rather than the assets themselves.

Takeovers in the United Kingdom are governed by the City Code on Takeovers and Mergers. The code applies to offers for, and other transactions involving a change in control of, companies with their registered office in (or which are considered to be resident in) the United Kingdom, the Channel Islands or the Isle of Man, if any of their securities are admitted to trading on a regulated market or a multilateral trading facility in the United Kingdom or on any stock exchange in the Channel Islands or the Isle of Man. The code also applies to companies whose shares are traded on the Alternative Investment Market or the ISDX Growth Market, regardless of whether they have their central management and control overseas. The code does not apply to private companies, unless there has been some marketing of their shares to the public in the previous 10 years.

The code applies to takeover and merger transactions, however they are effected, including by means of a statutory merger or court-approved scheme of arrangement. It imposes a set of statutory rules on all such transactions in relation to the form, structure and timetable of the transaction, in order to ensure the fair and equitable treatment of shareholders in the target company.

In addition, a number of other UK statutory and regulatory provisions apply to a transaction where the target company is publicly listed. These include:

- insider dealing provisions under the Criminal Justice Act 1993 and Financial Services Act 2000;
- market abuse and financial regulations under the Financial Services and Markets Act 2000;
- shareholder consents under the Listing Rules;
- disclosure and transparency obligations under the Disclosure Rule and Transparency Rules and the Prospectus Rules; and
- merger controls under the Competition Act 1998, the Enterprise Act 2002 and the EU Merger Regulation.

The vast majority of M&A transactions take the form of private company and asset acquisitions. As a consequence, this chapter primarily focuses on structuring private M&A transactions.

3. Share sales and asset sales – making the choice

If a party intends to acquire or dispose of an upstream interest, one of the first issues to be addressed is whether the interest will be transferred by means of a share sale or an asset sale. In a share sale, the interest that is being sold is the shares in the company that owns the upstream interest(s) that the purchaser wishes to buy. In an asset sale, the interest that is being sold is the upstream interest itself and any associated assets that the purchaser wishes to buy.

A number of factors will influence the decision of the parties to structure the transaction as a share sale or an asset sale.

3.1 Assets and liabilities

What a purchaser acquires in a share sale and an asset sale is fundamentally different.

In a share sale, the share purchase agreement (SPA) effects an indirect transfer of the upstream interest through the sale of the share capital of the target company that holds the relevant upstream interest. The purchaser therefore acquires all rights and liabilities of the target company (known and unknown), including those arising prior to the acquisition. The purchaser will generally need to undertake extensive due diligence into the financial, legal, tax and commercial position of the target company and seek disclosure from the seller of all liabilities of the target company in order to identify and quantify the risks associated with the purchase of that company.

In an asset sale, there is instead a direct transfer of the relevant upstream interest. The purchaser will acquire only those assets, rights and liabilities expressly transferred to it in the sale and purchase agreement. There are limited exceptions to this principle: in certain jurisdictions, regulatory requirements impose additional liabilities on the holder of an asset. In the United Kingdom, for example, liability for the decommissioning of an installation can be imposed on any party entitled to derive a financial or other benefit from that installation. Notwithstanding these limited exceptions, asset sales offer the purchaser the advantage of being able to cherry-pick the assets that have the greatest financial or strategic value to it and to insulate itself from most unwanted liabilities that may be associated with those assets.

3.2 Complexity

While an asset sale allows the purchaser to select only those assets that it perceives to be of value, it also brings with it the additional complication of requiring the purchaser to identify each of the assets it wishes to acquire. This may be a relatively simple task where an upstream interest is in the exploration phase of its lifecycle, but becomes considerably more complex where an upstream interest has moved into the development or production phase. Without careful scrutiny of the contractual arrangements associated with a particular upstream interest, a purchaser may discover too late that the perceived value of the upstream interest has been substantially eroded by the omission from the sale and purchase agreement of a key contractual arrangement that underpins the upstream interest. Furthermore, in an asset sale, there may be a number of different types of asset being transferred (eg, concession interests, trading arrangements, real property and/or intellectual property), with different procedures and registrations required to effect a valid transfer of title for each type of asset.

A share sale is ostensibly simpler. It involves the transfer of only one asset – the shares in the target company – and the transfer of title to those shares from the seller to the purchaser can usually be effected relatively simply by registration in the members' registry of that target company. However, a share sale can also be extremely complex. Where a business has grown organically, the assets and services required to operate that business may not all be situated neatly in the target company ready for sale. A pre-sale reorganisation may therefore be required to clean up an existing subsidiary to ready it for sale or to establish a new special purpose vehicle to package up upstream interests that were formerly sitting in a number of different subsidiaries for the sale process. A post-sale reorganisation may equally be required by the purchaser once the sale process has completed. This may be driven by the need to move the target company to a more appropriate place in the group structure of the purchaser (since the tax structuring of the original acquisition may have resulted in the target company sitting in a sub-optimal place from an operational perspective). Equally, where the target company was previously a trading company in the seller's group, the purchaser may wish to transfer the constituent assets into a known or clean entity and liquidate the target company in order to remove from its books a company that it knows little about. Whether effected pre or post sale, any reorganisation of the target company will need proper documentation. Intra-group transfer arrangements may be structured as either an asset sale or a share sale; but regardless of the approach, the documents will typically be much shorter than in a true arm's-length sale. Care will also need to be taken in the structuring of the consideration of any intra-group transfer to ensure there is no unintended undervaluation of the transferred interests that could trigger company law issues and invalidate the transaction or expose the directors to civil or criminal liabilities.

3.3 Third-party consents

Asset sales involve a change in the asset holder and generally existing contracts or trading arrangements do not automatically transfer to the purchaser. Transfers will invariably require the consent of third parties to the various contracts, adding time to the sale process and creating scope for those third parties to impose new terms to gain advantage from the change, or even to refuse the transfer.

In a share sale, the relationship between the target company and its contractual counterparties and suppliers does not change. This considerably reduces the number of third-party consents which may be required to effect a transfer of the target company and consequently reduces the potential for value impairment of the underlying business as a result of the transfer. In this respect, share sales are often simpler to implement than asset sales.

In certain circumstances, however, the requirement to obtain consent may be triggered not only by a change in ownership of the upstream interest itself, but also on a share sale as a result of a change in ownership of the ultimate owner of the upstream interest – so-called 'change in control' clauses. In the oil and gas industry, the underlying concession which grants title to the upstream interest will often contain such a clause. Thus, host government consent is likely to be required on both an asset sale and a share sale. Change of control clauses may also be incorporated in other contractual arrangements relevant to the upstream interest; a careful analysis of those arrangements should be undertaken as part of the acquisition due diligence process.

3.4 Pre-emption rights

Pre-emption raises specific concerns in oil and gas acquisition transactions, as joint operating agreements commonly include a pre-emption right to allow existing co-venturers to control the entry of a new participant into the joint venture. Typically, pre-emption rights under a joint operating agreement are triggered only on an asset sale and require the selling party to offer its co-venturers a priority right to acquire the upstream interest offered for sale on the same terms and conditions as those agreed to by a third-party purchaser. If a pre-emption right applies, the purchaser will need to ensure that any co-venturer's right to pre-empt a transfer under the joint operating agreement is waived as a condition precedent to the purchaser's obligation to acquire the upstream interest.

While less common, pre-emption may also apply on a share sale where a co-venturer's right to pre-empt is triggered by a change of control in the asset-holding company. In such case, the asset-holding company is required to offer its co-venturers a right to acquire the upstream interest offered for a monetary amount equivalent to the value ascribed to the upstream interest in the share sale. The valuation method and a mechanism to resolve any valuation disputes will need to be clearly described in the sale and purchase agreement.

3.5 Taxation

The tax consequences arising on a share sale are quite different from those arising on an asset sale. As a result, taxation is often one of the most influential factors in structuring the acquisition or disposal of upstream interests.

As a broad generalisation, the tax advantages of a share sale will usually be preferable for a seller, whereas the tax advantages of an asset sale will usually be preferable for a purchaser. However, the specific circumstances of the companies and assets involved will be the determining factor.

4. Documenting an asset sale

Asset sales can broadly be categorised into four different types reflecting the form, nature and timing of the consideration paid by the purchaser for the asset:

- sale and purchase;
- farm-in/farm-out;
- earn-in; and
- exchange of assets.

4.1 Sale and purchase

In the simplest formulation, the seller agrees to transfer some or all of its interest in an upstream interest and the purchaser agrees to pay to the seller an upfront cash consideration upon completion of the sale of the upstream interest. The basis on which the consideration is paid for the asset and the terms of the agreement reached between the seller and the purchaser for the transfer will be documented in a sale and purchase agreement. Such agreements typically do not include any restrictions or requirements in relation to the ongoing obligations (or work commitments) of the purchaser as defined under the terms of the underlying concession and joint operating agreement.

4.2 Farm-in/Farm-out

A form of asset acquisition which is almost exclusively used in the oil and gas industry is the farm-in/farm-out (where the choice of terminology is dependent upon the party in question's perspective). In general terms, a farm-out is a form of asset sale whereby the seller (or farming-out party) agrees to transfer part of its interest in an upstream interest to the purchaser (the farming-in party), while continuing to retain part of the upstream interest. The farm-out construction enables the farming-out party to reduce its exposure to an upstream interest and to finance the work commitments it is obliged to deliver under the terms of the underlying concession and the joint operating agreement.

The distinguishing feature of a conventional farm-out agreement is the link between the consideration due from the farming-in party and the ongoing obligations (or work commitments) of the farming-out party as defined under the terms of the underlying concession and joint operating agreement. The consideration due from the farming-in party for such transfer can be structured as either:

- a performance obligation – the actual performance of certain work commitments that would otherwise be required of the farming-out party; or
- a payment obligation – the payment of a defined share of the costs that would otherwise be incurred by the farming-out party in respect of those work commitments.

Where the consideration for a farm-out is structured as a performance obligation, the purchaser will assume responsibility in the farm-out agreement to perform certain of the work commitments in respect of the upstream interests. Care will need to be taken to define the farm-out obligation clearly – for example, the drilling of a well to a defined depth. Typically, the purchaser will not physically perform the work obligation itself because international oil and gas exploration is often complex and requires specialist technical knowledge (and because the purchaser might not be the appointed operator). The works could be subcontracted (by the purchaser or, where a number of parties own interests in the upstream interests, by the appointed operator) to a suitably qualified third-party contractor. The farm-out agreement will recite the purchaser's obligation to pay the seller's share of the costs of performing those works.

Where the consideration for a farm-out is structured as a payment obligation, part of that sum may represent a premium to be paid by the purchaser for the right to acquire the upstream interest partway through its lifecycle rather than from the outset. This premium is often described as a 'promote' and represents the ratio between the proportion of the expenditure that will be assumed by the farming-in party and the proportion of the interest it will receive as a result of the farm-in. The consideration might be structured as a 'carry' where the purchaser agrees to pay the seller's share of the costs associated with the performance of certain of the future work commitments in respect of the upstream interests. The carry arrangement will need to clearly define the costs to be incurred, the extent of the carry offered by the purchaser to the seller (including a possible cap on the intended carry costs) and whether any part of the carried costs that are unspent should be paid over to the seller or should remain with the purchaser.

4.3 Earn-ins

Under a conventional farm-in/farm-out structure, the upstream interest is transferred to the purchaser at the same time as or before payment of the consideration or performance of the works by the purchaser. This structure exposes the seller to the additional risk that the purchaser will subsequently fail to perform its obligations in respect of the consideration due in respect of the upstream interest. The farm-out agreement may therefore contain provisions that require the purchaser to reassign the upstream interest to the seller in the event of a failure of consideration. Reassignments can be difficult to achieve. They typically take place when a deal has gone sour and one or more of the parties involved is not incentivised to unwind the transaction, and they typically require further government and other third-party consents, which can be difficult and time consuming to obtain.

Under an earn-in structure, title to the upstream interest will not transfer to the purchaser until it has performed the work commitments. The earn-in structure provides clear benefits for farming-out parties, in that it mitigates the risk of non-performance or unsatisfactory performance by a farming-in party and obviates the need to address potentially complicated retransfer arrangements. If the farming-in party defaults on its consideration obligations under an earn-in structure, there will be no transfer to unwind.

While the earn-in structure carries with it more risk for the farming-in party, sometimes it may be necessary. Even if the commercial dynamics of the deal do not prevail in the farming-out party's favour, an earn-in structure may be needed if the parties are unable to obtain the requisite government consents for a transfer until certain work commitments have been performed.

4.4 Asset exchanges

An asset exchange structure is a further alternative to a traditional sale and purchase arrangement. An asset exchange involves the exchange of upstream interests between the contracting parties as mutual consideration.

Where a transaction is structured as an asset exchange, there is no clear delineation between the seller and the purchaser. Each party will act as seller of its respective asset and purchaser of the other's asset. This mutuality of roles means that the asset exchange agreement will need to address the giving of reciprocal warranties, representations and indemnities between the parties and contain an appropriate mechanism for reconciling any claims arising in respect of an interest, with an ability for the parties to net off their respective claims. It may also be that the exchanged assets are not equal in value, in which case additional cash payment may need to be factored into the completion mechanics of the transaction.

Another concern for both parties will be to ensure that completion of the transaction occurs simultaneously in respect of all assets being exchanged. Where the asset exchange is documented under one agreement, this can be achieved by reciting matters such as third-party consents as conditions to completion. Where the transaction is documented as two separate agreements, this could be achieved by expressing the consideration due under one agreement to be completion of the transaction under the other agreement (and *vice versa*).

5. Documenting a share sale

Although the transfer of ownership in the shares of the target company is effected by simple share transfer forms, the understanding reached by the seller and the purchaser in respect of the sale of those shares is documented by means of an SPA. The additional risk assumed by the purchaser by virtue of acquiring the target company, with all its past and future liabilities, usually has an impact on the nature of the SPA. The SPA will typically have more extensive warranties – including tax warranties, which will be dealt with along with other tax issues in a tax deed.

The nature of upstream interests may also mean that a share sale is sometimes unavoidable. Where ownership of infrastructure is held by companies owned by joint ventures across a number of different upstream concessions, the transfer of the seller's interest in those infrastructure companies will need to be effected by means of a share sale. The result may be that a combined asset and share sale is required to transfer all assets associated with those upstream interests effectively.

6. Structure and documentation of sale process

Regardless of whether a transaction is structured as a share sale or an asset sale, the sales process will generally follow a fairly standard route, with clearly identifiable stages. Where a public takeover or merger is being considered, the UK Takeover Code imports a distinct form and process for a sale. This has not been addressed for the purposes of this chapter.

6.1 Preparation and due diligence

The initial step is for the seller to establish a data room containing relevant information on the target assets or company being offered for sale. In order to gain access to that data room, a prospective purchaser will need to enter into a confidentiality agreement with the seller which not only reflects the confidentiality requirements of the seller, but also (to the extent that the seller is permitted to make such disclosure to a potential purchaser) passes down any applicable confidentiality obligations the seller has to third parties in respect of the upstream interests.

The seller may choose to run the sales process as an auction or tender process, thereby generating competition between prospective purchasers and optimising its chances of receiving a competitive offer for the interests. Whether the sale process is run as an auction or not, the seller will typically prepare the initial seller-friendly draft of the relevant sale and purchase agreement, SPA or farm-out agreement (henceforth referred to as a 'sale agreement', for ease of reference) and any ancillary agreements (which may include a joint operating agreement, if the interest to be sold will no longer be a 100%-owned asset), and invite the purchaser to submit its comments on the draft as part of its offer.

The next step in the process is for any prospective purchaser to conduct its due diligence process into the information disclosed by the seller. The purpose of this due diligence process is to identify any issues affecting the upstream interests or contained within the target company, which in turn will be used to inform the purchaser's valuation of the interests and any additional protections that the purchaser may wish to incorporate in the sale agreement. The due diligence process will also be used to verify that the target assets or company offered for sale constitutes the full value chain required by the purchaser to realise future value from those interests. In an asset sale, the purchaser will be concerned that the due diligence process properly identifies all assets and contracts necessary for the proper operation of the upstream assets post-completion of the sale. In a share sale, the purchaser will be more concerned that the due diligence process identifies any unknown residual liabilities in the target company that it may inherit. In each case, but especially in relation to a target company that has a long history, the cost of the due diligence can be disproportionate in comparison to the actual value ascribed to the asset. The purchaser in this case may attempt to take comfort through a combination of indemnities and warranties from the seller to avoid prolonged and expensive due diligence.

Where the purchaser is acquiring a non-operated interest, the purchaser's primary concern will be to understand the extent of the financial obligations it will assume as a result of the transfer and any controls a non-operator may have over the actions of the operator. When operated interests are being acquired by the purchaser, the purchaser will additionally be concerned to understand the operational obligations it will assume and how these align with its existing group operations. As a result, the acquisition of operated interests may require more extensive due diligence to be conducted by the purchaser.

Completion of the purchaser's due diligence will then lead to the purchaser either withdrawing from the process or submitting an offer setting out the terms on which it is willing to purchase the upstream interests. This will typically be outlined in an offer letter. That offer, if accepted by the seller, will then trigger the next stage of the sale process: negotiation of the sale agreement.

6.2 Negotiation of the sale agreement

The sale agreement is the cornerstone of the sales process and represents the outcome of the commercial, legal and pricing negotiations. That said, the form and content of a sale agreement – whether intended for a share sale or asset sale of upstream interests – is typically quite standard and includes the following key elements.

(a) Parties to the agreement

In the simplest M&A transactions, there may be only two parties to the sale agreement: the purchaser and the seller. The situation can be made more complicated by the existence of multiple sellers – for example, where the target company has more than one shareholder and each shareholder seller will need to enter into the agreement to sell. Where there are multiple sellers, the purchaser will want the sellers to be jointly and severally liable for the sale agreement obligations, especially in relation to the warranties and indemnities.

(b) Transfer and conditions to transfer

One of the first operative provisions in a sale agreement is the seller's offer to transfer the interest in exchange for payment of the consideration by the purchaser and the purchaser's acceptance of such transfer. This provision will typically define the interest being transferred and recite the date at which the parties have agreed to treat the interest as having been transferred from the seller to the purchaser. This may be the date on which the transfer is completed, but is commonly an earlier date such as the signature date of the sale agreement or an earlier 'economic date' mutually agreed by the parties.

Typically, the effectiveness of the transfer will be conditional on the satisfaction or waiver by a certain longstop date of a number of conditions precedent to the transfer. These usually include:

- receipt of any necessary governmental or regulatory approvals;
- third-party consents;
- the waiver or expiry of any applicable pre-emption rights; and
- the execution of consent notices and agreements to assign or novate any relevant agreements to the purchaser by those third parties.

In a share sale process, such consents will be considerably fewer because the only asset being transferred is the shares in the company, leaving the underlying contracts untouched.

In an earn-in agreement, in addition to the parties satisfying the procedural conditions, the purchaser will be required to perform the earn-in obligations and only then will the purchaser receive the relevant interest from the seller.

(c) Consideration

At the heart of any sale agreement is the purchase price. The payment of consideration by the purchaser to the seller can be structured very differently depending on market conditions, the relevant bargaining strengths of the parties, the value of the assets and any issues that may have come to light as a result of the purchaser's due diligence.

The simplest formulation is for a lump-sum cash consideration to be paid by the purchaser to the seller upon satisfaction of all conditions to the effectiveness of the transfer. The sale agreement will often provide for completion accounts to be prepared, usually under the control of the purchaser, to enable the consideration to be adjusted by reference to a pre-determined target position. The seller may require the purchaser to pay a percentage of the consideration as a deposit on signature of the sale agreement and the balance of the consideration on completion. Where the purchaser is asked by the seller to pay a deposit, the circumstances under which such deposit will be repaid to the purchaser need to be clearly defined.

Another formulation, typically used where the parties differ in their valuation of the target asset or company, is where the purchaser pays all or part of the consideration following the completion date, contingent upon the occurrence of a defined trigger event. Both the purchaser and the seller will be keen to ensure that the trigger event or events are clearly defined, and that the sale agreement includes a mechanism to resolve disputes should they disagree about whether a trigger event has occurred. In upstream transactions, it is also not uncommon to structure deferred consideration as an ongoing royalty payable by the purchaser to the seller or as a defined lump sum linked to start-up or ramp-up of production levels from an upstream interest.

As noted above, a unique feature of the farm-in and earn-in structures in the oil and gas industry is that the consideration for the transfer is commonly linked to the performance of or payment for a defined share of the work obligations set out in the underlying concession and joint operating agreement, such as the completion of seismic work or the drilling of a well.

Any element of deferred consideration payable by the purchaser following the transfer of the interest creates a risk of purchaser payment failure for the seller, which it may seek to mitigate through the inclusion of an obligation on the purchaser to provide some form of collateral support for its obligations. Equally, any payment made by the purchaser prior to completion raises the prospect of seller reimbursement risk in the event that there is a failure to complete the transaction. The purchaser may seek some form of collateral support from the seller to mitigate this risk or may require that any pre-completion payments be held in escrow by an independent escrow agent to the mutual order of the parties.

The sale agreement may also need to include provision for the adjustment of the consideration amount to reflect expenditures and income incurred between the economic date of the sale agreement and the date of completion.

(d) Interim period

The interim period covers the period of time between signing of the sale agreement and the date on which the conditions to the effectiveness of the transfer are satisfied (the completion date). The length of the interim period will be determined by the time required to satisfy or waive the conditions precedent. During the interim period, the seller will retain title to and operational control over the upstream interests (title and control transfer to the purchaser only at completion), and so the purchaser will look to incorporate interim period covenants in the sale agreement that constrain the seller's management of the upstream interests during the interim period in order to protect the value of those assets. A balance will need to be struck between the purchaser's desire to protect the value of the investment it intends to make in the interests and the reality that the seller may be constrained by the terms of its underlying concession and joint operating agreement. Typically, the purchaser's only remedy under the sale agreement in the event of a breach by the seller of the interim period protections is to make a claim for damages.

(e) ***Material adverse change***

The primary function of a material adverse change (MAC) clause in the sale agreement is to give the purchaser an opportunity to exit from its obligation to complete the transfer where there is a high risk of a material deterioration in the value of the asset or target company during the interim period. A MAC clause passes completion risk to the seller, allowing the purchaser to renegotiate the terms of the sale agreement or simply refuse to complete the transfer.

If the principle of a MAC clause is accepted by the seller, the scope of the clause will be a matter for negotiation between the parties. A MAC clause will typically refer to circumstances beyond the control of the purchaser (a deterioration in market circumstances or other macro-level events), and the purchaser will seek to extend its application as widely as possible. By contrast, the seller will wish to qualify a MAC clause, often requiring that the purchaser's right to terminate the sale agreement will be triggered only where the MAC event reduces the value of the upstream interests by a defined amount.

(f) ***Representations and warranties***

Typically, a sale agreement will contain a number of representations and warranties given by the seller in favour of the purchaser in respect of the seller's title and capacity to transfer the upstream interest, as well as other representations and warranties as to the circumstances related to the interest and tax position of the interest. How often these representations and warranties are repeated will be negotiated by the parties, with the purchaser wanting them to be given at signature and repeated at completion. Under English law, the breach of a representation or warranty will give the purchaser a right to claim damages against the seller, and additionally the breach of a representation could give the purchaser the right to rescind the sale agreement. Typically, however, the seller will seek to exclude the purchaser's right to rescind the agreement as a result of a breach of representation or will qualify any such right of rescission heavily by reference to the material adverse effect such a breach has had on the value of the upstream interest. The seller will also seek to limit its liability to pay damages for a breach of a representation or warranty in a number of different ways, as described below.

Seller's knowledge: The seller will often seek to limit the scope of its liability by qualifying any representations or warranties by reference to its actual knowledge.

This is a particularly important limitation for the seller where it does not control the matter represented or warranted (eg, where the upstream interest concerned is a non-operated interest, the seller will be reluctant to offer an unqualified warranty that all necessary consents have been obtained by the operator). How widely the seller's knowledge is defined will be a matter for negotiation between the parties, but it is not uncommon for the term to be defined by reference to the knowledge of a number of named individuals.

Time limits: It is common for the seller to include a fixed time period in which the purchaser must bring any claim. Standard time limits range from six to 24 months from the completion date for representations and warranties related to title and operational matters. The time limit to claim in respect of tax representations and warranties could be longer (commonly six years, recognising the right of tax authorities to reopen tax affairs up to six years after tax has been incurred).

Monetary limits: The seller will also seek to impose monetary caps on the purchaser's right to claim. This may include a *de minimis* threshold which must be reached before the purchaser is entitled to bring a claim and an aggregate cap on the seller's liability for all breaches of representations or warranties.

Other exclusions: The seller may also introduce a number of other exclusions to its liability which will preclude the purchaser from bringing a claim against the seller. These may be blanket exclusions such as an exclusion of the seller's liability for consequential losses or an exclusion of the seller's liability where the purchaser has an ability to recover the loss from a third party, such as an insurer.

One of the reasons a purchaser requires extensive representations and warranties from a seller is to encourage the seller to make full and proper disclosure of any matter or circumstances affecting the interest to be transferred. Typically, the sale agreement will be accompanied by a seller's disclosure letter which will recite specific and general disclosures against the seller's representations and warranties, qualifying those representations and warranties and precluding the purchaser from bringing a claim in respect of any matter so disclosed.

(g) Allocation of liability

Both the seller and the purchaser will be keen to apportion liability as between themselves to limit their liability to the other in respect of periods in which they do not benefit from the asset. Typically, the sale agreement will provide that the seller will retain the benefit of and liabilities arising from the upstream interest prior to the economic date recited in the sale agreement. The purchaser will then assume the benefit of and liabilities arising from the upstream interest on or after the economic date. This allocation of liability will be supported by reciprocal indemnities given by each party.

There are some limited exceptions to this general principle. For example, the seller may often require the purchaser to assume liability for and indemnify the seller against environmental and/or decommissioning costs in order to avoid any future residual liability in respect of those transferred interests. Equally, if the purchaser's due diligence process has resulted in the identification of specific and unexpected liabilities associated with the interest, it may seek specific indemnity protection from the seller against those liabilities. In each instance, the indemnities bring the benefit of 'pound-for-pound' recovery of any losses and relieve the claiming party of the common law requirement to mitigate the loss.

6.3 Completion

The final stage in the sales process is completion. Completion is the point at which the title to and risk in the upstream interests pass to the purchaser and all or part of the consideration is paid by the purchaser to the seller. The sale agreement will describe the mechanics for completion, setting out the respective obligations and deliverables of the parties. In the case of an asset sale, the completion documentation may be extensive, as title to each transferring asset will need to be transferred at completion.

Following completion, the assets will be owned by the purchaser, but there may be certain post-completion matters to attend to that may require the seller's cooperation, if not its involvement. These may include certain registrations and other notifications to perfect the purchaser's title to the interests, the payment of transfer taxes and other more general transitional operational matters.

Private equity investment in the oil and gas industry

Maarten Overmars
Simon Tysoe
David Ziyambi
Latham & Watkins

1. Introduction

Private equity's increasing interest in the oil and gas sector over the last decade has been a notable factor in the development of oil and gas M&A. Many sellers in the oil and gas sector (especially sellers of exploration and production (E&P) assets) historically viewed private equity as a slightly curious, and possibly transitory, 'bit-part' player in the oil and gas M&A ecology. In contrast, today the M&A processes of E&P sellers are designed to accommodate and, in some cases, to target private equity investors. Consequently, awareness of the preferences of, and techniques adopted by, private equity firms and portfolio companies backed by them are an integral part of understanding oil and gas M&A today.

This chapter gives an overview of how private equity tends to invest in E&P assets and answers three questions:

- What is private equity's interest in the oil and gas business and how has it changed over the past decade?
- In the context of oil and gas M&A, what – if anything – makes the private equity investor different from any other investor?
- Perhaps most pertinently, what is it about oil and gas – and particularly upstream oil and gas – that requires private equity investors to adjust their traditional approach to transactions in other industries?

In addressing these questions, this chapter looks exclusively at investments in E&P assets and companies (ie, upstream oil and gas), referring to investments in midstream, downstream or oilfield services (OFS) by way of contrast, where appropriate. It also outlines the key features of the two most popular structures for private equity investment in upstream oil and gas:

- the traditional 'buy-out' structure, under which the private equity investor backs a management team, takes a majority position in the management team's company and provides funding for the acquisition and development of the oil and gas assets currently owned by that company or shortly to be acquired by it; and
- a joint venture structure, whereby a private equity investor forms a joint venture with an oil and gas operating company under which the operating company provides its skills and services and its existing assets, and the private equity investor agrees to invest capital (including leverage) for the development of those assets in return for a certain equity return.

Before turning to the structure of investments, however, this chapter outlines a short history of private equity's interest in oil and gas.

2. Private equity and oil and gas – the journey upstream

As was rightly noted in the previous edition of this book, private equity investors have shown increasing interest in investment in the oil and gas industry for many years now. Traditionally, mainstream private equity's interest in the industry centred on OFS and energy infrastructure assets rather than upstream E&P assets, although there were numerous intermittent exceptions that suggested that upstream investment could be both viable and attractive. Over the course of the last 10 years, interest has expanded to E&P assets in a much more sustained manner as, like a Conrad hero, private equity pushes upstream. Reliable figures are hard to find, but Table 1 sets out the results of the authors' own survey of Mergermarket. The figures show the percentage of global energy deals in which a buyer was classified as having financial services as its core business, which therefore includes private equity funds, hedge funds, banks and sovereign wealth funds – many of which share similar investment share techniques, such as the use of special purpose vehicles, leverage and tax-efficient structures.

Table 1. Acquirers in announced M&A transactions classified as 'financial services' entities

Period	E&P services and equipment (OFS) sub-sector	Oil and gas E&P sub-sector
1 Jan 2006 to 31 Dec 2007	18%	10%
1 Jan 2012 to 31 Dec 2015	27%	19%
1 Jan 2016 to 31 Dec 2017	26%	22%

The figures show that private equity and similar investors have had a longer history in the industry than some would surmise. In addition, private equity has had (and retains) a strong interest in OFS – a business which shares more characteristics with other oil and gas businesses than E&P does. However, the most noticeable feature in Table 1 is the rapid increase in investment in E&P from 2012 onwards.

A number of factors have contributed to this journey. The first is the discarding of inhibition. Traditional private equity investors have been wary of investing in upstream companies due to an unwillingness to take 'reservoir risks' – by which we mean the risk that commercial quantities of oil and gas simply will not be found or, if found, will not be extractable on a commercial basis. Over the last 10 years, technological innovations pioneered in the United States have encouraged a re-evaluation of this conservative approach. The development of fracking has enabled access to oil and gas locked into shale rock, thereby significantly reducing the risk of any given oil and gas target area turning out not to contain commercial quantities of oil and gas. Shale is the abundant source rock from which quantities of oil and natural gas migrate into traditional reservoirs of more porous rock strata over millions of years. These reservoirs are the target for traditional oil and gas exploration drilling. The identification of these reservoirs is a matter of great technical skill and judgement, and there are numerous examples of reservoirs simply not being as promising as they originally looked. However, the advent of horizontal drilling and fracking technologies permitted oil and gas companies to drill along rather than through oil-bearing strata, and to excite the shale rock itself, fracturing the rock and releasing quantities of oil and gas that had been trapped between strata.

The second factor has been the abundance of opportunity. The financial crisis of 2008 generally reduced access to traditional funding sources for E&P. Traditional debt financing had become more scarce for oil and gas companies as stricter lending standards were imposed both in the United States and elsewhere. Access to the equity markets as a source of funds for oil and gas companies also became more constrained (and the equity markets have remained closed to oil and gas companies listed outside of the United States for some time now). As a result, a funding gap was created into which private equity naturally advanced. From 2010 to 2014, private equity investment in the oil and gas industry generally – and in the US upstream space in particular – expanded rapidly, with large deals being struck and ever-greater sums of money being raised by funds focused on investing in the sector.

Then, quite suddenly, over the course of the second six months of 2014, oil prices fell by nearly half. This oil price collapse had two major effects on the industry:

- It exacerbated the lack of liquidity that had affected the oil and gas industry since the financial crisis of 2008; and
- The prices fell for investment in what had previously been an increasingly overheated market.

With oil and gas companies forced to sell assets to raise much-needed cash for their business, and with many corporate buyers out of the market due to their own financial problems, private equity moved from being a funder to being a buyer. It was not just the abundance of assets, but also their quality that attracted interest, since the financial condition of many companies forced them to go beyond the usual list of 'non-core' assets to dispose of very attractive businesses. The potential for putting together high-quality portfolios at an acquisition price that could help to ensure a compelling return upon exit led to a countercyclical but inevitable uptick in interest from private equity in the oil and gas space.

The third, and most crucial, factor that drove private equity upstream was an increase in both the supply of, and the demand for, targets. The search for higher returns led private equity companies to look closely at upstream investments. Since the downturn in the oil price in the latter half of 2014, making a case for investment in more 'traditional' private equity targets in OFS or energy infrastructure had become more challenging. OFS companies suffered greatly from the cutbacks in expenditure by oil and gas companies globally. Seismic and drilling were particularly hard hit, with exploration budgets being slashed and much development drilling put on hold. Even supposedly 'non-discretionary' spending on maintenance was deferred; or if it was carried out, the rates which service companies could command for such services were reduced and profit margins squeezed. A great many drill rigs and service vessels were retired or mothballed.

At the opposite end of the spectrum, oil and gas-related infrastructure gradually became a victim of its own success. Many oil and gas companies were obliged to continue producing oil and gas to generate cash to service existing debt, albeit at prices which meant that they lost money. Oil and gas infrastructure, especially tariff-based pipelines, continued to generate profits notwithstanding the deterioration in commodity prices. In addition, the demand for oil storage spiked as traders took advantage of the oversupply and stored oil in the anticipation of a turnaround in oil prices. The combination of these factors, plus the continued interest in energy infrastructure assets from infrastructure funds, meant that competition for such assets became (and has remained) very strong, increasing prices and therefore decreasing the likely return on the investment. Upstream assets, on the other hand, had more closely followed the value of the commodity itself and OFS became cheaper. Unlike OFS, however, the value of upstream assets typically recovers quickly upon the recovery of the underlying commodity price. Conversely, OFS rely on an uptick in activity which is typically signalled by the return of the commodity price, but with the actual value increase in OFS likely to lag behind the uptick in the price of oil and gas at some distance.

3. Key drivers for private equity investment

Having looked at the assets in which private equity investors have invested in recent years, it is worth considering the features of private equity funds that drive, and to some extent constrain, the decisions as to what they invest in and the manner in which they do so.

3.1 Nature of fund

From the outset, it is worth bearing in mind that private equity investors come to the oil and gas industry with a slightly different mindset from that of other participants. First, and most importantly, they do not have a strategic interest in the development of oil and gas. Although the fund, and its investors, may be keenly interested in oil and gas assets, their key driver is to generate a certain return of capital on any equity invested. The manner in which this is done is largely indifferent to the oil and gas fund itself. Secondly, unlike for major E&P companies, there is no overwhelming demand to replace reserves of oil and gas, or to give the market good news stories in relation to certain developments – although both of those things may be considered as part of the value of any investment in such companies by a private equity investor. Of course, a number of investment techniques used by private equity have been adopted by other 'financial investors', particularly sovereign wealth funds. Such investments by sovereign wealth funds also tend to have ancillary drivers, such as a desire to gain operating experience or to gain access to new markets or new technology. For a pure private equity investor, however, such ancillary motivations are unlikely to sway an investment.

The third key point is that a typical private equity investor – by which we mean a fund structured as a fixed-life, self-liquidating limited partnership – will be very much focused on its ultimate goal of a successful exit from its investment. The private equity investor wants to sell the shares that it owns in the company through a trade sale or via a public offering, or in some other way to recapitalise the assets it owns in order to return funds to the investors. A fund will not only be very focused on the possibility of such an exit, but will also be concerned as to the timing of such an exit. The pressure is twofold. First, the fund itself will have a finite life – usually 10 years plus a possible short extension. Further, individual investments have a lifespan, since private equity funds typically have a period within which, as a rule, they must show a return to their investors by increasing the value of and then exiting their portfolio company investment – the time from the initial investment to the exit being referred to as a 'hold period'. Hold periods vary from fund to fund and depend on the activity in the market, but are typically between three and six years.[1] Therefore, any investment needs to demonstrate not only the ability to generate an adequate return, but also the ability to do so within time parameters which fit with the investment horizon of the fund. It is with particular reference to the need to show a return within a certain period that the recent focus on upstream assets has become so intense. As noted above, although OFS investments typically follow the price of the underlying commodity, they do so at a time lag which reflects the period that the commodity price takes to recover. However, upstream assets – especially those in the development phase – might offer the ability to add value more quickly and therefore generate a better overall return within the time horizon of private equity investors.

The recent sectoral focus has prompted considerable interest in adapting the traditional investment approach and using funds with longer hold periods or even using permanent capital vehicles (PCVs). A PCV is an unlimited-life, open or closed-ended fund which is typically structured as an investment company, although limited partnerships are also used. Table 2 on the next page compares some of the key features of a PCV as opposed to a traditional fund.

The flexibility of the PCV structure has a number of attractions for managers dealing with long-term investments in cyclical markets such as oil and gas. Under a traditional structure, fund managers have 10 to 12 years from raising the fund to winding it up and therefore the fund portfolio and strategy will need to reflect this. Given the longer investment horizons of the PCV, longer-term strategies may be pursued and good assets retained, if still performing, and the risk of being forced to sell assets during a downturn is reduced. The flexibility to raise additional funds in subsequent investment rounds or on an ongoing basis, rather than solely at the outset of the fund, presents the possibility of more marketable rounds once the fund's portfolio is assembled. From an investor's perspective, the position is more nuanced. Liquidity remains a concern and the need for the capital to be permanent must be balanced with the investors' need to liquidate their investment. One solution is for the PCV to be listed on a stock exchange, allowing the investors to realise their investment by secondary sale while retaining capital in the PCV.

1 Bain & Company's *Global Private Equity Report 2017*, 2004–16 annual medians.

Table 2. Features of PVCs versus traditional funds

	Typical fund	**PCV**
Fundraising period	12–18 months, after which no new commitments are sought.	May fundraise either on an ongoing basis or in several rounds of fundraising.
Lifecycle	Limited life – typically 10 years with a one or two-year extension.	May continue indefinitely.
Hold period	Three to six years.	More flexible.
Proceeds	Will usually distribute realised proceeds.	May have the flexibility to reinvest in future projects.
Redemption rights	Will not usually contain voluntary redemption rights, but capital returned at end of life.	May allow investors rights to redeem their interests (although likely restricted). More likely to have the right to sell and fund may be listed.

Whatever the nature of the fund, private equity investors are subject to stringent internal regulatory and compliance regimes. This manifests itself in a number of ways – firstly and most obviously by the extensive 'know your customer' due diligence that a private equity investor will need to do on the management team, co-investors, target entity or other participants in a M&A transaction. Second, a number of elements in any transaction in the oil and gas industry, especially those in emerging markets, may present significant challenges to the compliance regimes and require a private equity investor to carry out significant work in order to satisfy itself. Given the private equity investor's position as a fiduciary for its investors, the private equity fund is invariably unable to 'take a view' on such issues and contractual protection may well be necessary.

3.2 The importance of leverage

In order to meet expectations on the return of capital on any equity invested, private equity investors typically require leverage in the form of debt to be a proportion of the investment. In upstream assets, this debt element has traditionally been provided by banks providing credit facilities that are sized based on the level of reserves estimated by a consultant to be extractable from such assets. Such reserves-based lending (RBL) can be augmented or replaced by a bond issuance, particularly after all upstream assets have become operational and are producing. Oil and gas financing in the context of M&A is discussed in more detail elsewhere in this book; however, one of the main prerequisites of a successful RBL financing in the current market is that the borrower has oil and gas assets that are currently producing oil and gas and therefore has an existing income stream. Deviation from this prerequisite begins to stray into the realm of pure project finance or structured finance (eg, through forward sale structures), each of which entails a level of completion risk with which private equity investors have not yet become comfortable, except in limited circumstances. For example, a private equity investor may decide to invest in a target with only development assets using equity alone, but its business plan will almost invariably include bringing those assets to production in the short term, raising debt financing against cash flows generated by such production and using a large portion of such debt financing to return capital to the fund. Indeed, by investing in an asset which still requires capital to bring it into production in a market where capital is scarce, private equity investors may well leverage an enhanced return on their investment.

3.3 Quality of management team

An overriding driver for private equity investors is the quality of the management team or operating company in which they will invest. Although a private equity fund likes to take a controlling interest in its investment and will likely have fund personnel who are very familiar with oil and gas, it will not have – nor will it have the capacity or intention to have – day-to-day involvement in the target's business. The quality of the management team or operating company – and, in particular, its efficiency – will therefore be of crucial importance. In the buy-out market, a key driver of value creation is the prospect of bringing increased efficiency to operations and hence increasing profitability.

What will also be of importance is the ability of the private equity investor to incentivise management through issuing some form of sweetened equity so that the interests of the management team and the private equity investors are aligned. Frequently, the private equity investment will be primarily an investment in the management team itself, since the management company may have no assets at the point of investment and possibly no clear line of sight to such assets. The ultimate expression of this approach is the special purpose acquisition company, a listed management vehicle established with a view to acquiring assets in the future.

4. Due diligence and structuring

As may be apparent from the preceding paragraph, a decision to proceed with detailed due diligence on a target is taken only after a period of screening during which the investment's 'fit' is analysed. It is a decision not to be taken lightly, since private equity investors undertake very thorough due diligence on all aspects of the potential transaction. This will likely entail legal, commercial, environmental and technical due diligence, as well as insurance and anti-bribery, corruption and sanctions diligence. Outlined below are a number of key due diligence issues, with some context as to why they are of particular relevance to private equity investors and the banks from which they will raise debt finance, whose interest in and exposure to oil and gas investments are aligned with those of the private equity investors in most respects. The list is non-exhaustive and will vary from investment to investment.

4.1 Target and management

As noted above, the starting point – and sometimes the ending point – of any investment is a thorough evaluation of the management team. Where a private equity fund is investing in a management team, the track record of such a team – both generally and in relation to the specific assets which the target company owns or plans to own – is of crucial importance. In the United States, where backing of management teams for upstream projects has a longer pedigree than elsewhere, there are a number of management teams that have been backed several times in the past and their familiarity with the way in which private equity invests, manages and ultimately exits a particular investment, as well as the fund's familiarity with their operational experience, is beneficial.

Where a private equity investor is looking to invest in partnership with an operating company, similar considerations apply. The quality of the operator – one with a strong track record of bringing projects through to production on time and on budget – is important. Further, there will need to be alignment between the investor on the one hand and the operator on the other as to the strategic direction of any partnership. Most energy-focused private equity funds have a particular focus on certain jurisdictions and/or certain technologies. Indeed, many funds may have a restriction on the proportion of assets that they may have in, for instance, countries outside the Organisation for Economic Cooperation and Development (OECD). It is important to ensure that the operator's outlook aligns with the investor's outlook, both at the point of investment and going forward.

4.2 Anti-bribery and corruption

Most large private equity funds are subject to anti-corruption laws, and especially the US Foreign Corrupt Practices Act 1977 and the UK Bribery Act 2010. Each of these statutes has broad scope and can visit liability on investors for the wrongdoings of their employees and the employees of operating companies in both the United Kingdom and United States, as well as in foreign jurisdictions where investment assets are based. A private equity investor taking a majority stake in a target company will therefore need to satisfy itself that the historic activities of the company have complied with such anti-corruption laws and, given the scope of the relevant legislation, will need to consider performing due diligence on partners or contractors to confirm their compliance with such laws. In addition, to the extent that the fund is subject to legislation to which the target company is not itself subject, the private equity fund will need to ensure that, post-acquisition, the target company abides by the higher level of obligations.

4.3 Regulatory issues

Like any oil and gas investor, a private equity investor will need to understand the legal framework of oil and gas production in the relevant jurisdiction. This is inevitably a broad task, but a number of key items will be on any investor's list of questions.

First, what is the fiscal regime in the relevant jurisdiction? There is no preferred form of regime – private equity investors, like all oil and gas investors, understand that a production sharing regime maybe as investor friendly as a tax and royalty regime, and *vice versa* – but it will be crucial to understand this regime in detail so that the investor's financial model can be properly constructed. Non-fiscal terms, but terms that nonetheless have a financial implication – such as local content and domestic supply obligations – will need to be understood and factored in as best they can be.

Secondly, consent rights will be of particular interest to a private equity investor. Of course, a host government's right to exercise discretion over whether the private equity investor may or may not acquire the company will be a key item of due diligence for the investor, both in the context of the initial acquisition and in understanding any potential constraints around the exit from the investment. However, questions of consent are more far reaching. For instance, the framework of consent around the development of commercial resources under the terms of an applicable licence may well have implications for the speed at which a particular investment may be brought to production. Whereas for many oil and gas investors a period of delay may well be acceptable, the private equity investor's additional constraint of a time horizon in which to realise its investment brings this issue more acutely into focus.

Finally, the ability of the operating company freely to export and sell its production for dollars in the open market and to receive the proceeds of such sales offshore, and/or its ability to repatriate money promptly out of the host country without having to comply with strict currency control requirements, will be crucially important considerations.

4.4 Partners

Most oil and gas upstream activities are carried out by unincorporated joint venture arrangements between a number of participants. Each of these participants is jointly and severally liable for the obligations of the other vis-à-vis the government. Therefore, a proper understanding of the credit risk associated with such co-venturers must be factored in. In addition, where the private equity target operating company is not itself carrying out the operations, but one of the partners is instead acting as the operator, an understanding of its capabilities and track record is fundamental. In certain cases, especially where the investment involves a large development project, due diligence on both the operator and the contractors carrying out the project will be important in mitigating completion and/or operations risk. This goes not only to their technical capability and financial strength, but also to the terms of the contracts under which the development is taking place and also – especially in the context of the UK Bribery Act 2010 – their compliance with anti-bribery and corruption laws.

4.5 Corporate veil issues

High on the list of items for any private equity general counsel when looking at a potential investment will be whether local or international law, or any other arrangement, might give rise to a liability on the target company which might 'pierce the corporate veil' and lead to a liability on the fund itself or its third-party investors. The two main areas in which such liability might in principle arise concern environmental issues, particularly relating to large oil spills, and liability for the safe decommissioning of oil and gas facilities.

In relation to environmental matters, any private equity investor will require thorough due diligence in relation to the compliance of any target company with local and, as applicable, international environmental standards, in order to understand any potential liabilities. Consistency and clarity in the local law as regards environmental matters are also important, although there is an understanding that a government's response to a true ecological disaster will not necessarily be constrained by existing legislation. However, adequate mitigation measures – including high operating standards and, where applicable, appropriate environmental liability insurance – will help to mitigate exposure.

Decommissioning exposure is a classic example of a liability which private equity is keen to quantify and ring-fence. For example, under the UK North Sea decommissioning regime, not only is an operating company liable – jointly and separately – for its own share of decommissioning obligations and those of any of its co-venturers which goes into default, but so too are its holding companies. In fact, the UK legislation is such that any private equity fund holding a majority position in an operating company with North Sea assets could in theory face direct liability for the decommissioning of those assets or, where the assets are held in a joint venture, for the co-venturer's share of such liability. In order to avoid such exposure under current legislation, many investments in the North Sea have been structured as joint investments by funds so that no one private equity fund owns an overall majority position in the underlying operating company.

4.6 Tax and other structuring

A private equity investor will spend some time carrying out tax structuring due diligence to ensure that an adequate network of taxation treaties is in place such that funds extracted from the investment can be repatriated to the fund, often through an indirect route, without the risk of double taxation. This tax structuring will likely drive the selection of the corporate vehicle through which the private equity investor will invest, as well as its jurisdiction of incorporation. The structuring will need to consider not only the fund's tax position and ensure that the return to the funds is tax efficient, but also the tax position of the management team.

In addition to tax structuring, consideration may be given to whether existing bilateral investment treaties can be used. A bilateral investment treaty offers the private equity investor a degree of protection against direct and indirect expropriation by the host government, as well as potentially offering other investor rights. Where no bilateral investment treaty exists between the relevant host government and the jurisdiction in which the private equity fund operates, it might be possible to form the investment acquisition investment vehicle in a jurisdiction which benefits from such a treaty. Care should be taken to ensure there is some nexus to avoid the accusation of forum shopping.

In addition to the due diligence undertaken by the private equity fund, most acquisitions will require bank financing and the banks themselves will carry out due diligence. Typically, such acquisition financing will be of a limited recourse type, with the banks' recourse being solely to the target business. Therefore, the banks' due diligence will be similar in scope and extent to the purchaser's own due diligence.

5. Implementing the transaction

Assuming that the potential investment has successfully passed through the due diligence phase and the fund has decided to proceed, the private equity fund will set about documenting the transaction.

5.1 Transaction Model 1 – the buy-out model

Let us first assume that the fund is backing a management team, and that the team has secured the acquisition of certain E&P assets. In such a buy-out transaction the principal documents will be:

- the sale and purchase agreement (SPA);
- the investment agreement;
- the equity commitment letter; and
- the debt financing documents.

(a) Sale and purchase agreement

This document is dealt with at length elsewhere in this book; however, a number of items that flow from the acquisition structure will inform the draft. First, a special purpose vehicle acquisition company, and not the fund itself, will enter into the SPA. Second, the SPA will need to accommodate the debt financing element of the acquisition. Part of this will be cooperation language to ensure that the seller procures that the target assists with the financing. More controversially, the question of what will happen to the SPA if the debt financing is not obtained will need to be considered. Few sellers will be willing to allow a buyer simply to terminate the SPA should the financing falter. Equally, the residual risk that financing might fail means that the directors of the special purpose vehicle acquisition company will be extremely wary of signing an SPA which nonetheless commits them to complete even if the debt financing piece is not in place. The most satisfactory solution is for the acquisition company to secure certain funds from the banks, as discussed below; but other options that limit the acquisition company's exposure but nonetheless clearly motivate the purchaser to make appropriate efforts to secure financing, such as the agreement of a break fee, might also be considered.

(b) Investment agreement

The investment agreement sets out the terms on which the private equity investor will invest in the acquisition company alongside the managers, creating an alignment of interests between the private equity investor and the managers. The document performs three important functions. First, it acts as an SPA/subscription agreement in relation to the investment by the private equity investor and therefore contains certain warranties from the management. Typically, as well as usual capacity and authority warranties, these will include warranties on the business plans and other information provided by the managers as part of the sales process. Although the management will customarily give warranties, they will likely have little in the way of assets should a claim be made. Therefore, from the fund's point of view, these warranties are really more for information. The fund's prime recourse in the event of breach will be against the managers' shares in the acquisition company, thereby effectively removing them from the company.

Secondly, the investment agreement acts as a shareholders' agreement in relation to the acquisition company, setting out the way in which the company is to be managed, the role and responsibilities of the board, the obligations of the management and so forth. The private equity fund or funds will end up owning the vast majority of the shares in the acquisition company, so their control tends to be almost absolute, with the managers having only very limited minority protections.

Third, and most importantly, the investment agreement, along with the constitutional documents of the acquisition company, will contain the equity incentive package offered to management. Management incentive packages offered on upstream transactions are usually structured along the same lines as those offered on a classic private equity buy-out model, as follows:

- The most valuable part of remuneration occurs on a successful exit;
- The management starts to receive enhanced remuneration if and when the private equity receives its target internal rate of return (IRR) and/or target multiple on invested capital as part of that exit; and
- The management receives an increasingly greater return if the fund beats its target return.

However, a number of facets of the upstream business mean that certain terms of the incentive package tend to differ. Since E&P investments are typically higher risk than buy-outs in other industries, with a greater risk that the IRR required by the private equity investor will not be met, the return to the management on a successful exit will be considerably higher than that in a typical buy-out in other industries. A high multiple on exit may cause valuation issues for the management equity, in that their investment was insufficient at the outset and that therefore their return is not truly a return on an investment, but a benefit of being an employee of the company. This may in turn lead to tax issues for the managers, as elements of their payment are viewed as income rather than capital gains and are therefore subject to higher taxation.

Given the relatively short history of private equity investment in E&P outside of the United States, a confident assertion of what is market is not possible. However, from a fund's point of view, the management incentive package – even if generous – requires the management team to have some financial 'skin in the game' by investing their own money or, failing that, money borrowed from the fund. For managers new to private equity, which make up the majority of non-US teams, this may seem unusual and the process of negotiation may be longer than that in other industries.

(c) ***Equity commitment letter***

The equity commitment letter is the fundamental agreement between the private equity fund and the management entity under which the fund agrees to fund both the acquisition of assets and the activities of the company going forward. The letter may be drafted with a very specific acquisition in mind, such as in the classic buy-out model, or might instead offer the acquisition company a line of equity for use in future, as yet undefined acquisitions. Once the acquisition company draws down on the letter, the private equity fund will be issued with more equity in the acquisition company. Given the importance placed by private equity investors on keeping the obligations of the fund limited, the terms of the private equity fund's obligations under the equity commitment letter will be carefully limited in terms of value, time and conditions. In an acquisition, as well as the equity commitment letter being addressed to the acquisition company, the seller may seek to be an addressee of the letter so that it may call upon the equity commitment letter directly – for instance, if the acquisition company breaches its obligations under the SPA and as a result thereof closing does not take place. The equity commitment letter may or may not have conditions upon it over and above those set out in the SPA. For instance, many equity commitment letters are themselves conditional upon the debt financing element of the acquisition becoming unconditional. This increased conditionality, if not already factored in and mitigated, produces risks both for the seller and for the acquisition company.

In upstream transactions, the equity commitment letter may further be set up as a proxy for a guarantee by not only addressing the obligation to pay the acquisition consideration, but also standing behind other ongoing obligations under the SPA. Principal among these in an upstream transaction is any indemnity offered to the seller in respect of decommissioning and/or environmental liabilities associated with the assets or entities being acquired. While a private equity fund will be extremely hesitant to offer such support, in theory a level of support limited both in value and in time might be considered by a fund – in particular, to avoid the need to post other forms of collateral such as an escrow or a bank guarantee. The importance of fully understanding and negotiating the terms of the equity commitment letter in the context of an upstream transaction is vitally important for the fund, for the management and for any seller dealing with a private equity buyer.

(d) ***Debt financing documents***

As noted above, debt financing is very important in private equity transactions in order to achieve the leverage required to produce the fund's desired return on investment. The process and terms of typical oil and gas financing are discussed elsewhere in this book. However, it is worth noting that the loan documentation used for the traditional RBL model traditionally places considerably more control in the hands of the lenders than the typical leverage buy-out documentation that most private equity funds are familiar with. This is understandable given that RBL facilities are, by their nature, limited in recourse and lenders' diligence requirements typically increase in inverse proportion to the level of recourse they have to the borrower group and its assets. The added complication of completion risk where an investment includes (or consists totally of) development assets will lead lenders to require even more detailed diligence around the stakeholders in the investment, resulting in a longer list of conditions to drawdown that will give the lenders further comfort regarding the investment's ability to deliver a fixed-income return over time.

As well as balancing the competing demands of lender and borrower, there are often structural issues to be considered. Lenders typically expect the borrower group to grant a security package of both shares and assets, such as interests in the group's underlying oil and gas licences. Where this needs to be done by a target company in the context of its acquisition, issues of unlawful financial assistance or corporate benefit might arise, particularly in jurisdictions outside the OECD. Identifying these issues at an early stage, usually in conjunction with local legal counsel, is of paramount importance, as such issues may determine the structure of a transaction, or indeed its feasibility. Government consent for the creation of such asset level security is also likely to be required and obtaining such consent will typically be a condition to any debt financing. In order to minimise the potential gap between the SPA and the financing, such consents (and any other consents required by the lenders in connection with the debt financing) should be factored into the completion deliverables in the SPA.

5.2 Transaction Model 2 – the joint venture model

Let us now assume that the private equity firm is not adopting a buy-out approach, but rather investing in an existing E&P operating company to form a joint venture. While this approach has been widely used, there is much less of a 'typical' structure for such investments, although there are certain common features. First, instead of acquiring a company with a view to generating a return through its eventual sale, the private equity investor will agree to fund the operator's development activities, in return for which it will be looking for a certain IRR to be paid out of the cash flows of the joint venture. The technique used to achieve this economic result differs from transaction to transaction. In a typical shale-play joint venture in the United States, often referred to as a 'DrillCo' arrangement, the fund will take ownership of a working interest in certain acreage owned by the operator in return for bearing a defined share of development costs. The operator will carry out all the work and the fund will receive cash flows from the developed well; upon the required IRR being achieved, the working interest will revert in whole or (more likely) in part to the operator. The same economic effect can be achieved at a corporate level through the use of, for instance, equity commitment, redeemable preference shares or a mixture of equity and shareholder debt. Second, the level of control over the operations will need to be agreed. As noted, private equity funds do not wish to have operational control, but in the buy-out model they are used to having financial control over the company. In the joint venture model, this might not be achievable due to the fund's less dominant commercial position compared to a buy-out. This potentially sets up a lack of alignment. One key issue is costs and production – especially for shale wells, but more generally too. On one hand, the operator is often motivated to bring on wells and maximise production – primarily because of the need to generate cash flows, especially where the operator has debt to service. If the operator is listed, the announcement of new production wells may well increase the company's stock price. Further, as an operational matter, the operator will likely resist any suggestion that the fund can veto its well programme. On the other hand, the total costs of development of the well may be high and if the price of oil or gas is not sufficient, the fund's IRR will not be met. Therefore, some joint ventures include provisions stopping the fund being obliged to fund developments if, for instance, the oil price is below a certain level, with the operator being to some extent free to seek other funding as required. Such mechanisms work reasonably well for shale plays where the drilling time is short. In conventional plays – especially offshore, where drilling takes much longer and lead times are more extended – such flexibility is harder to achieve.

6. Conclusion

Since the last edition of this book, private equity investment in E&P has greatly increased and has become a significant part of the M&A landscape. As usual, private equity has been imaginative in its approach; and while the structure of private equity has in part informed the assets into which they have invested, funds have modified certain aspects of this approach – and indeed in some cases have modified their own structure in order to better fit the oil and gas industry. We can expect more innovation over the coming years, as many of the investments made in recent years come towards their exit point and a secondary market between oil and gas-focused funds becomes feasible.

Share purchase agreements

Alexander Reid
HFW

1. Introduction

1.1 Share purchase agreements in the oil and gas sector

Share purchase agreements (SPAs) may be encountered in various contexts in the oil and gas sector. Like asset purchase agreements, they are used to buy and sell petroleum assets, whether upstream, midstream or downstream. On a share sale, it is the shares in the asset-holding company (the target company) that are purchased, rather than the assets directly.

In the oil and gas sector, given the size, value and complexity of the assets in question, there are often a number of entities holding interests in any one asset or project. Project participants may hold their interest through an incorporated or an unincorporated joint venture. In the former case, a share sale will be required in order to transfer a project participant's interest (its shareholding) in the special purpose company (incorporated for the specific project) that holds the assets. In the case of an unincorporated joint venture, a project participant may hold its individual interest through its own special purpose company. In this case, the parties may structure the transaction as a sale of the shares in the special purpose company, rather than that company's direct interest in the project assets. This chapter focuses primarily on the latter case, which is the more common structure in the upstream sector.

1.2 Share purchase versus asset purchase

Share sales are often more efficient and straightforward processes as compared with asset sales. At a very basic level, there is only one asset (the shares) which needs to be transferred. Hence, it is not necessary to expressly identify the various underlying assets that are subject to the sale, or to apportion the purchase price as between them, in the SPA.[1] A share sale will be most appropriate where the target company is a special purpose vehicle, holding only those assets that are the subject of the sale. If the target company holds additional assets which the seller does not wish to sell or the buyer does not wish to acquire, the seller will need to conduct pre-transaction restructuring to transfer those assets out of the target company.

From the seller's perspective, a share sale generally has the advantage of

* The publisher acknowledges Catherine Byers as the co-author to this chapter in the previous edition.

1 Apportionment may not be strictly necessary, depending on the governing law of the asset purchase agreement, but it will typically be desirable, from both a legal and a tax perspective.

providing a clean break from all liabilities connected with the ownership and use of the assets, since those liabilities will generally transfer with the target company.[2] The buyer will need to rely on its due diligence and the contractual protection in the SPA to control its risk exposure in respect of such liabilities.

A share sale may also limit the need to acquire waivers of pre-emption rights. Where the subject of the sale is an interest in an unincorporated joint venture, pre-emption rights or other restrictions on transfer under the joint operating agreement (the customary document governing the operation of the joint venture) may not be triggered, since joint operating agreements do not always contain restrictions on changes of control in the interest-holding company.

As noted above, transferring the shares in the target company will have the added advantage that any assets of the target – such as employees, expertise and IP rights registered in the name of the target company – will transfer with the ownership of the shares. This may be particularly important in the context of an upstream transaction if the target company is the operator. In such circumstances, the buyer may wish to retain the current operator team or the services of key individuals in order to help continue operations and the process of obtaining any host government and/or joint operating agreement consents required in connection with the change in ownership.

Although not discussed in detail in this chapter, consideration will need to be given to the tax implications of a share sale as compared with an asset sale. The target company may have the benefit of tax losses, credits or allowances which can be used to reduce the tax liabilities of other members of its group. Where these pass to a buyer on a share sale, the seller may expect them to be taken into account in the purchase price.

A share acquisition, however, may not always be the most appropriate method of structuring the transaction. The extent of the liabilities of the target company which would otherwise be inherited by the buyer on a share acquisition (eg, employment, pensions and tax liabilities, litigation, environmental, health and safety liabilities and operational risks, such as major damage to production facilities pre-completion) may outweigh the benefits of relative simplicity and speed. In addition, the transfer of shares may attract a stamp duty charge or other similar transfer taxes, depending on the jurisdiction of incorporation of the target company. Finally, because the host government of the petroleum contract often views a change of control as an assignment of interest, it may levy a profit or capital gains tax on the sale.

1.3 Decommissioning obligations

The most significant area of concern for the buyer of shares in an upstream transaction will often be the extent of the target company's decommissioning and abandonment obligations. Under many petroleum regimes, responsibility for decommissioning lies with the entities that hold the project assets at the time decommissioning is to take place. While the joint operating agreement will usually

---

2 However, there may be exceptions to this – for example, in relation to decommissioning and abandonment liabilities.

provide that the project participants bear this liability in proportion to their participating interests, their liability to the host government for decommissioning is usually joint and several. As such, the buyer could bear a disproportionate share of the liability. In some host countries, project participants are required – often after the mid-point of a petroleum field's expected life – to make regular payments out of project revenues into a reserves fund to meet future decommissioning costs. Thus, the buyer will assume the proportionate contribution to the fund which reflects its period of ownership. However, it is likely that the buyer (together with the other project participants) will remain liable for any deficiency in the fund at the end of the project. Ultimately, the buyer will factor decommissioning liability into its negotiation of the headline purchase price. In a buyer's market, particularly in respect of more mature assets where such liabilities may exceed the residual value of the resources, a buyer may negotiate that the seller should retain some liability in respect of such obligations.

2. The sale process

The process for the sale and purchase of oil and gas assets (whether by a share or asset purchase) does not differ materially from that followed in other sectors. The majority of share sales and purchases in the oil and gas sector relate to private, non-listed companies (typically special purpose companies established by oil and gas companies to hold interests in specific projects).

Notably, upstream transactions usually involve obtaining host government consents, which will affect the process and will need to be considered at an early stage. Such approvals are required due to the state's sovereign ownership and the national importance of petroleum resources. The consent requirements will typically be contained in the 'petroleum contract' relating to the project rights (ie, the production sharing agreement, risk service agreement, concession agreement or licence under which the state granted the right to explore and exploit the relevant petroleum resource) or the applicable legislation. The consent requirements will generally be formulated as the right of the host government to approve any direct transfer of project rights and (relevant to share sales) any change of control in the project rights-holding entity.

In some jurisdictions, however, the host government views a change of control in the holder of an interest in a petroleum contract as an assignment. Therefore, government consent may be required even though the petroleum contract may be silent on the point. The parties should consider at an early stage, once a deal is in prospect, when first contact should be made with the relevant governmental authority in relation to the transaction to ensure that there are no difficulties in obtaining the requisite consent, which in certain countries may take a number of months to obtain. Official submission of any application is likely to take place after signing the SPA and will be a condition to completion.

3. The sale and purchase agreement

Where the sale is being conducted by way of a competitive process, the first draft of the SPA will be prepared by the seller. In other cases, there is no hard and fast rule as to which party will have initial control of the SPA drafting, and this will usually be subject to the respective bargaining strength of the parties or past practice in associated transactions (if any). Clearly, each party will have a preference for preparing the first draft to ensure that any provisions favourable to it are included from the start of negotiations. A number of the key provisions are considered below.

3.1 Parties

The buying and selling entities should be identified at an early stage, if possible. It is common for buyers to use a special purpose company to carry out the purchase. This may be for reasons such as practicality or tax structuring, or to take advantage of bilateral investment treaties between the host government and the country in which the special purpose company is incorporated. This practice means that the selling entity may also be a special purpose company.

The seller and buyer may wish to conduct due diligence on each other's purchasing or selling entity respectively, and obtain opinions on the authority and the capacity of that entity to enter into the transaction. The seller and buyer will also need to consider whether third-party financial support of the purchasing or selling entity's obligations will be required (eg, in the form of a parent company guarantee). On the seller side, these obligations are primarily the ongoing obligations under the warranties and indemnities. On the buyer side, there may be obligations to pay deferred or adjusted consideration and other ongoing obligations such as tax and other counter-indemnities.

3.2 Agreement to sell

The SPA will state that the buyer and seller are respectively obliged to buy and sell the target shares on the terms of the SPA, free from encumbrances, together with all rights attaching to the shares. An express carve-out can be made for any encumbrances that the buyer is willing to accept (although this is unusual):

> *On and subject to the terms and conditions of this Agreement, the Seller shall sell and the Buyer shall buy the Sale Shares free from all Encumbrances[, save for any Permitted Encumbrances,] and together with all rights that attach (or in the future may attach) thereto including, in particular, the right to receive all dividends and distributions declared, made or paid [on or after the Effective Date].*

3.3 Pre-emption right waivers

On the sale of shares in an incorporated joint venture, the other project participants are likely to have a pre-emption right under the shareholders' agreement (which may be the same document as the joint operating agreement) in respect of the shares being sold. The pre-emption right will require the seller to give to the other project participants formal 'pre-emption notice' of the proposed sale, the price and other material terms. The other project participants will then have a specified time period in which they may notify the seller that they wish to acquire the seller's shares. Should the pre-emption procedure be instigated, it could result in the buyer losing the shares if the other project participants exercise their pre-emption rights. In practice, therefore, it is preferable for the parties to obtain advance waivers from the project participants in respect of their rights under the pre-emption procedure, thus permitting the transaction to proceed without the need to follow the pre-emption process. The buyer should also require the seller to undertake that any other necessary waivers have been obtained.

The Seller hereby waives all rights of pre-emption and any other rights or restrictions over any of the Sale Shares conferred on it by the Constitutional Documents of the Target Company or in any other way and shall procure that any such rights conferred on any other person are waived no later than Completion.

In the rarer cases that the joint operating agreement for an unincorporated joint venture specifies that pre-emption rights apply on a change of control in a company which holds a participating interest, it is likely to be the project interest itself that must be offered to the other project participants, rather than the shares in the company, since the seller shareholder is not party to or bound by the joint operating agreement.

3.4 Purchase price

(a) Determination of purchase price

The SPA will state the purchase price payable for the target shares. If the purchase price is fixed and payable in cash, this clause will be straightforward. In practice, however, target companies will frequently be valued by reference to the net present value of future income streams[3] (so-called 'enterprise value'), adjusted to reflect the net debt or working capital position of the target company on a specified 'effective date', as determined on an accrual basis of accounting. The effective date is the date from which the economic risk and benefit in the target company and its assets are to pass from the seller to the buyer. In the upstream sector, it is usual to agree an effective date which will facilitate the accounting treatment (eg, the end of an accounting cycle or immediately prior to the commencement of a new work programme and budget). The SPA will usually require the buyer to pay the seller interest on the enterprise value (as adjusted to reflect the effective date net debt or working capital position) for the period from the effective date until the date of completion.

In order to ascertain the adjusted value, financial statements made up to the effective date will be required. If the effective date coincides with the most recent financial year end of the target company, then the audited annual accounts may be used (if these are already available). In other circumstances, effective date financial statements will need to be prepared.

(b) Restrictions on value leakage and apportionments

The SPA will include provisions restricting the seller from extracting value from the target company between the effective date and completion (eg, by payment of dividends) and/or requiring additional adjustments to be made to the extent that the

---

3 If the target company holds a petroleum contract which is a production sharing agreement, the target company's entitlement to cost oil will be a material value item.

seller provides or receives benefits to or from the target company respectively in the period between the effective date and completion.

The SPA may also contain general provisions allocating receipts and liabilities accruing before the effective date to the seller, and receipts and liabilities accruing after the effective date to the buyer. The SPA will oblige the parties to make payments to each other (by means of an adjustment to the purchase price) in respect of all receipts and liabilities received or incurred by them which are for the account of the other party pursuant to such allocation.

(c) ***Deferred consideration***

Where the future performance of the target company is unpredictable such that its value cannot be estimated, the purchase price may include an 'earn-out' mechanism, where a portion of the purchase price is deferred and calculated to be payable by reference to the target company's performance in a specified period after completion. However, earn-outs are uncommon in upstream transactions, since the value of the target company depends primarily on future production levels. Indeed, it is common practice in an upstream transaction for the seller to give no warranty regarding, and to specifically exclude liability for, petroleum reserves, levels of production, energy prices, the physical condition of any facilities, or any economic, geoscientific or cost/expenditure forecasts. All of the foregoing are for the buyer's evaluation and determination.

3.5 Completion conditions

Certain matters will need to be addressed by the parties before completion can take place. It is generally preferable to address any such issues prior to the SPA being signed. However, the parties may be unwilling to address particular matters (eg, host government consents) until they have the protection of a binding agreement – for example, due to the expense or publicity involved in addressing them. These matters will be listed in the SPA as conditions to completion.

Some conditions relate to matters which could affect the validity of the transaction, result in penalties or have other adverse consequences if not satisfied (eg, governmental consents). Others may be purely for the benefit of one or other party, in which case their inclusion may depend solely on the relative negotiation strength of the parties (although some such conditions are more market standard than others).

The SPA will identify the party responsible for fulfilling each condition (although where completion relates to governmental consents or otherwise depends on the cooperation of third parties, this will generally be a 'reasonable endeavours' rather than an absolute obligation). The parties should be obliged to cooperate and provide each other with any information and support required towards fulfilment of the conditions, together with an obligation to inform the other party upon a condition being fulfilled or of any circumstances which would prevent the condition's fulfilment. The SPA will stipulate that completion must occur within a specified number of days once the last of the conditions has been fulfilled and will contain a 'long-stop' date on which the SPA will terminate (or can be terminated unilaterally by either party) if the conditions have not been fulfilled by that time. Where achievement of a condition is purely for the benefit of one particular party, that party may be permitted to waive it (eg, waiver of a material adverse change (MAC) condition by the buyer).

Common conditions on an upstream share sale include the following:

Subject to waiver in accordance with clause [x], Completion is subject to and conditional upon:....

(a) Governmental consents

....the written consent to the Transaction by the [relevant authority] of [jurisdiction] in accordance with applicable law and the terms of the [petroleum contract];...

As noted above, the consent of the host government will generally be required under the petroleum contract or applicable legislation if the share sale will result in a change of control of the asset-holding entity. Anti-monopoly consents may also be required. Certain strategic investment laws of the host state may also apply if the project concerns the exploitation of resources considered strategically important to the host country. These laws may limit the participation of foreign investors in such projects (particularly if those investors are owned or controlled by foreign governments) or make such participation subject to a screening process.

(b) Other third-party consents

Where either party is a company whose shares are traded publicly, there may be a regulatory requirement to obtain approval of the transaction by the party's shareholders – particularly if the transaction value is significant as compared with the value of that party's corporate group or otherwise under the rules of the applicable stock exchange. Shareholder approvals may alternatively be required by a party's constitutional documents or shareholder agreements. Change of control consents may also be required under key agreements.

(c) Pre-sale reorganisation

.....completion of the transfer by the Target Company of the [Excluded Assets] pursuant to the [reorganisation/hive-out agreement] dated [x];

If a preliminary restructuring is required, the seller may not wish to carry out such restructuring until the SPA has been signed, due to the costs involved. As such, it will frequently be treated as a condition to completion.

(d) Release of seller guarantees

....irrevocable and unconditional (save for any condition relating to the sale of the Sale Shares under this Agreement) release of all of its obligations and liabilities under the [Target Company Guarantee(s)]....

The seller may have given funding or other guarantees to the host government in respect of the target company, which it will require to be released. The host government will usually require a replacement guarantee from the buyer before doing so and it is unlikely that the buyer will provide this prior to completion. In such circumstances, rather than including a condition in the SPA, the relevant provisions in the SPA may alternatively be formulated as an obligation on the buyer to provide the relevant replacement guarantee at completion itself (such that the seller can procure release of its own guarantee as soon as possible after completion) on terms that, if a claim is made under the seller's guarantee before the seller can procure its release, the buyer will indemnify the seller.

(e) ***Release of charges and encumbrances***

The shares and assets of the target company may have been charged to lenders of the seller's group, as security for the group's loan facilities. The buyer will wish to ensure that the shares and assets have been released from such charges by completion. However, lenders may be unwilling to grant such releases before completion has occurred (particularly if the purchase price needs to be used towards the repayment of loans).

(f) ***Material adverse change***

Finally, a buyer may seek to include a condition that no MAC occurs in respect of the target company between signature of the SPA and expected completion. If included, the buyer will not be required to complete if a MAC occurs. The provision therefore alters the balance of risk between the seller and buyer in the period between signing the SPA and completion. The parties will need to give careful thought to what constitutes a MAC. This may be defined in terms of a significant specified percentage reduction in the future EBITDA (earnings from operations before interest, taxes, depreciation and amortisation) of the target company as compared with current levels.

In an upstream transaction, a MAC clause has traditionally not been as common due to the nature of the target company's business, and may be resisted by the seller due to its inherent risk and the customary levels of liability insurance. The one exception might be a major event occurring prior to completion which causes a cessation or curtailment of production for a significant period (often longer than a year). However, in a buyer-friendly environment, such clauses may be seen more frequently.

3.6 Interim period obligations

Where conditions are included in the SPA, there will be a gap between its signature and completion. The parties will need to set out in the SPA their respective rights and obligations during this interim period.

(a) ***Conduct of operations***

Both parties will have an interest in the conduct of operations of the target company during this period. The buyer has a vested interest in the target company from the date the SPA is signed and will be keen to ensure that the seller takes no action that could adversely affect the value of the target company. Conversely, the seller will not wish to cede control at a time when it continues to own the shares and the transaction remains contingent on outstanding conditions. SPAs typically reflect a compromise of these interests, in the form of a positive obligation on the seller to continue to conduct operations in the ordinary course, together with a list of actions that the seller must not take in the interim period unless it first obtains the consent of the buyer. This list will include actions such as paying dividends, entering into or amending key agreements, incurring significant capital expenditure, divesting any significant assets, commencing or settling litigation and hiring key employees. It will also include certain fundamental corporate actions, such as changing the constitution of the target company, issuing new shares or making other alterations to the share capital structure of the target company. Frequently, there will also be a positive obligation to keep the buyer updated as to material developments in relation to the target company's operations, and to provide the buyer with any specific information requested by the buyer regarding the continuing operations (subject usually to a reasonableness qualification or materiality thresholds).

On an acquisition of a joint venture interest, the extent of the list will depend on the seller's ability to control such actions under the governance provisions of the relevant operating agreement. The SPA may include an express right of the buyer to attend operating committee meetings with the seller as an observer (if permitted by the joint operating agreement) and limitations on the seller voting on resolutions of the joint operating committee without the buyer's previous consent.

(b) Insurance

In the interim period the target company will be run at the buyer's risk, which vests (subject to completion) from the effective date. It will therefore be important to the buyer that the target company maintains insurance against material operational risks and third-party liabilities during this period.

(c) Funding

Funding of the project in the interim period must also be considered. If the project is already in production, the target company may be cash positive and able to fund any ongoing expenditure it is required to make in relation to the project. If the project is at an earlier stage, the target company may still require shareholder or third-party funding.

Assuming that the effective date has already occurred, such funding is ultimately for the buyer's account. However, it is usual for any such interim period funding to be provided by the seller, with subsequent repayment by the buyer of this funding (together with interest) on completion. Depending on how the funding was provided, the repayment could be made by an upward adjustment to the purchase price. However, where the seller has provided the funding by shareholder loan (as is common), it may be preferable for tax reasons to assign the loan (together with the interest) at value to the buyer. Alternatively, the buyer may prefer to provide loan funding directly to the target company on completion, from which the seller's loan (together with interest) can be immediately repaid. In such case the documentation may allow for the relevant amount to be paid directly from the buyer to the seller, rather than flowing through the target company.

Alternatively, if the target company is cash positive, the seller may need to account to the buyer for use of the target company's funds in the interim period – for example, when the seller's group has cash pooling arrangements whereby the target company's funds may be used by other companies in the group pursuant to intra-group loans. In such case, the seller will usually be required to ensure that the balance of any intra-group loans made by the target company is zero by completion, and to account to the buyer for interest for the period during which any seller's group companies had use of those sums. Depending on the terms on which the intra-group loans were made, the seller may pay interest directly to the target company along with the repayment of principal, in accordance with those terms, or to the buyer as a downward purchase price adjustment.

(d) ***Management charges***

Where the target company is a special purpose vehicle, established simply to hold the seller's interest in a project, the target company may not have its own personnel, management or administrative capability. Instead, it may rely on management and administrative services provided by other members of the seller's group, for which the seller will usually charge a fee. This fee may depend on varying factors, such as the time spent by the seller's personnel dealing with matters relating to the target company. Assuming that the effective date has already occurred prior to signing (such that the economic risk has already passed to the buyer), the buyer will wish to control the extent of these fees. This may be achieved by agreeing fixed or capped amounts chargeable to the target company by the seller in respect of each week or month in the interim period.

(e) ***Preparation of completion statements***

In contrast to M&A transactions in other sectors, where the price adjustment calculations may occur post-completion (eg, by way of completion accounts), the upstream SPA will usually require the seller to prepare a completion statement shortly before completion. The completion statement will be prepared once the completion conditions have been met and the completion date can therefore be ascertained. The completion statement will set out the enterprise value previously agreed between the seller and the buyer and the seller's calculations of the relevant adjustment values, discussed above, by reference to the effective date, including:

- the effective date working capital and debt adjustments (if the effective date accounts were already available at the time the SPA was signed, these values may already have been ascertained and agreed between the seller and buyer);
- interest on the enterprise value, after adjusting for the effective date working capital and debt, from the effective date until the completion date;
- apportionments as between the parties in respect of receipts and liabilities accruing prior to and after the effective date;
- any funding provided by the seller in the interim period (together with interest);
- (to the extent not repaid by the seller's group prior to completion) any funding provided by the target company to other companies in the seller's group during the interim period, together with interest;
- the value to the seller of any tax benefits which will pass with the target company on completion;
- any interim period management fees; and
- any other adjustments specific to the transaction.

The completion statement will state the final purchase price to be paid by the buyer on completion, based on the above adjustments. The SPA will also set out a post-completion review mechanism for such statements in the event that the buyer disagrees with them.

3.7 Completion obligations

The SPA will set out the actions which must be performed by the parties on the completion date.

(a) Share transfer mechanics

The main completion obligations are that of the seller to transfer the target shares and that of the buyer to pay the adjusted purchase price (subject to any further adjustment necessitated by the post-completion review mechanism, discussed in section 4.8). The procedure for the transfer of shares will depend on the laws of the jurisdiction in which the target company is incorporated. Typically, the seller will sign a form of share transfer instrument, which it must then submit to the target company (together with any share certificates evidencing the seller's ownership of the shares), in order that the transfer can be entered in the target company's register of members to effect the change in ownership.

> *At Completion, the Seller shall deliver, or shall procure the delivery, to the Purchaser of a duly executed transfer of the Sale Shares in favour of the Buyer (or its nominee(s)) together with the certificates for the Sale Shares or, in the case of any lost certificate, an indemnity in a form satisfactory to the Buyer.*

In some jurisdictions, stamp duty or similar transfer taxes may be payable on the transfer before the legal change of ownership can occur. In those circumstances, the SPA may envisage a form of trust arrangement whereby the seller holds the target shares to the order of the buyer in the interim.

(b) Administrative and management changes

The seller will be under an obligation to remove its representatives from the board of directors and other management bodies of the target company, and to remove its signatories from any bank mandates and appoint persons nominated by the buyer in their place. Where the seller is selling the entire share capital of the target company, it may also pass a resolution to change the target company's name if the current name suggests any connection with the seller.

Where the seller is selling shares in an incorporated joint venture (such that the parties to the shareholders' agreement and, if different, the joint operating agreement will change), the buyer will need to accede as a party to such agreement. The relevant agreement will usually provide a procedure for doing this, whereby the buyer enters into a deed of adherence with the other parties, in which the buyer undertakes to adhere to the agreement's terms.

(c) Failure to complete

The SPA will include provisions governing the parties' rights and obligations where the other party refuses to complete or is unable to comply materially with its completion obligations. Typically, the non-defaulting party will be permitted to waive the respective completion requirement, postpone completion or terminate the SPA and seek damages.

3.8 Post-completion obligations

The SPA will contain various post-completion obligations of the parties.

(a) *Review of completion statements*

The SPA will give the buyer the opportunity to invoke a dispute resolution procedure post-completion if it disagrees with the amounts or items contained in the completion statements. This will usually involve referral of the matter to an independent expert if the parties have been unable to resolve amicably any disagreement over the completion statements within a limited time period. Once the completion statements have been definitively ascertained (whether by the parties' agreement or expert determination), any further resultant purchase price adjustment will become payable.

(b) *Provision of information*

The seller may require ongoing access to the records of the target company after completion, to the extent that such records relate to the seller's period of ownership (eg, to satisfy information requests from tax or regulatory authorities). The SPA will usually give the seller the right to be provided with access to such information for a limited number of years after completion. Often, this timeframe is related to the period in which the relevant tax authority may reopen its files on the target company in respect of previous tax years. The seller's right will be subject to reasonableness requirements as to the extent of the information requests and to advance notice to be given the buyer.

(c) *Other post-completion obligations*

Various filings with public registries may be required in relation to matters dealt with at completion (eg, in relation to any change of name of the target company). Typically, it will be the buyer that is required to make (or ensure that the target company makes) any such filings. The seller may also be under a positive obligation to hold the shares to the order of the buyer if (for tax or other reasons) the legal change in ownership cannot be perfected until after completion.

4. Warranties and indemnities

4.1 Warranties

Warranties are statements of fact made in the SPA as to the condition of the target company, its operations and assets. They are the main contractual tool by which the buyer gains legal assurance as to the state of the target company and protects itself against unknown risks relating to the target company and its operations. Although it will have conducted due diligence, a buyer may not have an effective legal remedy against the seller where the buyer has relied on due diligence information which, it is subsequently discovered, was inaccurate or incomplete. In contrast, the buyer will have a right to monetary compensation where it transpires that a warranty made by the seller in the SPA was untrue.

4.2 Purpose of warranties

Warranties serve a dual purpose. First, warranties are used as a means of risk allocation to shift the 'buyer beware' risk from the buyer back to the seller. The inclusion of a seller's warranty as to a certain state of affairs will mean that the seller, rather than the buyer, bears the risk where the true state of affairs differs. The seller, with its greater knowledge and experience of the business, may place a lower value on certain risks than the buyer and so will be in a better position to bear that risk.

Second, warranties may also be used to fill gaps in due diligence. For example, where the seller has been unable to provide evidence as to the existence or absence of a certain state of affairs during the due diligence process, the buyer may require the seller to provide a warranty as to such matters in the SPA. This may elicit disclosures from the seller setting out exceptions to the warranties. However, warranties should not be considered a substitute for a full investigation of any potential risks before it purchases the asset.

4.3 Scope

The warranty catalogue in an SPA can be extensive. It will usually be contained in a schedule to the SPA with the main body of the SPA containing a statement by the seller that the warranties in the schedule are true. Warranties will be given as at the signing date of the SPA and may also be repeated by the seller on completion. In the former case it is the buyer that bears the risk of an adverse change in the target company's affairs occurring after signing which makes the warranties untrue on completion. In the latter case, it is the seller that bears this risk (since the buyer will have a right to claim damages for any breach of warranty arising in that interim period).[4] In the authors' experience, it is usual for warranties to be repeated on completion to the extent that they relate to circumstances which are within the seller's control or to title or good standing of the petroleum contract. Such cases will often trigger a discussion over whether the seller should be entitled to make further disclosures against warranties between signing and completion and the consequences of any such updated disclosure.

The most fundamental warranties concern the capacity and status of the seller, and title to the shares.

The Seller is the sole legal and beneficial owner of the Sale Shares.

....

The Sale Shares constitute [100]% of the allotted and issued share capital of the [Target Company], are fully paid or credited as fully paid and are free from all Encumbrances.

Warranties are also typically given in relation to accounts, contractual matters (including any change of control issues), litigation, compliance with laws, finance

---

4 However, the buyer will not usually have a right to terminate unless expressly agreed in the SPA (see section 4.4).

matters and indebtedness, insolvency, property, employment matters and pensions, intellectual property, effect of sale and tax – although this is a non-exhaustive list.

On an upstream sale, the most fundamental asset will be the project rights and the buyer will focus on the key warranties relating to these rights, including that the target company's title to the project rights and the project rights have been validly granted in accordance with the laws of the host country and the governing law of the petroleum contract.

The [Target Company] is the legal and beneficial owner free from all Encumbrances of the Interest.[5]

The buyer will also seek warranties that there have been no breaches of the petroleum contract or other circumstances that could lead to those project rights being withdrawn, and that all the other key agreements relating to the asset are in place and valid:

The Interest Documents and all the [Target Company's] rights, benefits and interests under or deriving therefrom have been validly granted and are in full force and effect......

The Interest Documents are the only material agreements which govern or relate to the creation, existence and validity of the Interest, and are the only material agreements to the Target Company is party relating to the Interest.

Warranties may also state that such agreements do not include any unduly onerous terms for the buyer, that no party is in breach of their terms, and that there are no other circumstances that could lead to their premature termination.

There will also likely be specific warranties as to the status of any required licences, permits and approvals, as well as health and safety issues and environmental matters such as oil spillage. A comparatively lighter touch is usually taken to the other typical commercial warranties, although this may depend on the bargaining strength of the buyer.

4.4 Remedies for breach

The compensation payable for breach of warranty may be calculated with reference to the difference in the value of the target company (and therefore the shares purchased) and the value had the warranty been true. Alternatively, it may be calculated on an indemnity basis, where the seller must indemnify the buyer, on a pound-for-pound basis, for all losses and expenses incurred by the target company as a result of the breach of warranty. The governing law and the express terms of the SPA will determine which of the two applies. The two bases may result in very different calculations, depending on the extent to which a breach of warranty affects the overall value of the project operations. The former is the established position under an English law contract for the purchase of shares. However, the latter – which is generally the more advantageous for a buyer and is established practice in the United States – is increasingly prevalent, in particular where international parties are involved. When considering the measure of damages recoverable, much will depend on the basis on which the target company was valued and the actual loss which may

5 Where 'Interest' is the percentage interest in the target upstream asset or licence.

be incurred by breach of warranty. It may be appropriate, on the individual facts, to agree to apply different measures of damages to different categories of warranty or to include limits of liability.

The buyer may be able to negotiate a termination right if a material breach of warranty is discovered before completion. If agreed, this is often subject to the seller's right to remedy such breach, if capable of remedy, within a reasonable timeframe.

4.5 Indemnities

Indemnities operate to protect the buyer against specific risks identified during the due diligence process by compensating the buyer on a pound-for-pound basis. For example, if the target company is involved in high-value litigation, the buyer might seek an indemnity from the seller in respect of all resulting costs and liabilities and in return the seller may require conduct of the litigation.

In addition, if the target company has a history of operations unconnected with the project assets or, where restructuring has been undertaken, to move assets out of the target company prior to the sale, the buyer may require indemnities in relation to residual liabilities relating to these operations or assets on the basis that they have no connection with the assets that the buyer is acquiring and it is therefore inappropriate for the buyer to acquire such liabilities. Indemnities, rather than warranties, are used for specific risks because of the wider scope of compensation available to the buyer and uncertainty surrounding a buyer's ability to claim under a warranty where it was aware of the circumstances giving rise to the risk.

4.6 Counter-indemnities

Like warranties, indemnities can be used to transfer risk. This can cut both ways. For example, the seller may seek to use counter-indemnities to ensure that it achieves a clean break from liability in certain limited high-risk areas (most frequently decommissioning and environment). The risk of residual liability attaching to the seller is limited on a share sale, since the liabilities relating to the ownership and use of the assets will generally transfer with the target company. However, there are some exceptions. For example, under some regimes, previous parties to petroleum contracts or licences and their affiliates (ie, the seller) can ultimately be held liable for decommissioning costs if these cannot be satisfied by the current licensees and their affiliates. The seller's residual risk in these areas can be mitigated by obtaining a counter-indemnity from the buyer (covering liability arising from circumstances occurring both before and after completion) in such areas. There may be a carve-out for liability caused by highly culpable behaviour of the seller, such as wilful misconduct.

While this may appear to place an unfair burden on the buyer, such indemnities are frequently accepted in practice on upstream transactions in the areas of decommissioning (which may extend to providing a letter of credit or guarantee)[6]

6 This is particularly relevant in the case of decommissioning, since the seller's residual liability is likely to arise specifically in circumstances where the target company and the buyer are not financially capable of satisfying the decommissioning liabilities themselves.

and the environment, and arguably reflect a generally accepted industry approach to risk allocation in these areas. However, in a buyer's market, it may be negotiated that the seller retains some of this risk through mutual indemnities. In any event, the seller will nevertheless be required to give warranties that it is unaware of any circumstances which may give rise to such liabilities. The interplay between such warranties and the indemnities will need to be considered on the individual facts.

On a share purchase, it is also common for the parties to enter into a tax indemnity, which will apportion pre and post-transaction liability to taxes between the seller and the buyer respectively. In practice, the relevant provisions will be complex and may therefore be contained in a separate document.

5. Limitations of liability

It is customary to agree certain limits on the liability of the seller for claims under the SPA. These will be in addition to any general limitations in the agreement, such as materiality or knowledge qualifiers contained in the warranties given by the seller and any matters properly disclosed to the buyer. The scope of these limitations is often subject to a great deal of negotiation between the parties. The seller will always be seeking to limit its exposure under the SPA; whereas the buyer will be keen to ensure that, should an actionable claim for breach arise (which in itself will be subject to negotiation), there will be no further significant barriers to recovery.

5.1 Time limits

In the absence of express agreement to the contrary, the statutory limitation periods for bringing a claim under the warranties will apply. Under English law, for example, these will be six years for contracts under hand and 12 years for deeds. It is standard practice for the parties to agree to shorten these limits anywhere from 12 months to three years for general claims (usually to cover at least one accounting cycle following completion), with a longer period for tax (eg, up to seven years in the United Kingdom, due to the tax authorities' power to reopen tax affairs), and certain other matters of particular concern to the buyer, such as title. A seller may also seek further certainty as to its exposure by imposing additional time limits in which any identified potential claims should be brought. Any such provision should make it clear that compliance with the time limits will be a condition of the seller's liability. A buyer will wish to avoid agreeing to any such fetter on its rights if a *bona fide* claim arises.

5.2 Financial limits

It is commonplace to include a minimum amount for actionable claims, to avoid trivial claims and wasted costs. This can be a fairly low number depending on the litigious appetite of the parties. The parties would also usually expect to negotiate a separate threshold (or basket) which a claim, or collection of claims in aggregate, would have to exceed before the liability of the seller is triggered. A sensible starting point here may be 1% to 2% of the total consideration, although this may vary by reference to the size of the transaction and agreed thresholds of materiality. The buyer will want to ensure that it will be entitled to recover the whole amount of any qualifying claim(s) and not just the excess amount.

In addition, the seller will wish to cap its overall liability to an agreed amount. This is often heavily negotiated. A logical approach from the buyer's perspective would be that, if at all, the seller's liability should be limited to the consideration received by it under the SPA. However, practice has developed such that a cap may be agreed ranging anywhere from as little as 20% to 100% of the consideration depending on the value of the transaction, the bargaining strength of the parties and the nature of the losses actually recoverable under the SPA. Multiple sellers will seek to limit their liability by reference to the proportion of the total consideration received by them respectively.

5.3 Additional limitation provisions

Other limitations may include limiting or excluding liability for losses arising due to a change in law or acts by the buyer, or losses recoverable under insurance. Any negotiation of limitations on liability will be intrinsically linked to the scope of the exposure of the seller under the SPA, current market practice and the nature of the losses actually recoverable under the SPA and applicable governing law. It is often more productive for these limitations to be presented as a package, with reference (if appropriate) to the scope of relevant warranty and indemnity coverage, rather than as a series of individual items to be negotiated in isolation. For policy reasons, it is not possible under various legal jurisdictions to limit or exclude liability for fraud, and any attempt to do so may risk invalidating the rest of the agreed exclusions or limitations.

6. Disclosure

As discussed above, the seller will give the buyer a suite of warranties in the SPA about the target company and assets being sold. The SPA will provide that those warranties are given subject to matters disclosed in the disclosure letter. The disclosure letter is therefore a key document, as it is the seller's opportunity to qualify the warranties it is giving and therefore qualify its liability accordingly. The drafting of the disclosure letter is often not prioritised in the sale process, as the main focus usually falls on the SPA. However, the content of the disclosure letter itself may have significant implications. If a seller fails to disclose a matter adequately, it may be subject to claims which it could have avoided. Equally, if a buyer fails to review the disclosures properly, it may inadvertently concede its right to bring a claim for breach of warranty.

It is in the seller's interest to disclose as much as possible in the disclosure letter through a combination of general disclosures – matters that are or would be apparent from sources generally available to the buyer – and specific factual disclosures relating to the target. The seller will be seeking in the disclosure letter to impute the buyer with knowledge of as much information as possible on any breaches or potential breaches of warranty in order to minimise the grounds upon which the buyer may bring a subsequent action for breach of warranty.

Under English law, it is uncertain whether a buyer that has actual knowledge of a potential breach of warranty at the time of acquisition will succeed in bringing a claim for such breach even if the subject matter of the breach was not disclosed in the disclosure letter. Therefore, if the buyer is aware of an undisclosed potential breach, it would be prudent to seek an indemnity or price reduction rather than assume that a breach of warranty claim will be available to it.

7. Boilerplate clauses

Last but not least, the SPA will also contain a series of boilerplate clauses. Some common examples include confidentiality, agreed and/or mandatory announcements, assignment, provisions for notice (allowing for practical application given the cross-border nature of many transactions), bearing of transaction costs, the grant of any third-party rights, entire agreement or 'integration' clauses and, of course, governing law and jurisdiction. While these clauses are often not subject to the same level of scrutiny as the principal operative provisions, their importance should not be overlooked in the negotiation of the SPA. This is equally the case for share sale agreements in the upstream sector; the standard wording for such clauses may not always be applicable to the circumstances in hand.

Asset sale and purchase agreements

John C LaMaster
Akin Gump Strauss Hauer & Feld LLP

1. Introduction

An asset sale and purchase takes place when a purchaser acquires assets directly from the seller which owns those assets. This chapter focuses on the types of asset transactions that typically take place in the oil and gas industry, being the acquisition of participating interests in one or more host country upstream petroleum agreements (UPAs) such as licences, concessions or production sharing contracts, together with associated contracts such as joint operating agreements (JOAs), and related assets such as geological and geophysical data, facilities and equipment.

Each asset transaction presents a unique set of facts and circumstances, including matters such as the allocation of risk between the parties and the economic terms of the transaction. As a result, there is no prescribed or standard form of an asset sale and purchase agreement (ASPA) – although the author is a member of the Association of International Petroleum Negotiators' (AIPN) Asset SPA Drafting Committee, which is preparing a model form ASPA that may, over time, develop into a standard form document used by the industry.

A farmout agreement is a specialised form of oil and gas ASPA.[1] The distinguishing characteristic of a farmout agreement is that the transferor will transfer part of its participating interest in a UPA to a transferee, in return for that transferee performing and/or paying for certain works that otherwise would have been performed and/or paid for by the transferor – for example, the drilling of a well. In this regard, a farmout agreement is fundamentally an asset sale and purchase, albeit with a different form of consideration.

Rather than discussing every provision that is common to most ASPAs, this chapter focuses on those parts of an ASPA that are unique to, or that frequently raise issues in, an upstream oil and gas asset sale and purchase.

2. Allocation of liabilities

In an asset transaction, as a general rule, the seller will retain all pre-completion liabilities and the buyer will assume all post-completion liabilities with respect to the specific assets being transferred. It is also possible, however, to structure an asset transaction and draft the relevant documents to alter this general rule regarding the allocation of liabilities.

1 Farmout agreements are discussed in more detail in section 8 below.

One way to alter the general rule is for the buyer and the seller to agree an economic effective date, being a different date from the completion date, on which the liabilities are assumed by the buyer. An example of this type of contractual provision is as follows:

Notwithstanding the date of this Agreement or the date on which the Assignment is executed or approved by the Government, the effective date of this Agreement as between the Parties (the "Effective Date") shall be deemed to be [insert date]. The consideration payable by the Buyer reflects the Effective Date.

In some cases, the buyer may want to identify with specificity all of the liabilities and obligations that it will assume with respect to the purchased assets, and leave all other liabilities and obligations with the seller. From a seller's standpoint, this approach at first glance seems very pro-buyer. However, it can be tempered by including among the assumed liabilities and obligations those arising in the ordinary course of business with respect to the relevant assets. An example of this type of contractual provision is as follows:

On the Closing Date, but effective as of the Effective Date, the Buyer shall assume and agree to discharge only the following liabilities and obligations of the Seller (the "Assumed Liabilities"): [enumerate list]. All liabilities and obligations of the Seller other than the Assumed Liabilities (the "Retained Liabilities") shall remain the sole responsibility of and shall be retained, paid, performed and discharged solely by the Seller.

It is also possible to structure the transaction to provide that the buyer will assume some specific pre-completion liabilities, or that the seller will retain some post-completion liabilities. For example, it is not uncommon for a buyer to agree to assume known pre-completion liabilities that have been disclosed to the buyer, even though the buyer would derive no benefit from the assumption. An example would be a known environmental liability. In this case, the buyer would have had the opportunity to assess and quantify the liability, and take it into account in the purchase price.

It is less common for a buyer in an oil and gas asset transaction to agree to assume unknown pre-completion liabilities. However, this can sometimes be the case even in an asset transaction. For example, in acquisitions from super-major international oil companies or in situations where the seller has disproportionate bargaining power, the seller may take the position that the buyer must assume all liabilities, past, present and future. Sometimes this assumption is limited to environmental and decommissioning liabilities, although these are often the most significant potential unknown liabilities. In this situation, the buyer is left to rely on its due diligence investigation of the relevant assets.

It is possible that certain types of liabilities may follow the assets as a matter of law. For example, under some environmental laws, a buyer may become liable for remediation with respect to pre-completion activities of a seller in cases where the seller can no longer be held liable (eg, where a seller has subsequently become insolvent). Similarly, in jurisdictions with sophisticated decommissioning laws, pursuant to the operation of law a buyer is likely to assume responsibility to remove infrastructure that has been put in place by the seller and other predecessors-in-title.

It is also common for sellers to retain certain known post-completion liabilities. For example, if a buyer has identified during its due diligence investigation that the seller is involved in litigation, then the buyer may require the seller to retain all liabilities with respect to such litigation and to indemnify the buyer against all such liabilities. In this case, the seller would want to retain control of the litigation post-completion and may need ongoing access to records relating to the subject of the litigation.

3. Provisions typically found in an ASPA

The provisions of an ASPA for an oil and gas transaction will in many respects be similar to those of a sale and purchase agreement for any other type of asset transaction. The following sections discuss those specific provisions that are unique to, or that commonly arise as issues in, an agreement for an upstream oil and gas asset sale and purchase.

3.1 Description of the assets

A buyer in an asset transaction will acquire only those assets described with specificity in the ASPA. This is one way in which an ASPA differs from a share sale and purchase agreement. In a share sale and purchase agreement, only one class of asset (the shares) needs to be described. In an ASPA, it is essential that the assets are described comprehensively and that the participating, working and/or cost-bearing percentage interests to be acquired are described with specificity. In a transaction involving multiple assets, this can be a burdensome process, although it is seldom a point of contention. It is sometimes also necessary to apportion the purchase price between the various assets in the ASPA. For example, in a transaction where only certain assets are subject to pre-emption rights, it will be important that those assets are allocated a specific price at which a third party can exercise its pre-emption right. Apportionment between different oil and gas interests for multi-asset transactions may also be important for tax reasons.

For an upstream transaction, the principal asset being acquired will be the participating interests in the relevant UPA. This could be a licence, a concession agreement, a production sharing contract, a risk service agreement or some combination thereof (eg, a licence plus a production sharing contract). The assets will also typically include the relevant participating interests under the applicable JOA (and, possibly, unitisation agreements). Depending on the state of exploration and development of the relevant asset, there may also be other contractual rights, entered into either by the operator or by the individual JOA partners, such as production sales and transportation agreements, drilling contracts and other service agreements. Also depending on the state of exploration and development of the relevant asset, there may be physical assets such as geological, geophysical and other technical data, as well as platforms, pipelines and other facilities. If the transaction also includes transfer of operatorship, the buyer will need to acquire the assets held by the seller in its capacity as the operator.

Where less than all of the seller's assets are being sold, and where there could possibly be an overlap between the assets being sold and the assets being retained, it may be necessary to include a list of excluded assets. Where an ASPA includes both a list of included assets and a list of excluded assets, it is usually necessary to give one of the lists priority over the other; this could be done, for example, by making one list exhaustive and the other list illustrative.

The following is an example of a description of assets in a transaction where just a UPA and an associated JOA are being sold:

> *Upon the terms and subject to the conditions set forth in this Agreement, at Completion, but with effect from the Effective Date, the Seller shall sell, convey, assign and transfer to the Buyer, free and clear of Encumbrances other than Permitted Encumbrances, an undivided [•]% Participating Interest in and to the Contract and the JOA.*

3.2 Purchase price

The consideration in an ASPA can take several different forms. Of course, a cash consideration is common and straightforward. The consideration may also take the form of other assets. For example, the buyer and the seller may be swapping similar upstream assets on a like-for-like basis, or perhaps with a cash-balancing component. A swap transaction can sometimes be simpler to document than other asset transactions, because both parties will have a mutual interest to ensure that the ASPA is not too pro-seller or pro-buyer. Consideration can also take the form of a promissory note or interests in shares. One form of consideration that is relatively unique to upstream oil and gas transactions is a promote. This occurs when a seller sells part, but not all, of its interests in an asset. A promote can take the form of a carried interest – for example, where the buyer agrees to pay certain well costs on behalf of the seller – or the reimbursement of historic costs (see section 8 below).

It is possible that some or all of the consideration may be deferred until after completion of the sale and purchase. This is obviously the case where a promissory note forms all or part of the consideration. However, the parties may also agree to a retention mechanism whereby some portion of the purchase price is held back by the buyer to ensure that funds will be available if there are any future warranty claims by the buyer. These retained funds could be held in an escrow arrangement. Similarly, if a promissory note forms all or part of the purchase price, the buyer may have a right to offset any claims against the seller against amounts due under the promissory note.

In the volatile oil price environment that has existed since around 2014, M&A activity has declined in the upstream oil and gas industry. This is largely due to the inability of buyers and sellers to agree on the valuation of assets. For example, a seller may have a higher expectation of future oil commodity prices than a buyer, leading to a valuation or purchase price gap. One way to bridge this gap is to provide for an earnout. Earnouts are provisions in sale and purchase agreements, or in standalone earnout agreements, that provide for a contingent purchase price payable at some point in the future, after completion of the sale and purchase. The earnout could last for a specified period of time or may terminate once a specified amount has been paid out. Although an earnout based on a single factor such as the future oil commodity price may be simple, the drafting of earnouts can become very complicated. For example, many complications will arise if the earnout is calculated based on the buyer's post-completion earnings from operations before interest, taxes, depreciation and amortisation. Similarly, if the earnout is payable in the buyer's shares rather than in cash, the parties will need to resolve valuation issues regarding not only the earnout, but also the buyer's shares (assuming it is a private company not having its shares traded on a stock exchange). Another issue that arises is whether interest is payable on the earnout; a seller may argue that interest should be payable on the basis that the earnout payment is a deferred part of the purchase price.

The purchase price may be subject to post-completion adjustment. For example, in the sale and purchase of a producing upstream asset, the post-completion adjustment can ensure that expenses and revenues are properly allocated as between the buyer and the seller as of the completion date. Alternatively, the parties may agree on an economic effective date on which the economic risk and reward of the assets transfer from the seller to the buyer, usually on an accrual basis of accounting. The economic effective date is typically a date prior to the completion date and is often based on a convenient accounting date, such as a month-end or quarter-end date. In this case, the post-completion adjustment will be calculated as of the economic effective date rather than the completion date. Any revenues received by the seller, and any costs or expenses incurred by the seller, relating to the period between the economic effective date and the completion date will be for the account of the buyer. In a sale and purchase of a producing asset, there may also be adjustments for historic imbalances (underlifts or overlifts) in production. Lastly, the issue of whether interest is payable on any post-completion adjustment is frequently negotiated, and would seem to be a reasonable inclusion in circumstances where the post-completion adjustment could result in a payment by either the buyer or the seller. The AIPN Model Form Farmout Agreement includes a simple adjustment mechanism as follows:

> *Farmor and Farmee agree that they shall make whatever adjustments and payments from one to the other to reflect the Assignment as of the Effective Date, notwithstanding any cost recovery allocations, tax deductions or other benefits or payments received from the Government thereafter as a result of the application of the Contract or any applicable laws of the Government which reflect the Approval Date (and not the Effective Date).*[2]

Post-completion purchase price adjustment mechanisms are typically much more complicated, and are carefully drafted to match the facts and circumstances of the relevant transaction.

3.3 Warranties

From a buyer's standpoint, warranties serve three functions in an ASPA. First, they serve a due diligence and information-gathering function for the buyer. A properly drafted set of warranties will set out the key assumptions that the buyer has made in establishing the purchase price and deciding to enter into the transaction. The seller is then required to disclose information against the warranties prior to the buyer

2 AIPN Model Form Farmout Agreement (2004).

signing the ASPA and thereby prior to the buyer making a binding commitment to buy the assets. This disclosure can alert the buyer to any problems it may have been unaware of, and may provide the basis for the buyer to renegotiate the purchase price, seek specific indemnities or even walk away from the transaction.

The second function of the warranties is to establish a mechanism whereby the buyer can terminate the transaction even after the ASPA has been signed. This is typically accomplished by the interplay between the warranties and the conditions precedent. A usual and customary condition precedent to completion is that the seller's warranties are true and correct in all material respects at completion; this is often referred to as the 'bring down' condition precedent (see the example in section 6 below). If the conditions precedent have not been satisfied by a specified longstop date, then the ASPA may terminate. The ASPA may provide that this termination automatically occurs on the longstop date. More commonly, the ASPA will give either party the right to terminate on or after the longstop date. In cases where the conditions precedent have not been satisfied due to a breach by one of the parties, the ASPA may give only the non-breaching party a right to terminate. As a result, if some material facts or circumstances occur or become known between signing and completion of the ASPA which constitute a breach of the seller's warranties, and if the seller has not remedied that breach before the longstop date, the buyer will have a right to terminate because the conditions precedent have not been satisfied.

The third function of the warranties is to give the buyer post-completion recourse against the seller if any of the warranties prove to be untrue at signing or completion, and if the valuation of the target assets would have differed as a result. The compensation recoverable for a breach of warranty will depend in part on the governing law of the ASPA. Under English law, recovery can be on a diminution basis, whereby the buyer recovers an amount equal to the difference between the value of the assets subject to untrue warranty and the value of the assets had the warranty been true. Alternatively, recovery can be on an indemnity basis, whereby as well as claiming the difference in value, the buyer recovers any other losses it suffered on a pound-for-pound or dollar-for-dollar basis. The two formulations may result in different valuations for different breaches of warranties. The latter formulation is more favourable to buyers.

The seller's warranties contain detailed information regarding the assets to be acquired and are much more comprehensive than the buyer's warranties. However, the seller's warranties in an ASPA will typically be less extensive than in a share sale and purchase agreement, because the seller will not need to give detailed warranties regarding a target company. The seller and the buyer will also typically give each other a series of identical warranties – for example, regarding their respective corporate organisation and corporate authorisation to enter into the ASPA and to consummate the transactions contemplated thereby.

As a general rule, a buyer may receive more thorough warranties regarding operational matters from a seller which is an operator than from a seller which is a non-operator. A non-operator seller may refuse to give warranties regarding operational matters or may want to qualify those warranties to the knowledge of the seller.

A buyer may be tempted to negotiate and rely on extensive warranties from the seller, in place of a thorough due diligence investigation. However, this would be ill advised, for several reasons. It is better to identify problems upfront than have to deal with them post-completion. There is always a level of uncertainty regarding recoverability of post-completion claims – for example, as a result of financial and time limits included in the ASPA, as discussed in section 3.4. Also, post-completion claims, if disputed, can result in expensive arbitration or litigation, as well as in excessive demands on management time. In any case, under current practice it is usual for a seller to include the entire contents of its data room in the seller's disclosures against the warranties; in that case, the buyer will be deemed to have the same level of knowledge as if it had conducted a thorough due diligence investigation of the contents of the data room and will thus be prevented from making a warranty claim in relation to a matter that it would have been aware of had it properly conducted due diligence.

It is worth noting a difference in practice between US lawyers and English solicitors with respect to representations and warranties. US lawyers sometimes distinguish representations from warranties on the basis that representations are limited to statements as to existing circumstances, whereas warranties can also cover future circumstances.[3] In practice, however, US lawyers tend to use the words 'representations' and 'warranties' interchangeably, and sellers typically make 'representations and warranties' in ASPAs. English solicitors, on the other hand, are careful to distinguish representations from warranties, on the basis that misrepresentations can give rise to specific contractual remedies such as rescission. As a result, sellers in English law ASPAs typically give only warranties, not representations.

The legal principles regarding warranties are no different in the sale and purchase of upstream oil and gas assets from the sale and purchase of any other asset. An ASPA will typically contain standard seller's warranties regarding matters such as litigation, compliance with laws, anti-bribery and taxes. However, there are also some warranties that are specific to oil and gas transactions, including the following.

(a) Title to UPA and JOA

Perhaps the most important warranty confirms that the seller is a party to the licence or other UPA, and has a specified percentage interest in such licence or other UPA and in the JOA. The appropriate standard is 'good title' rather than 'good and marketable title', as marketability can be affected by a multitude of things, such as the typical requirement to obtain government consent to transfer an upstream asset (see section 5.1 below). The assets should also be warranted to be free from any encumbrances, charges, royalties and third-party rights, except as set forth in the relevant UPA and in the JOA. The AIPN Model Form Farmout Agreement includes the following title warranty:

It is the legal and beneficial owner of a [•]% undivided interest in the Contract, free and

3 James C Freund (1975), *Anatomy of a Merger: Strategies and Techniques for Negotiating Corporate Acquisitions*, at 153.

clear of any liens, claims, burdens or encumbrances, other than liens, claims, burdens or encumbrances in favour of the Government provided by Law or the terms of the Contract.[4]

(b) Title to other assets

If there are assets other than the UPA and the JOA, the seller should warrant title to those assets as well:

The Farmor owns and has the right to use the other Assets, free and clear of any liens, claims, burdens or encumbrances, except such imperfections of title, easements, and encumbrances, if any, which would not, individually or in the aggregate, have a material adverse effect on the Assets. The Farmor has not assigned, sold, mortgaged or otherwise transferred any of its rights in the Assets or contracted to do any of the above.[5]

Where the seller is a non-operator, and where the operator will have acquired the relevant assets, the seller may argue that its warranties regarding those assets should be qualified by the seller's knowledge.

(c) Agreements

Typically, the seller will warrant a complete list of all agreements (or at least all material agreements) affecting or relating to the assets being purchased and sold, and that true and complete copies thereof have been disclosed to the buyer. If the list includes only material agreements, then it is important to define what is meant by 'material'; this can be done, for example, by reference to a threshold dollar amount of the remaining financial commitment of the seller under the contract.[6] The warranties typically include statements that the agreements are in full force and effect, and that the seller – and to the seller's knowledge, no other party – is in default thereunder. A buyer may also request a warranty regarding relevant transfer restrictions in such agreements, such as governmental and third-party consent requirements and pre-emption rights; although a seller may take the view that the relevant agreements have been disclosed to the buyer and it is for the buyer to conduct its own analysis. Examples of warranties regarding agreements are as follows:

The Contract contains the entirety of the contractual obligations of Farmor to the Government, and no other understanding or agreement exists between the Farmor and the Government in relation to the subject matter of this Agreement.

Farmor has provided Farmee with complete and correct copies of all material Specified Instruments and all amendments thereto. Where Farmor has provided any translation of a document, Farmor makes no, and disclaims any, representation or warranty as to the accuracy of the translation. All payments and obligations due under the Specified Instruments have been paid or performed and all such agreements are in full force and effect. Neither Farmor, nor to the knowledge of Farmor, any other party is

4 This provision is taken from the AIPN Revision Draft, dated 13 May 2015, which is a proposed update to the 2004 Model Form Farmout Agreement set forth at www.aipn.org.

5 This provision is taken from the AIPN Revision Draft, dated 13 May 2015, which is a proposed update to the 2004 Model Form Farmout Agreement set forth at www.aipn.org.

6 *Model Asset Purchase Agreement with Commentary* (American Bar Association 2001), p118.

in default under any of the Specified Instruments. No event has occurred or failed to occur which constitutes, or which, with the giving of notice or the passage of time or both, would constitute, a default, violation, or breach under any of the Specified Instruments. To the knowledge of Farmor, no other party to any of the Specified Instruments has given or has threatened to give notice of any action to alter, terminate or rescind or procure a judicial reformation of any of the Specified Instruments.[7]

(d) Status of minimum work obligations

With respect to an upstream asset that is still in an exploration phase (and, in some cases, even in the development phase), the seller should warrant that all minimum work obligations and minimum expenditure obligations under the UPA that have been required to be completed up to the completion date of the sale and purchase have in fact been completed. An example is as follows:

All accrued obligations and liabilities imposed by the Licence(s) (including without limitation, work obligations) have been duly fulfilled and discharged and there are no outstanding work obligations to be fulfilled under the Licence(s) and the Secretary of State has not given notice to the Seller of any intention to require further works to be conducted (whether in relation to exploration or development) or to call for the submission of or impose a development programme or abandonment programme.[8]

(e) Technical data

The seller may warrant its title to geological, geophysical and other technical data, and that such data is transferable to the buyer. The example above in section 3.3(b) is broad enough to include title to this type of data. However, the seller typically will not give any warranties regarding the quality, contents or any interpretations of such data. At most, a seller may give limited warranties regarding the raw data it provided to the engineers preparing its reserve report:

Seller has made available to [•] (the "Reserves Engineer") prior to the issuance of their report dated [•] (the "Reserves Report") all relevant information requested by the Reserves Engineer, which information did not, at the time such information was provided, contain any material misrepresentation. Seller has no knowledge of any material adverse change in any information provided to the Reserves Engineer since the date of the Reserves Report.

More commonly, a seller will disclaim any warranties regarding the quality, contents or any interpretations of any geological, geophysical and other technical data. For example:

Save as expressly provided in the Warranties, there are no representations or warranties relating to the accuracy, completeness or materiality of any information, data or other materials (written or oral) now, heretofore or hereafter furnished to the Buyer or any of its Affiliates, officers, employees, agents, representatives or advisors by or on behalf of the Seller or any of its Affiliates. Without limitation to the foregoing, there are no

---

7 These provisions are taken from the AIPN Revision Draft, dated 13 May 2015, which is a proposed update to the 2004 Model Form Farmout Agreement set forth at www.aipn.org.

8 Oil & Gas UK (formerly United Kingdom Offshore Operators Association) Model Form Acquisition & Disposal Sale & Purchase Agreement, Schedule 1, paragraph 1.3.

representations and warranties relating to: production rates; decline rates; geological or geophysical data or interpretations; the quality, quantity, recoverability or cost of recovery of any Petroleum reserves; any product pricing assumptions; or the ability to sell, market or export Petroleum.

(f) ***Environmental***

The seller should give warranties regarding compliance with environmental laws, and that it has not received any notices of alleged non-compliance. The scope of these warranties will depend somewhat on the facts of the transaction and may include, for example, information regarding abandoned or suspended wells. Environmental warranties are also often somewhat jurisdiction specific.

Sellers should be aware that buyers often propose environmental warranties that use overbroad definitions. For example, commonly proposed definitions of 'environmental laws' include codes of conduct and best practices, which are not in fact laws and can be much broader than laws. Also, definitions of 'hazardous substances' or 'contaminants' can often be so broad as to include spilt soft drinks. Sellers should resist these overbroad definitions on the basis that they can lead to unintentional liability under the warranties.

The following is an example of environmental warranties from a heavily negotiated transaction in Oman, including some broad definitions:

(a) Save with respect to minor deviations from the requirements of any Environmental Laws binding on the Operator and the Seller (including their respective officers) which give rise to immaterial consequences for the Operator and the Seller, to the Knowledge of the Seller, the Seller and the Operator are in compliance with Environmental Laws.

(b) The Seller is not subject to any existing, pending or, to the Knowledge of the Seller, threatened action, suit, investigation, inquiry or proceeding of any Governmental Authority under any Environmental Law. To the Knowledge of the Seller, the Operator is not subject to any existing, pending or threatened action, suit, investigation, inquiry or proceeding of any Governmental Authority under any Environmental Law.

(c) To the Knowledge of the Seller, all permits, licences or similar authorisations, if any, required to be obtained or filed under any Environmental Law ("Environmental Permits") have been duly obtained or filed. To the Knowledge of the Seller, all of the Environmental Permits that have been obtained are in full force and effect and all of the Environmental Permits that have been filed for, if any, are currently pending before a Governmental Authority. Save with respect to minor deviations from the requirements of any Environmental Permits which give rise to immaterial consequences for the Seller and the Operator, to the Knowledge of the Seller, the Seller and the Operator are in compliance with the terms and conditions of all Environmental Permits that have been obtained.

(d) The Seller and, to the Knowledge of the Seller, the Operator have not: (i) entered into or been subject to any consent, decree, compliance order or administrative order under any Environmental Laws; or (ii) within the past two years received any written request for information, written notice, demand letter, written administrative

inquiry, or formal or informal written complaint or written claim or suit from any Governmental Authority with respect to any violation of Environmental Laws.

(e) For purposes of this Paragraph [•] the following terms shall have the following meanings:

"Environment" means all or any of the following media: land (including without limitation surface and sub-surface soil, sand, gravel and other naturally occurring substances, together with buildings, structures or receptacles in, on, under or over it), water (including without limitation surface, coastal and groundwaters, wells, felajs, wadis, aquifers, rain water and water stored or produced in hydraulic installations, and any other definitions of water used in Environmental Laws), and air (including without limitation the atmosphere within any naturally occurring underground structure or man-made receptacle above or below ground).

"Environmental Laws" means all international, regional, national, federal, European Union, state and local laws, treaties, conventions, protocols, laws, by-laws, decrees, ministerial decisions, regulations, legally binding guidelines and legally binding codes of practice, including any amendments thereto, in each case as in effect on the date hereof, and binding interpretations thereto made by court decisions or administrative orders, in each case as in effect on the date hereof, as applicable to the business activities of the Seller and the Operator (including the exploitation of Petroleum and all activity conducted under or pursuant to the Interest Documents), relating to: (a) restoration; (b) pollution; or (c) protection of human health or safety or the Environment.

(f) Notwithstanding anything to the contrary in this Agreement, the warranties set forth in this Paragraph [•] are the only warranties of the Seller in any way relating to Environmental Laws and/or Environmental Permits.

(g) Actions under UPA and/or JOA

Depending on the facts of the transaction and the state of exploration and development of the specific assets, the buyer may seek some other specific oil and gas warranties. For example, the following is an example of a warranty regarding production imbalances (ie, one JOA party lifting a larger amount of production than its participating interest entitlement):

Farmor has no obligation to deliver Hydrocarbon production (or cash in lieu thereof) to other owners of the Participating Interests in the Contract as a result of past sales by Farmor or its predecessors in excess of the share of production to which they were entitled.[9]

The following is an example of a warranty regarding the lack of non-consent and sole risk operations (ie, the exercise of an option typically included in JOAs that joint operations are conducted by less than all of the parties):

No operations are being conducted or have been conducted with respect to the Farmout Interests as to which Farmor has elected to be a non-consenting party under the Joint Operating Agreement.

9 This provision was taken from the AIPN Revision Draft, dated 13 May 2015, which is a proposed update to the 2004 Model Form Farmout Agreement set forth at www.aipn.org.

No operations are being conducted or have been conducted with respect to the Farmout Interests as sole risk operations under the Joint Operating Agreement.[10]

The following is an example of a warranty regarding the lack of any withdrawal or assignment:

Neither the Seller nor any of its Affiliates have given to or received from any other party thereto any notice of withdrawal from any of the Interest Documents or any notice of any proposed assignment of interest arising thereunder, which notice is in either case still current.

In cases where the seller is not the operator, the buyer may want a specific warranty regarding the status of the operator:

The Operator has not given any notice of resignation as operator under the JOA and, to the Knowledge of the Seller, the Operator is not intending to resign, nor, to the Knowledge of the Seller, is the Operator in default of any of the Interest Documents such as to entitle the other parties to the JOA to remove it as operator. To the Knowledge of the Seller, the Operator, in its capacity as operator under the JOA, has not entered into any transaction, agreement or arrangement outside the ordinary course of business.

(h) Additional warranties from the buyer

As mentioned above, a buyer may give additional warranties to the seller regarding the buyer's financial and technical capabilities. These are potentially important for two reasons:

- The buyer's financial and technical capabilities are important in relation to the parties securing governmental consent to the transfer; and
- If the sale is of only part of the seller's interest, the buyer's financial and technical capabilities are of interest to the seller in its capacity as a future joint venture partner with the buyer.

Technical capabilities will obviously be important if the buyer will become the operator of the joint venture. Examples of these warranties are as follows:

The Buyer has sufficient cash, available lines of credit or other sources of immediately available funds to enable it to fulfil all of its obligations under the Contract, the JOA and this Agreement.

The Buyer has the technical capability, personnel and resources to fulfil its obligations under the Contract and the JOA.

3.4 Limitations on warranties

(a) Disclaimers

In an upstream oil and gas transaction, a seller will typically disclaim any warranties regarding any reserve reports, the quantum of reserves, levels of production or reservoir performance, as these are subjective matters that the buyer should investigate as part of its technical due diligence. An example of a disclaimer

10 These provisions are taken from the AIPN Revision Draft, dated 13 May 2015, which is a proposed update to the 2004 Model Form Farmout Agreement set forth at www.aipn.org.

regarding technical information is set forth above in section 3.3(e). A seller may also attempt to disclaim any warranties regarding the physical condition of any facilities or equipment. The following is an extensive disclaimer regarding the physical condition of facilities and equipment from a transaction covering oil and gas assets in Texas (a common law jurisdiction) and Louisiana (a civil law jurisdiction):

> *NOTWITHSTANDING ANYTHING TO THE CONTRARY IN THIS AGREEMENT, SELLER EXPRESSLY DISCLAIMS AND NEGATES AS TO PERSONAL PROPERTY, EQUIPMENT AND FIXTURES CONSTITUTING A PART OF THE OIL AND GAS PROPERTIES OR OTHER ASSETS (i) ANY IMPLIED OR EXPRESS WARRANTY OF MERCHANTABILITY, (ii) ANY IMPLIED OR EXPRESS WARRANTY OF FITNESS FOR A PARTICULAR PURPOSE, (iii) ANY IMPLIED OR EXPRESS WARRANTY OR CONFORMITY TO MODELS OR SAMPLES OF MATERIALS, (iv) ANY RIGHTS OF PURCHASERS UNDER APPROPRIATE STATUTES TO CLAIM DIMINUTION OF CONSIDERATION, (v) ANY CLAIMS BY PURCHASERS FOR DAMAGES BECAUSE OF REDHIBITORY VICES OR DEFECTS OR OTHER VICES OR DEFECTS, WHETHER KNOWN OR UNKNOWN AS OF THE EFFECTIVE DATE OR THE CLOSING DATE, AND (vi) ANY AND ALL IMPLIED WARRANTIES EXISTING UNDER APPLICABLE LAW; IT BEING THE EXPRESS INTENTION OF BOTH PURCHASER AND SELLER THAT THE PERSONAL PROPERTY, EQUIPMENT AND OTHER FIXTURES INCLUDED WITHIN THE OIL AND GAS PROPERTIES AND OTHER ASSETS ARE HEREBY CONVEYED TO PURCHASER IN THEIR PRESENT CONDITION AND STATE OF REPAIR, "AS IS" AND "WHERE IS" WITH ALL FAULTS, AND THAT PURCHASER HAS MADE OR CAUSED TO BE MADE SUCH INSPECTIONS AS PURCHASER DEEMS APPROPRIATE. SELLER AND PURCHASER AGREE THAT, TO THE EXTENT REQUIRED BY APPLICABLE LAW TO BE EFFECTIVE, THE DISCLAIMERS OF CERTAIN WARRANTIES CONTAINED IN THIS SECTION ARE "CONSPICUOUS" DISCLAIMERS FOR THE PURPOSES OF ANY APPLICABLE LAW, RULE OR ORDER.*

(b) Knowledge limitations

A seller may also want to limit some of its warranties 'to the seller's knowledge'. The seller's reasoning is that it is willing to be liable for those matters it is aware of, but not for matters of which it has no knowledge. From a buyer's standpoint, a knowledge qualifier should be acceptable only in circumstances where the seller may not actually have the relevant knowledge and where the buyer is not relying on the warranty as an absolute guarantee.

Examples of where a knowledge qualifier is appropriate include warranties regarding litigation and contractual defaults. A typical litigation warranty will require the seller to state that there are no pending or threatened lawsuits. The seller should give an absolute warranty regarding pending lawsuits, but it is generally acceptable to use a knowledge qualifier with respect to threatened lawsuits. The reasoning is that the seller should know about all pending lawsuits, but may not be aware that a third party is plotting to file a lawsuit against it. For example:

> *There are no actions, suits, litigation, arbitration or similar proceedings pending or, to the Knowledge of the Seller, threatened against the Seller in any court or before any Governmental Authority, or before any arbitrator, with respect to the Assets.*

Similarly, a seller should warrant that it is not in default of any material contracts, but it is generally acceptable to use a knowledge qualifier with respect to other parties being in default. Again, the reasoning is that the seller cannot reasonably be aware of all possible breaches by third parties. For example:

With respect to each Material Contract: (a) the Seller has duly performed and complied in all material respects with each of its obligations thereunder; (b) to the Knowledge of the Seller, there are no grounds for rescission, avoidance, repudiation or termination and the Seller has not received any notice of termination; and (c) to the Knowledge of the Seller, none of the other parties thereto is in default or is likely to become in default thereunder.

Except with respect to the foregoing examples, there is no standard practice for determining which warranties, if any, should be qualified by the seller's knowledge.[11] It is clear, however, that a knowledge qualifier is not appropriate where the seller is relying on the warranty as an absolute guarantee. For example, a title warranty should not be limited by knowledge. In this case, the seller should bear the full risk of any title deficiencies, regardless of whether the seller knew of the deficiencies.

It is common to define two elements of the seller's knowledge. First, the ASPA can refer to the specific persons whose knowledge is relevant – for example, the seller's shareholders, directors, officers and/or employees. These persons can be identified by name or by job title. Frequently, the listed persons include the seller's deal team – for example, the lead negotiator, the persons who put together the data room and perhaps even the seller's in-house lawyer for the deal. Second, the ASPA can define the seller's knowledge with respect to whether there is a duty of the relevant persons to investigate. A pro-buyer formulation would define the seller's knowledge 'after reasonable investigation'. A pro-seller formulation would define the seller's knowledge 'without any duty of independent investigation'.[12] The following is an example of a definition of 'knowledge':

"Knowledge" – an individual will be deemed to have Knowledge of a particular fact or other matter if: (a) that individual is actually aware of that fact or matter; or (b) a prudent individual could be expected to discover or otherwise become aware of that fact or matter in the course of conducting a reasonably comprehensive investigation regarding the accuracy of any representation or warranty contained in this Agreement.[13]

(c) *Materiality limitations*

A seller may want to limit some of its warranties with concepts of materiality, on the basis that the seller should not be responsible for, and the parties should not waste their time on, 'immaterial' matters. There are two common traps regarding the use of materiality qualifiers.

First, it is important to be precise with respect to the location and usage of a materiality qualifier. It is quite different for a seller to warrant that "there has been no material breach of any contract", as opposed to "there has been no breach of any

11 *Model Asset Purchase Agreement with Commentary* (American Bar Association 2001), p29.
12 Martin D Ginsburg *et al* (1994), *Mergers, Acquisitions and Leveraged Buyouts*, at 33 and 34.
13 *Model Asset Purchase Agreement with Commentary* (American Bar Association 2001), p28.

material contract". The former could be untrue if there were a breach of a minor contract, whereas the latter could be untrue if there were an immaterial breach of a significant contract. In this particular case, it may make sense to provide that "there has been no material breach of any material contract".

Second, it is important to watch out for double materiality. This can arise in cases where the parties have agreed to baskets – for example, a basket that prevents claims below a specified amount. Where individual warranties have materiality qualifiers, it may be unclear when the basket amount is met. The problem can also arise where a 'bring down' condition precedent provides that the warranties are true and correct in all material respects. Where individual warranties have materiality qualifiers, the aggregate level of materiality necessary to render the condition precedent unsatisfied can be unintentionally large. For these reasons, buyers often argue that sellers should not include materiality qualifiers in individual warranties and instead should rely on the materiality provided by the baskets and the conditions precedent.[14]

(d) Disclosure

The seller will typically be entitled to make disclosures against the warranties. This is usually achieved by the preparation and delivery by the seller to the buyer of a disclosure letter. The disclosure letter is normally delivered at the signing of the ASPA, although its contents will have been reviewed and negotiated by the parties prior to that time as part of the overall ASPA negotiations. Alternatively, the disclosures could appear in a schedule to the ASPA.

In either case, the disclosures have the effect of setting forth exceptions to the warranties and thereby modify the warranties. Section 3.3 above describes the three functions of the warranties from a buyer's standpoint. The disclosures together with the warranties serve a due diligence and information-gathering function for the buyer. The disclosures, however, will preclude the buyer from refusing to close the sale and purchase on the basis that the 'bring down' condition precedent is not satisfied, because the disclosures render the relevant warranties true and correct. Furthermore, the disclosures will prevent post-completion claims by the buyer under the warranties with respect to the matters so disclosed. The disclosures therefore have the effect of shifting the risk of the matters disclosed from the seller to the buyer. If any matter so disclosed is unacceptable to the buyer, such as ongoing litigation, the buyer may request indemnification from the seller with respect to that specific matter, may renegotiate the purchase price or may simply refuse to sign the ASPA.[15]

Disclosure letters are usually delivered at the time the ASPA is signed. However, in any ASPA involving transfer of a UPA, there will be a requirement to obtain governmental consent to the transfer (as further discussed below in section 5.1), with the result that there will be a period of time – which may be substantial – between signing and completion. Events may occur or come to light during this interim

14 'Double dipping' is discussed in *Model Asset Purchase Agreement with Commentary* (American Bar Association 2001), p226; and Lou R Kling and Eileen T Nugent, *Negotiated Acquisitions of Companies, Subsidiaries and Divisions*, Law Journal Press 2005, §15.03 footnote 1.

15 Lou R Kling and Eileen T Nugent, *Negotiated Acquisitions of Companies, Subsidiaries and Divisions*, Law Journal Press 2005, §§10.01 – 10.02.

period that constitute a breach of the warranties. Most ASPAs include a provision requiring the seller to notify the buyer of any such events and/or to supplement the disclosure letter to disclose details regarding the event. This notification and/or supplement should not, however, be given effect for purposes of the 'bring down' condition precedent that the seller's warranties are true and correct at completion. To do so would shift the risk of the occurrence of events during the interim period between signing and completion from the seller to the buyer. Whether or not the event has the effect of precluding post-completion claims by the buyer is more complicated. On the one hand, if the disclosed event is unacceptable to the buyer, the buyer has the remedy of not completing the transaction by means of the 'bring down' condition precedent. On the other hand, the disclosed event, if material, changes the benefit of the bargain expected by the buyer when it signed the ASPA and, at least in the buyer's view, it should retain post-completion recourse with respect to the newly disclosed event.[16]

(e) ***Baskets***

A 'basket' or a 'cushion' provision states that a buyer will be entitled to recover damages only if those damages exceed a certain amount. The purposes of a basket are twofold. First, the basket is a recognition that there are bound to be some minor mistakes or inaccuracies in the seller's warranties. Second, the basket prevents arguments or disputes with respect to *de minimis* amounts.[17]

Baskets can be either thresholds or deductibles. When a basket is a threshold, once the specified amount is met, the buyer may recover the full amount back to the first pound or dollar. When a basket is a deductible, once the specified amount is met, the buyer may recover only the amount in excess of the specified amount.[18] In this regard, the simplest analogy is that a basket that is a deductible is similar to typical car insurance.

Baskets are often drafted in two layers. The first layer applies to individual claims and the second layer applies to aggregate claims. When layering baskets in this manner, it is possible to mix and match the baskets as thresholds or deductibles. It is not uncommon for the individual basket to be a deductible and for the aggregate basket to be a threshold. The question in this case is whether, once the aggregate basket amount is achieved, the buyer will be entitled also to recover amounts under the individual basket amount. In the following example, the individual basket amount is a deductible and the aggregate basket amount is a threshold. However, once the aggregate basket amount is achieved, the buyer can recover the full amount of the damages other than amounts below the individual basket amount.

(a) In no event shall the Seller be liable in any way whatsoever to the Buyer in respect of any breach of the Warranties (excluding in respect of any Tax Warranties) unless

---

16 Lou R Kling and Eileen T Nugent, *Negotiated Acquisitions of Companies, Subsidiaries and Divisions*, Law Journal Press 2005, §10.05.

17 *Model Asset Purchase Agreement with Commentary* (American Bar Association 2001), p226; Lou R Kling and Eileen T Nugent, *Negotiated Acquisitions of Companies, Subsidiaries and Divisions*, Law Journal Press 2005, §15.03.

18 Martin D Ginsburg *et al* (1994), *Mergers, Acquisitions and Leveraged Buyouts*, at 13; *Model Asset Purchase Agreement with Commentary* (American Bar Association 2001), p226.

the Buyer has suffered Losses with respect to such breach in an amount in excess of [•] Pounds Sterling (£[•]) (the "Individual Basket Amount"), in which event the Buyer shall be entitled to recover only the amount of Losses in excess of the Individual Basket Amount (subject to Paragraph (b) below).

(b) In no event shall the Seller be liable in any way whatsoever to the Buyer with respect to any breach of the Warranties (excluding in respect of any Tax Warranties) unless the Buyer has suffered Losses in the aggregate in excess of [•] Pounds Sterling (£[•]) (the "Aggregate Basket Amount"), at which point the Buyer shall be entitled to recover all such Losses other than amounts below the Individual Basket Amount.

The logic of this example, from a seller's standpoint, is that the parties did not intend to argue regarding *de minimis* claims, and the fact that the individual basket amount is a deductible carries out that intent. A buyer could argue, however, that although it is acceptable to disregard individual immaterial losses, once the aggregate amount of the losses becomes by definition material, then the entire amount should be recoverable.[19]

As noted above in section 3.4(c), if the individual warranties include materiality qualifications and the ASPA also includes one or more baskets, then this could result in double materiality (or 'double dipping'). One way to address this is to provide that, for purposes of determining whether the basket amounts have been met or exceeded, the materiality qualifications in the individual warranties should be disregarded.

It is common to exclude certain matters from the baskets altogether. For example, the example first cited above in section 3.4(e) carved out tax warranties. It is also common to carve out title warranties and sometimes essential warranties such as environmental or anti-bribery and corruption. Alternatively, the parties could negotiate separate baskets for different types of liability.[20]

It is also common to provide that the baskets are applicable only to the warranties, and are not applicable to breach of covenants or undertakings in the ASPA. For example, the example first cited above in section 3.4(e) applies only to the warranties.

Once the concept of one or more baskets has been agreed by the seller and the buyer, the obvious question is the amount. The amount is typically a function of the purchase price (ie, the bigger the deal, the bigger the baskets); but aside from that, it is difficult to make many generalities regarding the amount of the baskets. Some surveys of public M&A deals include this type of information;[21] but in the author's experience, the amount of the baskets will depend on the relative bargaining power of the parties more than any other factor. Obviously, the seller wants the baskets to be as high as possible, whereas the buyer wants them to be as low as possible. From a tactical standpoint, it makes sense for a buyer to postpone negotiating the amount of the baskets until after it sees the entire suite of negotiated warranties and disclosures.[22]

---

19 James C Freund (1975), *Anatomy of a Merger: Strategies and Techniques for Negotiating Corporate Acquisitions*, at 372.

20 *Model Asset Purchase Agreement with Commentary* (American Bar Association 2001), p227.

21 For example, the Business Law Section of the American Bar Association publishes an annual *Strategic Buyer/Public Target M&A Deal Points Study*.

22 James C Freund (1975), *Anatomy of a Merger: Strategies and Techniques for Negotiating Corporate Acquisitions*, at 371.

(f) *Cap on overall liability*

Sellers may also seek an upper limit, or ceiling or cap, on their overall liability under the ASPA. This concept is not uncommon in oil and gas services agreements (eg, seismic acquisition agreements and drilling contracts), and over the years seems to have spread over into oil and gas ASPAs. The cap is often set at an amount equal to the overall consideration or some fraction thereof. This is particularly the case where the seller is a private equity fund or a family business, where the proceeds of the sale are typically distributed to the investors or family members. Such sellers would have difficulties in collecting distributions back from such persons.[23]

The following is an example of a cap provision that provides for different caps for different liabilities:

In no event shall the Seller be liable in any way whatsoever to the Buyer in contract, tort, negligence, breach of statutory duty or otherwise for any Losses under this Agreement, to the extent such Losses in aggregate exceed:

(a) 100% of the Purchase Price in relation to the Warranties of the Seller set forth in Clauses [•] (Organisation of the Seller), [•] (Authorisation of Transaction), [•] (Noncontravention), [•] (Title to Shares), [•] (Environmental) and [•] (Tax); or

(b) in all other cases (including without limitation breach of all Warranties other than those listed in sub-paragraph (ii) above), [•] percent ([•]%)[24] *of the Purchase Price, after which point the Seller will have no obligation or liability to the Buyer for any further Losses.*

(g) *Survival*

It is usual for an ASPA to specify a period of time following completion in which the buyer must assert any claim for breach of warranty. The rationale is the same as that underlying a statute of limitations; at some point in time, a seller is entitled to the certainty and peace of mind that no further claims will be forthcoming. Against this must be weighed the buyer's right to a reasonable period of time in which to discover the basis for any claim.[25]

The parties may agree different survival periods for different types of claims. For example, it is customary that the survival period for asserting tax claims is equal to the relevant statute of limitations for the applicable tax authority to assert a claim, plus a period of time after expiry of the statute of limitations to allow the buyer to assert a claim against the seller in the case where the tax authority has asserted a claim at the last minute. It is also often the case that claims for critical warranties such as title and environmental have longer survival periods than claims for other warranties.

The duration of the survival period or survival periods is negotiable and typically depends on the relative bargaining positions of the parties. A common benchmark is

---

23 Lou R Kling and Eileen T Nugent, *Negotiated Acquisitions of Companies, Subsidiaries and Divisions*, Law Journal Press 2005, §15.03.

24 In the author's experience, this percentage amount is negotiable and depends primarily on the relative bargaining power of the parties. It is not uncommon for this percentage amount to be below 50%.

25 James C Freund (1975), *Anatomy of a Merger: Strategies and Techniques for Negotiating Corporate Acquisitions*, at 372; *Model Asset Purchase Agreement with Commentary* (American Bar Association 2001), p228.

a period of time to allow the buyer's independent auditors to conduct at least one, and possibly two, post-completion annual audits, as these audits are likely to identify any claims.[26]

In cases where all or part of the consideration is payable after completion, such as by means of a promissory note or an earnout, or where part of the purchase price is held in escrow, the buyer will want to ensure that the survival period is at least as long as the tenure of the promissory note, earnout or escrow, in order to facilitate the possible set-off of any claims against the promissory note, earnout or escrow.[27]

The following is an example of a provision establishing different survival periods for different types of claims:

In no event shall any amounts be recovered from the Seller for breach of any Warranty or in contract, tort, negligence, breach of statutory duty or otherwise for any matter for which a written notice of claim specifying in such reasonable detail as is reasonably available to the Buyer at the time such notice is provided, the specific nature of the Losses and the estimated amount of such Losses (to the extent estimable) ("Claim Notice") is not delivered to the Seller prior to 1700 local time at the address set out at Clause [•] on or before the last day of the applicable Survival Period. The "Survival Period" shall be as follows:

(a) with respect to any claim under the Tax Warranties, or any Tax Claim, the period specified in the Tax Deed;

(b) with respect to any claim under the Warranties other than the Tax Warranties, a period of 12 months from the Completion Date;

(c) with respect to any claim under Clause [•] or Clause [•], the seven year time period set forth in such Clauses; and

(d) with respect to any other provision of this Agreement, a period of 12 months from the Completion Date.

The expiration of any Survival Period set forth in this Clause shall not affect any claim timely asserted in good faith in a valid Claim Notice prior to the expiration of such Survival Period.

(h) Buyer's knowledge of breach

Sellers are sometimes concerned that a buyer may, during its pre-signing due diligence, learn of a fact or circumstance that could constitute a breach of one of the seller's warranties. In this case, the seller does not want the buyer to proceed to signing the ASPA without first disclosing that fact or circumstance to the seller, because without such disclosure the seller would be proceeding unknowingly into a breach situation. A buyer in this ambush situation is sometimes referred to euphemistically as 'laying behind the log'. The seller's typical solution is to provide that the buyer cannot make a claim to the extent that it had knowledge of the breach prior to signing the ASPA:

No amount shall be recovered from the Seller for the breach or untruth of any of the

---

26 James C Freund (1975), *Anatomy of a Merger: Strategies and Techniques for Negotiating Corporate Acquisitions*, at 374; *Model Asset Purchase Agreement with Commentary* (American Bar Association 2001), p229.

27 *Model Asset Purchase Agreement with Commentary* (American Bar Association 2001), p229.

Warranties to the extent that such breach or untruth was within the Knowledge of the Buyer at or prior to the date of this Agreement.

(i) ***No rescission***

Under English law, a misrepresentation can give rise to a right of rescission. Given the harshness of this remedy and the difficulties encountered in unwinding a transaction, most English law sale and purchase agreements disclaim any right of rescission:

The Buyer shall not be entitled to rescission of this Agreement in any circumstances, including without limitation as a result of breach or untruth of any of the warranties.

(j) ***Other limitations***

The limitations on the seller's liability can stretch on for pages, and are seemingly limited only by the imagination of the seller and the seller's lawyers and the willingness of the buyer and the buyer's lawyers to wade through them. Other limitations on liabilities include:

- waivers of consequential damages;
- obligations to mitigate losses; and
- where a claim is based on a liability that is contingent only, a limitation that no claim may be asserted unless and until such contingent liability becomes an actual liability.

These limitations in an ASPA are typically similar to those in a share sale and purchase agreement.

4. Indemnification

In connection with a discussion of warranties and limitations on warranties, it is worth considering a difference in practice between US lawyers and English solicitors with respect to indemnification.

In US practice, it is common for sellers to provide general indemnities to the buyer with respect to any losses, claims and demands arising from breach of the seller's representations, warranties or covenants in the ASPA. Although a buyer would typically have recourse against a seller for these breaches in any case, indemnities are often provided for several reasons, including:

- to make it clear that the representations and warranties survive completion of the sale and purchase;
- to ensure that certain types of expenses, such as attorneys' fees, incurred in connection with a claim will be recoverable; and
- to set forth specific procedures for the handling of claims, such as procedures for handling third-party lawsuits or claims.[28]

It is also common to include specific indemnities for particular areas of concern identified by the buyer during its due diligence investigation of the assets. For

28 James C Freund (1975), *Anatomy of a Merger: Strategies and Techniques for Negotiating Corporate Acquisitions*, at 160.

example, if the buyer has discovered that there is ongoing litigation against the seller, the risk of which the buyer is not willing to assume, then the seller may agree to indemnify the buyer against any adverse consequences of that litigation.

Under English law practice, general indemnities with respect to any losses, claims and demands arising from breach of the seller's warranties or covenants in the ASPA would be more unusual. This is because, under English law, an indemnity changes the scope of recovery by the buyer. A buyer with the benefit of an indemnity will be entitled to recover for a breach of warranty on a pound-for-pound or dollar-for-dollar basis; whereas a buyer without the benefit of an indemnity may recover only an amount equal to the difference between the value of the assets subject to the untrue warranty and the value of the assets had the warranty been true, which may be a lesser amount. Although general indemnities are therefore uncommon in English law ASPAs, it is still common to include specific indemnities for specific areas of concern, such as the example regarding identified litigation referred to in the preceding paragraph.

5. Transfer restrictions in the context of an asset sale and purchase

The principal disadvantage of an asset sale and purchase involving upstream oil and gas properties is that the transaction tends to trigger various transfer restrictions, including requirements to obtain approvals to the transfer from governmental authorities and joint venture participants, as well as possible pre-emption rights.

5.1 Governmental consent

UPAs such as licences, concessions and production sharing contracts are granted by governmental authorities to persons which have demonstrated their financial and technical capability to undertake the relevant petroleum operations. As such, the governmental authority has a strong interest in ensuring that the UPA is not transferred to a third party without the requisite financial and technical capabilities. As a result, it is universal under relevant petroleum legislation and UPAs that an asset transfer of a UPA will require the approval of the relevant governmental authority.[29]

This is one reason why upstream petroleum purchases and sales are sometimes structured as share transfers rather than asset transfers. It is possible that a share transfer may not require governmental approval, although this is increasingly unlikely as modern upstream petroleum legislation and UPAs are more likely to regulate changes of control. Also, even in the absence of specific change of control provisions, governmental entities are likely to interpret existing legislation and agreements as requiring governmental approval even for a share transfer.[30]

It is an unfortunate fact that – at least in some jurisdictions – the requirement to obtain governmental consent can sometimes create an opportunity for a government to extract concessions, such as modifications of the relevant UPA, in return for granting its consent. The parties often address this possibility with the following provision:

---

29 Claude Duval *et al* (2009), *International Petroleum Exploration and Exploitation Agreements: Legal, Economic and Policy Aspects*, at 161.

30 Lou R Kling and Eileen T Nugent, *Negotiated Acquisitions of Companies, Subsidiaries and Divisions*, Law Journal Press 2005, §2.08[3].

If the Government imposes conditions for approval of the Assignment in excess of those which are usually imposed in similar circumstances or which approval contains unusual and onerous conditions which either Party is not willing to accept, then subject to any reimbursement as provided herein, the affected Party may terminate this Agreement without any further obligation or liability to the other Party in accordance with the provisions of Article 3.3.[31]

5.2 Third-party consent to transfer

JOAs governing oil and gas joint ventures typically have detailed provisions regulating the transfer of interests in the relevant UPA and the JOA. Upstream petroleum operations are expensive, complicated and long term by their nature. Furthermore, it is typical for all joint venture participants to be jointly and severally liable for all obligations to the host country arising under the UPA. For these reasons, participants have a keen interest in knowing the identity and financial and technical capabilities of their joint venture participants. As a result, transfers are often restricted in various ways.

The most common restriction is a requirement that any transfer of the relevant assets be subject to consent of the joint venture participants. The JOA will typically require the seller to provide information to the non-transferring joint venture participants regarding the financial and technical capabilities of the proposed buyer. The joint venture participants then have the right to approve the transfer or not. The extent to which approval can be withheld will depend on the terms of the relevant JOA. Some JOAs provide that consent can be withheld only if the buyer has insufficient financial or technical capabilities, whereas others may simply state that consent cannot be unreasonably withheld. In either case, the approval right is personal to each non-transferring joint venture participant – that is, the approval is not a matter that is subject to a passmark vote under the JOA.

The JOA transfer restrictions may be less restrictive in cases of transfers from an existing joint venture participant to one of its affiliates. However, it is common for the JOA to provide in this case that the seller must remain jointly and severally liable with the affiliate transferee for all obligations under the JOA. The non-transferring joint venture participants may agree to release the seller from this continuing liability if the affiliate transferee can demonstrate that it has financial and technical capabilities at least equal to those of the seller. The JOA may further provide that the interests must be transferred back to the seller in the event that the transferee ceases to be an affiliate of the seller.

If a buyer wants to assume operatorship, this will also require consent of the non-transferring joint venture participants. However, in this case, under many forms of JOA such as the AIPN 2012 Model Form, the approval of the successor operator is by means of the operating committee and a passmark vote rather than by personal approval of each non-transferring joint venture participant.[32] Transfer of operatorship will generally also require governmental consent.

---

31 AIPN Model Form Farmout Agreement (2004), optional provision Article 3.4.
32 AIPN Model Form Joint Operating Agreement (2012), Article 4.11.A.

Finally, depending on the state of exploration and development of the relevant upstream oil and gas asset, there may also be third-party consent requirements under other contracts, such as drilling contracts, unitisation agreements, production sales and transportation agreements or other service agreements. In the case of a producing field, the number of these third-party consent requirements could be significant. These third-party consents could also be critical to the overall transaction in cases where all or some of the relevant agreements are material to the assets and/or are on favourable economic terms.[33]

A practical 'chicken and egg' issue sometimes arises with respect to third-party consents. A third party may be unwilling to consent to the proposed transfer and proposed buyer prior to completion of the sale and purchase – that is, at a time when the interest has not actually transferred. The seller and the buyer may not be willing to complete the sale and purchase without the third party's consent in hand. And it is often not possible or desirable to have the third party present at the completion. The practical solution is either to make the relevant consent document conditional upon completion having occurred or to make the consent document unconditional, but date it as of the completion date and have it held in escrow until completion.

5.3 Pre-emption

A pre-emption right is a right for a non-transferring joint venture participant to acquire all or a proportionate part of the interests of a transferring joint venture participant in priority to any third-party buyer. Pre-emption rights can take a variety of forms and in each case it is important to read closely the exact terms of the relevant provisions in order to ascertain whether the pre-emption rights apply to a specified transaction.

It is sometimes said that pre-emption rights only really matter to buyers, because the seller will successfully dispose of its interests regardless of whether the buyer is an existing joint venture participant exercising a pre-emption right or a third-party buyer. However, this overlooks the fact that third-party buyers are potentially deterred from bidding on upstream assets that are subject to pre-emption rights, on the basis that they are unwilling to exert time and money on an acquisition that could be pre-empted, whereas they may have alternative investment opportunities that are not subject to pre-emption and therefore appear to be more certain. In this regard, the existence of pre-emption rights can have a detrimental effect on the marketability of upstream participating interests and may even affect their monetary value.

Pre-emption clauses typically take one of two forms:

- A classic right of pre-emption provides that, once a seller has agreed to a sale and purchase with a third-party buyer, the seller must then offer that deal to its joint venture participants, which will have a specified period of time to match the offer. In this way, the existing joint venture participants have a priority right over any new entrants. In analysing this type of pre-emption

33 Lou R Kling and Eileen T Nugent, *Negotiated Acquisitions of Companies, Subsidiaries and Divisions*, Law Journal Press 2005, §2.08[2].

clause, it is important to focus on what event triggers the right of pre-emption. In some cases the trigger may be an agreement in principle between the seller and the buyer (eg, an accepted offer letter or heads of terms), whereas in other cases the trigger may be a fully negotiated ASPA.
- A right of first refusal, sometimes also referred to as a right of first negotiation, requires a seller to offer the interests to be transferred to its joint venture participants prior to striking any deal with a third-party buyer. The seller and its joint venture participants then typically have a specified period of time in which to agree the terms of a sale and purchase, failing which the seller is allowed to market its interest free of the pre-emption right, provided that it does not sell to a buyer on lesser terms than those offered by any existing joint venture participant.

In each of these formats, if more than one existing joint venture participant wants to participate in the pre-emption, then the JOA will typically provide that the seller's interests will be allocated among the pre-empting joint venture participants pro rata to their existing percentage interests or on such other basis as the pre-empting joint venture participants may agree.

Some UPAs or host country petroleum codes also include rights of pre-emption in favour of the government or its national oil company. These are becoming more prevalent as 'resource nationalism' drives oil-producing countries to attempt to exert greater control over their natural resources.

Depending on how a pre-emption clause is drafted, it may be possible to structure a sale and purchase to avoid the pre-emption rights. For example, it would be unusual for a pre-emption clause to apply to a share transfer. In this regard, it is sometimes possible to do in two steps what otherwise could not be done in one step: that is, a seller could transfer its interests to an affiliate, which is typically a permitted transfer under a JOA, and then sell the shares in that affiliate to the third-party buyer free from any pre-emption right. This loophole is often closed by JOA provisions that allow transfers to affiliates of the seller, but require retransfer back to the seller if the affiliate ceases to be an affiliate of the seller.

A pre-emption clause can sometimes be avoided by means of an offer of non-cash consideration, such as an asset swap. In this case, the pre-emption right may not apply because the existing joint venture participants cannot physically match the consideration offered by the third-party buyer. Other non-cash consideration could include shares or other equity interests. Additionally, some pre-emption clauses do not apply to package deals, where the assets that are subject to the pre-emption right are being sold together with a larger package of other oil and gas properties. In each case, careful consideration must be given to the details of the pre-emption clause.

In transactions where pre-emption is involved, ASPAs typically include covenants or undertakings describing how to deal with the pre-emption:

Farmor shall provide notice to each holder of a Pre-Emptive Right that is triggered by the execution of this Agreement within [•] Business Days after the Effective Date in accordance with the terms and conditions of the Specified Instrument that gives rise to such Pre-Emptive Right. Any Pre-Emptive Right must be exercised subject to all terms and conditions set forth in this Agreement, including the obligation to assume and perform all of the obligations of the Farmee hereunder.

Each such notice shall request the waiver of such Pre-Emptive Right, and the Farmor shall use reasonable efforts to secure such waiver as soon as reasonably practicable; provided that in no event shall Farmor be obligated to make any payments or undertake obligations for the benefit of the holder of any Pre-Emptive Right in order to obtain such waiver.

If Farmor receives notice that it reasonably believes is a valid exercise of a Pre-emptive Right, it shall promptly notify Farmee and provide it with a copy of the notice and written confirmation of the date on which it was received and the means of delivery.[34]

Whether this covenant or undertaking should be coupled with a termination right if the pre-emption is exercised will depend on whether the asset subject to the pre-emption is material in the context of the overall transaction.

5.4 Other transfer restrictions

It is common for upstream petroleum legislation and UPAs to restrict the right of transfer during the exploration phase, on the basis that the original parties should be responsible for completing the minimum work obligations.[35]

It is also common for upstream petroleum legislation, UPAs and JOAs to require that each party hold a minimum participating interest – often in the range of 5% to 10% – below which no transfers are permitted (except to a zero participating interest). An example is the UK policy on the fragmentation of licence interests, which states that "in some circumstances the creation of very small licence interests may be of questionable advantage to the [UK North Sea]".[36] The logic for these restrictions is that a multitude of small participants can render operations unworkable from an administrative standpoint and can also complicate voting arrangements under JOAs.

A typical JOA will prohibit transfers of interests other than an 'undivided' interest. One purpose of this restriction is to prevent a party from assigning rights apart from obligations. Another purpose is to prevent assignments of only part of a licensed area, which could require splitting JOAs to govern parts of the licence that are owned by different participants.

6. Conditions precedent[37]

One of the fundamental decisions to be made in structuring an ASPA is whether to have a simultaneous signing and completion or signing followed by deferred completion sometime thereafter. Given the universal requirement for governmental approval of an asset sale and purchase involving a UPA, a deferred completion is a

34 This provision is taken from the AIPN Revision Draft, dated 13 May 2015, which is a proposed update to the 2004 Model Form Farmout Agreement set forth at www.aipn.org.

35 Claude Duval *et al* (2009), *International Petroleum Exploration and Exploitation Agreements: Legal, Economic and Policy Aspects*, at 306.

36 Department of Energy and Climate Change, *Oil and Gas: Petroleum licensing guidance*, 4 December 2012.

37 For a complete discussion of conditions precedent, see J LaMaster and C Moran, *Oil and Gas Sale and Purchase Agreements – SPAs for International Oil and Gas Acquisitions and Divestitures*, at p39.

practical necessity. As a result, an ASPA for an oil and gas transaction will typically contain a number of conditions precedent to completion, with the result that there will be a period of time between signing the ASPA and completion of the transactions contemplated by the ASPA.

It is advisable to avoid conditions precedent that give either party a *de facto* option not to proceed with the transaction. These types of conditions precedent typically include some subjective element in favour of the party to which that condition precedent runs. For example, an ASPA that has a condition precedent for a party's board approval creates a *de facto* option in favour of that party, because if that party has a change of heart regarding the transaction, then it can always have its board turn it down. Similarly, conditions precedent that the buyer shall have completed its financing of the transaction, or that the buyer shall have completed its due diligence investigation and that the results of such investigation are acceptable to it, can create 'outs' in favour of the buyer. If any of these types of conditions precedent must be included, it is best to include a specified timeframe by which they must be satisfied or waived. For example, a condition precedent regarding due diligence could provide that the buyer must confirm on or before a specified date that it has completed its due diligence to its satisfaction, after which that condition precedent falls away. In this manner, the seller is relieved of the subjective condition precedent at an earlier stage than the longstop date that might otherwise apply to the remainder of the conditions precedent.

Where an ASPA includes conditions precedent to completion, the parties may want to impose a limit on the period of time between signing of the ASPA and completion of the transactions contemplated by the ASPA. This is typically done by inclusion of a longstop date. If the conditions precedent are not satisfied or waived, and completion has not occurred on or before the longstop date, the ASPA may automatically terminate. More commonly, the ASPA will give either party the right to terminate on or after the longstop date. In cases where the conditions precedent have not been satisfied due to a breach of warranty or covenant by one of the parties, the SPA may give only the non-breaching party a right to terminate the ASPA. For example:

> *If the Conditions Precedent are not satisfied by [date], then either Party has the right to terminate this Agreement by giving notice to the other Party in accordance with the provisions of Article 10. In the event of termination pursuant to this Article 3.3, the proposed Assignment shall terminate, shall be rendered void and shall have no force or effect.*[38]

A typical set of conditions precedent to completion in an ASPA for upstream oil and gas assets would include all or some of the following:

> *Completion hereunder is subject to the satisfaction or waiver of each of the following conditions (collectively, the "Conditions Precedent"):*
>
> *(a) the Parties obtain the approval of the Government to the Assignment and the change of operatorship in writing as required under the Contract;*
>
> *(b) the Parties shall have obtained the approval of the Operating Committee under the JOA to the appointment of the Buyer as successor Operator under the JOA;*

38 AIPN Model Form Farmout Agreement (2004), Article 3.3.

(c) the Parties shall have obtained the third party consents and approvals identified in Schedule [•], and such consents and approvals shall be in full force and effect;
(d) Seller has obtained a waiver in writing from each of the co-venturers under the JOA of their pre-emptive rights pursuant to the provisions of Article [•] of the JOA or expiry of the time periods for any such co-venturers to attempt to acquire the Asset in accordance with such provisions;
(e) the relevant Persons shall have entered into the JOA Novation Agreement and the Ancillary Agreements;
(f) each of the Seller's warranties shall have been accurate in all material respects as of the date of this Agreement, and shall be accurate in all material respects as of the Completion Date, as if then made, without giving effect to any supplement to the Disclosure Letter;
(g) each of the covenants and obligations that the Seller is required to perform or to comply with pursuant to this Agreement at or prior to Completion shall have been duly performed and complied with in all material respects;
(h) the Buyer shall have obtained on terms and conditions satisfactory to it all of the financing it needs in order to consummate the Transaction and to fund the working capital requirements of the Buyer after Completion; and
(i) there shall not have occurred any Material Adverse Change between the Signing Date and the Completion Date.

7. Ancillary transfer documents

In a share sale and purchase, no transfer documents are necessary to transfer specific assets to the new owner, because those assets will remain the property of the target company. The only transfer document that is typically necessary is the share transfer for the shares in the target company.

Conversely, in an asset sale and purchase, it is customary for there to be transfer documents for the various assets being sold and purchased. There are several reasons for this practice. First, in the case of upstream assets involving a UPA, there will always be a requirement for governmental consent, so there will always be a period of time between signing of the ASPA and completion of the sale and purchase. Because of this time gap, the ASPA itself is typically not used as the legal agreement to effectuate completion of the legal transfer. Instead, the ASPA typically lists certain actions to be taken at completion, including delivery of certain assignments and novations. Second, buyers will want evidence of the actual transfers, especially with regard to the UPA. These transfer documents can then be used as evidence of the transfers *vis-à-vis* governmental authorities and third parties, instead of having to disclose the entire terms of the ASPA. Third, joint venture participants and other third parties will want the buyer to assume the seller's obligations under various field agreements, such as JOAs, and *vis-à-vis* these third parties the assumptions must be in separate assignments and novations rather than in the ASPA. Lastly, assets such as offshore vessels often require jurisdiction-specific transfer and registration documents.

The documents required to complete an upstream oil and gas asset sale and purchase will vary from jurisdiction to jurisdiction. However, there will generally always be an assignment of the UPA and a novation of the JOA.

In jurisdictions following English law practices and in agreements governed by English law, a distinction is drawn between transfers of rights and transfers of obligations. While it may be possible to transfer rights under an agreement without the consent of the other parties to that agreement, it is not possible to transfer obligations under that agreement without such consent. The transfer of rights and obligations requires a novation of the relevant agreement, which must be entered into by the seller, the buyer and all other parties to the relevant agreement. The novation will release the seller from its liabilities under the relevant agreement and will substitute the buyer in place of the seller, as if the buyer had always been a party to the relevant agreement. This is the customary procedure with respect to international JOAs governed by English law.[39]

In cases where abandonment or decommissioning security has already been established, the buyer will need to ascertain how it will participate in that security. The buyer may need to put in place a letter of credit or enter into a trust arrangement. If so, these will typically be required as deliverables at completion of the sale and purchase.

8. The special case of the farmout agreement

As mentioned above, a farmout agreement is a specialised form of ASPA. The distinguishing characteristic of a farmout agreement is that the transferor will transfer part of its participating interest in a UPA to a transferee in return for that transferee performing and/or paying for certain works that otherwise would have been performed and/or paid for by the transferor – for example, the acquisition of seismic data or the drilling of a well. In this way, the farmor spreads the risks of the petroleum operations or finances works that it could not otherwise afford to undertake.

Farmout terminology can be confusing to the uninitiated. The transaction is often referred to as a 'farmout' from the perspective of the transferor, but as a 'farmin' from the perspective of the transferee. The transferor is typically referred to as the 'farmor' or, less commonly, 'farminor' or 'farmoutor'. The transferee is typically referred to as the 'farmee' or, less commonly, 'farminee' or 'farmoutee'.

Farmout agreements are sometimes drafted in a shorter form than other ASPAs, even sometimes in the form of a letter agreement.[40] The reason for this seems more a matter of historical practice than a matter of best practice. A farmout agreement is fundamentally an asset sale and purchase, and there is no compelling reason why a farmout agreement should not contain the types of provisions that are customarily found in an ASPA. For example, the AIPN 2004 model form farmout agreement does not include certain limitations on the farmor's liability, such as time limits for making claims, baskets or a financial limit or cap on liability. A farmor may want to consider including these types of provisions in its farmout agreement.

The timing of the actual assignment under a farmout agreement can be an important issue. Some farmout agreements provide that the farmee will earn its

---

39 Peter Roberts (2010), *Joint Operating Agreements*, at 130.

40 Claude Duval *et al* (2009), *International Petroleum Exploration and Exploitation Agreements: Legal, Economic and Policy Aspects*, at 306.

participating interests only upon completion of the works to be undertaken by the farmee. This is often referred to as an 'earn-in' and the result is that completion of the works is in effect a suspensive condition to completion of the assignment. This formulation is more favourable to the farmor and raises the material risk for the farmee that the host government may not consent to the assignment even after the works have been completed. The alternative is to provide that the farmee acquires its participating interests prior to completion of the works. This formulation is more favourable to the farmee, but requires that the farmout agreement include provisions for reassignment of the participating interests back to the farmor in the event that the farmee does not complete the works. In some jurisdictions the government will not consent to the transfer until the works are completed. Given that there is no universally accepted form of farmout agreement, this point is a matter for negotiation on a deal-by-deal basis.

The consideration in a farmout agreement can take many forms. As noted above, the defining characteristic of a farmout agreement is that the farmee agrees to undertake and/or pay for some works that would otherwise be undertaken and/or paid for by the farmor. These works can include undertaking and/or paying for the acquisition and interpretation of seismic data, the drilling of one or more exploration wells or the drilling of one or more appraisal wells. The farmee typically pays 100% of the costs and expenses of such works, and in effect 'carries' the farmor.

The ratio between the amount of costs to be borne by the farmee and the percentage of participating interest to be acquired by the farmee is often referred to as the 'promote'. A transaction where the farmee has agreed to pay 100% of the costs of an exploration well or other works and will acquire 100% of the farmor's participating interests is referred to as a 'ground floor' deal. More commonly, the farmor will retain some participating interests. So, for example, if the farmee has agreed to pay 100% of the costs of an exploration well or other works, but will earn only 50% of the farmor's participating interests, that will be a two-for-one promote. If the farmee has agreed to pay 100% of the costs of an exploration well or other works, but will earn only 33% of the farmor's participating interests, that will be a three-for-one promote.[41]

Other forms of consideration in farmout agreements include the farmee agreeing to pay to the farmor all or a portion of the historical costs and expenses incurred by the farmor in connection with the prospect. In this case, the farmee is typically given audit rights under the terms of the applicable JOA in order to confirm such expenditure.

Farmout agreements can become very complicated, with combinations of works to be performed and/or paid for and other types of consideration to be paid, and various types of interests to be earned and retained. These terms and conditions are limited only by the creativity of the commercial and legal teams negotiating the transaction. From a legal perspective, drafting and negotiating complicated farmout agreements can be an enjoyable challenge.

41 Martyn R David (1996), *Upstream Oil and Gas Agreements*, at 34.

Public takeovers

Mary Bartle
David Lewis
Clifford Chance LLP

---

1. Introduction

Public takeover activity in the United Kingdom increased in 2014 and 2015, and since then has remained broadly stable in terms of deal volume, despite the prospective withdrawal of the United Kingdom from the European Union. Notwithstanding increased general takeover activity levels and the 2015 Royal Dutch Shell plc offer for BG Group plc valued at £48 billion, there have been few takeovers of exploration and production (E&P) companies in recent years. As the price of oil took a dive in the second half of 2014 and volatility continued until late 2016, when oil prices stabilised, the prediction that cost efficiencies might drive E&P consolidation failed to fully materialise in the UK public takeover market.

Takeovers of public companies in the United Kingdom look and feel very different from private treaty transactions as a result of the United Kingdom's legal and regulatory framework – and in particular, the UK City Code on Takeovers and Mergers. It is critical that any party considering making a bid for a UK public E&P company understands such framework and the aspects of it that particularly affect bids for companies in that sector. Failure to do so can have a significant impact on the outcome of any such bid.

The main points to consider in public takeovers are:

- board recommendation;
- host country approvals;
- the ability to walk away;
- deal certainty;
- the formal sale process;
- teaming up; and
- the target's flexibility.

1.1 Board recommendation

Securing a recommendation of the target board as early as possible is typically vital. The bidder may be unable to obtain due diligence information on the target if it does not have the target board on side. Without such information, it can be difficult for a bidder to validate its valuation and to assess the implications for the assets of the proposed change of control, particularly where the value of the target is derived from a small number of key assets or licences.

Obtaining the support of the target board early in the process has become arguably even more important since the introduction into the Takeover Code in

2011 of the automatic 'put up or shut up' (PUSU) regime. If a target is required to make an announcement which commences the offer period, it must identify in that announcement all potential bidders with which it is in talks or from which it has received an approach (that has not been unequivocally rejected). Such named bidders automatically become subject to a 28-day PUSU deadline, which requires the bidder either to launch a firm bid (ie, release a firm intention announcement) or publicly confirm that it does not intend to make a bid within 28 days of such announcement. Such deadline can be extended if the UK Panel on Takeovers and Mergers, at the request of the target, consents to such extension. Although there is no doubt that targets can use this tool to their advantage, target boards in recommended deals have generally been willing to grant an extension where such bidders genuinely need more time to complete their pre-bid preparations. In an unsolicited scenario, however, bidders face the risk of being timed out by a target board unwilling to support an extension.

1.2 Host country approvals

Navigating the political environment in the local jurisdictions in which the target operates is critical to the success of a bid. In some cases, due to the terms of the local exploration licence, a bidder risks the loss of such licence if it acquires the target without the host government's consent. Even where there is no contractual or legal obligation to obtain the government's consent, bidders typically take the view that the ongoing relationship with the host government is vital to the future prospects of a project and wish to secure the support of the host government in any event. It can be challenging for a bidder to secure the support of the relevant host governments and regulators without cooperation from the target and, as a bidder must proceed with its bid once it has released its firm intention announcement (see below), the importance of getting the target board on side early in the process cannot be overemphasised.

1.3 The ability to walk away

A key principle of the Takeover Code is that a bidder must proceed with its bid once it has released its firm intention announcement. Although it is customary for a bidder to include a host of detailed conditions to its bid, in practice it is extremely difficult for a bidder to withdraw from a bid following such an announcement. This has two particularly important implications. First, bidders typically want to obtain an indication of support from the host government before the firm intention announcement is made so as to reduce the risk of the government either refusing consent (resulting in the loss of the licence) or seeking to extract some value in return for its consent. Second, bidders need to understand that they are effectively taking the risk of the business from the time of the firm intention announcement with very limited controls over it. There are no specific warranties or indemnities given by the target or its shareholders. This can prove troubling for some potential bidders, particularly those with limited experience of these types of deal and those more familiar with private treaty agreements containing enforceable walk-away rights and detailed warranty schedules.

1.4 Deal certainty

There is limited scope for a bidder to secure certainty of deal execution. Other than in exceptional circumstances, break fees and other deal execution measures given by the target – such as non-solicitation undertakings, matching rights and restrictions on the target board switching its recommendation – are prohibited. In the absence of deal protection measures, stake building and securing irrevocable undertakings are the main tools at the disposal of bidders. However, although the tactical benefits of stake building may be obvious, pre-bid stake building remains the exception rather than the rule in UK takeovers. This is often due to the complex web of legal and commercial challenges that stake building presents. As a result, it is significantly more common for bidders to seek to obtain irrevocable undertakings or letters of intent to support the bid as an alternative to stake building.

1.5 The formal sale process

The formal sale process has proved quite popular with target E&P companies since its introduction in September 2011. A formal sale process is much closer to a US-style sell-side auction of a public company and is quite different from the traditional way of executing a bid in the United Kingdom. It allows the target to announce that it is seeking one or more potential offerors for the company by means of a formal sale process. Where a formal sale process announcement is made, the Takeover Panel will normally grant dispensation from the requirement to name any potential offeror participating in that process and from the 28-day PUSU regime referred to above. The panel may also grant dispensation from the prohibition on the target paying an inducement fee, provided that the inducement fee meets certain requirements, including that it is paid only to one offeror in the process (at the time of a firm offer) and is *de minimis* in value.

Why this sale process has to date proved particularly attractive to E&P targets is an interesting question. In general, the formal sale process has increased in popularity in recent years, with a number of processes resulting in successful bids. However, of the E&P formal sale processes launched since 2014, all have been withdrawn without a successful firm offer for the target – although in the case of the formal sale process of Salamander Energy plc announced in May 2014 (in relation to which Clifford Chance LLP acted for Salamander), the process could have resulted in an offer had Salamander not agreed to dispose of a 40% interest in its B8/38 concession (including the Bualuang field) and the surrounding G4/50 concession to SONA Petroleum Berhad. Upon announcing the disposal in July 2014, Salamander terminated the formal sale process. Shortly after the conclusion of the formal sale process, Salamander announced in October 2014 that it had received a possible offer from Ophir Energy plc, and that it had also received an approach from a consortium led by Compañía Española de Petróleos, SAU and Strategic Energy (Global) Limited. In November 2014 Ophir made a firm offer for Salamander, which completed in March 2015, following termination of the agreement with SONA in relation to its asset disposal.

In addition to the scarcity of firm offers resulting from the formal sale processes announced by E&P companies since 2014, it is important to note that all of the formal sale processes announced during such period were announced as part of wider strategic reviews, where a sale of the company was identified as one of the possible outcomes of that review. Consequently, it is likely that the recent popularity of this process for E&P companies has been the result of a shift in strategic focus of certain E&P companies in light of macro-economic factors affecting the sector.

1.6 Teaming up

It is not uncommon for a potential acquirer to endeavour to team up with another industry player in connection with a potential transaction to share risks or avoid a bidding contest. However, in a public bid scenario, a bidder must be mindful of the implications of doing so. If the third party is a 'concert party' of the bidder (see section 3.6), the actions of such a third party can have serious implications for the bid. There are a broad range of repercussions, one of the most important being that if a bidder and its concert parties acquire an interest in shares that carry 30% or more of the voting rights of the target, the bidder may be required to make a mandatory cash (or cash alternative) offer, subject to very limited conditionality. This would present a material departure if the initial proposed transaction contemplated share consideration. Mandatory offers are fairly unpopular with bidders for the reasons outlined later in this chapter.

1.7 Target's flexibility

There are very limited defensive tactics available to a target company in a Takeover Code transaction. In fact, once a target has reason to believe that a *bona fide* offer might be imminent, the target cannot take any action that could frustrate a bid without the approval of its shareholders. This prevents targets from, among other things, acquiring or disposing of material assets and entering into contracts outside the ordinary course of business, such as farm-in arrangements. As the restriction takes effect early (ie, once a target has a reason to believe that a *bona fide* bid might be imminent), target companies that are regularly approached by interested parties should continuously assess how they operate their businesses.

We explore these aspects further in this chapter as well as focusing on some key features of the regulatory framework applicable to a bid for an E&P company.

2. The application of the Takeover Code

As mentioned in section 1, takeovers of UK public companies are highly regulated, in particular through the Takeover Code. The Takeover Code is a set of principles and rules designed to provide a flexible framework and to ensure fair and equivalent treatment of shareholders of the target company. It has a statutory footing and the Takeover Panel – an independent body which issues and administers the Takeover Code – can impose various sanctions if a party fails to comply with it (see below). It is therefore essential to establish at the outset of a potential transaction whether the target company is subject to the Takeover Code.

The Takeover Code applies to takeovers and mergers (however effected) of companies that have their registered office in the United Kingdom, the Channel Islands or the Isle of Man, and have their securities admitted to either:

- a UK regulated market (eg, the London Stock Exchange's main market for listed securities or the ISDX Main Board);
- a UK multilateral trading facility (eg, AIM or the ISDX Growth Market); or
- any stock exchange in the Channel Islands or Isle of Man.

The Takeover Code also applies to takeovers of untraded public companies which are resident in the United Kingdom, the Channel Islands or the Isle of Man and takeovers of certain private companies having public company characteristics. In addition to regulating takeovers and mergers, the Takeover Code is concerned with regulating other transactions which have as their objective or potential effect obtaining or consolidating control of such companies, as well as partial offers to shareholders for securities in the relevant companies.

As of 8 January 2018, specific provisions of the Takeover Code also apply to sales of all or substantially all of the target's assets in competition with an offer under the Takeover Code. In addition, certain rules under the Takeover Code restrict a person subject to it from, for a designated period, among other things, announcing an offer or possible offer for the target company or making any statement which raises or confirms the possibility that an offer might be made for the target company. As of 8 January 2018, the Takeover Code was amended to prevent a person subject to those rules from avoiding their application by purchasing assets which are 'significant' in relation to the target company. In assessing whether assets are significant, the Takeover Panel will have regard to consideration, assets and profits tests where relative values of more than 75% are normally regarded as significant.

The Takeover Panel has a wide range of enforcement powers and sanctions at its disposal. These include non-statutory enforcement powers, such as private or public censure, or barring a person from engaging in any takeover-related activity for a defined period (known as 'cold shouldering'), as well as statutory enforcement powers, such as production of documents, compliance rulings, compensation rulings, disciplinary action and financial penalties. The panel can also apply to court for enforcement. The first case of the exercise of the panel's powers to seek enforcement of a rule-based requirement under Section 955 of the Companies Act 2006 was released in 2017 in *Panel on Takeovers and Mergers v King* [2017] CSOH 156. In that case, the Outer House of the Court of Session in Scotland granted an order sought by the panel to require respondent David King to comply with the panel's rulings that he should announce a mandatory offer under Rule 9 of the Takeover Code for all shares of Rangers International Football Club plc not already owned by him and his concert parties.

3. Pre-bid planning

The pre-bid planning stage is one of the most critical stages of the bid process. Although successfully managing this stage of the process cannot necessarily ensure a successful outcome, it may prevent the potential bid falling at the first hurdle. In view of the key issues highlighted above, avoiding premature disclosure of a potential deal for an E&P company governed by the Takeover Code is critical. Some of the key matters for consideration at this stage are set out below.

3.1 Announcement obligations and PUSU

The Takeover Code places considerable emphasis on the importance of secrecy before the initial offer-related announcement. For example, if a bidder wishes to approach more than six external parties, excluding certain persons such as financial, legal and other immediate advisers (but including, for example, potential debt or equity finance providers), it must consult with the Takeover Panel. Subject to the relevant exclusions, if more than six parties have been approached in connection with an offer or possible offer, the panel will normally require an announcement to be made to avoid the risk of a false market being created should a leak of price-sensitive information occur.

If there is a leak which results in the target becoming the subject of rumour or speculation (whether or not the potential bidder is named) or there is an untoward movement in the target's share price,[1] the panel must be consulted and will determine whether an announcement is required. If there is no evidence of a leak, a bidder's financial adviser will usually seek to persuade the panel that the share price movement is not the result of a leak, but rather a consequence of some other fact or circumstance, such as general market and sector movements or the recent release of price-sensitive information relating to the target. The initial offer-related announcement confirming a possible offer will push the target into an offer period, which triggers the application of numerous provisions in the Takeover Code.

A number of other events may also require an announcement to be made; these are principally designed to minimise the risk of a false market in the target's shares. A diagram summarising the announcement requirements is set out in Figure 1.

Before a potential bidder has approached the target, the bidder is responsible for making any required announcement. That responsibility then shifts to the target following an approach (unless the target unequivocally rejects the approach). While responsibility rests with the bidder or the target, the bid parties and their financial advisers must closely monitor the target's share price so that they are well positioned to identify any untoward movements and bring them to the panel's attention.

If the target is required to make the announcement which commences the offer period, it must identify all potential bidders from which it has received an approach, and such named bidders automatically become subject to a 28-day PUSU deadline unless the target has initiated a formal sale process (see section 1.5 above). This means that the bidder must release a firm intention announcement or publicly confirm that it does not intend to make a bid (known as a 'no intention to bid' statement) within 28 days of such announcement, unless the panel, at the request of the target, consents to an extension of the deadline. Where detailed due diligence is essential – for example, of seismic data and/or a good understanding of a host government's likely reaction to a change of control of a target which has an indirect interest in the country in question – this 28-day limited window can create real leverage for the target and put significant pressure on the bidder. For this reason, there have been only a handful of hostile transactions in the E&P space recently.

1 A movement of 10% above the lowest price since an approach has been made to the target or 5% in a single day is generally regarded as 'untoward' for these purposes.

Figure 1. Announcement requirements

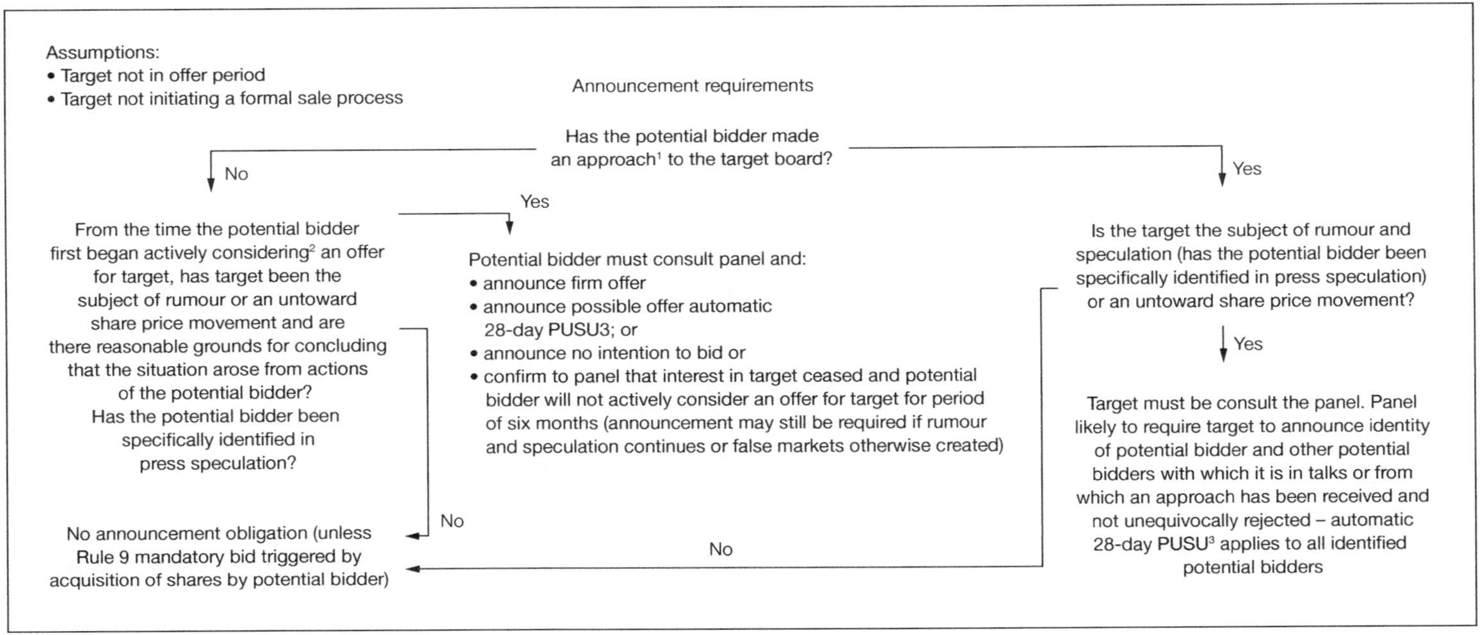

1 The panel considers an 'approach' to be made as soon as a potential bidder (or someone acting on its behalf) informs a director, representative or adviser of the target company that it is considering the possibility of making an offer. This could be at a very preliminary stage in the bidder's preparations. It does not matter whether the approach is informal or no more than broadly indicative. There is no requirement for an approach to be made in writing, or for an indicative offer price (or any terms or conditions) to be specified, and it could be made as part of a conversation on unrelated matters.

2 The panel will consider an offer being 'actively considered' at the point at which the assessment of a potential target moves from being routine to something more focused and intense.

3 Unless PUSU period extended at the request of the target in respect of one or more bidders.

As mentioned above, although there is no doubt that a target can use this hard deadline to its advantage, target boards have generally been willing to grant an extension of the PUSU period where a bidder genuinely needs more time and is welcome. Of course, the position is very different in the context of a hostile scenario where bidders do face the risk of running out of time.

In certain circumstances, the Takeover Panel may grant a dispensation from the requirement to make an announcement where the potential bidder agrees to 'down tools' and cease any active consideration of an offer for the target. An agreement to down tools or the making of a no intention to bid statement generally results in the bidder being unable to make an offer for the target for six months, save in specified circumstances.

If an announcement obligation is triggered, the bidder is not normally required to announce a firm intention to make a bid, except where a mandatory offer has been triggered (see section 3.6). If the bidder is not ready to commit to proceed with the offer (eg, if it is still in negotiations with the target board or does not have committed financing in place), a brief holding announcement that talks are in place can be made.

3.2 Recommended or hostile?

The most significant factor which influences the likely success of a bid, absent a higher competing offer, is whether it is recommended by the target board. If the bid is hostile or unsolicited, there is often a fierce battle in the public arena where its outcome sometimes remains unknown until the final day of the bid.

Careful tactical planning is required before a potential bidder seeks a recommendation. As part of this planning, the bidder will need to consider whether it would be willing to launch a hostile bid if its advances are rejected by the board of the target.

Upon receiving the approach, the target board will consider whether it is in the interests of the company as a whole to entertain the proposal, taking into account its obligation under the Takeover Code not to deny shareholders the opportunity to decide on the merits of a *bona fide* bid. It is not unusual for target boards to reject the first or even numerous approaches. There may be a number of rounds before the target board can conclude that the bid price and other terms being offered could potentially form the basis of a recommendable bid.

If the target board concludes that it will entertain the bid further, it will normally provide due diligence information to the bidder and its advisers once the bidder has entered into a suitable confidentiality agreement (see section 3.3).

It is common for targets to seek to include 'standstill' provisions in the confidentiality agreement. These provisions usually restrict the bidder from making a hostile offer for the target and/or acquiring securities in the target without its consent for a period (typically six to 18 months), subject to any carve-outs that may be agreed between the parties. These have the effect of giving the target some control over the bid process and prevent the bidder from acquiring a strategic stake (which could deter competing bidders).

Once it becomes aware that a *bona fide* offer might be imminent, the target board is prohibited from taking any action that could frustrate an offer without the approval of its shareholders. Rule 21.1(a) of the Takeover Code sets out a non-exhaustive list of the types of action which would be prohibited, including the acquisition or disposal of assets of a material amount and the entering into of contracts other than in the ordinary course of business. This would generally capture any significant farm-in arrangement or the disposal of a licence which is material to the business, as well as abnormal increases in the terms of service of directors of the target. The 'rubber hits the road' under this rule if a company has been proposing farm-in arrangements to a number of interested parties and one of them decides that it wishes to consider making an offer. This would mean that proceeding with a farm-out with another party would require shareholder consent in circumstances where it may not otherwise.

If a target board rejects an early-stage approach (or approaches), it is free subsequently to recommend the bid at any time in the bid process.

3.3 Due diligence

As in the case of a private acquisition, a potential bidder will want to undertake detailed due diligence on the target before deciding whether to proceed with the transaction. Before approaching the target, a bidder and its advisers will usually review publicly available information, including financial statements, public documents and announcements, especially any reserve engineer reports.

The level of non-public information that a bidder can expect to receive will depend on whether the target board expects to recommend the bid.

In the case of an unsolicited bid situation, the publicly available information may be the only information available to the potential bidder. The Takeover Code does not, as a general rule, require a target to provide information to an unwelcome bidder, except under the 'equality of information' provisions described below. This can make it challenging for a bidder to launch a hostile bid for an E&P company, particularly if a significant proportion of the value of the target is derived from a small number of key assets or licences. If the latest seismic or other technical data and the key contracts (eg, licence agreements, joint operating agreements, farm-in/farm-out agreements, pre-emption agreements) are not available to a bidder, it can be difficult for the bidder to support its valuation and to understand the implications for the assets of the proposed change of control. It is by no means impossible, however – as borne out by hostile bids such as Centrica's bid for Venture Production plc in 2011 and Korea National Oil Corporation's bid for Dana Petroleum plc in 2010, although the principal assets of the target entities in each case were in the North Sea where the licensing regime and degree of government intervention (or not) in transactions were well understood and far from opaque.

In a recommended situation, the target will normally provide some information about its business and the review of this information will take place before the formal offer announcement is made (but potentially after the deal has become public knowledge). Obtaining all of the information that a bidder may want is not always straightforward, however, as targets are commonly wary of providing extensive information, particularly at the outset. This is in part due to the fact that the

Takeover Code contains 'equality of information' provisions: if information has been given to an offeror or potential offeror (whether publicly identified or not), and another offeror or *bona fide* potential offeror requests such information, then such requesting party must be provided with the information, even if it is less welcome (as long as it signs a basic confidentiality agreement). As it is not permitted to require such a bidder to enter into standstill provisions of the kind described above as a condition to the provision of the information, the target effectively loses some control of the bid process from that moment. The test of 'potential offeror' is not a difficult one to pass and as a result, targets are often reluctant to share commercially sensitive technical (or other) data with a offeror or *bona fide* potential offeror on the basis that it may have to be disclosed to a genuine competitor or state-owned government enterprise, if subsequently requested.

3.4 Break fees and other deal protection measures

Under the Takeover Code, a target is generally prohibited (subject to some specific exemptions) from entering into 'offer-related arrangements' in favour of the bidder and its concert parties during an offer or when an offer is reasonably in contemplation. 'Offer-related arrangements' are defined broadly to include any agreement, arrangement or commitment in connection with an offer. The prohibition captures various deal protection measures, such as non-solicitation undertakings, matching rights and restrictions on the target board changing its recommendation.

Such arrangements also include, among other things, break fees, work or diligence fees and arrangements with a similar effect to a break fee. There are some very limited exceptions to this general prohibition, which are shown in the route map in Figure 2.

There have been very few examples of the Takeover Panel allowing target boards to enter into break fee or other offer-related arrangements since the prohibition was introduced. At the time of writing, the only three examples of bids where break fees were agreed involved independent E&P companies – Cove Energy plc in 2012 and Valiant Petroleum plc and Lochard Energy Group plc in 2013. These companies put themselves up for sale via the formal sale process under the Takeover Code (see section 7 for more details), which is one of the few circumstances in which the panel may consent to a break fee.

In the absence of such deal protection measures, stake building and securing irrevocable undertakings and letters of intent from target directors and shareholders are the main tools at a bidder's disposal to reduce execution risk.

Pre-bid stake building provides a number of tactical advantages. It may deter rivals, give the bidder a first mover advantage and, on a contractual offer, increase the chances of acquiring ultimate control of the target. It may reduce the overall cost of the bid if the bidder can acquire shares at a price lower than the eventual offer, and can also provide some downside protection against the bidder's deal costs if its stake is ultimately acquired by a competing bidder at a price higher than that paid for it.

However, pre-bid stake building remains relatively uncommon in UK takeovers. Although there has been more consideration of this tactic since offer-related arrangements were prohibited, it commonly does not convert into execution due to

Figure 2. Deal protection measures permitted and prohibited by the Takeover Code

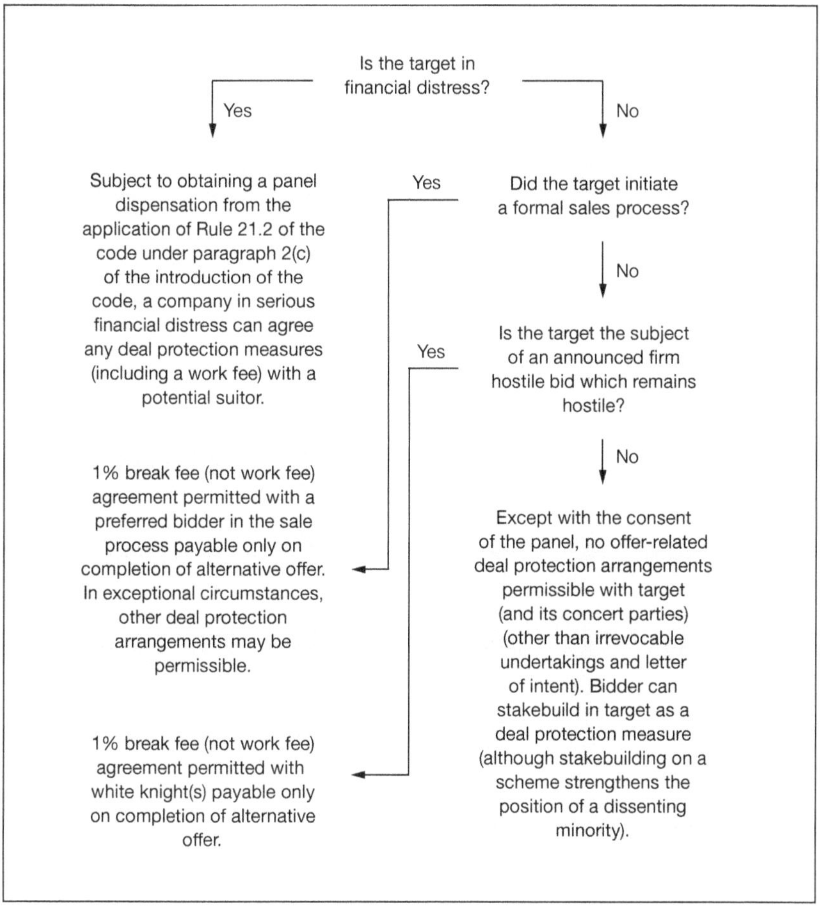

the difficulty of navigating the complex web of legal and commercial challenges that stake building presents. Moreover, bidders are often reluctant to risk a loss on their investment if their bid fails and no competing bidder emerges.

Consequently, bidders more commonly seek to obtain irrevocable undertakings or letters of intent to accept the offer (or vote in favour of the scheme) as an alternative to stake building. Irrevocable undertakings are normally provided by directors of the target in recommended bids. Bidders also usually seek to obtain irrevocable undertakings from institutional shareholders prior to announcement so as to demonstrate strong support for the bid.

3.5 Securing the support of host governments

As highlighted above, the importance of navigating the political context in the local jurisdictions in which the target operates at an early stage cannot be underestimated.

The consent of the host government (as the issuer of the exploration licence) is typically required for a change of control of the licence holder, often a subsidiary of the target company, but it is not always clear that indirect changes of control are caught. There may also be an 'antitrust' (ie, merger control) filing required in the country in question and the commensurate risk that this may be held up should the bidder not have the host government support. Even if consent is not strictly required under the licence or otherwise, bidders typically take the view that they still wish to secure the support of the host government. As a result, it is important that bidders seek to engage with governments at the earliest opportunity and usually do so together with the target board.

We have seen host governments in emerging markets, particularly in Africa, using their consent rights as an opportunity to extract additional benefits or payments from target companies in these circumstances. For example, in the formal sale process for Cove Energy plc referred to above, the Mozambique government used the consent request as an opportunity to impose a tax charge of 12.8% on the transaction. In that case, Cove had approached the Mozambique government in the initial stages to discuss the potential takeover and to seek the government's endorsement of various potential bidders. It was fortunate for PTTEP (as the ultimately successful bidder) that the tax charge was imposed public prior to it launching its firm offer (and hence it was factored into its bid price), as the Takeover Panel may not have allowed PTTEP to adjust its offer downwards or to walk away from the bid if it had become aware of the tax charge later in the process. This case highlights the importance of engaging with host governments prior to a bidder releasing its firm intention announcement.

3.6 Arrangements with third parties

If a bidder is contemplating involving a third party, such as an industry player, in the bid, it is important to consider the implications of doing so. On the assumption that the parties are not joint offerors, the third party may be a concert party of the bidder under the Takeover Code. The third party will be a concert party if such parties, pursuant to an agreement or understanding (whether formal or informal), cooperate to obtain or consolidate control of a company or to frustrate the successful outcome of an offer for a company. The Takeover Code presumes that certain categories of persons will be acting in concert with one another unless the contrary is established. For example, a company will be presumed to be acting in concert with its parent, subsidiaries and 'associated companies', its directors, and its defined benefit pension schemes. A company will be presumed to be acting in concert with its corporate joint venture partners (and such joint venture partner's parent, subsidiaries and associated companies) if both the company and the joint venture partner control 20% or more of the equity share capital of a joint venture company. However, in recent years the panel has allowed this presumption to be rebutted in certain circumstances, including if the joint venture partners and the joint ventures are on arm's-length terms and the joint venture partner and the Takeover Code company do not have the ability to control or influence one another and are otherwise independent of one another. Since joint ventures are so common in the E&P sector, this is an important issue to assess early in the bid process.

Actions by a concert party of a bidder can have serious implications for a bid. There is a broad range of repercussions – one of the most important of which is that if a bidder and its concert parties together hold more than 30% of the target and thereafter acquire any further stake in the target, the bidder is required to make a mandatory cash offer. Mandatory offers are fairly unpopular with bidders for various reasons, but largely because they require bidders to offer cash (or a cash alternative) and the bid can be subject only to a 50% plus acceptance condition rather than the normal 90% threshold (see section 6).

In addition, acquisitions of target shares by concert parties can result in a floor on the offer price, as well as potentially affecting the nature of the consideration that may be offered by the bidder.

4. Financing and cash confirmation

Cash (either alone or in some cases with bidder securities) has been the most common form of consideration offered by bidders for E&P companies over recent years.

Where cash is offered, the Takeover Code requires that the bidder's financial adviser be satisfied that the cash is in place before the offer is formally announced, as it must confirm in the firm intention announcement (and the bid document) that sufficient cash resources are, and will continue to be, available to the bidder to finance the offer on 'certain funds' terms. In some cases, financial advisers may require cash to be placed in a ring-fenced account during the offer; or if acquisition finance is being put in place, the financing must not be subject to unacceptable conditions precedent or a material adverse change condition. Conditions precedent not related to the offer or not within the bidder's control are not typically permitted.

The financial adviser takes its responsibility seriously, as any failure by it to check the bidder's position sufficiently could result in the panel requiring the financial adviser to pay the cash itself.

5. Structure of the bid

A UK takeover will usually be structured as either a contractual offer or a court-approved scheme of arrangement.

A contractual offer is made by the bidder to all target shareholders and, when the offer becomes unconditional, target shareholders which have accepted the offer are bound to transfer their shares to the bidder. In order for an offer to succeed, the bidder needs to receive acceptances in respect of over 50% of the voting shares. However, as the bidder must acquire 90% of the shares (for a UK offer, although this threshold may vary depending on the jurisdiction of incorporation of the target) to which the offer relates in order to acquire the remaining shares through the squeeze-out process, the bidder usually sets the acceptance condition at 90%. In practice, the bidder will often waive that acceptance condition at some point after it has secured acceptances, together with shares it already owns, over more than 50% of the shares, as the bidder can generally expect to receive a further wave of acceptances after such time.

A scheme of arrangement is a statutory procedure under the UK Companies Act 2006 (or equivalent legislation of the country in which the company is incorporated) under which a takeover can be effected by the passing of resolutions by target shareholders and with the approval of the court. A scheme for an English company requires the approval of a majority in number representing 75% in value of each class of target shareholder voting on the necessary resolutions and once approved, all shareholders are bound by the scheme. If the requisite threshold is not met, the scheme will fail and the bidder will acquire no target shares.

The structure ultimately chosen will depend on a number of deal-specific factors, including the likelihood of an interloper emerging, the shareholder base of the target and its support for the deal, and whether it is a recommended bid. Recommended bids, particularly those of a high value, are more commonly implemented by a scheme of arrangement.

Hostile bids are generally structured as contractual offers. This is because a scheme of arrangement is a target-led process and, although it is theoretically possible to implement a scheme without the support of the target board, there would be significant practical difficulties in doing so. The contractual offer structure was hence chosen in the following hostile E&P takeovers: Essar Global Fund Limited's offer for Essar Energy plc in 2014, Korea National Oil Corporation's takeover of Dana Petroleum plc in 2010 and Centrica's takeover of Venture Production plc in 2009. Competing offers are also generally structured as contractual offers, as they are perceived as being more flexible and the bidder has more control over the bid. By way of example, Shell – the first mover in the formal sale process of Cove Energy plc referred to above – chose to make its (ultimately unsuccessful) bid via a contractual offer due to the desire to be fleet-footed in the face of an interloper.

Bidders can switch between offer and scheme (and *vice versa*), subject to Takeover Panel consent. For example, a recommended bid which starts out as a scheme may, with the panel's consent, be switched to a contractual offer if a competitive bid situation arises, thereby allowing the bidder greater flexibility to adjust its offer terms.

6. Launching the bid

6.1 Announcing the bid and the formal offer

The first public step in the process (absent a leak or other holding announcement) is the release of the firm intention announcement. From such time, the bidder must then proceed with the bid, other than in wholly exceptional circumstances. The announcement must contain the principal terms and conditions of the bid (see below). A cash offeror must have its acquisition financing fully locked down at the time of the announcement of the firm intention.

The formal bid is then made, in the case of a contractual offer, by an offer document and, in the case of a scheme of arrangement, by a scheme circular. All target shareholders must be sent a copy of this document, normally within 28 days of the firm intention announcement.

6.2 Types of condition and pre-condition

It is typical for a bidder to seek to make its bid subject to a broad range of conditions (or less commonly, pre-conditions (see below)), which must normally be objective in nature. Under the Takeover Code, the bidder has an obligation to use all reasonable efforts to ensure the satisfaction of any conditions or pre-conditions to which the bid is subject. However, on a recommended bid, it will be open to the parties to agree contractually to place a more onerous standard on the bidder related to satisfaction of conditions (eg, an 'all steps necessary' or 'best efforts' standard). This can provide the target with more protection where the deal is subject to risky conditions.

Rather than describing in detail the range of conditions commonly included in bids, we focus in this section on those categories of condition of particular importance in the context of bids for E&P targets.

The first category is regulatory, governmental and other third-party consents. As highlighted earlier in this chapter, it is common for consent to be required of the host government (as the issuer of the licence to be acquired indirectly). As a result, bidders commonly include receipt of any such governmental consents as conditions to the offer. It may also be necessary to include conditions relating to antitrust approvals. The requirement for the consent of other third parties, such as co-licensees, could be addressed through conditions, although pre-emption rights contained in joint operating agreements are not normally triggered by an indirect change of control of a licensee. In practice, the impact of not getting such consent would need to be virtually deal-destroying for such a condition to be capable of being invoked (see below).

The second category is conditions relating to the target's business. These are generally comprehensive and appear similar in scope to the warranties that a purchaser might expect to receive on a private company acquisition, such as a material adverse change condition. However, for the reasons set out below, a bidder should not be lulled into a false sense of security.

Third, where the target's principal current or potential revenue streams derive from an important asset or group of assets, there may be specific conditions related to an asset. For example, in Ophir's offer for Salamander in 2014, it was a condition to completion that a previously agreed disposal to SONA of an effective 40% interest in the B8/38 concession containing the Bualuang oil field and the surrounding G4/50 concession be terminated in accordance with the condition. In January 2015, Ophir and Salamander announced that this condition had been satisfied.

There may be circumstances in which it is more appropriate for a bidder to include in the firm intention announcement a pre-condition to making the bid. The Takeover Panel must consent to the inclusion of a pre-condition and will usually do so if it relates to material official authorisations or regulatory clearances relating to the bid (normally where the timeframe for obtaining and/or the outcome in respect of such clearance cannot easily be accommodated within the Takeover Code timeframe). The Royal Dutch Shell plc offer for BG Group plc in 2015 contained a number of pre-conditions relating to competition authority clearances. The panel has discretion to permit other pre-conditions, although the circumstances in which it is willing to do so are fairly limited.

6.3 Withdrawing from a bid

A fundamental feature of the Takeover Code is that a bidder must proceed with its bid once it has released its firm intention announcement. This underpins the Takeover Panel's aim of reducing the risk of false markets developing, as shareholders can rely on that announcement. It also explains why acquisition financing must be fully locked down on announcement.

In policing potential withdrawals, the panel assesses whether a proposed withdrawal is genuine and reasonable, and whether the circumstances are of material significance to the bidder in the context of the bid. As the panel applies a very high materiality threshold when making its assessment, in practice it is extremely difficult to obtain the panel's consent to invoke a condition (other than the acceptance condition, the scheme condition or the regulatory conditions) and walk away from the bid. If a government or other regulatory body agrees to grant its consent, but such consent is granted with onerous conditions attached, the panel will apply its high materiality threshold when assessing the implications of those onerous conditions on the bidder and whether it should be entitled to withdraw its bid.

An example that highlights the stance taken by the panel to a request by a bidder to withdraw from a bid was the offer by ONGC Videsh Limited (OVL) – which was 74% indirectly owned by the government of India – for Imperial Energy in 2008. The offer was subject to two pre-conditions relating to the approval under Russian law of foreign investments. On 11 November 2008, OVL announced the satisfaction of the pre-conditions and hence was due to post its offer document within the Takeover Code-stipulated 28 days. OVL sought an extension to the publication date, citing the Mumbai terrorist attacks as a reason why the appropriate Indian governmental committee had not had a chance to approve publication of the offer document. The panel ruled that no extension should be granted, on the basis that it is not appropriate for bidders (or persons controlling them) to have a unilateral right to introduce further pre-conditions.

OVL did not appeal the panel's decision and sent its offer document within the 28 days. There was considerable media speculation that OVL's real reason for applying for an extension to the publication date was to enable it to seek to renegotiate the price or withdraw from the deal (as, due to a dramatic fall in the oil price, Imperial Energy's shares would have been trading at a much lower price absent OVL's bid). In its announcement on 9 December 2008, the board of Imperial Energy strongly recommended that Imperial Energy shareholders accept the offer as soon as possible in order to achieve the 90% acceptance condition by the first closing date. The 90% acceptance condition was satisfied by that date, so OVL was unable to lapse its offer on the first closing date and its offer became wholly unconditional.

7. Formal sale processes

As explained in the introduction, a process by which companies put themselves up for sale is proving quite popular with E&P targets. A formal sale process involves the target putting itself up for sale; this often occurs if the target is in financial difficulty or has been approached by one or more potential bidders.

In addition to potentially improving the chances of securing a higher bid price, formal sale processes have proved attractive as they open the door to a number of dispensations not available to other Takeover Code transactions. In particular, the target can seek the Takeover Panel's dispensation from naming all bidders which have approached the target in its announcement that commences the offer period and a dispensation from imposing the automatic 28-day PUSU deadline. The panel may also grant dispensation from the prohibition on the target paying an inducement fee, provided that the inducement fee meets certain requirements, including that it is paid only to one offeror in the process (at the time of a firm offer) and is *de minimis* in value.

In practice, targets have (not surprisingly) focused on securing the dispensations allowing anonymity for potential bidders and the removal of the PUSU deadlines so as to assist the target's management of a private auction process. That said, on occasion, the panel has been willing to consent to targets agreeing to inducement fees, such as in the case of Shell's bid for Cove discussed above, Ithaca Energy's bid for Valiant Petroleum announced on 1 March 2013 and Parkmead's bid for Lochard Energy plc announced on 23 May 2013.

The target commences the formal sale process by releasing an announcement which puts up the 'for sale' sign. In 2017 the Takeover Panel issued Practice Statement 31, which contains specific content requirements for any such announcement. Any potential bidder is entitled to participate in the process, although the target may require the party to execute a suitable confidentiality agreement. Such confidentiality agreement may contain standstill provisions and other restrictions designed to control the sale process, such as restricting bidders from unilaterally approaching governmental bodies, regulators and/or other third parties whose consent is required for the proposed change of control. In addition, the panel has indicated that it will permit a target to require a potential offeror to undertake not to request any information under the equality of information provisions in the Takeover Code (described above), provided that this undertaking applies only until the earlier of a third-party firm intention announcement or the conclusion of the offer period. These restrictions are intended to put all bidders on a level playing field – the principle generally applied by the panel when monitoring the progress of the formal sale process. Bidders will then typically be provided with details of the process, including the deadline by which bids must be received, and given access to a data room.

The formal sale process is concluded in one of two ways. If the target board does not receive a bid that it is willing to recommend, the formal sale process is terminated. If it does receive an acceptable bid, the preferred bidder will release a recommended firm intention announcement. However, the release of such announcement is not necessarily the end of the story. The recommended bid must be conducted as a normal Takeover Code-regulated bid, leaving the door open for any participant in the sale process (or other third party, for that matter) to launch a competing bid and for the board to switch its recommendation.

The formal sale process of Cove Energy demonstrates how the 'winner' of the formal sale process is not necessarily the successful acquirer. In April 2012 it was announced that Shell had won the formal sale process and that Shell's bid for Cove was unanimously recommended by the Cove board. On the first closing date of Shell's bid, PTTEP announced a higher offer for Cove, at which point the Cove board switched its recommendation to PTTEP. As Shell decided not to increase its offer, PTTEP successfully acquired Cove in August 2012.

8. Defensive tactics

Unlike in many other jurisdictions, there is fairly limited scope under the Takeover Code for the target to take defensive measures against a bid. As explained above, the Takeover Code prohibits the target from taking any action which would effectively result in the offer being frustrated or its shareholders being denied the opportunity to decide on its merits.

If the target board believes that the bid undervalues the company or is otherwise deficient, all it can do is persuade its shareholders to reject the bid. The target will do this by distributing a separate defence document in which the board sets out its reasons for not recommending the offer.

Financing oil and gas M&A transactions

Robert Aulsebrook
Akin Gump Strauss Hauer & Feld LLP

1. Introduction

A key component of any acquisition of oil and gas assets is the consideration of the likely acquisition costs and the sources of financing for those costs. Acquisition costs include not only the likely purchase price of the target, but also due diligence costs, potential restructuring costs, adviser fees and the cost of obtaining finance to fund the acquisition (including interest, fees and related funding costs).

Where the purchaser requires external financing, it will normally have a number of options to consider. These options will vary in attractiveness depending on the cost of the financing (which must be considered as part of the total acquisition cost), the extent to which new stakeholders will be introduced into the business (both debt and equity), and the likely constraints that will be placed on that business by the finance providers.

1.1 Purchasers

The types and sources of available finance will vary depending on the nature of the purchaser. If the purchaser is a public company, it may be able to access public debt and equity markets to raise finance. Private purchasers will have more limited options and will look to private providers of debt or equity (banks or other financial investors) or their own shareholders for funds. In some cases, the purchaser may be a private equity or financial investor which is acquiring the assets with the expectation of reselling them in the future for a profit.

1.2 Acquisition price

The projected acquisition price of the relevant oil and gas assets (the 'target') will also be a factor in determining the types and source of finance. Where the acquisition price is relatively low, the purchaser may be able to raise the finance from a single source (eg, a bank or shareholder). On the other hand, as the projected price increases, the purchaser may have to rely on multiple sources and types of finance, which increases the complexity of the financing.

1.3 Target assets

The nature of the assets being acquired will have an impact on the types and source of available financing. The target may be a corporate entity (or group of related corporate entities) which owns the relevant oil and gas assets, or it may comprise the assets themselves. The relevant assets may include exploration or production licences, real property, plant and equipment, contractual rights, intellectual property, stock, book debts and/or other assets.

In many cases, the financing may only need to cover the acquisition costs of the purchaser – particularly where the target is already producing revenues and has sufficient financing in place to cover its costs. In other cases, the purchaser may need to arrange additional financing to meet specific requirements of the target following completion, such as providing working capital, funding a particular capital investment or refinancing existing indebtedness.

Where the target is in the development phase and requires significant investment to develop an asset or reach commercial levels of production, the purchaser may need to arrange separate financing to meet these costs.

1.4 Location of assets

The location of assets, including the legal jurisdiction in which they are situated, will influence the sources and types of finance. As many oil and gas projects are located in developing countries, some involving substantial political risk, the financing options in those jurisdictions will be limited to financiers with experience in those markets and where the financing structure appropriately mitigates any unacceptable risks. In particular cases, the financiers may include international development banks or the financing may benefit from political risk insurance or other external credit support.

2. Sources of finance

The sources of finance for an acquisition may be one or more of the following.

2.1 Purchaser's balance sheet

There may be some cases where a purchaser can finance the entire acquisition of an asset from its own balance sheet, either because the target assets are relatively low in value or because the purchaser has an excess of cash reserves (eg, after selling other assets). In most cases, however – particularly where the assets are relatively high value – a purchaser will look to external sources of finance to fund some or all of the cost of acquisition.

2.2 Equity financing

One source of financing that may be available to a purchaser is equity finance. This funding may take different forms depending on the corporate shareholding structure of the purchaser and the other sources of finance.

In many cases, a purchaser will look to its current shareholders as a source of finance. This financing may be raised pursuant to a rights issue or, if the shareholding group is relatively small or the purchaser is a wholly owned special purpose vehicle (SPV), less formally through contributions of new equity, quasi-equity (eg, redeemable preference shares) or subordinated shareholder loans.

Alternatively, companies may be able to attract equity finance from third parties. Financing may be raised by means of a private placement to one or more persons, or from a financial investor taking a minority equity stake in the target or the purchaser in the expectation of earning a higher return on a future sale. Public companies (or private companies going public) may also be able to raise finance through equity markets with a public offer of shares.

Although equity financing is not required for all acquisitions, the parties providing debt financing will require a certain level of equity financing in cases where their recourse is limited to the target assets (eg, in a leveraged buy-out or private equity acquisition).

2.3 Credit facilities

Purchasers may be able to fund the cost of acquiring the target by borrowing from third-party banks or other financial investors under a credit arrangement. If the acquisition cost is relatively low, the purchaser may be able to borrow funds on a bilateral basis from a single lender which intends to hold the loan to maturity. In other cases – particularly where the acquisition costs are higher – the purchaser may borrow under standard market loan agreements (produced by the Loan Market Association, the Loan Syndications & Trading Association or a similar body) from one or more banks, which will sell down or syndicate their participation in the financing to a wider group of lenders.

Where the purchaser requires the funds at short notice, the purchaser may obtain temporary financing, in the form of a bridge loan, from one or a few lenders to finance the acquisition of the target. A bridge loan is generally required where the purchaser intends to finance the acquisition on a longer-term basis by means of publicly traded debt securities (including eurobonds or high-yield debt securities).

The purchaser will also need to consider whether additional financing is required for the target following the acquisition. It will consider whether any current financing the target has in place should be refinanced either at the time of the acquisition or thereafter, including in situations where the acquisition triggers early pre-payment provisions in the target's existing finance arrangements. In addition, the purchaser will consider whether the target requires any other financing going forward (eg, covering working capital, overdrafts, operating expenses, capital expenditures, letters of credit or bank guarantees).

2.4 Debt securities and convertible debt securities

Certain purchasers may be able to fund an acquisition by issuing debt securities. Smaller enterprises may issue loan notes to financial investors whose terms may not differ significantly from loan terms. In other cases, the loan notes may be convertible into equity in the purchaser or the target to provide the financial investor with potential equity returns, possibly in contemplation of a public offering. Public companies or large private companies may issue publicly traded loan notes or bonds (including eurobonds) to fund acquisitions (although the amount of time required to arrange the issuance and sale of these securities usually makes them appropriate only for refinancing other acquisition financing).

2.5 Off-balance-sheet financing

The purchaser may be able to use off-balance-sheet financing, such as private equity or project finance, to fund an acquisition. In these cases, the lenders' recourse will be restricted to the cash flows and asset values of the target business, and they will take security over the relevant assets to secure the purchaser's obligations to repay the financing and preserve the priority of their claims against other creditors.

3. Key advisers

Each of the parties to an acquisition and related financing – the purchaser, the seller and the finance providers – will be assisted by one or more sets of external advisers which provide specialist advice not available within its organisation. The external advice usually required on an oil and gas acquisition relates to valuation, taxation, legal documentation and structuring, arranging finance and due diligence.

3.1 Financial advisers

Generally, the seller and purchaser will have their own financial advisers, which may assist them in evaluating the target business and related due diligence. The seller's financial adviser may also be responsible for organising any sale or auction of assets, including evaluating any bids or proposals received from potential purchasers.

The purchaser's financial adviser may help it to scrutinise the target's revenues and cash flows, capital and operating expenditures, and tax and other liabilities. In addition, the financial adviser will advise on the acquisition costs (including purchase price and related costs) and, where applicable, assist in preparing the purchaser's bid. It will also usually advise on the available financing options and the related terms and structuring of any financing. In many cases, the purchaser's financial adviser will also take a lead role in arranging and providing the financing, although this is a distinct role requiring a separate mandate.

3.2 Legal advisers

The seller, the purchaser and the finance providers will each be advised by one or more teams of lawyers on various aspects of the transaction.

In relation to the acquisition, the seller and purchaser will be advised by their own lawyers on the terms of the acquisition agreement under their respective governing law. If the target and its assets are located in a different jurisdiction, the purchaser will need further legal advice to ensure that any local law issues affecting the assets are identified in the legal due diligence and addressed or remedied.

Each party will want its legal advisers to confirm that any transfer of assets complies with applicable law. This may require advice on the local law relating to licences, property rights, employment, intellectual property, tax and the environment. Although the finance providers will not usually be involved in the acquisition, they will generally require their own lawyers to conduct due diligence on the acquisition and may raise concerns for the purchaser that require addressing with the seller in order to secure the financing.

In relation to the financing, the purchaser and the finance providers will usually each be represented by external lawyers qualified in the jurisdiction of the law governing the finance documents (eg, English or New York law). If the financing involves the issuance of securities, they will require advice on the relevant law in any jurisdiction where the securities will be offered and/or listed. In addition, the purchaser and the finance providers will each be advised by lawyers in the jurisdictions where the obligors are incorporated and any security is provided.

3.3 Tax advisers

Each of the parties may be advised by its own separate tax advisers, although in some cases relevant tax advice may be provided by a party's legal advisers. The seller and the purchaser will each need to consider the tax issues relevant to the acquisition of the target, including any sales or stamp taxes depending on the assets and jurisdictions. In addition, the purchaser will want to ensure that the financing is structured in a manner that minimises the possibility of tax being withheld on payments under the relevant finance documents.

3.4 Environmental advisers

The purchaser may require environmental advisers to assist in the due diligence process, in regards to potential liability for both pre-existing environmental problems and future decommissioning costs. In addition, the financiers may require the purchaser to ensure that an environmental adviser is engaged throughout the term of the financing, to provide ongoing environmental assessments, confirm compliance with environmental or social welfare obligations, propose action plans to remedy environmental problems and monitor implementation of those plans.

4. M&A finance process

4.1 Initiation of sale process

The initial sale process will differ from deal to deal. In many cases, the sale process will be initiated by the seller, which may contact one or more potential purchasers or which may organise a formal auction (usually with the help of a financial adviser). In this instance, the seller may prepare an information memorandum which describes the target's assets and liabilities, and its historic financial performance and future financial prospects (including possibly a business plan).

In other cases, a purchaser may approach the target's owner with a proposal or offer to purchase the target. If the target's owner is interested in pursuing the proposal or accepting the offer, or where the seller has arranged an auction, the potential purchaser may be allowed to conduct limited due diligence, including site visits and/or meeting with the target's management.

4.2 Arranging finance

As the sale process progresses – pursuant either to an auction or to less formal negotiations between the parties – the seller will generally expect the purchaser to demonstrate a high level of commitment and capability to complete the deal before entering into exclusive negotiations. In particular, the seller will normally require the purchaser to demonstrate that it has the necessary finance available (in some cases, on a firm commitment or certain funds basis) to fund the acquisition.

Early in the sale process, the purchaser will need to begin the process of arranging finance involving most or all of the following steps:

- The purchaser may engage a financial adviser (typically, an investment bank or similar adviser) in relation to the acquisition, which will advise on the possible sources and cost of finance.
- The purchaser (or its financial adviser) will contact possible sources of finance and provide them with information on the proposed acquisition, including any seller's information memorandum or business plan. The finance providers will be asked to provide indicative offers and proposed levels of funding.
- The purchaser will mandate a financial institution (often its financial adviser) or more than one financial institution (often including the financial adviser) to arrange the finance required. The mandate will include a term sheet and will usually be subject to standard conditions, including credit committee approval, satisfaction of know-your-customer requirements, agreement on documentation and no material adverse change in the credit market or business condition of the purchaser (and possibly the target).
- As the sale process progresses, the financiers may be expected to confirm that conditions relating to due diligence, internal approvals and material adverse change have been satisfied and no longer apply. The seller may require this as a condition to agreeing a heads of terms and exclusivity with the purchaser.

In certain cases, a seller may approach a bank in advance of initiating the sale process to agree terms on which that bank would be willing to finance the acquisition of the target. These terms may be presented to potential purchasers together with the information memorandum to enhance the possibility of a successful sale.

4.3 Due diligence

During the due diligence phase, the purchaser, its financiers and often the seller will examine the financial, operational and legal situation of the target in order to confirm the viability of the sale and the assumptions underlying the purchase price. This process will generally overlap with the arranging of financing and continue during the documentation phase.

Before the sale process starts, the seller may undertake its own due diligence on the target assets or business, particularly where a competitive tender is planned. Relevant information collected during this process may be included in an information memorandum and provided to potential purchasers. It may include financial and legal due diligence reports and highlight any issues that the seller believes should be disclosed upfront. Additional information may be identified and placed in a data room (often accessible electronically) in advance, and made available to particular potential purchasers and their financiers.

In some cases, a purchaser and its financiers may rely principally (although not exclusively) on the seller's due diligence, particularly where the information provided is detailed and up to date. However, ordinarily the purchaser will conduct its own due diligence to ensure that it has sufficient information on which to assess the target business and identify any material risks.

The financiers will also conduct their own due diligence on the target. At a minimum, the financiers will review the acquisition agreement to confirm that:

- the purchaser will acquire the relevant assets;
- the seller's warranties, indemnities and undertakings are sufficient; and
- the conditions to the purchase will be satisfied on or before the time the financing is provided.

They will also review any due diligence reports prepared by the seller's or the purchaser's advisers, and in some cases may base their lending decisions on the contents of these reports. If the financiers' recourse is limited to the target business, their due diligence will be far more extensive and more similar in scope to the purchaser's due diligence.

While a purchaser will carry out its due diligence directly, it will also appoint external advisers to perform additional due diligence in specific areas. It will have its financial adviser review in detail the financial information provided by the seller to verify the target's financial status and health and support the buyer's valuation analysis. The purchaser's legal advisers in each relevant jurisdiction will examine the target's legal situation in detail – including, where relevant:

- its corporate structure;
- key supply, processing, transportation and offtake contracts;
- outstanding financing arrangements;
- licences and permits;
- real property rights;
- regulatory and environmental issues;
- litigation and disputes; and
- legal aspects of insurance and tax.

In addition, the purchaser may appoint other types of consultant to advise on particular aspects of the target and its business, including market surveys, environmental issues, insurance issues and taxation.

4.4 Legal documentation

Generally, each of the seller, the purchaser and the financiers will appoint its own legal counsel to advise on the transaction and prepare the necessary agreements, including the following:

- Acquisition agreement – this will vary depending on the type of assets being acquired and could be either a share purchase agreement or an asset purchase agreement.
- Finance documents – these will vary depending on the type(s) of financing being provided. There may be one or more credit facility agreements, note documentation, an inter-creditor agreement, security agreements and/or hedging agreements.
- Sponsor support documents – if the borrower is an SPV or acquisition subsidiary with no substantial assets, the financiers will usually require a guarantee from a corporate parent company and/or adequate security or

other credit support. In cases where the financiers are providing only a portion of the required finance for an acquisition, the sponsor may be required to provide the balance in the form of an equity contribution or by subordinated loans to the borrower.

- Shareholders' agreement – if multiple purchasers are acquiring the target (or if the purchaser is acquiring less than all of the target), the various shareholders may enter into a shareholders' agreement to govern their relations (including future financing) and regulate future disposals.

For the purposes of preparing the legal documentation, the parties may rely on advice from a variety of specialist advisers, including accountants, tax advisers, environmental advisers, employment and property lawyers, and local counsel in the jurisdiction(s) where the principal assets are located.

4.5 Signing and closing

The seller and purchaser will generally desire that the acquisition completes at the same time as signing of the legal documentation. However, there may be conditions (eg, government consent, waiver of pre-emption rights, competition or merger clearance) that can be satisfied only after signing. Once all conditions to the acquisition and financing have been satisfied, the purchaser will receive the financing and pay the purchase price (or relevant part thereof) to the seller, and title to the target shares or assets will be transferred to the purchaser.

4.6 Syndication and refinancing

If the financing is relatively large, the relevant lenders may wish to sell down some or all of their participations in the financing (to the extent permitted under the facility documentation). These sales may occur pursuant to a formal syndication process (in which case the purchaser's cooperation may be required), or by independent sales by lenders in the secondary loan market. The arrangers may put together an information package with input from the purchaser, including details of the target business, a business plan, the due diligence reports and relevant legal documentation.

In some cases, the financing may be provided under bridge financing from one or more lenders. Bridge loans have a short term (they can be as short as 30 days, but more usually up to six months and in any case not more than 12 months). In such cases, the purchaser and the bridge lenders will usually have agreed the form of longer-term financing that the purchaser will arrange in order to take out the bridge financing. This may be in the form of a syndicated loan or, for certain purchasers, loan notes or other debt securities.

4.7 Post-completion

Following completion, the target business will be owned by the purchaser. While the acquisition financing remains outstanding, the terms of that financing will require the purchaser to comply with various covenants in the finance documents that will restrict the purchaser in the conduct of its business and/or the target business.

5. Financing structure

The financing structure will be driven by several factors, including:

- the recourse of the lenders;
- the presence of junior or subordinated creditors in the financing structure; and
- tax issues affecting the acquisition and the financing.

5.1 Recourse of lenders

In a standard corporate financing, the lenders may provide finance to a creditworthy company in the purchaser's corporate group, which may itself be the purchaser or which passes the financing along the relevant acquisition vehicle. Alternatively, the lenders may make the loan directly to a subsidiary in the purchaser's group whose purpose is to raise finance or which has been formed to be the acquisition vehicle, in either case on the basis of a corporate guarantee given by a creditworthy company in the group.

In cases where the financiers' recourse in respect of the financing will be limited to the target business, they will normally require a significant equity contribution to the acquisition from the purchaser and security and other credit support to be provided in respect of the target business. The acquisition and related financing will normally be structured by using one or more newly formed SPVs that will acquire the target business and borrow the relevant financing. Frequently, the acquisition vehicle(s) will be owned by a second SPV which is in turn owned by the equity providers, so that they are structurally subordinate to the financiers. In this case, in addition to security over the target business, the financiers will take security over the shares of the acquisition vehicle(s) and require restrictions in the finance documents on the conduct of the target business.

5.2 Junior and subordinated creditors

In some cases, the combination of the purchaser's funds and senior debt will be insufficient to cover the acquisition costs of the purchaser. If there is a shortfall (a funding gap), it may be necessary for the purchaser to make it up with junior or mezzanine debt. This debt, which is subordinated to the senior debt, is generally more expensive and has a longer maturity profile.

There are several ways that junior debt can be subordinated to senior debt. First, the senior creditors and junior creditors may enter into an inter-creditor agreement (or a subordination agreement) that will restrict the junior creditors from being repaid prior to the senior creditors. This is referred to as 'contractual subordination'. Second, junior debt may be placed in holding companies above the company drawing the senior debt. This places the senior debt closer to the operating business (and therefore the relevant assets and revenues), and is referred to as 'structural subordination'. Third, senior creditors may be granted security over assets either in priority to junior creditors (which may hold second-ranking security) or to the exclusion of junior creditors (which are therefore unsecured).

5.3 Tax considerations

As with the acquisition structure, the financing structure will be affected by tax considerations. The relevant borrower in the funding structure will want to ensure that any repayment of the financing (particularly, payment of interest and dividends) will be free from withholding tax in the jurisdiction where it is tax resident. This will be ensured when either:

- the borrower is in a jurisdiction which does not impose withholding tax on interest and other payments; or
- a relevant double tax treaty exempts the payments from withholding tax or deductions. Where a double tax treaty is relevant, the jurisdiction of the relevant equity holders and financiers will also be relevant.

6. Key financing documents

6.1 Equity documents

If the purchaser has a strong balance sheet, it may be able to borrow funds itself or by guaranteeing funds loaned to another group member or finance SPV. If the transaction is structured using private equity or limited-recourse financing, where the financiers have recourse only to the target and its assets, they will expect a significant equity investment from the sponsor into the acquisition vehicle or target business.

The relevant equity documents will depend on the type of equity or quasi-equity to be contributed. Where the equity provider will receive share capital, the relevant documents will include the articles of association (or similar constitutive documents) of the relevant acquisition company and, where relevant, a subscription agreement, a shareholders' agreement and/or an investment agreement. If the equity will be invested in the form of subordinated loan capital, there may be a loan agreement; or if the loan capital is held in the form of securities, there will be loan notes, an instrument creating the loan notes and a subscription or investment agreement.

6.2 Debt mandate documents

At the beginning of the process to raise debt finance, the purchaser will usually enter into a mandate letter with one or more financial institutions that will arrange the finance (the 'lead arrangers'). Although the specific terms are negotiable, the mandate letter will be a standard market form for the relevant finance. The mandate letter will stipulate whether the lead arrangers have a firm underwriting commitment or will arrange financing on a best efforts basis. In addition, the mandate letter will normally contain a term sheet setting out the key terms agreed by the arrangers with the purchaser for the financing.

6.3 Credit facility agreement

Where the purchaser is borrowing funds from banks or other financial institutions, the main financing document will be a credit facility agreement, which may be based on a form applicable in the relevant loan market. Where the funding is provided in different tranches but is otherwise subject to the same warranties, covenants and events of default, the funding may all be provided within the same facility agreement. However, where some of the funding will be provided by junior creditors that receive more limited warranties, covenants or enforcement rights, that funding will normally be documented under a standalone credit facility agreement.

6.4 Guarantees and security agreements

Unless the borrower has a strong enough balance sheet to support the external finance it is obtaining, the financiers will expect parties related to the borrower to provide guarantees or other credit support for the financing. If the borrower is an acquisition SPV or a finance subsidiary of the purchaser's group, the financiers may be content only with a guarantee from a creditworthy member of the purchaser's group.

Where the financiers are concerned about the ability of the purchaser to repay the financing, or where their recourse is limited to the target business, they will generally require extensive security over the assets of the target business. Depending on the assets, the security will include some or all of the following:

- the shares or other ownership interests in the purchaser (normally a newly formed SPV) and/or any companies being acquired. Security over shares or similar ownership interests in companies and similar entities is generally taken under the law of the jurisdiction of incorporation or organisation of the relevant entities. In some jurisdictions, the availability of security over shares is restricted by rules against provision of financial assistance by companies in the acquisition of their own shares. In addition, in some jurisdictions, local tax rules may affect the scope and structure of security granted over shares;
- the purchaser's rights under the acquisition agreement, including the benefit of warranties and the right to claim under any indemnities. In practice, the seller will normally be unwilling to permit the purchaser to assign the acquisition agreement to the lenders, so this will be subject to negotiation; and/or
- the assets and properties being acquired or otherwise held by the purchaser and the target. If these assets include real property, land rights, bank accounts and certain other assets, the relevant security agreement will normally be governed by the law of the jurisdiction in which such property is located. Other security may be governed by the law of the jurisdiction governing the primary facility agreement.

6.5 Inter-creditor agreement

If the purchaser has attracted debt finance from more than one source (including intra-group loans), the rights of the different classes of creditors may be regulated by an inter-creditor agreement. This will usually set out the following terms:

- the ranking and priority of the relevant tranches of finance;
- the ranking and priority of security;
- subordination of claims of junior creditors on insolvency;
- the right of each class of creditor to receive payments from the borrower and the right of senior creditors to block payments to junior creditors in certain cases;

- the right of each class of creditor (subject to any relevant restrictions) to take any action to enforce the terms of their finance documents following a default by the obligors, including acceleration of their debt;
- the right of each class of creditor (subject to any relevant restrictions) to take any action to enforce any claims against the obligors, including the initiation of legal or insolvency proceedings;
- the right of each class of creditor (subject to any relevant restrictions) to enforce any guarantees or security given in support of their financing; and/or
- the right of any class of creditor (subject to any relevant restrictions) to amend the terms of their finance documents.

6.6 Hedging arrangements

The purchaser will need to consider whether any portion of the financing will expose it to unacceptable interest rate or exchange rate risks. In some cases, the lenders may require the purchaser to hedge these risks as a condition of the financing.

Long-term financing that bears interest at a variable rate will expose the borrower to the risk that the basis for the interest rate calculation (eg, the London Inter-bank Offered Rate or any benchmark that replaces it) could significantly increase over the life of the financing. Any such increase could in turn make it more difficult for the borrower to service and ultimately repay the debt. To hedge this risk, the borrower can enter into an interest rate swap, which changes the floating interest rate into a fixed interest rate for all or a substantial portion of the financing.

Moreover, where the purchaser or the relevant target business earns substantial revenues in a currency that differs from the currency of the relevant financing, there is a risk that changes in exchange rates after the borrowing of the funds will effectively increase the amount it is required to pay when the revenues are converted into the currency of the financing. The borrower in this case can enter into a currency swap, which locks in the exchange rate at which the currency will be converted.

Interest rate and currency swaps are entered into pursuant to a standard form International Swaps and Derivatives Association master agreement between the borrower (or a related party) and the relevant swap counterparties. In most cases, the swap counterparties will also be lenders to the acquisition financing and will usually be secured to the same extent as the lenders on the financing.

In relation to an interest rate swap, the swap documentation will provide that the relevant party (either the borrower or the hedge counterparty, depending on whether the interest rate has increased or decreased) pays the other party the difference between the amount of interest payable at the floating rate and the fixed rate. In relation to a currency swap, the relevant party will pay the other party the difference between the amount that would be payable at the exchange rate in effect on the date the swap was entered into and the amount payable at the exchange rate on the date of the relevant payment.

7. Key debt financing terms

Where finance is obtained in the loan market, the key debt financing terms will be set out in a facility agreement entered into between the relevant parties. On the purchaser's side, the principal borrower will normally be the acquisition vehicle, while members of the target group may also be borrowers on working capital or other facilities, and one or more members of the purchaser's group and/or the target group may be party to the agreement as guarantors of the financing. On the financiers' side, the original lenders to the financing will sign the facility agreement, while other lenders may become parties after signing by receiving transfers of participations in the financing from the original lenders or participate in the financing through standalone sub-participation agreements. Further, in most cases, the persons providing administrative services in respect of the facility (eg, a facility agent or security trustee) will also be party to the facility agreement.

The credit agreement will normally be in a standard form used in the relevant finance market. In London, the Loan Market Association maintains a variety of forms for various types of financings, including investment grade and leveraged financing. The key terms are set out below.

7.1 Conditions precedent

The conditions precedent ensure that the lenders have received all relevant documents and confirmed the completion of all relevant actions before they are obliged to provide the financing. In particular, the lenders will want to ensure that the following conditions have been satisfied:

- All finance and security documents relevant to the financing have been executed and any documents required to perfect security have been delivered;
- All documents relating to any other debt financing have been executed and the conditions therein have been satisfied;
- All documents relating to any equity financing have been executed and the relevant funding has been advanced;
- The acquisition agreement has been executed and all conditions to the acquisition have been satisfied;
- Corporate authorities for all relevant obligors have been delivered, including any necessary resolutions, copies of constitutional documents and powers of attorney, and specimen signatures of persons authorised to sign for those obligors;
- Due diligence reports and legal opinions in a form satisfactory to the lenders have been received;
- Recent financial statements (normally audited) for the obligors and the target have been received; and/or
- Other confirmations in respect of indebtedness or security relating to the target group have been delivered.

7.2 Mandatory pre-payment

The facility agreement will stipulate the circumstances (the 'mandatory pre-payment events') in which the facility is required by be repaid early by the relevant borrowers. Mandatory pre-payment events are distinct from events of default, although in some cases their effect can be the same – that is, repayment of the entire facility prior to its scheduled maturity. In other cases, only a portion of the facility, or only particular lenders, may be required to be pre-paid. Common mandatory pre-payment events include:

- a change in control of the borrower or the target business;
- a specified liquidity event, such as an initial public offering or private sale of shares in the target business;
- the sale of particular assets or assets of a minimum value;
- application of excess cash generated by the target business in a particular financial year (a 'cash sweep');
- application of the proceeds of any claim against the seller under the acquisition agreement; and/or
- application of the proceeds of particular insurance claims relating to the target assets.

7.3 Representations and warranties

Each of the borrowers will be required in the facility agreement to give various representations and warranties relating to itself, its group and the target. The representations will be made on the signing date of the facility agreement. Thereafter, some or all of them will be repeated when a drawdown notice is presented and when a drawdown is advanced by the lenders, and it is a condition of each drawdown that the relevant representations are true. Some or all of the representations will also be made periodically throughout the duration of the financing. If any of the representations are not true when they are made or repeated, the lenders will have the right to declare a default on the financing.

Typically, representations cover the following areas:

- Each relevant company is duly incorporated;
- Each relevant company has the power and authority to perform its obligations under the finance documents;
- The obligations of obligors under the finance documents are binding;
- Execution and performance of the finance documents do not conflict with any other legal or contractual obligations or the articles of association;
- The choice of law of the finance documents is a valid choice of law and judgments or, where relevant, arbitral awards are enforceable in any relevant jurisdictions (including jurisdictions where relevant obligors are incorporated or resident);
- All required authorisations have been obtained for performance of the finance documents and their admissibility in court, and for conduct of the target business;
- No relevant company can claim immunity from legal proceedings;
- Any information disclosed to the lenders by or on behalf of the borrower, including information relating to the target, is true and accurate in all material respects;
- Specific warranties regarding the target business and assets may be given;
- No stamp duty, filing or similar fees are payable in respect of the finance documents;

- No withholding tax is payable on payments to be made under the finance documents;
- No insolvency proceedings have been commenced against any relevant company;
- The latest audited accounts are true and accurate, and there has been no material adverse change to the relevant companies or group since the date of those financial statements;
- No litigation exists or has been threatened against the borrower's group or the target;
- No laws have been breached by the borrower's group or the target;
- The assets or project complies with applicable environmental laws;
- Any security given is valid and has the priority it is expressed to have;
- All taxes which are due and payable have been paid; and/or
- Obligations under the finance documents are *pari passu* with the borrower's other unsecured and unsubordinated obligations.

The wording of the representations will be based on standard market wording and contain any relevant materiality or other qualifications agreed between the borrower and the lenders. To the extent that the borrower is unable to give any particular representation in the form required by the lenders, it may be required to make specific disclosures that qualify the representation.

7.4 Covenants

The borrower will be required by the lenders to undertake various obligations that restrict how it operates its business (including the target business). These obligations fall into four general categories: information undertakings, financial covenants, positive undertakings and negative undertakings.

(a) Information undertakings

The lenders will require the borrower to provide various types of information to them while the financing remains outstanding. This information permits the lenders to monitor the financial performance of the borrower and its business, and includes the following:

- annual audited financial statements for each obligor and for the borrower's group;
- unaudited half-yearly and quarterly (and sometimes monthly) management accounts;
- notice of defaults or material adverse events;
- notice of any material litigation, environmental claims or disputes under transaction documents;
- documents sent to creditors (and sometimes shareholders) generally;
- any information required from time to time by the lenders to comply with know-your-customer requirements; and/or
- any other information reasonably requested by the lenders regarding the borrower or its business.

The financial statements are generally required to be delivered together with a certificate from the borrower's directors confirming the borrower's and each relevant company's compliance with any financial covenants.

(b) ***Financial covenants***

Frequently, the facility agreement contains one or more financial covenants that the borrower or its group is required to comply with while the financing remains outstanding. These covenants measure the group's financial performance or position by reference to financial ratios using information from the group's financial statements, as well as other sources. The covenants will vary depending on the type of financing and borrower profile. They will typically be tested quarterly or half-yearly on particular dates (referred to as 'testing dates').

Typical financial covenants include the following:

- leverage ratios measuring the outstanding net debt of the borrower or the borrower's group against earnings (typically earnings before interest, taxes, depreciation and amortisation (EBITDA)) or assets;
- debt service coverage ratios measuring the operating revenues of the borrower or its group during a particular time period against corresponding liabilities falling due. These ratios may relate to particular periods occurring during the life of the facility (eg, next 12 months or previous 12 months), to the period from the current testing date through to the final maturity date of the facility or, in some cases, for the field life of the underlying oil and gas project;
- in some instances, if the target relates to an underlying oil and gas field development project, a 'reserve tail' requiring that a certain percentage of the approved petroleum reserves remain unextracted following the final maturity date of the loan;
- interest cover ratios measuring earnings (typically EBITDA) against interest payments falling due during a particular period;
- net worth covenants requiring the borrower's group to maintain a minimum consolidated net worth of the group at specified amounts during specified periods following completion; and/or
- capital expenditure covenants restricting the borrower's group from incurring capital expenditures in an amount greater than a specified threshold in any financial year.

In many cases, failure to meet a financial covenant will trigger an event of default. By their nature, because most financial covenants are based on historic financial information, it will not be possible for the borrower to remedy any breach. However, depending on the financial covenant, there may be cases where a breach can be 'cured' by repaying a portion of the underlying debt or injecting additional capital into the borrower's business (an 'equity cure').

(c) ***Positive undertakings***

Other general covenants that apply to the borrower and its group following completion are categorised as positive undertakings and negative undertakings. Positive undertakings require the borrower to ensure that certain obligations are affirmatively complied with at all times while the loan remains outstanding. The number and detail of these undertakings will depend on the transaction and nature of the borrower's group, and may include some or all of the following:

- Develop and operate the underlying project in accordance with the terms of any relevant business plan or transaction documents, and in accordance with prudent oil and gas industry practices;
- File tax returns and pay all taxes as they fall due;
- Maintain corporate existence;
- Comply with applicable law and constitutional documents;
- Comply with environmental laws and regulations and any environmental requirements in the facility agreement;
- Obtain and maintain all authorisations and consents required in connection with the group's business and any underlying oil and gas project, and required to ensure the legality, validity and admissibility in evidence of the finance documents;
- Maintain insurance;
- Maintain assets in good working order and acquire or maintain all assets or rights required to operate or develop the underlying oil and gas project;
- Permit lenders and their advisers access to books and records, and premises;
- Ensure that lenders' claims against relevant obligors remain *pari passu* with the claims of all other unsecured and unsubordinated creditors;
- Ensure that any security provided to secure the obligor's obligations remains valid, perfected and with the same priority in favour of the relevant finance parties;
- Use the proceeds of the financing only for purposes of acquiring the target and any other permitted purposes;
- Diligently defend claims against the target business;
- Replace or renew material project agreements relating to any underlying oil and gas project;
- Comply with laws relating to anti-corruption, anti-money laundering and sanctions; and/or
- Maintain all required bank accounts and operate them in accordance with any agreed terms.

(d) Negative undertakings

Negative covenants restrict the borrower or its group from taking certain actions. These restrictions are designed principally to preserve the value of the business of the borrower and target. Typical negative covenants include the following:

- a negative pledge (subject to exceptions) that prevents the borrower or its group from granting security over its assets in favour of other creditors;
- restrictions on disposing assets (subject to exceptions);
- restrictions on incurring additional financial indebtedness or granting guarantees (subject to exceptions);

- restrictions on entering into hedging arrangements;
- restrictions on granting loans or credit to other persons;
- restrictions on transactions with affiliates;
- restrictions on mergers and reorganisations;
- restrictions on joint ventures;
- restrictions on acquisitions and investments;
- restrictions on amending, terminating or granting waivers under material agreements relating to any underlying oil and gas project;
- restrictions on changing the business of the borrower or the target;
- restrictions on amending articles of association;
- restrictions on operating bank accounts;
- restrictions on making distributions or restricted payments; and/or
- restrictions on paying junior or subordinated debt.

7.5 Events of default

The credit facility agreement will contain a detailed list of events that will cause a default if they occur and entitle the lenders to take enforcement action against the borrower. Typical events of default include the following:

- failure to pay any amount when due under the finance documents;
- breach of representation when made or repeated by any relevant obligor;
- breach of a financial covenant;
- specific breaches relating to environmental undertakings;
- breach of any other obligation under the finance documents;
- failure to pay any other financial indebtedness when due (cross-default) or a requirement to repay any other financial indebtedness before its schedule maturity due to a default (cross-acceleration), frequently subject to certain minimum thresholds;
- insolvency of any obligor or other group company;
- insolvency proceedings instituted against any obligor or other group company;
- cessation of business by any obligor;
- failure to pay any claim following a judgment or award, usually above a certain threshold;
- where it has become illegal for any obligor to perform its obligations under any finance document or any material transaction document relating to an underlying oil and gas project;
- where any security ceases to be valid and binding or retain the priority it is expressed to have;
- where any material consents or authorisations are revoked or terminated;
- expropriation or nationalisation of material assets or the underlying oil and gas project;
- failure to reach completion on an underlying oil and gas project within the contemplated timeframe for completion;
- abandonment of any underlying oil and gas project;
- where the whole or a material part of an underlying oil and gas project is lost,

destroyed or damaged and insurance is insufficient to reinstate the project within an agreed timeframe;
- where any finance document or transaction document relating to an underlying oil and gas project ceases to be in full force and effect;
- a material adverse change in the business, operations, assets or prospects of the borrower or the borrower's group, in the ability of the obligors to perform their obligations under the finance documents, or in the legality, validity or enforceability of the finance documents;
- where a *force majeure* event suspends all or a material part of an underlying oil and gas project which continues for more than an agreed number of days; and/or
- the occurrence of material litigation.

Many events of default will be subject to materiality thresholds and cure periods agreed by the borrower with the lenders.

Following an event of default, the lenders can elect to require the borrower to repay the outstanding amount of the facility and enforce any rights it may have under any guarantee or security agreement.

Anti-corruption initiatives in upstream oil and gas[1]

Tamer A Soliman
Mayer Brown

1. Introduction

Multinational companies operating in the upstream oil and gas industry face significant anti-corruption compliance issues. These include the challenges of complying with the requirements of the US Foreign Corrupt Practices Act (FCPA),[2] the UK Bribery Act[3] and similar anti-corruption laws.

Enacted in 1977, the FCPA prohibits giving, offering, promising or authorising the provision of "anything of value"[4] (ie, bribing), directly or indirectly, to a "foreign official"[5] to obtain or retain business, secure an improper advantage or cause a foreign public official to exercise improperly his or her authority.[6] In addition, the FCPA requires companies to keep accurate books and records and to establish and maintain adequate internal controls.[7] The UK Bribery Act generally prohibits the

---

* The publisher acknowledges Jaelyn Edwards Judelson, Nnedinma Ifudu Nweke and Sarah Banco as co-authors to the Anti-corruption chapter in *Oil & Gas in Africa: A Legal and Commercial Analysis of the Upstream Industry* published by Globe Law and Business (May 2015), on which this chapter is based.

1 A previous version of this chapter was first published in Hammerson and LaMaster (eds), *Oil and Gas in Africa: A Legal and Commercial Analysis* (Globe Law and Business, 2015).

2 Foreign Corrupt Practices Act of 1977, 15 USC, Sections 78dd-1 and 78dd-2 (1994), amended by Pub L No 105-366, 112 Stat 3302 (1998).

3 Bribery Act 2010 (United Kingdom).

4 The phrase "anything of value" is not explicitly defined in the FCPA, but the identical phrase under the domestic US bribery statute has been broadly construed to include both tangible and intangible benefits. See, for example, *United States v Moore*, 525 F 3d 1033, at 1048 (11th Cir 2008) (rejecting the defendant's objection to a jury instruction defining sex as a "thing of value", which "unambiguously covers intangible considerations"); *United States v Gorman*, 807 F 2d 1299, at 1304-1305 (6th Cir 1986) (holding that loans and promises of future employment are "things of value"); *United States v Williams*, 705 F 2d 603, at 622-623 (2d Cir 1983) (approving jury instruction that stock could be a "thing of value" if the defendant believed it had value, even though the shares had no commercial value, and noting that "the phrase 'anything of value' in bribery and related statutes has consistently been given a broad meaning"). See US Department of Justice (DoJ), *A Resource Guide to the US Foreign Corrupt Practices, Act*, at 74, note 86 (2012) (DoJ Resource Guide), available at www.justice.gov/criminal/fraud/fcpa/ guidance/.

5 The FCPA defines a 'foreign official' as "any officer or employee of a foreign government or any department, agency, or instrumentality thereof, or of a public international organization, or any person acting in an official capacity for or on behalf of any such government or department, agency, or instrumentality, or for or on behalf of any such public international organization". See Securities Exchange Act of 1934, 15 USC, Sections 78dd-1(f)(1)(A) and 30A(f)(1)(A); see also 15 USC, Sections 78dd-2(h)(2)(A) and 78dd-3(f)(2)(A).

6 FCPA, note 2 above. The FCPA applies to:
- persons that have issued registered securities in the United States ('issuers');
- entities incorporated in the United States and US citizens and permanent residents ('domestic concerns');
- foreign nationals or businesses in the United States; and
- foreign directors, officers, employees, agents or shareholders acting on behalf of an issuer or domestic concern.

See 15 USC, Sections 78dd-1, 78dd-2 and 78dd-3.

7 FCPA, note 2 above.

same activity as the FCPA but prohibits additional actions, including receiving a bribe from a foreign public official (ie, passive bribery) and giving or receiving a bribe from a private individual (ie, commercial bribery).[8] In addition, unlike the FCPA, the UK Bribery Act creates strict liability for companies that fail to have adequate controls in place to prevent corrupt activity.[9] Local anti-corruption laws must be considered in connection with any potential compliance issue as well, albeit in the context of aggressive enforcement of the FCPA by the United States, as well as growing international cooperation in investigations and enforcement activity.

Other national, regional and inter-governmental bodies around the world have established anti-corruption legal frameworks, such as international and regional protocols, since the United States enacted the FCPA in 1977. Notably, the World Bank and the International Monetary Fund (IMF) have used their influence to develop and implement a number of anti-corruption measures focused on fighting corruption at both state government and business levels. Anti-corruption legal frameworks and measures are referred to in this chapter as 'anti-corruption initiatives'.

This chapter discusses the most common anti-corruption challenges[10] that multinational oil and gas companies encounter when operating in the upstream oil and gas industry, and assesses the lessons and impact of the major anti-corruption enforcement actions and initiatives designed to respond to those challenges. This chapter focuses on sub-Saharan Africa,[11] which is a major source of significant economic opportunities for multinational companies, but also a challenging environment in which to comply with anti-corruption initiatives.

2. Anti-corruption challenges in sub-Saharan Africa

Multinational companies operating in the oil and gas industry in sub-Saharan Africa generally face some of the highest levels of corruption in any industry in the world. According to Transparency International's 2017 Corruption Perceptions Index (CPI), approximately 90% of sub-Saharan African countries scored below 50,[12] making sub-Saharan Africa one of the two most corrupt regions in the world.[13] By comparison, 95% of Eastern Europe and Central Asia and 84% of the Middle East and North Africa

---

8 UK Bribery Act, note 3 above. Enacted in 2010, the UK Bribery Act applies to:
- British nationals;
- persons ordinarily resident in the United Kingdom;
- entities, wherever formed, which carry on business or part of a business in the United Kingdom; and
- persons or entities which commit any element of the offence in the United Kingdom.

See Section 12(4).

9 *Ibid*, Section 7.

10 This chapter addresses 'transnational anti-corruption challenges' or anti-corruption challenges arising from laws that address corruption of foreign officials, as opposed to laws that address corruption of domestic officials.

11 The United Nations defines 'sub-Saharan Africa' to refer to all of Africa except Morocco, Algeria, Tunisia, Libya, and Egypt. See UN Statistics Division Composition of Macro Geographical (Continental) Regions, Geographical Sub-regions, and Selected Economic and Other Groupings (31 October 2013), http://unstats.un.org/unsd/methods/m49/m49regin.htm#ftna.

12 A country or territory's score indicates the perceived level of public sector corruption on a scale of 0 to 100; 0 means that a country is perceived as highly corrupt and 100 means that it is perceived as free from corruption. A score of below 50 indicates a high risk of corruption.

13 See Transparency International, Corruption Perceptions Index 2013 at 10, https://files.transparency.org/content/download/2185/13756/file/2017_CPI_Brochure_EN.PDF.

14 *Ibid*.

scored below 50 on the CPI.[14] The World Bank ranked sub-Saharan Africa's control of corruption in the bottom 30% to 33% globally between 1996 and 2012, putting it on par with Southeast Asia.[15] In addition, according to Transparency International's 2011 Bribe Payers Index, the oil and gas industry ranks as one of the most likely industries to pay bribes to foreign officials.[16]

The high level of corruption in sub-Saharan Africa, particularly in the oil and gas industry, creates unique challenges for multinational companies in trying to conduct profitable businesses without falling foul of the FCPA, the UK Bribery Act and similar anti-corruption laws. Some key challenges in this context are discussed below.

2.1 Lack of information

One common anti-corruption challenge that oil and gas companies face in many parts of sub-Saharan Africa stems from a lack of information that is crucial for compliance. There are several aspects to this problem.

The first is the lack of transparency on local laws, policies and practices, including tax, customs duties and clearance, and immigration laws. This widespread problem is particularly acute in the emerging oil and gas sectors in the region. Many governments are formulating or developing energy policies for newly emerging sectors, and without the benefit of experience. Lack of transparency and clarity can lead to opportunities for bribery in two ways. A lack of clarity regarding legal standards, rights and obligations creates opportunities for abuse of authority through arbitrary delay or onerous interpretations. In some cases, the lack of transparency has also led to a different kind of problem: companies may unknowingly violate the law and come under pressure to make unplanned back-payments or to pay penalties to local governments.[17] Under the tight time and budgetary pressures of oil and gas exploration and development projects, employees and agents may be incentivised to pay kickbacks or bribes to local officials in order to resolve quickly any delays caused by demands for back-payments or penalties.

The second aspect is the common need to rely on third-party middlemen in such an environment. The more opaque the legal and regulatory environment, the greater the need for 'insiders' who can help to navigate the system. Of course, this is not unique to sub-Saharan Africa, and indeed does not necessarily lead to corruption. Reliance on middlemen and insiders, however, creates a particularly acute problem where there is neither a set of laws and standards nor rigorous enforcement of government oversight of conflicts of interest and corruption. In that environment, third-party agents and representatives have a strong incentive to abuse influence or engage in corrupt practices to secure business and lucrative success fees. These parties

---

15 See World Bank, Worldwide Governance Indicators, available at http://info.worldbank.org/governance/wgi/index.aspx#reports. The World Bank ranks countries for control of corruption, considering the existence of anti-corruption regimes, the quality of enforcement and the prevalence of common forms of corruption on a country-by-country and a regional basis.

16 See Transparency International, Bribe Payers Index Report 2011 at 15, www.transparency.org/bpi2011/results. The Bribe Payers Index ranks the likelihood of companies from 28 leading economies paying bribes while acquiring or conducting business abroad.

17 See Layne Christensen Company, Cease and Desist Order, Admin Proc File 3-16216 (27 October2014). See also note 128 below.

may, in turn, create compliance risks if not carefully managed through compliance mechanisms and controls.

Often compounding this problem is the lack of resources and public records that can be crucial for counterparty and third-party due diligence in the anti-corruption context. Companies wishing to ensure compliance face challenges in many parts of sub-Saharan Africa, due to a lack of readily accessible and reliable resources, including information on the background, affiliations and ultimate ownership – as well as the credentials, capabilities and reputability – of third-party agents. Thus, even if a company wishes to hire a legitimate third party to help it navigate local laws, companies often cannot meet FCPA enforcement officials' expectations with regard to due diligence.[18] The short supply of qualified third parties and the increase in FCPA enforcement actions against third parties further complicate the matter.[19] For example, a sophisticated freight forwarding and logistics company withdrew its operations from Nigeria after it pleaded guilty to violating the FCPA, noting that the "ongoing uncertain and hard-to-assess legal environment in Nigeria" made it difficult to provide effective services to its customers without violating anti-corruption laws.[20]

2.2 Local content laws

Local content laws (ie, laws requiring foreign companies to partner with local entities) are prevalent in sub-Saharan Africa, particularly in the oil and gas industry.[21] While these laws are meant to stimulate local economic growth, they also create opportunities for bribes and kickbacks because foreign companies are often required to partner with local entities with direct or indirect government ties and, in some cases, without sufficient capability or incentive to perform in a manner commensurate with their share in a venture. In many cases, local entities in the oil and gas industry in sub-Saharan Africa are state owned. Even local entities without state ownership may be considered an 'instrumentality' of the state through indirect control (and therefore involve a 'foreign official' for purposes of the FCPA), such as board appointments for government officials or ownership of the local entity by a government official in his or her individual capacity.

Other laws in sub-Saharan Africa may not require foreign companies to partner with local entities, but may instead require that foreign companies operate through locally registered subsidiaries.[22] Local subsidiaries are often geographically isolated from

18 Complaint, paragraphs 31-36, *Securities and Exchange Commission v Halliburton Company*, 4:09-cv-00399 (SD Tex 2009).

19 *Information, US v Panalpina, Inc*, 4:10-cr-00765 (SD Tex 2010); see also *Information, US v Panalpina World Transport (Holding) Ltd*, 4:10-cr-00769 (SD Tex 2010).

20 "Panalpina reports dynamic growth in the first half year" (30 July 2008), www.panalpina.com/www/global/en/home/news_media/news_archive_folder/08_07_30.html.

21 See Reagan R Demas, "Doing Business in Africa While Ensuring Compliance with the FCPA", in Baker & McKenzie, *Inside the FCPA: The Corruption & Compliance Quarterly, North America, Winter 2012*, at 1, www.bakermckenzie.com/files/Uploads/Documents/Global%20Corporate%20Compliance/nl_na_insidefcpawinter_jan12.pdf; see also PricewaterhouseCoopers, *From Promise to Performance: Africa oil & gas review* (June 2013), at 6, www.pwc.com/en_NG/ng/pdf/pwc-africa-oil-and-gas-review.pdf.

22 See Demas, *op cit* (note 20 above).

23 See Ernst & Young, *Managing bribery and corruption risks in the oil and gas industry* (2014), at 7, www.ey.com/Publication/vwLUAssets/EY-Managing-bribery-and-corruption-risk-in-the-oil-and-gas-industry/$FILE/EY-Managing-bribery-and-corruption-risk-in-the-oil-and-gas-industry.pdf.

parent companies, thus creating additional challenges for anti-corruption monitoring and increased opportunities for bribery.[23] Despite the heightened risks and challenges created by these local partnerships, FCPA enforcement officials still expect parent companies to implement effective control mechanisms over their foreign subsidiaries' activities in order adequately to detect, investigate or deter corrupt payments.[24]

2.3 Customs laws

The pressure to meet exploration, development and production timelines in the oil and gas industry also creates incentives for both companies and government officials to engage in bribery in relation to customs laws. For example, companies may have staff and equipment that are mobilised, but unable to work until critical equipment can be cleared through customs. Understanding this pressure, customs officials often request processing fees to perform routine duties. Between 2007 and 2013, US enforcement officials settled with 12 companies, one freight forwarder and several of its customers for a scheme involving the bribery of Nigerian Customs Service (NCS) officials.[25]

3. Anti-corruption enforcement efforts in sub-Saharan Africa

3.1 Domestic/local anti-corruption law enforcement

A detailed review of the domestic legal and enforcement regimes of each country in sub-Saharan Africa is beyond the scope of this chapter. However, companies facing potential corruption issues must carefully weigh and be aware of both the general corruption enforcement environment and the potential impact of applicable local law on their in-country operations and transactions.

In this regard, several points are noteworthy. Most states in the region have enacted laws that prohibit, to one degree or another, the giving and receiving of domestic bribes. While not as common, foreign bribery is also prohibited in certain jurisdictions (eg, South Africa). In general, however, implementation and enforcement are still at a nascent stage, and there is often a perception that enforcement activity is hindered by a number of factors. These include:

- lack of resources for enforcement;
- conflict of interest among political decision makers; and
- the exercise of political influence to hinder enforcement activity.

Certain jurisdictions have adopted national corruption commissions and are undertaking initiatives to address corruption, including in the oil and gas sector. In

---

24 Complaint, paragraphs 31-36, note 18 above. See also the following: information at paragraphs 9-15, *US v Weatherford Int'l Ltd*, 4:13-cr-00733 (SD Tex 2013); information at paragraph 31, *Securities and Exchange Commission v ENI, SpA*, 4:10-cv-02414 (SD Tex 2010).

25 See US DoJ press release, "Three Vetco International Ltd Subsidiaries Plead Guilty to Foreign Bribery and Agree to Pay $26 Million in Criminal Fines" (6 February 2007), www.justice.gov/opa/pr/2007/February/07_crm_075.html. See also US DoJ press release, "Oil Services Companies and a Freight Forwarding Company Agree to Resolve Foreign Bribery Investigations and to Pay More Than $156 Million in Criminal Penalties" (4 November 2010), www.justice.gov/opa/pr/oil-services-companies-and-freight-forwarding-company-agree-resolve-foreign-bribery; US DoJ press release, "Parker Drilling Company Resolves FCPA Investigation and Agrees to Pay $11.76 Million Penalty" (16 April 2013), www.justice.gov/opa/pr/2013/April/13-crm-431.html.

southern Africa in particular, growing attention has been paid to the widespread public outcry over potential corruption in the nascent energy sector. For example, in January 2016 President Buhari of Nigeria – a country that has been associated with a significant number of FCPA enforcement matters – introduced several proposed bills aimed at reforming and expanding the country's money-laundering law, as well as establishing whistleblower protections and enhancing mutual legal assistance for international investigations. On 30 November 2014, the Tanzanian Parliament voted to dismiss senior officials of the Tanzanian government, including the minister of energy, in connection with allegations of corruption.[26] More recently, on 16 March 2018 South African prosecutors announced that they were bringing corruption charges against former President Jacob Zuma.

Even in countries with a relatively developed anti-corruption law framework, the enforcement track record is either unclear or weak. South Africa – the only African country to have ratified the Organisation for Economic Cooperation and Development (OECD) Convention on Bribery – was recently chided by the OECD for a lax enforcement record. In its most recent report on South Africa's anti-corruption legal regime, the OECD noted that since joining the convention in 2007 and establishing a "well-drafted" corruption law, the country has yet to prosecute a single case of foreign bribery.[27]

3.2 Lessons from FCPA/UK Bribery Act enforcement in sub-Saharan Africa

Although several national governments and international organisations have established and implemented legal frameworks to combat corruption, rigorous enforcement of the FCPA has had the most significant effect on multinational oil and gas companies' approach to compliance in the region. Five of the 10 largest historical FCPA settlements are a result of enforcement actions against multinational oil and gas companies.[28] These enforcement actions have resulted in companies paying hundreds of millions of dollars in fines and high-level executives, managers and other employees being held personally liable, including serving prison sentences. These are discussed in the case studies below.

By contrast, UK Bribery Act enforcement in sub-Saharan Africa has been far more limited to date. In July 2017 the UK Serious Fraud Office (SFO) announced that it had opened a corruption investigation into global mining firm Rio Tinto.[29] The announcement stated that the SFO was investigating "suspected corruption in the conduct of business in the Republic of Guinea by the Rio Tinto group, its employees and others associated with it". Rio Tinto had several months earlier launched an internal investigation into payments of $10.5 million to a third-party consultant

---

26 See Kimberly Bennet, "Tanzanian Parliament Votes on PM Resignation Amid Corruption Scandal", *The Jurist* (30 November 2014), http://jurist.org/paperchase/2014/11/tanzania-parliament-votes-on-pm-resignation-amid-corruption-scandal.php.

27 See OECD Working Group on Bribery, *Phase 3 Report on Implementing the OECD Anti-Bribery Convention in South Africa* (March 2014).

28 See Richard L Cassin, "Keppel Offshore Lands 7th on Our Top Ten List", FCPA Blog (26 December 2017), available at www.fcpablog.com/blog/2017/12/26/keppel-offshore-lands-seventh-on-our-top-ten-list.html.

29 www.sfo.gov.uk/2017/07/24/sfo-opens-investigation-into-the-rio-tinto-group/.

with close ties to the Guinean president in connection with the renewal of its Simandou iron ore mining rights. Outside the African context, however, the SFO has shown a willingness to aggressively pursue major investigations and impose significant penalties. On 17 January 2017 the SFO and Rolls Royce PLC entered into a deferred prosecution agreement (DPA) following a four-year investigation into decades-long corruption practices, including in relation to projects relating to gas pipeline projects in Central Asia.[30] The agreement resulted in, among other things, a record fine of £671 million against the company. Notably, the investigation also led to individual guilty pleas and prosecutions in the United Kingdom and the United States by agents and intermediaries used by the company in connection with these practices.

In addition, the SFO announced in 2017 that it was investigating a number of companies and individuals – including KBR, Inc,[31] Petrofac PLC[32] and several individuals – in connection with its investigation of Unaoil, a third-party agent of SBM Offshore NV.[33] SBM, a Dutch-based manufacturer of offshore drilling equipment, and its US subsidiary entered into a $238 million settlement with the US Department of Justice (DoJ) in November 2017 based on allegations of bribery in several countries, including Angola and Equitorial Guinea.[34]

The long-term impact of the UK Bribery Act on anti-corruption compliance in sub-Saharan Africa remains to be seen. However, in light of the SFO's recent enforcement actions and announced investigations, the apparent trajectory of those matters and the SFO's stated intentions with regard to foreign bribery prosecutions and the significant corruption issues in sub-Saharan Africa, it is only a matter of time before the SFO brings a significant anti-corruption prosecution under the UK Bribery Act involving the region.

In the meantime, consideration of the enforcement history in several key FCPA actions is instructive with regard to the practical nature of anti-corruption compliance issues that arise in conducting business in sub-Saharan Africa.

3.3 Key FCPA enforcement cases

(a) Vetco

In early 2004 a group of private equity entities formed Vetco International Ltd and through this new entity sought to acquire from ABB Ltd several oil and gas companies and their subsidiaries, including ABB Vetco Gray Inc ('Vetco US'), ABB Vetco Gray UK Ltd ('Vetco UK'), Vetco Gray Controls Inc ('Vetco Inc') and Vetco Controls Ltd ('Vetco Ltd') (collectively, 'the acquired entities').[35] During the pre-acquisition due diligence, the acquirers identified illegal bribery activity in Nigeria by

---

30 www.sfo.gov.uk/cases/rolls-royce-plc.
31 www.sfo.gov.uk/cases/kbr-inc/
32 www.sfo.gov.uk/cases/petrofac-plc/
33 www.sfo.gov.uk/cases/unaoil/
34 www.justice.gov/opa/pr/sbm-offshore-nv-and-united-states-based-subsidiary-resolve-foreign-corrupt-practices-act-case. At the time of writing, SPM is also in negotiations with Brazilian authorities to finalise the terms of a settlement — expected to exceed $300 million – in connection with bribes to Petrobras.
35 See Information, paragraphs 2-4, *US v Vetco Gray Controls Inc*, 4:07-cr-00004 (SD Tex 2007).

some of the acquired entities relating to the obtaining of contracts.[36] After a joint investigation into this matter, the acquirers required ABB to disclose the conduct voluntarily to the DoJ and requested that the DoJ not take enforcement action against the acquirers for FCPA violations prior to the acquisition.[37]

On 6 July 2004 – prior to both the closing of the acquisition and the DoJ's response to the acquirers' request for non-prosecution – the DoJ and the Securities and Exchange Commission (SEC) settled with ABB, Vetco US and Vetco UK for violations of the FCPA in Nigeria.[38] According to court documents, between 1998 and 2001, Vetco US and Vetco UK paid $1 million in bribes to officials of the National Petroleum Investment Management Services (NAPIMS), a Nigerian government agency that evaluates and approves bidders for contract work on oil exploration projects in Nigeria, in exchange for confidential bid information and favourable consideration for its bids by NAPIMS.[39] Vetco US and Vetco UK paid bribes directly to NAPIMS officials. Vetco UK also paid bribes through a Nigerian agent with which it had a fraudulent consultancy agreement established to provide marketing and goodwill services.[40] The bribes comprised cash and gifts, such as country club memberships, mobile phone bill payments and paid shopping excursions in the United States.[41]

On 12 July 2004 – six days after the DoJ and SEC settlements – the DoJ responded to the acquirers' request for non-prosecution in FCPA Opinion Procedure Release 2004-02. In the opinion release, the DoJ stated its intent not to prosecute the acquirers or acquired entities for violations that occurred prior to 12 July 2004, provided that the acquirers met certain terms and conditions. These included effectively instituting and implementing a compliance system, training and other sufficient controls to deter and detect violations of the FCPA.[42] Despite the DoJ's requirements, four of the acquired entities settled with the DoJ and/or SEC between 2007 and 2008 for FCPA violations in Nigeria.

On 6 February 2007 Vetco Inc, Vetco Ltd and Vetco UK (again) pleaded guilty to conspiracy to violate the bribery provisions of the FCPA.[43] According to court documents, from September 2002 to April 2005, the companies hired and authorised Panalpina Inc – a major international freight forwarding and customs clearing company – to make approximately $2.1 million in corrupt payments to NCS officials for preferential treatment in customs clearance and collection of tariffs and duties.[44]

---

36 See US, Opinion Procedure Release, 04-02 (12 July 2004), www.justice.gov/criminal/fraud/fcpa/opinion/2004/0402.pdf.

37 *Ibid.*

38 See US press release, "ABB Vetco Gray Inc and ABB Vetco Gray UK Ltd Plead Guilty to Foreign Bribery Charges" (6 July 2004), www.justice.gov/archive/opa/pr/2004/July/04_crm_465.htm.

39 Information, paragraphs 3-37, *US v ABB Vetco Gray, Inc*, H-04-CR-279 (SD Tex 2004).

40 *Ibid.*

41 *Ibid.* Vetco US agreed to pay a criminal fine of $5.25 million to the DoJ. In addition, Vetco US and Vetco UK's parent company ABB agreed to pay the SEC $5.9 million in disgorgement of profits and a civil penalty of $10.5 million. See note 31 above.

42 *Ibid.*

43 See press release of 6 February 2007 at note 24 above.

44 Information, paragraphs 31–32, *US v Vetco Gray Controls Inc*, 4:07-cr-00004-1 (SD Tex 2007). Vetco Inc, Vetco Limited and Vetco UK agreed to pay criminal fines of $6 million, $8 million and $12 million respectively. See press release of 6 February 2007 at note 24 above.

In calculating Vetco UK's penalty, the DoJ noted Vetco UK's prior guilty plea, prior DoJ directives in 2004 and the acquirers' failure to comply with the opinion release.[45]

On 6 February 2007 Aibel Group Ltd, a subsidiary of Vetco UK, also entered into a DPA[46] with the DoJ for the same underlying conduct, but was not required to pay a criminal or civil fine or to disgorge profits. On 21 November 2008, however, Aibel admitted to non-compliance with its DPA and settled with the DoJ on the basis of the facts which the company had admitted in the 2007 DPA.[47] The DoJ noted that the case marked the third time that an entity affiliated with Vetco International had pleaded guilty to violations of the FCPA and that the acquirers had failed to follow the terms and conditions of the opinion release.[48]

(b) *Panalpina oil and gas industry sweep*

On 2 July 2007, in the wake of the 2007 Vetco settlements, the DoJ sent letters to 11 oil and gas companies requesting information about their dealings with Panalpina Inc.[49] On 4 November 2010 the DoJ and the SEC settled FCPA enforcement actions with Panalpina Inc and Panalpina World Transport (Holding) Ltd, a subsidiary of Panalpina Inc (collectively, 'Panalpina') and six of Panalpina's customers:

- Pride International, Inc;
- Royal Dutch Shell plc and its subsidiary Shell Nigeria Exploration and Production Company Ltd (collectively, 'Shell');
- Transocean, Inc;
- Tidewater Inc and its subsidiary Tidewater Marine International, Inc (collectively, 'Tidewater');
- Noble Corporation; and
- GlobalSantaFe Corp.[50]

On 16 April 2013 the DoJ and SEC settled with a seventh Panalpina customer, Parker Drilling Company.[51]

According to court documents, between 2002 and 2007 Panalpina offered an express courier service to its customers in Nigeria called Pancourier, through which Panalpina bribed NCS officials to circumvent certain time-intensive Nigerian customs laws, including required paperwork, inspection of products and customs

---

45 See note 24 above.

46 A DPA postpones prosecution of an FCPA violation in exchange for any or all of the following:
• payment of a monetary penalty;
• cooperation with the government;
• compliance with remediation requirements; and
• admission of relevant facts.
See DoJ Resource Guide, note 4 above.

47 See US DoJ press release, "Aibel Group Ltd Pleads Guilty to Foreign Bribery and Agrees to Pay $4.2 Million in Criminal Fines" (21 November 2008), www.justice.gov/opa/pr/2008/November/08-crm-1041.html.

48 *Ibid.*

49 See Gibson and Dunn, *2010 Year-End FCPA Update* (3 January 2011), www.gibsondunn.com/publications/pages/2010Year-EndFCPAUpdate.aspx.

50 See press release of 4 November 2010 at note 24 above; see also SEC press release, "SEC Charges Seven Oil Services and Freight Forwarding Companies for Widespread Bribery of Customs Officials", www.sec.gov/news/press/2010/2010-214.htm.

51 See press release of 16 April 2013 at note 24 above.

fees.[52] In addition, Panalpina offered an express service for extensions of initial Nigerian temporary import permits, which were time-sensitive permits required to import high-value, specialised equipment into Nigerian waters.[53] Specifically, Panalpina bribed NCS officials to obtain permit extensions that were not permitted under Nigerian law in order to help its customers avoid the time and cost of removing the equipment from Nigerian waters.[54]

In addition to its actions in Nigeria, between 2006 and 2008 Panalpina paid approximately $4.5 million in bribes to Angolan customs officials through a similar scheme, to induce them to overlook incomplete or inaccurate documentation or to avoid customs duties or fines.[55] Panalpina also paid millions of dollars in bribes to Angolan government officials to secure contracts.[56]

Panalpina, Pride, Shell, Transocean, Tidewater and Parker entered into DPAs and agreed to criminal penalties with the DoJ.[57] These entities also settled with the SEC, together with GlobalSantaFe Corp.[58] Noble, Panalpina's other customer charged in the case, also settled with the DoJ and SEC.[59] However, due to Noble's "early voluntary disclosure, thorough self-investigation of the underlying conduct, full cooperation" and "extensive remedial measures", the DoJ imposed a non-prosecution agreement (NPA)[60] and Noble was subject to a fine that was substantially lower than those imposed on Panalpina's other customers.[61]

(c) *Bonny Island project*

In 1990 the Nigerian government collaborated with three international oil and gas companies to create a joint venture to develop a liquefied natural gas project on an island off the coast of Nigeria called Bonny Island.[62] In 1991 four companies – MW Kellogg Limited, Snamprogetti Netherlands BV, JGC Corporation and Technip SA – formed a joint venture for the purposes of bidding on and performing engineering, procurement and construction (EPC) contracts for the Bonny Island project.[63] Between 2009 and 2013, the DoJ and SEC settled with all joint venture partners, one consulting company and three individuals in respect of a bribery scheme to win a series of EPC contracts related to the Bonny Island project.[64]

According to court documents, between 1995 and 2004 the joint venture paid or

---

52 Information, paragraphs 25–27, *US v Panalpina World Transport (Holding) Ltd*, note 18 above. Panalpina charged its customers a premium for the service and invoiced customers by recording bribes as 'local processing fees', 'interventions', 'special handling' and 'administration charges'.

53 *Ibid* at paragraphs 32–36.

54 *Ibid*. Panalpina invoiced its customers for the bribe payments and characterised the payments as 'TI interventions' or 'TI recycling' costs.

55 *Ibid* at paragraphs 40–42.

56 *Ibid* at paragraphs 43–45. To generate cash for the bribes, Panalpina invoiced an Angolan government-controlled entity for a non-existent employee who was allegedly dedicated to working on the logistics for a particular project (the 'ghost employee').

57 See press release of 4 November 2010 at note 24 above.

58 *Ibid*.

59 *Ibid*.

60 An NPA is similar to a DPA, except that the DoJ does not file criminal charges but rather maintains this right in order to allow the company to demonstrate good conduct during the term of the DPA. See *DoJ Resource Guide* (note 4 above) at 75.

61 See press release of 4 November 2010 at note 24 above.

62 Information, paragraph 14, *US v Kellogg Brown & Root LLC*, 09-00071 (SD Tex 2009).

63 *Ibid* at paragraph 4.

promised to pay Nigerian government officials, including those in the executive branch, in exchange for the award of four EPC contracts totalling $6 billion.[65] To carry out the bribery, the joint venture created a Portuguese-based 'special purpose corporation' that entered into fraudulent consulting agreements with Marubeni Corporation, a Japanese trading company, for the payment of bribes to lower-level Nigerian government officials; and with Tri-Star Investments Ltd, a shell corporation run by Jeffery Tesler, for the payment of bribes to higher-level Nigerian government officials.[66]

Kellogg, Brown & Root LLC (KBR) (the successor company to Kellogg), Snamprogetti, JGC, Technip and Marubeni entered into DPAs with the DoJ and agreed to pay criminal penalties. In addition, KBR and its former parent company Halliburton Company, Snamprogetti and its parent company ENI, SpA and Technip settled with the SEC.[67] Three individuals also settled with FCPA enforcement officials:

- Albert 'Jack' Stanley, a former officer and director of KBR;
- Wojciech J Chodan, a former sales vice president of Kellogg; and
- Tesler, a joint venture consultant with Tri-Star.[68]

Stanley and Tesler were sentenced to 30 and 21 months in prison respectively, plus supervised release, and each was ordered to pay hundreds of millions of dollars in combined fines and restitution.[69] Chodan was sentenced to one year of unsupervised probation and ordered to pay hundreds of thousands of dollars in combined fines and restitution.[70]

In addition, the UK SFO ordered Kellogg to pay a fine of $12 million.[71] "The SFO

---

64 See US DoJ press release, "Former Officer and Director of Global Engineering and Construction Company Pleads Guilty to Foreign Bribery and Kickback Charges" (3 September 2008), www.justice.gov/opa/pr/2008/September/08-crm-772.html. See also US DoJ press release, "Kellogg Brown & Root LLC Pleads Guilty to Foreign Bribery Charges and Agrees to Pay $402 Million Criminal Fine" (11 February 2009), www.justice.gov/opa/pr/2009/February/09-crm-112.html; US DoJ press release, "Technip S.A. Resolves Foreign Corrupt Practices Act Investigation and Agrees to Pay $240 Million Criminal Penalty" (28 June 2010), www.justice.gov/opa/pr/2010/June/10-crm-751.html; US DoJ press release, "Snamprogetti Netherlands BV Resolves Foreign Corrupt Practices Act Investigation and Agrees to Pay $240 Million Criminal Penalty" (7 July 2010), www.justice.gov/opa/pr/2010/July/10-crm-780.html; US DoJ press release, "UK Citizen Pleads Guilty to Conspiring to Bribe Nigerian Government Officials to Obtain Lucrative Contracts as Part of KBR Joint Venture Scheme" (6 December 2010), www.justice.gov/opa/pr/2010/December/10-crm-1391.html; US DoJ press release, "UK Solicitor Pleads Guilty for Role in Bribing Nigerian Government Officials as Part of KBR Joint Venture Scheme" (11 March 2011), www.justice.gov/opa/pr/2011/March/11-crm-313.html; US DoJ press release, "JGC Corporation Resolves Foreign Corrupt Practices Act Investigation and Agrees to Pay a $218.8 Million Criminal Penalty" (6 April 2011), www.justice.gov/opa/pr/2011/April/11-crm-431.html; US DoJ press release, "Marubeni Corporation Resolves Foreign Corrupt Practices Act Investigation and Agrees to Pay a $54.6 Million Criminal Penalty" (17 January 2012), available at www.justice.gov/opa/pr/2012/January/12-crm-060.html.

65 Information, paragraph15, note 55 above.

66 *Ibid*, at paragraphs 12–14.

67 See US SEC press release, "SEC Charges KBR and Halliburton for FCPA Violations" (11 February 2009), www.sec.gov/news/press/2009/2009-23.htm. See also US SEC press release, "SEC Charges Italian Company and Dutch Subsidiary in Scheme Bribing Nigerian Officials With Carloads of Cash" (7 July 2010), www.sec.gov/news/press/2010/2010-119.htm; US SEC press release, "SEC Charges Technip with FCPA Violations" (28 June 2010), www.sec.gov/news/press/2010/2010-110.htm.

68 See press releases of 3 September 2008, 6 December 2010 and 11 March 2011 at note 57 above.

69 See press releases of 3 September 2008 and 11 March 2011 at note 57 above.

70 See press release of 6 December 2010 at note 57 above.

71 See note 26 above.

recognized that [Kellogg] took no part in the criminal activity that generated the funds", but pursued the case because the funds due to Kellogg were share dividends payable from profits and revenues generated by contracts obtained through bribery and corruption.[72] In commenting on the case, the SFO noted that it demonstrated the range of tools that UK enforcement officials are prepared to use to prevent bribery.[73]

(d) *EGGS project*

In 2008 and 2013, the DoJ settled with the Willbros Group, Inc and Willbros International, Inc (collectively, 'Willbros') and Bilfinger SE, respectively, for conspiring to make corrupt payments and falsifying books and records relating to a project for the Eastern Gas Gathering System (EGGS) in Nigeria – a natural gas pipeline system operated through a joint venture between the Nigerian National Petroleum Corporation and two foreign oil companies.[74] According to court documents, Willbros and Bilfinger created a joint venture through which the companies' Nigerian-based subsidiaries made payments and promises to pay $6 million in bribes to Nigerian government officials between 2003 and 2007 in order to obtain a contract for the EGGS project.[75] To carry out the bribery scheme, Bilfinger and Willbros inflated their joint venture's bid for the EGGS contract by 3% and promised to pay Nigerian government officials the extra money if their joint venture won the contract.[76] The joint venture then submitted inflated invoices to the operator of the EGGS project and distributed 3% of the invoice payments to Nigerian government officials.[77]

Using fraudulent consultancy agreements, Willbros originally funnelled money to Nigerian government officials through two purported consultants operating consultancy companies in Nigeria.[78] However, a 2005 internal investigation at Willbros revealed the illegal activity and the company terminated the consultancy agreements.[79] Subsequently, certain individuals at Willbros were concerned that the failure to pay bribes to government officials would interrupt the company's Nigerian business.[80] These individuals orchestrated a series of internal and external company loans (including one from Bilfinger), extracted cash from a Willbros petty cash account in Nigeria and funnelled bribes indirectly to Nigerian officials through a second consultant.[81] Bilfinger paid bribes using cash from the office safe at one of its Nigerian-based subsidiaries.[82]

Willbros and Bilfinger each paid criminal fines and entered into DPAs with the

---

72 *Ibid.*
73 *Ibid.*
74 See US DoJ press release, "Willbros Group Inc. Enters Deferred Prosecution Agreement and Agrees to Pay $22 Million Penalty for FCPA Violations" (14 May 2008), www.justice.gov/opa/pr/2008/May/08-crm-417.html; see also US DoJ press release, "German Engineering Firm Bilfinger Resolves Foreign Corrupt Practices Act Charges and Agrees to Pay $32 Million Criminal Penalty" (11 December 2013), www.justice.gov/opa/pr/2013/December/13-crm-1297.html.
75 Information at paragraph 28, *US v Willbros Group, Inc*, 4:08-cr-00287 (SD Tex 2008).
76 *Ibid.*
77 *Ibid.*
78 *Ibid.*
79 *Ibid* at paragraph 32.
80 *Ibid* at paragraphs 32–36.
81 *Ibid.*
82 Information, paragraph 21, *US v Bilfinger SE*, 13-cr-00745 (SD Tex 2013).

DoJ, and Willbros also settled with the SEC.[83] The DoJ also filed charges against three former Willbros executives – Jim Bob Brown, Jason Steph and James Tillery – and a former Willbros consultant, Paul Novak.[84] Brown and Steph were sentenced to serve 12 and 15 months in prison respectively, and ordered to pay thousands of dollars in criminal fines.[85] Novak was sentenced to over one year in prison and ordered to pay a criminal fine of $1 million.[86] In connection with the DoJ investigation, the SEC also settled with Brown, Steph and two former, less senior Willbros managers.[87] Tillery remains a fugitive and has never been tried.[88]

(e) ***Weatherford***

On 26 November 2013 the DoJ and SEC settled with Weatherford International Ltd and its wholly owned subsidiary, Weatherford Services Ltd (collectively, 'Weatherford'), for FCPA violations in Angola and the Middle East.[89] According to court documents, Weatherford engaged in two bribery schemes in Angola between 2004 and 2008 to bribe Sociedade Nacional de Combustiveis de Angola, EP (Sonangol), a government-owned and controlled corporation with the sole right to explore, produce, manufacture, transport and market oil and gas in Angola.[90]

Under the first scheme, Weatherford established and operated a joint venture with two local entities controlled by Sonangol officials and their relatives and funnelled hundreds of thousands of dollars in payments to the officials and their relatives in exchange for lucrative contracts and inside information about competitors' pricing.[91] Despite indications of red flags and advice received from outside counsel to identify the beneficial owners of the joint venture, Weatherford did not conduct any meaningful due diligence before signing the final agreement with Sonangol.[92] In the second scheme, Weatherford bribed an Angolan official to renew Weatherford's oil and gas contracts.[93] Specifically, Weatherford entered into a

---

83 See press releases of 14 May 2008 and 11 December 2013 at note 67 above.

84 See US DoJ press release, "Former Executive of Willbros Subsidiary Pleads Guilty to Conspiring to Bribe Foreign Officials in Nigeria and Ecuador" (14 September 2006), www.justice.gov/opa/pr/2006/September/06_crm_621.html. See also US DoJ press release, "Former Executive of Willbros Subsidiary Pleads Guilty to Conspiring to Bribe Nigerian Government Officials" (5 November 2007), www.justice.gov/opa/pr/2007/November/07_crm_885.html; US DoJ press release, "Former Willbros International Executive and Consultant Charged in $6 Million Foreign Bribery Conspiracy" (19 December 2008), www.justice.gov/opa/pr/2008/December/08-crm-1137.html; US DoJ press release, "Former Willbros International Consultant Pleads Guilty to $6 Million Foreign Bribery Scheme" (12 November 2009), www.justice.gov/opa/pr/2009/November/09-crm-1220.html.

85 See *US v Jim Bob Brown*, 4:06-cr-00316-1 (SD Tex 2006), http://shearman.symplicity.com/? mode=form&lbid=187; see also *US v Jason Edward Steph*, 4:07-cr-00307-1 (SD Tex 2007), http://shearman.symplicity.com/?mode=form&lbid=189.

86 See *US v James K Tillery*, 4:08-cr-00022-1 (SD Tex 2008), available at http://shearman. symplicity.com/?mode=form&lbid=185.

87 See note 77 above.

88 See US DoJ press release, "Former Consultant for Willbros International Sentenced in Connection with Foreign Bribery Scheme" (3 May 2013), www.justice.gov/opa/pr/former-consultant-willbros-international-sentenced-connection-foreign-bribery-scheme.

89 See US DoJ press release, "Three Subsidiaries of Weatherford International Limited Agree to Plead Guilty to FCPA and Export Control Violations" (26 November 2013), www.justice.gov/opa/pr/2013/November/13-crm-1260.html.

90 Information, paragraphs 13–40, *US v Weatherford Services*, 4:13-cr-00734 (SD Tex 2013).

91 *Ibid.*

92 *Ibid.*

93 *Ibid* at paragraphs 41–46.

fake consultancy agreement with a freight forwarding agent and then generated fraudulent purchase orders for services that the freight forwarding agent never performed.[94] In turn, the freight forwarding agent generated fraudulent invoices and, when paid, passed at least some of the money on to the foreign official authorised to renew Weatherford's contracts.[95]

3.4 Impact of FCPA and UK Bribery Act enforcement actions

The cases outlined above support several observations about conducting business in the oil and gas industry in sub-Saharan Africa.

The oil and gas industry in sub-Saharan Africa is at high risk of corruption. In the *Bonny Island* cases, Stanley, Chodan and Tesler admitted in their plea agreements that although they knew that it was unlawful to bribe foreign officials, they believed that support of Nigerian government officials – including top-level executive branch officials and high-level petroleum ministry officials – was necessary to win the Bonny Island project EPC contracts.[96] In addition, Weatherford's original consultancy agreement with its Angolan freight forwarding agent included an FCPA clause prohibiting the freight forwarding agent from giving anything of value, directly or indirectly, to an official or employee of any government.[97] However, the freight forwarding agent rejected the FCPA clause, stating that "in view of the nature of the business I cannot accept the original wording".[98]

Enforcement officials expect companies to establish, implement and maintain an effective compliance programme that is commensurate with that risk. In *Weatherford* the DoJ specifically noted that the company operated in an industry with a "substantial risk profile", yet failed to establish internal controls in areas such as third-party due diligence, anti-corruption risk management and gifts, travel and entertainment.[99] The DoJ noted that prior to 2008, Weatherford had no dedicated compliance officer or compliance personnel. Furthermore, the company failed to translate its anti-corruption policy into any language other than English.[100] This scrutiny of compliance efforts, and the adequacy of compliance resources, can also be expected under the UK Bribery Act – under which 'failure to prevent' bribery is an offence.

The FCPA poses serious monetary risks for companies. In 2007 the fines imposed on the Vetco entities were unprecedentedly high. The joint venture partners in the *Bonny Island* cases agreed to fines that rank among the top 10 highest FCPA fines ever (KBR at number 2; Snamprogetti at number 6; Technip at number 7; and JGC at number 8), with KBR's fine being the largest ever imposed on a US company.[101]

---

94 *Ibid.*

95 *Ibid.*

96 See plea agreement at paragraph 18.c, *US v Albert Jackson Stanley*, 4:08-cr-00597 (SD Tex 2008). See also plea agreement at paragraph 18.c, *US v Wojciech J Chodan*, 4:09-cr-00098 (SD Tex 2010); plea agreement at paragraph 18.c, *US v Jeffrey Tesler*, 4:09-cr-00098 (SD Tex 2011).

97 Information, paragraph 45, *US v Weatherford Services*, note 83 above.

98 *Ibid.* Weatherford acquiesced by removing the FCPA clause and inserting one requiring the freight forwarding agent to "comply with all applicable laws, rules, and regulations issued by any governmental entity in the countries of business involved".

99 Information, paragraph 9, *US v Weatherford Int'l Ltd*, 4:13-cr-00733 (SD Tex 2013).

100 *Ibid* at paragraphs 10–15.

101 See note 24 above.

The cases outlined above also support the following general observations about the impact of the FCPA enforcement actions worldwide:

- Companies must be aware of competitors' activities that may signal industry-wide risks. In commenting on the *Panalpina* cases, the SEC stated that the investigations were triggered "after detecting widespread corruption in the oil services industry" (ie, the *Vetco* cases) and added that the agencies would "continue to focus on industrywide sweeps, and no industry is immune from investigation".[102]
- The FCPA has a broad jurisdictional reach. In the 2004 *Vetco UK* case, jurisdiction was based on the theory that a Vetco US employee acted as an agent for Vetco UK.[103] The SEC reached Panalpina by charging that it aided and abetted and acted as an agent of its US-issuer customers, even though Panalpina itself was not an issuer.[104] Historically, non-US companies have been the subject of more FCPA enforcement actions than US companies.
- Non-US citizen employees will be held liable for violations of the FCPA. The United States extradited Chodan and Tesler from the United Kingdom to prosecute them in the *Bonny Island* cases.[105]
- Parent companies must ensure that their subsidiaries are implementing policies and procedures. In the *Panalpina* cases, the SEC alleged that Halliburton had not ensured that KBR and Snamprogetti implemented agent policies and procedures.[106] With regard to Halliburton, the SEC alleged that it had conducted insufficient due diligence on Tesler because:
  - it never identified the beneficial owners of Tri-Star;
  - it did not seek to determine how Tesler would carry out his duties; and
  - it did not check all Tesler's references, some of which were false.[107]
- Due diligence procedures for agents must go beyond a basic questionnaire. In the SEC complaint against Technip, the SEC alleged that Technip had failed to conduct sufficient due diligence on agents because it only required that its agents should complete a written questionnaire seeking minimal background information and did not require additional procedures, such as conducting an interview or background check and following up on responses to the written questionnaire.[108] A Technip senior executive admitted that Technip's due diligence procedures were a perfunctory exercise, conducted so that Technip would have some documentation showing purported due diligence.[109]
- FCPA enforcement officials will prosecute companies that do not comply with DPAs. The *Vetco-Aibel* case marked the first time the DoJ declared a breach of an FCPA DPA and prosecuted a company on the basis of the facts

102 See press release of 4 November 2010 at note 24 above.
103 Information, paragraph 39, note 32 above.
104 Complaint, paragraph 9, *Securities and Exchange Commission v Panalpina, Inc*, 4:10-cv-4334 (SD Tex 2010).
105 See press releases of 6 December 2010 and 11 March 2011 at note 7 above.
106 Complaint, paragraphs 30–36, note 18 above; Complaint, paragraph 31, *SEC v ENI, SpA*, 10-cv-2414 (SD Tex 2010).
107 Complaint, paragraphs 30–36, note 18 above.
108 Complaint, paragraphs 30–31, *SEC v Technip SA*, 10-cv-02289 (SD Tex 2010).
109 *Ibid.*

admitted in the earlier agreement. Prosecution of companies for non-compliance with a DPA is particularly relevant in the M&A context when companies are assessing the risk of a proposed transaction and negotiating transaction documents.

- FCPA enforcement officials give meaningful credit to companies for voluntary disclosure and transparency. For example, after learning of the Panalpina investigation, Noble discovered the improper payments through an internal investigation of its operations in Nigeria and voluntarily informed the DoJ of its investigation and findings.[110] Noble received a NPA as opposed to a DPA and received a penalty well below the low end of the US Sentencing Guidelines.

4. Anti-corruption conventions and protocols

In addition to the FCPA and the UK Bribery Act, the international community has instituted measures to combat corruption in sub-Saharan Africa. When the FCPA first passed into law in 1977, US companies felt disadvantaged by its stringent provisions and feared losing business.[111] Shortly thereafter, the US government started lobbying for an international anti-corruption agreement to level the playing field.[112] It started by engaging in negotiations within the United Nations and then turned its attention to the OECD.[113] However, given the FCPA's advantageous terms to non-US companies, the United States struggled to negotiate an international agreement comparable to the FCPA until 1999, when the OECD finally agreed to the Convention on Combating Bribery of Foreign Public Officials in International Business Transactions.[114] In 2003 the United Nations and the African Union each agreed to an anti-corruption convention and, in addition, regional communities started to adopt anti-corruption protocols.

4.1 OECD anti-corruption convention

The OECD Convention on Combating Bribery of Foreign Public Officials in International Business Transactions, often called the OECD Anti-bribery Convention (ABC), entered into force in 1999. The ABC was the first legally binding global instrument to prohibit the bribery of foreign public officials and became the driving force behind most international anti-corruption initiatives. All 34 OECD member states and seven non-member states have ratified the ABC, including one sub-Saharan African country, South Africa.

The ABC strongly resembles the FCPA and generally requires member countries to criminalise the bribery of foreign public officials, including authorisation and

---

110 See press release of 4 November 2010 at note 24 above.

111 Jan Outers, Cedric Ryngaert and Ann Sofie Cloots, "The International Legal Framework against Corruption", (2013) 14 *Melbourne J of Int'l L* 205 at 209. Reports varied in their estimates of how much business was lost annually to non-US companies because of the FCPA, with estimates of up to $45 billion in 1995. See Margo Cleveland *et al*, "Trends in the International Fight against Bribery and Corruption", 90 *J of Int'l Ethics* 199 at 205 (2009).

112 Outers, Ryngaert & Cloots, *op cit* (note 104 above).

113 *Ibid.*

114 The OECD Convention on Combating Bribery of Foreign Public Officials in International Business Transactions came into effect in early 1999.

aiding and abetting of such bribery. It obliges member countries to investigate and, where appropriate, prosecute those that offer, promise or pay bribes to foreign public officials, as well as to impose heavy penalties. The OECD Working Group on Bribery in International Business Transactions is responsible for monitoring implementation of the ABC. Each member state periodically undergoes a rigorous peer review that includes an in-depth assessment of the state's domestic anti-bribery laws and their implementation and enforcement.

4.2 United Nations Convention Against Corruption

The United Nations Convention Against Corruption (UNCAC), which entered into force in December 2005, is the first global anti-corruption framework aimed at creating universal standards. In all, 171 countries have signed UNCAC, including most sub-Saharan African states, with the exception of Chad, Equatorial Guinea, Eritrea, Somalia, Sudan and South Sudan.

Like the ABC, UNCAC requires its signatories to criminalise bribery, but it goes much farther in both scope and specificity. Unlike the ABC's focus on supply-side bribery of public officials, the UNCAC definition of 'bribery' includes both the giving and receiving of bribes in the public and private sectors. UNCAC's private sector provisions are similar to those of the FCPA in establishing recordkeeping and internal controls standards, while also promoting corporate codes of conduct, compliance programmes and best practices for companies.[115] UNCAC also deals with several preventative measures, including:

- adopting policies to prevent corruption;
- designating a body to coordinate and oversee the implementation of policies;
- establishing appropriate procurement systems;
- using both civil and criminal law to facilitate the recovery of state assets; and
- developing enhanced accounting and auditing standards for the private sector.

In 2009 UNCAC also adopted a review mechanism that consists of peer review and country visits if necessary. Finally, UNCAC's international cooperation chapter, which is largely self-executing, establishes mandatory extradition obligations where there is dual criminality,[116] as well as guidelines for providing mutual legal assistance or transferring criminal proceedings "in the interests of the proper administration of justice".

4.3 African Union Convention on Preventing and Combating Corruption

In 2003 African heads of state adopted the African Union Convention on Preventing and Combating Corruption (AUCPCC). The AUCPCC, which came into force in August 2006, provides wide-ranging mandatory measures, including provisions on corruption prevention and criminalisation, regional cooperation, asset recovery,

---

115 Lucinda Low, "The United Nations Convention Against Corruption: The Globalization of Anticorruption Standards," Remarks at the Annual International Bar Association Conference: "The Awakening Giant of Anti-Corruption Enforcement" (4–5 May 2006), www.steptoe.com/assets/attachments/ 2599.pdf.

116 Dual criminality applies to an offence that is a crime in both the country requesting extradition and the country receiving the extradition request.

transparency of political fundraising and commercial corruption. However, the AUCPCC does not require sanctions or liability for legal persons. The AUCPCC established the African Union Advisory Board on Corruption to monitor implementation of the convention's requirements, but thus far the board has focused on establishing its own organisational structure, while its strategic plan indicates that it will take an additional year to build its organisational efficiency. The board's monitoring mechanism is not expected to be as rigorous as that of the ABC.

As the most comprehensive African-based regional anti-corruption convention, the AUCPCC signifies the consensus of African states in the areas of prevention and criminalisation of corruption and harmonises these states' anti-corruption measures with the objective of strengthening African development. Of the 54 member states in the African Union, 35 have ratified the AUCPCC.

More recently, at its 30th Assembly of Heads of State and Government in January 2018, the African Union held its annual summit under an anti-corruption theme and announced 2018 as 'African Anti-corruption Year'.[117]

4.4 African regional community anti-corruption protocols

The Southern African Development Community[118] (SADC) Protocol against Corruption, which entered into force in 2003, establishes five categories of obligation in order to promote and harmonise anti-corruption efforts at the national level:

- preventative measures (eg, codes of conduct for public officials and procurement transparency);
- criminalisation of bribery;
- anti-money laundering measures;
- cooperation; and
- implementation of anti-corruption efforts.

However, the SADC Protocol lacks an efficient implementation mechanism.[119] Of the 15 SADC member states, 13 have ratified the SADC Protocol.

The Economic Community of West African States (ECOWAS) Protocol Against Corruption, which is similar to the SADC Protocol, provides for a wide range of preventative measures. However, only Ghana has ratified the ECOWAS Protocol, and it has not yet entered into force.

Finally, the East African Community (EAC) – which comprises Uganda, Tanzania, Rwanda and Burundi – has drafted the Protocol on Preventing and Combating Corruption. However, differences among the EAC member states on whether to give prosecutorial powers to their respective anti-corruption agencies have hampered the signing of the convention.[120]

---

117 https://au.int/en/pressreleases/20180122/african-union-launch-2018-african-anti-corruption-year.

118 The SADC comprises Angola, Botswana, Democratic Republic of Congo, Lesotho, Madagascar, Malawi, Mauritius, Mozambique, Namibia, Seychelles, South Africa, Swaziland, Tanzania, Zambia and Zimbabwe.

119 Outers, Ryngaert & Cloots, *op cit* (note 104 above) at 231.

120 Fred Oluoch, "Regional agencies seek more powers to fight corruption", *The East African*, 28 June 2014, available at www.theeastafrican.co.ke/news/Regional-agencies-seek-more-powers-to-fight-corruption/-/2558/2364780/-/dbp3te/-/index.html.

4.5 Impact of anti-corruption conventions and protocols

Given the relatively recent implementation of anti-corruption conventions and protocols in sub-Saharan Africa, the impact of these initiatives remains to be seen. However, the authors offer a few observations on the current and potential impact of the anti-corruption conventions and protocols previously discussed:

- Despite almost no participation by African states, the ABC is relevant for multinational oil and gas companies operating in sub-Saharan Africa because state parties to the ABC, including several OECD member states and Russia, are home to several large multinational oil and gas companies.
- According to Transparency International, the implementation of UNCAC is a "promising but uneven start with room for improvement in a number of areas".[121] It notes several specific areas of concern for UNCAC implementation:
  - establishing a follow-up process to address member states' implementation of the recommendations made in country reports;
  - speeding up the review process;
  - increasing transparency by publishing more of the country reports from the review process; and
  - providing technical assistance to governments of member states.[122]
- Along with UNCAC, the AUCPCC has the potential to have the greatest impact on the African content. However, the implementation of comprehensive and strong national anti-corruption laws across Africa is still nascent.
- The collective resources of the United Nations and the African Union in implementing, enforcing and harmonising anti-corruption measures may prove more beneficial for the African continent than the SADC, ECOWAS and EAC regional protocols. However, regional alliances have historically proved to be more effective in Africa, such as in the economic context.

4.6 Other international developments: World Bank and IMF

In the midst of the United States' efforts to negotiate an international anti-corruption agreement, the World Bank in the early 1990s became aware of the fact that a "substantial part of its loans were diverted through corrupt practices".[123] Historically, despite its influence in the world of politics and economic relations, the World Bank had not engaged in anti-corruption initiatives because it believed that anti-corruption constituted a policy issue beyond the scope of its charter.[124] However, in 1996 the World Bank declared corruption a "cancer" and deployed a number of administrative instruments to combat fraud and corruption.[125]

---

121 See Transparency International, United Nations Convention Against Corruption: Progress Report 2013 at 4, available at www.transparency.org/whatwedo/pub/un_convention_against_corruption_progress_report_ 2013.

122 *Ibid.*

123 Outers, Ryngaert & Cloots, *op cit* (note 104 above) at 213.

124 *Ibid.*

125 *Ibid,* at 214.

In 2007 the World Bank adopted a new strategy to combat corruption on the basis of three pillars.[126] First, the World Bank supports initiatives to help countries strengthen their governance, including initiatives in effectiveness, transparency and accountability.[127] Second, the World Bank aims to improve the impact of its own development funds by improving the integrity of its own projects.[128] Third, the World Bank works with other international actors to coordinate and harmonise approaches in countries where governance poses a significant challenge for development.[129]

One key feature of the World Bank's administrative instruments has been its suspension and debarment system. Under this system, the World Bank has imposed 359 suspensions and debarred or otherwise sanctioned 368 firms or individuals as of 30 June 2015.[130] Two-thirds of the bank's reported sanctions decisions affect just five sectors – healthcare, transportation, agriculture, water and energy.[131] Geographically, the suspended entities have had projects spanning the globe, although the World Bank has homed in on Africa, which has been the subject of one-third of the total number of investigations conducted by the bank.[132] Finally, although the World Bank's public statements focus on bribery and other forms of corruption, the vast majority of its sanctions cases to date have involved various types of low-level fraud that are easier to prove, such as forgery or misrepresentations in bidding documents.[133]

Like the World Bank, the IMF originally perceived governance issues as being outside of its economic goals and hesitated in pursuing anti-corruption initiatives.[134] Between 1996 and 1997, however, "the IMF acknowledged the economic impact of corruption...and followed the World Bank" in incorporating good governance into its standards and practices.[135] The IMF issued a formal Transparency Policy and launched other efforts, such as its Standards and Codes Initiative, to promote anti-corruption efforts. The IMF also utilises conditionality provisions in its aid agreements.

The historically high volume of international development funds flowing into high-risk sectors in sub-Saharan Africa has made the World Bank and IMF powerful advocates in the fight against corruption in the region. The direct impact of World Bank and IMF initiatives is difficult to measure. However, these two organisations have undoubtedly helped to reshape the global anti-corruption discourse through their unique and influential position in world politics and economics.

---

126 See "The World Bank's Sanctions System: Tackling Corruption Through a Two-Tier Administrative Sanctions Process", http://go.worldbank.org/EB6JXKU4Z0 (last updated 24 November 2014).
127 *Ibid.*
128 *Ibid.*
129 *Ibid.*
130 See *World Bank Office of Suspension and Debarment, Report on Functions, Data and Lessons Learned 2007-2015*, second ed (2015) at 25, http://documents.worldbank.org/curated/en/153431468196176596/pdf/104658-WP-PUBLIC-OSD-Report-Second-Edition.pdf.
131 See Freshfields Bruckhaus Deringer, "World Bank sanctions investigations: blacklist revisited" (August 2013), www.freshfields.com/uploadedFiles/SiteWide/Knowledge/World%20Bank%20sanctions%20-%20blacklist%20revisted.pdf.
132 *Ibid.*
133 See World Bank Office of Suspension and Debarment report (note 122 above) at 29.
134 Outers, Ryngaert & Cloots, *op cit* (note 104 above) at 214.
135 *Ibid.*

5. Conclusion

Although the level of corruption in sub-Saharan Africa has dropped somewhat in the past decade, corruption remains a major business challenge and poses legal, commercial and reputational risks for multinational oil and gas companies operating in the region.[136] Although FCPA and UK Bribery Act enforcement actions have incentivised many multinational companies to change their behaviour in operating in sub-Saharan Africa, it is clear that these enforcement actions are not enough. Eliminating corruption will require continued effort by the international community through the regional and international anti-corruption initiatives described above. In particular, efforts by the member states of organisations in sub-Saharan Africa and major economic players in the region other than the United States, such as China, will be necessary. As the international community continues to develop and implement anti-corruption initiatives, companies must continue to evolve their understanding of compliance requirements and adapt their controls to the particular risks, business practices and challenges arising in the region.

136 On October 27 2014, the SEC:

> *charged a global water management, construction, and drilling company headquartered in Texas with violating the Foreign Corrupt Practices Act (FCPA) by making improper payments to foreign officials in several African countries in order to obtain beneficial treatment and reduce its tax liability.... According to the SEC's order instituting settled administrative proceedings, Layne's misconduct occurred from 2005 to 2010. In addition to favorable tax treatment, the improper payments helped the company obtain customs clearance, work permits and relief from inspections by immigration and labour officials in various African countries.*

See US SEC press release, "SEC Charges Texas-Based Layne Christensen Company With FCPA Violations" (27 October 2014), www.sec.gov/News/PressRelease/Detail/PressRelease/1370543291857. See also note 16 above.

Disputes in oil and gas M&A transactions

Mark Beeley
Orrick, Herrington & Sutcliffe (UK) LLP

1. Introduction

M&A transactions have always given rise to disputes – whether because one party to the transaction is struck with remorse and tries to avoid the deal it has entered into, or because of arguments that the assets or shares which have been sold are not as promised in some fashion. M&A transactions in the oil and gas sector are no exception – indeed, if anything, there is more scope for dispute, as the inherent uncertainty as to the underlying resources leads to even more temptation (or need) to try to revisit the deal, irrespective of how carefully the contractual documents were drafted and how in-depth the prior due diligence was.

Given the general availability of specific performance where a seller refuses to complete a transaction (presuming a sale of shares in a company or unique underlying assets), claims to force completion are generally rare. However, claims arising from the buyer's failure to complete (perhaps because it cannot find the money or because it has learnt something new which has given it buyer's remorse) are common; as are claims arising post-completion, often with arguments that representations and warranties were breached or over who is responsible for subsequently arising (or late-discovered) liabilities.

This chapter provides an overview and introduction to both the substance of such matters and the mechanisms by which they are typically resolved.

2. Common dispute resolution modalities in oil and gas M&A

Although arbitration remains by far the most common dispute resolution mechanism for general oil and gas-related contracts, three different dispute resolution mechanisms are frequently employed in oil and gas M&A agreements:

- submissions of disputes to a domestic court;
- international arbitration; and
- expert determination.

These three primary mechanisms may be bolstered by other alternative dispute resolution techniques (eg, mandatory meetings of management teams, mediation or conciliation) as part of 'stepped' (or 'tiered') dispute resolution regimes; but collectively they represent the primary routes for disputes to be substantively resolved where a negotiated settlement is not achievable without some formal process. That said, most disputes in this area are normally compromised between the parties long before judgment or an award is in sight.

2.1 Court litigation

It is difficult to generalise as to domestic court litigation processes. What is common in London will be very strange and contrary to practice only 200 miles away in Paris. However, the drivers to submit disputes to a domestic court are largely the same whichever court is chosen. There are typically three:

- First, the court may have direct jurisdiction over the asset being sold. If there is a risk of a purchase of a company not completing, there may be an attraction in ensuring that disputes go to the court where the target company is incorporated, to ensure that the court of that jurisdiction can give a mandatory direction to the relevant corporate registry to register the change in ownership.
- Second, despite recent efforts by institutions to revise rules and encourage early decision making in arbitration, as well as making emergency arbitrators available and similar initiatives, there remains a reluctance among arbitrators to grant summary or default judgment.[1] The courts, on the other hand, generally have a full range of summary disposition powers available to them, allowing for the prompt resolution of disputes which are relatively open and shut, or where one party has chosen not to participate.
- Third, court systems generally offer at least one level of appeal against any ruling. This gives some parties a level of comfort that ultimately the 'right' answer will be reached, which is not always the case in arbitration. The trade-off is a lack of finality and having access to a review mechanism is often second guessed with hindsight, depending on which side of the first-instance determination a party finds itself.

The courts of England and New York tend to be the most frequently selected options. They represent reasonably quick forums with well-understood procedures, respected judges and specialist commercial lists. For matters involving Chinese parties, Hong Kong offers similar charms and enhanced enforcement prospects. The Dubai International Financial Centre Court is increasingly fulfilling a similar function for matters in the Middle East. Other court systems can be selected where there is a particular need for the court to have direct jurisdiction over the assets. Paris and Amsterdam fulfil similar roles in the civil law world, although there is a general preference for common law jurisdictions and regimes in the area of high-stakes transactions, given the perceived certainty (or predictability) that these offer.

This tension between the need for control/power over (i) the subject matter of the transaction and (ii) the parties to the agreement can sometimes be met by submission to the jurisdiction of particular courts on a non-exclusive basis. This can provide flexibility and multiple potential forums which can be selected from when a dispute arises, but may also give rise to 'races to the courthouse' and the tactical commencement of multiple proceedings.

Whether the decision is taken to have exclusive or non-exclusive submission to

---

1 Typically, for fear of giving rise to a challenge for having denied a party a reasonable or full opportunity to present its case.

the jurisdiction of a particular court, care should be taken to ensure that the chosen court will actually exercise that jurisdiction. If a party is not domiciled in the jurisdiction, strong consideration should be given to requiring process agents within the court's jurisdiction to ensure that no delays or uncertainties arise from the need to convince a court to exercise jurisdiction over a foreign party at what may be a crucial time.

A submission to the court is normally a relatively straightforward piece of boilerplate. An example for submission to the English court follows:

The courts of England and Wales have exclusive jurisdiction to settle any dispute arising out of or in connection with this Agreement (including a dispute regarding the existence, validity or termination of this Agreement).

2.2 Arbitration

While the old refrain that arbitration is 'cheaper, quicker and confidential' may no longer hold true in most respects, it remains a popular choice for agreements involving the oil and gas sector. It represents a reliable means of keeping parties out of courts which may not be as neutral, efficient or reliable as the parties would like. It also offers an end product which is effectively enforceable globally under the auspices of the New York Convention.[2] While a domestic court judgment of the English courts may be enforced across the European Union[3] and with some certainty in the fellow common law jurisdictions, it has nothing like the reach of a New York Convention-compliant arbitral award – which is enforceable under a standardised regime in 157 countries.[4]

Popular juridical seats of arbitration for disputes in this sector include London, Paris, New York, Hong Kong, Singapore, Stockholm and Dubai.[5] However, this list is by no means exhaustive or curtailing, and a plethora of arbitration bodies now exist in every region. Similarly, a wide range of arbitration rules and institutions to administer them are available to parties. For disputes of this nature, however, the LCIA[6] and the International Chamber of Commerce (ICC) International Court of Arbitration tend to be the most popular. By way of example, the LCIA's 2016 annual report showed that a little over one-fifth of all arbitrations commenced under its rules that year involved the energy sector, with a similar percentage of disputes (viewed across all sectors) involving sale and purchase-type agreements.

Arbitration agreements in these types of contract range from the basic clauses recommended by the institutions to highly bespoke arrangements. Common features include:

- prescriptive qualifications that the future arbitrators must possess;
- time limits for the rendering of awards; and
- express contemplation of the mechanisms by which emergency relief can be given.

---

2 The New York Convention on the Recognition and Enforcement of Foreign Arbitral Awards 1958.
3 Although there is obvious future uncertainty as to the position post Brexit.
4 As at the end of November 2017.
5 Both under the 'onshore' federal regime and 'offshore' in the Dubai International Financial Centre.
6 Formerly known as the London Court of International Arbitration.

An example of an arbitration clause at its (near-) simplest follows, being the LCIA's own standard form arbitration clause:

Any dispute arising out of or in connection with this contract, including any question regarding its existence, validity or termination, shall be referred to and finally resolved by arbitration under the LCIA Rules, which Rules are deemed to be incorporated by reference into this clause. The number of arbitrators shall be [one/three]. The seat, or legal place, of arbitration shall be [City and/or Country]. The language to be used in the arbitral proceedings shall be [ ].[7]

However, there is no inherent jurisdiction in any arbitration tribunal and accordingly it can be wise to take the time to specify the powers and procedures of the tribunal, either through the deliberate choice of the rules of an arbitral institution or through the designing of a bespoke scheme. The choice of juridical seat can also have a significant impact on the working of any arbitration.

Unlike court submission clauses, arbitration agreements are increasingly not a matter of boilerplate and significant future wasted costs can be incurred if they are not tailored to the circumstances at hand.

2.3 Expert determination

Expert determination has been described as "a means by which the parties to a contract jointly instruct a third party to decide an issue between them".[8] In such terms, it sounds very much like arbitration, but the reality is quite different. The expert (who will normally not be a lawyer, but rather an accountant or perhaps a reservoir engineer or investment banker) typically delivers his determination in 30 or perhaps 60 days, need not afford the parties every opportunity to make submissions, typically need not give reasons and is employed to take as rough and ready a view as the situation may call for. Typically, absent fraud or a clear departure from the expert's instructions, the resulting determination cannot be appealed and is treated thereafter as a binding part of the contract. Like a classic commodities 'look/sniff' arbitration, it is rough and ready justice, but one to which parties are subject only where they have decided (either at the time or in advance) that such an approach is appropriate for an issue – often driven by a decision either that a matter financially does not justify the full expense and theatre of the court or arbitration, or that a genuinely industry and experience-driven view is required (eg, the replacement of a discontinued index as part of a gas sales pricing mechanism).

Expert determination is very much a feature of the common law world, although many Western European legal systems have equivalent concepts. Large swathes of the world (eg, South America and China) do not recognise the concept, though, so care should be taken to ensure that expert determination is recognised under the selected substantive law of any contract. If there is any uncertainty, either change the substantive law or ensure that a particularly detailed contractual scheme is expressly included, backed up by recourse to arbitration in the event of any dispute.

---

7 As found on 27 December 2017 at www.lcia.org/Dispute_Resolution_Services/LCIA_Recommended_Clauses.aspx.

8 Kendal, Freedman & Farrell, *Expert Determination*, 4th ed, para 1.1.1.

In relation to oil and gas M&A transactions, expert determinations are most commonly used in two contexts – both within the broad church of post-closing price adjustments. As with general M&A, it is by no means uncommon for disputes as to the proper accounting of assets (eg, closing date balances) to be resolved by way of expert determination, with the expert normally being an accountant. Similarly, price adjustments keyed to reserve estimates often call for reservoir engineers to make binding determinations.

Expert determination clauses are particularly contract-specific creatures, varying with the nature of the contemplated dispute and the supporting governing law. However, arbitration bodies such as the LCIA and the ICC (in addition to ever-obliging law firms) are increasingly willing to assist with such processes, and both offer model clauses which may at least serve as starting points for unfamiliar draftspersons.

2.4 Unexpected hitches

Of course, the best-laid plans of mice and men often go awry. While the parties to a particular transaction can carefully legislate the forum in which they wish their disputes to be resolved, such agreements do not (normally) bind third parties that may seek to intervene in the transaction for their own purposes. Sudden juxtapositions can arise, with a third party suing in the courts to stop the transaction closing or with a buyer seeking relief from an arbitral tribunal to force the seller to close regardless. Conflicting results and mismatches in achievable speed may be unfortunate realities in such circumstances. There can be considerable advantage in being the first mover in such a scenario.

3. Common disputes in oil and gas M&A

Ultimately, disputes in oil and gas M&A transactions (as opposed to operations) are contractual matters – with the exception of accusations of tortious misrepresentation, tortious interference and/or fraud. Accordingly, they are for the most part not unique. All too often, the question is whether what was sold was what was promised or whether required payments have been made. That said, certain scenarios do repeatedly arise which raise issues with a particular oil and gas industry flavour. Some of these are reviewed below.

3.1 Pre-emption/right of first refusal

A common feature of joint operating agreements (JOAs) is a pre-emption or right of first refusal clause. At its simplest, it provides that if a JOA party is to sell its interest to a third party, then the other JOA partners have a right to pre-empt the sale on equivalent terms. On one level, the seller might not care – it will be getting rid of its interest in any event and should be getting paid at the same level. However, all too often, assets form part of larger deals, meaning that the exercise of a pre-emption right in one JOA can cause the wider package deal to fall apart.

Canny sellers therefore engage in sophisticated structuring to seek to create deals which are not pre-emptable. Common tactics include:

- structuring the sale at the company rather than asset level (relying on the fact that many pre-emption clauses of years past dealt only with sales of the underlying asset and not changes of control); and

- structuring deals to include asset swaps rather than simple cash consideration on the basis that it is arguably not possible to offer a matchable consideration.

While there are certainly disputes where genuine rights to pre-empt have been overlooked or overridden, joint venture partners can often view the need to give notice of pre-emption as an opportunity to extract value. Often hard-nosed (or unscrupulous) parties will threaten to pre-empt mischievously, on the assumption that they can extract value as a price for letting the deal go through. Aggressive players will threaten (or indeed seek) injunctions against the underlying transaction, threaten the prospective buyers with lawsuits for tortiously interfering with their contractual rights and assert equitable interests in the property being sold. Assertions of injunctions and constructive trusts can put significant pressure on sellers trying to reach closing before longstop dates. Buyers must either form robust views as to the emptiness of these threats or risk buying assets to which they might not ultimately have title – perhaps leading them to seek additional protection from sellers (whether by indemnity or price adjustment).

3.2 Breach of warranty

As with any sale, breaches of warranty are common issues in oil and gas transactions. This is particularly the case where the underlying business is so uncertain. Given that reserves can only ever be estimated, future oil prices only ever predicted and seismic data only ever interpreted, warranties as to the underlying business can be particularly dangerous to give.

While it may seem an open and shut question as to whether a warranty was true when it was given, disputes may still be found in relation to:

- any warranty which contains any subjective or uncertain element (warranties that conditions would not be 'materially different' are particularly prone to this sort of issue); or
- whether the necessary pre-conditions to a warranty claim are met (frequently, transaction documents contain time limits, claim value thresholds and notice requirements which must all be complied with, and which a defendant that has decided to dig in and fight will no doubt probe for any failure of the claimant to achieve strict compliance with).

Disputes also arise as to whether a claim can be brought where the buyer must have known, or ought to have known, that the warranty was false when it was made (which may or may not affect the ability to rely on the warranty, depending on the governing law). Such arguments then lead to minute examinations as to what may or may not have been found in the pre-signing data room and due diligence (presuming that copies of the same still exist or are reconstructable), and often strained interpretations of vague line items in disclosure letters.

Of course, beyond questions of liability, further disputes will often arise as to the value of the loss consequent on the breach of warranty. This issue involves the normal questions of causation and remoteness, but is often complicated by contractual exclusions of certain kinds of loss, exclusive remedy clauses and imprecise usage of terms such as 'consequential loss'. English law, at least, has seen a much more literal interpretation of such exclusions in the last few years than the many decades of prior case law might suggest.

3.3 Breach of standstill/non-circumvention agreement

The documents which support the due diligence ahead of transactions can also give rise to claims. Confidentiality agreements allowing access to data rooms commonly contain various forms of restrictions. So-called 'standstills' prevent potential purchasers from using the data relating to the target field to evaluate other similarly situated fields. Interim joint bidding or partnering agreements contain non-circumvention agreements, preventing partners from cutting each other out of the deal.

Much like violations of pre-emption clauses, these sorts of disputes give rise to the threat of injunctions, subsequent damages and, in rare cases, issues of constructive trusts and similar constructs. Such disputes are also ripe for accusations of tortious interference against an involved third party.

Where parties fail to obtain injunctions to prevent the apprehended transaction closing, claims for damages remain. However, the calculation of damages and proving of an actual loss can be particularly problematic in such circumstances (what is the value to you of stopping someone else buying an asset which you were not going to buy yourself?), requiring recourse to mechanisms such as 'hypothetical bargain'/'negotiating' damages.

3.4 Post-closing adjustments

It is not uncommon for elements of the purchase price to remain uncertain even at the point of closing. This is particularly the case where exploration activities are still ongoing on fields and there is genuine uncertainty around the levels of hydrocarbon reserves that will ultimately be proven. Where the price has been based around the level of reserves, it is not uncommon for mechanisms (normally in the form of modified expert determinations) to come into play where those reserves are revalued at certain subsequent points – normally with two reserve estimates being contemporaneously prepared and either mid-points being taken or a further report (from a third expert) being provided for to break any deadlocks. Such matters inevitably lead to further disputes, with accusations of biased reports being submitted, misleading information being provided or mistaken approaches being taken to the underlying data.

3.5 Tax claims

Tax claims tend to present as:

- breaches of warranty (eg, a statement as to the existing tax position of the target company proves to be false);
- claims for indemnification for disclosed or undisclosed tax claims raised

against the target company which are subject to a 'your watch/my watch' indemnification regime; and

- disputes in relation to the taxes which arise from the transaction itself – particularly where one or both parties have made an assumption as to how the relevant authorities will treat the sale and purchase, and that assumption proves to be false. This final category has given rise to significant claims in recent years, particularly where the transaction touches on developing markets. Both India and China have provided examples of sales of offshore companies which ultimately hold hydrocarbon assets in-country, where the host government has made the decision (whether backed by then-existing legislation or otherwise) to levy tax on the sale as though it had been an in-country sale of assets.

Such disputes tend to involve wars on multiple fronts. Not only will the buyer and the seller seek to claim indemnification from each other and argue as to on whose watch the unforeseen tax liability arose, but there will also typically be litigation before the domestic tax tribunal and perhaps international arbitration brought against the host state under an investment agreement, a bilateral investment treaty or a multilateral investment treaty (eg, the Energy Charter Treaty).

3.6 Bribery and corruption issues

Bribery and corruption are increasingly topical matters, with the advent of the United Kingdom's Bribery Act 2010 on top of the long-existing US Foreign Corrupt Practices Act leading to a surge in pre-transaction due diligence and supporting warranties and indemnitees.

While on one level this might simply be thought of as another risk which a warranty or indemnity might cover, the nature of this risk raises serious questions as to the extent to which the buyer of a target company might be protected from a criminal liability which it has now inherited. Given the size of the potential fines where the enforcement authorities pursue cases and the costs of defending against any investigation, serious consideration must be given to the question of whether an indemnity against prior wrongful conduct of the target company will be enforced under the relevant governing law, or whether there is a viable argument that a party cannot be indemnified for a criminal wrong. Further complications arise given the near-universal trend for accused corporations to reach settlements rather than try enforcement actions – does the indemnity stretch to voluntary settlements? What is reasonable and prudent conduct of an indemnitee in such circumstances, where the risk of losing even a mistaken suit can destroy the company – not to mention the attendant reputational damage given the almost universally public nature of these processes?

Further issues arise where buyers encounter material in pre-acquisition due diligence suggesting that corrupt activity might be present in a target company (eg, the payment of bribes to win business). Under many regulatory regimes, there is a duty on the involved lawyers to make disclosures to the relevant authorities in such circumstances (ie, where there is a suspicion of money laundering – being the dealing in the proceeds of a criminal act). Such disclosures typically must be made secretly and the transaction may not proceed unless clearance is given – although the seller cannot be 'tipped off' that a report has been made. The tension between being unable to progress the transaction and being unable to tell the seller why can cause particular problems where an issue is identified late in the day.

3.7 Overriding royalty interests

It is not uncommon for a party which is exiting an oil and gas asset to retain an 'overriding royalty interest' as part of the consideration. This is often expressed as a right to receive a monetary payment equivalent to a certain percentage of the production from the field that was sold. Such rights frequently give rise to subsequent litigation over how the exact percentage is calculated (eg, as to whether the costs of transporting the oil to the offtake point can be deducted from the amount of production being assessed). Parties will seize on any ambiguity to argue for a narrow (or expansive, depending on which foot the shoe is on) definition.

This is an area where the choice of substantive law may be key. By way of example, Texas law has a rich body of cases construing such interests and a series of 'default' presumptions which will apply in construing any grant. However, that substantive law has grown out of the broader context of Texas law considering such matters as the grant of a property right. In other jurisdictions, where the producing party never has direct title to the hydrocarbons being produced, applying the Texas common law rules may produce some surprising results. By way of contrast, English law does not have a similar body of detailed jurisprudence concerning such interests and the overriding royalty agreement will be construed using the standard rules of interpretation which would apply to any contract.

4. Conclusion

Oil and gas transactions are not unique from other M&A transactions in giving rise to potential disputes. However, given the sums involved, those disputes are probably more likely than not worth pursuing, despite the ever-increasing cost of modern litigation and arbitration. The issues involved frequently touch on multiple jurisdictions and legal systems, and frequently run the risk of third-party intervention – whether from the host state, a rival bidder or a joint venture partner. Accordingly, this is a field that particularly requires draftspersons and advisers to treat the dispute resolution clause as something other than boilerplate which need not be given particular attention in the drafting and negotiating process. Significant value can be protected if there is a comprehensive, joined-up dispute resolution regime, which has been specifically crafted with the individual parties and bearing the relevant assets (and likely potential disputes) in mind.

Where disputes do arise, the party which is best prepared tends to have the upper hand. A comprehensive and certain record of what was in the data room (and, in the days of e-data rooms, of who accessed which documents) will be a key part of any warranty claim. Scrupulous compliance with time limits, notification requirements and the like will avoid indemnity claims being lost through 'foot faults'. Knowledge of the other side's timetable and financial pressure points will assist any party asserting a right of first refusal with a view to extracting value; as will an awareness that typically, such disputes end in settlement rather than through the ruling of the judge. Post-closing disputes are normally post-closing adjustments by another name. Pre-closing disputes can lead to the collapse of the entire transaction, however, whether through a legal interdiction or the issues simply becoming too awkward or risky to commercially stomach. *Caveat venditor et emptor*?

Financial and tax due diligence

Chris Searle
BDO LLP

1. Introduction

Although it is unlikely to be a regulatory requirement even for public companies, it is considered best practice for acquirers – whether public or private – to commission an accounting firm to undertake financial and tax due diligence on a target company or business once the heads of terms have been agreed between the seller and the acquirer. The rationale for such due diligence is to provide comfort to the acquirer that there are no issues in the target's finances, accounts or tax affairs that might cause the acquirer either to terminate the acquisition or to renegotiate the purchase price downwards. Ultimately, it is up to the acquirer to decide whether to proceed with the acquisition and at what price, and the financial and tax due diligence is an important part of this decision-making process. The role that the accountant plays in undertaking such work is that of the 'investigating accountant'.

Because financial and tax due diligence is essentially discretionary, the scope of such work can be as wide or as narrow as the acquirer sees fit. A narrow scope is more likely if the target is a small, early-stage exploration company, while a fuller scope is more likely for a larger company that is in production. In addition, if the acquirer has significant knowledge of the target and/or has itself undertaken preliminary due diligence prior to making its offer, this is likely to reduce the scope of the financial and tax due diligence undertaken by the investigating accountant.

2. Summary of a full-scope financial and tax due diligence exercise

Set out below is a summary of a full-scope financial and tax due diligence exercise (an actual scope that would form part of the investigating accountant's engagement letter is set out at the end of this chapter).

2.1 History and commercial activities

This section of the financial due diligence exercise provides the acquirer with a review of the key drivers of the target's business, how it generates its revenue and to whom production is sold. It briefly summarises the history of the target and sets out its legal structure. It reviews how the business operates, summarises the stage of development of the target's oil and gas assets, and identifies the target's customers (if it is producing and selling oil and gas), including whether there is a dependence on a small number of customers. It reviews the financial aspects of any contracts with customers and with joint venture partners, and arrangements such as production sharing agreements and other agreements with host country governments. It also identifies the key suppliers and whether there are any alternatives to these key suppliers.

However, frequently in M&A transactions, the acquirer already possesses a significant amount of knowledge of the target prior to commissioning financial due diligence. As a result, the acquirer may consider that there is no need for the investigating accountant to include this section in its scope.

2.2 Management and personnel

This section identifies the key members of the target's management team, assesses whether there are any gaps within the team and summarises the terms and conditions of employment. It also assesses matters such as the rate of staff turnover and union representation.

The work undertaken in this respect will reveal any gaps in the target's management team that may need to be filled after completion and whether there is a succession plan in place for senior management approaching retirement. It also enables the acquirer to assess any differences between the terms and conditions of employment of its staff and of the target's staff that may have to be aligned after completion. In addition, should the acquirer be contemplating a reduction in the target's headcount, the information generated from this work is a useful starting point for calculating the cost of such an exercise.

Whether the acquirer includes this section in the investigating accountant's scope will depend on its prior knowledge of these matters.

2.3 Historical trading results

This section summarises the trading results shown in the financial statements for the last three completed financial years and explains trends in the income statement covering revenue, cost of sales and overheads. The investigating accountant will identify any exceptional factors affecting the results in any of the years, such as an impairment of an asset, in order to assess the true underlying profitability of the target. The investigating accountant will also assess whether seasonal factors affect the business. For example, drilling may not be possible in some areas in the rainy season and this will affect revenue and costs in these months. If the target is part of a larger group, the investigating accountant should identify the services provided by the larger group to the target and whether the cost is on an arm's-length basis. Either such services must be provided by the acquirer following completion or the acquirer will have to enter into an arrangement with the seller to provide these services for a time after completion.

If the financial statements of the target have been audited, a higher degree of confidence can be placed in them by the investigating accountant than if they have not been audited. The investigating accountant should point out to the acquirer in its report if the financial statements have not been audited and the elevated level of risk that the results might be misstated.

2.4 Current trading results

For the period in the current financial year to date, the investigating accountant will review the actual results in the income statement shown in the management accounts and compare them with the budget for this period and with the actual results in the corresponding period in the previous year. The comparison to budget and to the corresponding period in the prior year is useful in assessing the likely outcome for the current year as a whole that is undertaken in the review of the target's projections (see below).

2.5 Historical and current balance sheets

The investigating accountant will review each caption in the balance sheet at each year-end for the last three completed financial years and at the latest management accounts date, explaining what is in each category of asset and liability and the movements between the balance-sheet dates. In essence, this review is designed to provide comfort that assets in the balance sheet are not overstated or liabilities understated.

2.6 Historical cash flows

The investigating accountant will review the cash-flow statements for the last three financial years, preferably on a monthly basis, to assess seasonal trends in cash flow, seeking to explain the sources and uses of cash.

2.7 Accounting policy review

The investigating accountant will review the accounting policies disclosed in the target's financial statements in order to identify and assess material differences with the policies of the acquirer. There may be some undisclosed accounting policies that need to be identified and explained, most commonly on revenue recognition.

2.8 Accounting systems and controls

The investigating accountant will review the accounting and internal control system of the target to ensure that it can provide robust, timely and reliable management accounts, and that there are reasonable controls, especially over purchasing and cash payments. Improvements should be suggested where necessary.

2.9 Projections

The investigating accountant will review the target's projections or budget for the remainder of the current financial year and possibly the next financial year (if the latter have been prepared), in order to provide the acquirer with a view on whether the budgeted results are likely to be achieved, having regard to the results achieved in the current year to date reviewed under "Current trading".

2.10 Taxation

The investigating accountant will review the corporate tax, sales tax and payroll tax affairs of the target to provide comfort to the acquirer that the target's tax affairs are in order, and that there are no liabilities not disclosed in the target's financial statements. An exploration company is likely to possess tax losses and the investigating accountant should advise the acquirer on the best way that these can be preserved, since many jurisdictions have rules that can put such losses at risk after a change of control in the target.

3. Financial and tax due diligence process

3.1 Agree scope

The first step is for the acquirer and the investigating accountant to agree the scope of the financial and tax due diligence exercise. The best way to do this is for the investigating accountant to send the acquirer a standard full scope, as summarised above and as shown at the end of this chapter, and then meet to go through the scope, deleting items that are of no interest to the acquirer and adding items which are of interest, but which are not within the scope. The acquirer is likely to have had access to information on the target and perhaps to have undertaken some preliminary financial and tax due diligence itself. It may also be familiar with the business of the target. Such initial work and familiarity will help to inform agreement on the scope of the financial and tax due diligence.

3.2 Agree terms of engagement

Having agreed the scope, the investigating accountant will prepare an engagement letter addressed to the acquirer. The agreed scope will be attached to the letter as an appendix. The engagement letter will set out various matters, including fee arrangements for the agreed work and a cap on the accountant's liability for the work.

3.3 Determine level of access to target

From the investigating accountant's perspective, the ideal situation is to have full access to the target's head office, and other premises in the case of a larger group, so that the due diligence investigation can be carried out on site with unrestricted access to the target's management. There may be issues of confidentiality, in terms of the target's management wishing to keep the sale secret from employees; but there are ways in which this can be overcome – for example, by the investigating accountants adopting the guise of doing their work in connection with a bank financing the target.

However, increasingly nowadays, more sophisticated sellers and their advisers are running sale processes as auctions in order to maximise the price obtained for the target by keeping more than one bidder interested for as long as possible before granting exclusivity to one potential acquirer. Information is made available to acquirers and their advisers through an online data room. The seller will provide access to the online data to the various potential acquirers and their advisers. In this situation, there is likely to be limited access to the target.

3.4 Issue information request list to target

The investigating accountant will prepare an information request list based on the scope that has been agreed with the acquirer, which is then submitted to the target. If the due diligence work can be undertaken at the target's premises, the information can be collated there and made available to the investigating accountant.

In the case of an online data room, a set of information will be made available to all bidders. This will not necessarily accord with the information request list compiled by the investigating accountant, in which case the latter will upload questions and requests for further information into the online data room.

3.5 Fieldwork

Once information is made available by the target, the investigating accountant will commence fieldwork. This will involve analysing information provided and generating questions to be answered by the target's management. The fieldwork will run more smoothly if it is conducted on the target's premises because regular meetings can be held with the management team. The process is a little more problematic if it is being run via an online data room, since there will be a delay between questions being submitted and answers provided.

As the fieldwork progresses, the due diligence report will be drafted. Once the scope has been covered to the satisfaction of the team undertaking the fieldwork, the report will pass through the investigating accountant's quality control process, involving review by the senior team members. Once this has been done, it is best practice for a draft of the report, excluding the executive summary, to be sent to the target's management team, so that it can correct any factual inaccuracies that often occur during the fieldwork phase. For example, the management team may have misunderstood a question posed by the investigating accountant or the latter may have misunderstood an explanation provided by the former.

Once a meeting has been held between the investigating accountant and the target's management team to go through the latter's comments, the corrected report can be provided to the acquirer and a meeting held between the acquirer and the investigating accountant to discuss the report. A requirement for additional work may arise from this meeting. Once the report has been completed to the acquirer's satisfaction, it is ready to be signed by the investigating accountant.

3.6 Deal breakers

If, during the course of the fieldwork, the investigating accountant discovers an issue that is of such materiality that it may cause the acquirer to withdraw from the transaction or renegotiate the offer price, the investigating accountant should notify the acquirer immediately, rather than waiting for the acquirer to find out about the issue when it reads the due diligence report. In this way, the acquirer can decide whether to abort the acquisition or stop further due diligence work pending renegotiation of the purchase price.

3.7 Vendor due diligence

In recent years, vendor due diligence has become increasingly common in M&A transactions. In this process, the seller commissions and pays an investigating accountant to prepare a due diligence report on the target. The scope is similar to that outlined above. The advantage that vendor due diligence gives the seller is that it allows an auction process to be run to a later stage of the transaction before exclusivity is granted, thus in theory maximising the purchase price. The disadvantage to the acquirer is that there is always a suspicion that the investigating accountant preparing the vendor due diligence report has not been as rigorous in its analysis as an investigating accountant undertaking due diligence for an acquirer. In any event, by the time that an acquirer has been granted exclusivity, the draft vendor due diligence report is likely to need updating – certainly in respect of current trading – and it is considered best practice for an acquirer to appoint an investigating accountant to review the vendor due diligence report and to undertake 'top-up' due diligence on matters such as the latest management accounts.

3.8 Audit file review

If the financial statements of the target have been audited, the investigating accountant should ask to review the audit files for the last three years. This review can be a useful source of information (eg, analyses of balances in the financial statements), but should also reveal any weaknesses in the accounting and systems of the target, hopefully reported in a management letter. The audit files will also disclose adjustments to the year-end management accounts identified by the auditors. The quantum and nature of these provide a good guide to the reliability of the management accounts.

3.9 Review of sale and purchase agreement and completion mechanisms

Once the due diligence has been completed, the acquirer's accountants are frequently asked by the acquirer to review the accounting aspects of the sale and purchase agreement regarding the completion mechanics. Historically, it was usual for a set of completion accounts to be prepared and reviewed or audited. However, in recent years the use of a 'locked box' has become increasingly common. This method is described below.

Completion accounts are prepared as at the date of completion, usually by the acquirer, using a set of accounting policies specified in the sale and purchase agreement, and are then reviewed by the seller's accountants. The acquirer will seek to minimise the value of the net assets, since this should trigger a reduction in the purchase price for the acquisition; whereas the seller will seek to maximise the value of the net assets, since this will increase the price. Arguments over the accounts can last for many months and can even go to expert determination by a third-party accountant if the parties cannot agree.

In contrast, the date of the locked box is set some time before completion of the transaction at an actual recent balance-sheet date and the bidders use this balance sheet to set their price. The eventual acquirer takes the economic interest in the target from this locked box date (ie, before it legally owns the target). The sale and purchase agreement ensures that the seller does not remove any value, other than as set out in the sale and purchase agreement, from the target between the locked box date and the actual date of completion. This is known as 'leakage'. The seller will be paid an agreed 'day rate' between the locked box date and the actual completion date to compensate it for forgoing the economic interest in the target from the locked box date. The main advantage of a locked box is that it removes the need for completion accounts and the lengthy arguments that can sometimes ensue between the seller, the acquirer and their respective accountants over the completion accounts.

3.10 Post-acquisition due diligence

Once the transaction has completed, some acquirers may request their accountants to undertake some form of post-acquisition due diligence on the target in order to assist the acquirer's integration plans or help to identify which assets the acquirer retains and which it sells.

Appendix I: Scope of pre-acquisition due diligence report

Introduction

This section will contain an introduction to the report, including:

- our terms of reference;
- scope of the work, including any limitations;
- basis of information within the report;
- verification of factual accuracy; and
- access to key personnel.

Summary of findings

A concise summary of the contents of the report and the principal findings arising from our work.

History and commercial activities

A brief description of the history and development of the business and its current operation:

- Details of the legal structure of the business and its ownership.
- The business's current strategies with reference to the latest business plan or corporate brochures.
- A summary history of the business, including key events in its development.
- A description of the following areas:
    - activities and products or services, including new products or services which have been recently introduced or are planned;
    - customers and marketing, including terms of trade with customers, contracts with customers, pricing policy, gross margins, details of sales and marketing operations, marketing strategy, distribution channels, guarantees and warranty terms, quality policy; and
    - suppliers and production, including extent of reliance on key suppliers, contracts and terms of trade with suppliers.
- A description of the business locations, including the nature of tenure.
- Details of any legal agreements or actions affecting the group.

Organisation structure and employees

Details of the management structure and senior managers, together with the key characteristics of the workforce, highlighting strengths, weaknesses and constraining factors:

- A description of the management and reporting structure of the business.
- Details of the management and senior employees of the business, covering

their roles, experience and terms of employment, including remuneration package, length of service and service contracts.

- Identification of key personnel and succession plans.
- Details for other employees of:
  - current staffing levels in each area of operation and any proposed changes, details of staff turnover rates and any difficulties in recruitment;
  - salary/wage structure, terms of employment including holidays, pensions and other benefits, notice period etc;
  - dates of salary/wage reviews and current status of such;
  - details of profit sharing and bonus schemes;
  - recruitment and training policies; and
  - the extent of unionisation and commentary on any major disputes arising during the historical period (as defined below) and staff relations in general.
- Identification of any important relationships with outside contractors and professional advisers and the extent of the business's reliance upon them.
- Summary of pension schemes.

Historical trading results

Explanation and commentary on the significant factors behind the reported trading results for recent years and any exceptional or non-recurring items which have had a material impact:

- A summary of the historical results of the business covering the latest available three completed financial years (the 'historical period').
- An explanation of the major fluctuations in turnover and profits during the historical period, to identify seasonality and industry trends.
- An analysis of turnover by product/service, geographical markets and major customers for the historical period.
- A breakdown of gross profit analysed by each main activity for the historical period, together with an explanation as to significant variations.
- An analysis of overhead expenses, together with comments on significant fluctuations.
- A summary of intra-group trading and any related-party transactions.
- An explanation of, and comments on, trends disclosed by the results, to include relevant notes of any exceptional profits or losses and any other significant contributory factors.

Assets and liabilities

Commentary on the assets and liabilities of the business and, in particular, valuation bases and the basis of recognising liabilities:

- A summary of the balance sheets of the business during the historical period and at the latest management accounts date.
- A commentary on, and analysis of, the principal balance-sheet items, including:
  - non-current assets, to include an analysis of the net book value of fixed

assets by category, a commentary on capitalisation, revaluation and depreciation policies and details of capital expenditure, current capital commitments and any grants received;
- inventory, to include the basis of valuation, method of provisioning and stock turnover;
- accounts receivable, to include the basis of bad debt provisioning and bad debt history, ageing of debtors, debtor days and commentary on the adequacy or otherwise of the bad debt and credit note provisions;
- accounts payable, to include hire purchase/finance lease commitments, details of accruals and deferred income;
- details of bank facilities and security provided, and details of any penalty clauses included in the facilities agreement for withdrawing from such arrangements;
- details of any off-balance sheet financing;
- provisions for liabilities and charges, to include deferred taxation, the basis of providing for warranty costs and recent claims history; and
- details of any contingent liabilities.

Cash flows

A summary of recent cash-flow patterns and the significant factors affecting cash flow:

- A summary of the cash-flow statements of the business during the historical period.
- An analysis of the cash-flow statements and major cash-flow movements, including appropriate commentary thereon.
- Details of any seasonality in cash flow.

Current trading

Commentary on trading results for the period since the last completed financial period:

- A commentary on, and analysis of, the results shown by the latest management accounts, comparing them with budgeted results for the period and actual results for the corresponding period in the previous financial year.

Financial projections

Commentary on management's trading and cash-flow projections, the method of their compilation and key underlying assumptions, with particular reference to their relationship with current trading levels:

- A summary of the profit and cash-flow projections of the business.
- The procedures adopted in preparing the financial projections.
- A comparison of the opening balance sheet in the projections to the latest management accounts.
- A commentary on the assumptions material to the financial projections.
- A summary of the available bank facilities throughout the period of projections, commenting on the available headroom between the projected net funds/debt and facilities.

- A description of any financial covenants in the facility agreements and comments on the group's ability to comply with the covenants on the basis of the projections.
- The sensitivity of the projections to changes in key assumptions, together with any mitigating actions/factors.

Taxation

Details of the current status of the tax affairs of the business:

- A summary of the tax affairs of the company, including a commentary on the following:
    - the most recent corporation tax computations for which either:
- an agreed assessment has not yet been issued;
        - the period permitted under corporation tax self-assessment for Her Majesty's Revenue & Customs to raise enquiries has not yet ended; or
        - a notice of closure in respect of a corporation tax self-assessment enquiry has not yet been issued;
    - the effective rate of taxation;
    - provisions for corporate and deferred taxes;
    - tax losses, if any, and their likely future offset;
    - the results of the last VAT inspection;
    - the results of the last PAYE/NIC inspection; and
    - a commentary on any recent reconstructions, reorganisations and tax clearance applications.

Accounting policies and audit issues

Commentary on the acceptability of key accounting policies and practices:

- A commentary on the accounting policies adopted by the business and their detailed implementation, including compliance with [UK generally accepted accounting principles/International Financial Reporting Standards].
- Details of any changes in policy during the historical period.
- Identification of accounting policies that differ from those of the company and an assessment of the impact of restating the target's results using the company's policies.
- Details of the policy adopted in respect of the recognition of turnover and any other undisclosed policies and practices.
- Any control weaknesses identified in management letters and any adjustments made to management accounts to arrive at year-end audited accounts.

Management information and internal control

An overview of the substance and adequacy of management information and internal controls:

- A commentary on key management information prepared by the business.
- A commentary on responsibilities within the finance function.
- Details of the key internal controls operated by the business and the

frequency, basis of preparation and reliability of management accounts, including the reasonableness of any general assumptions made in their preparation.

- A brief overview of the accounting and operational computer systems used by the business, including, as appropriate:
  - hardware and operating systems;
  - software, commenting on the extent of bespoke software;
  - redundancy and robustness;
  - service, support and upgrade arrangements and contracts; and
  - disaster recovery and backup procedures.

To the extent that the above procedure identifies systems weaknesses or other issues, we will discuss with you the scope of any additional work that may be appropriate.

The views expressed in this chapter are the author's own, not those of BDO LLP.

Due diligence and warranties

Marc Hammerson
Caroline-Lucy Moran
Akin Gump Strauss Hauer & Feld LLP

1. Introduction

1.1 Reasons for due diligence and warranties

In a book focused on M&A, it is worth noting one view of the outcome of such activity: acquisitions too often produce disappointing results for buyers. Transactions fail to generate value. One study by the National Bureau of Economic Research calculates that $226 billion of shareholder wealth has been lost as a result of M&A over a 20-year period.[1] Post-acquisition write-downs are not uncommon.

This negative view is not universally held and the success or otherwise of a transaction for a buyer will depend on unique aspects of the deal. Nonetheless, the study serves as a reminder of the purpose of the techniques discussed below. This chapter focuses on two methods (one contractual, the other pre-contractual) intended to ensure that buyers realise the value anticipated from acquisitions.

Due diligence and warranties are different methods intended to achieve this goal. They complement and inform each other. Nearly all transactions – to varying extents – contain elements of both. Due diligence is the initial step in the buyer's information-gathering exercise. However, the subsequent negotiation of warranties (and the related seller disclosure process) often generates further information that assists the buyer's assessment of the transaction.

Each practice is designed to protect buyers.[2] They are required, in part, as a result of the principle of *caveat emptor* (let the buyer beware). This provides that, other than egregious behaviour (eg, fraud, undue influence, unconscionable conduct or misrepresentation),[3] English law does not (except for breach of express contractual terms) protect a buyer from an unsatisfactory outcome. In order to seek compensation, provisions must be included in the sale and purchase agreement (SPA). If the target assets or target company[4] turn out to be different from that

1 NBER working paper 9523 (March 2003), "Do shareholders of acquiring firms gain from acquisitions?" (a sample of 12,023 acquisitions of public companies between 1980 to 2001). This study is not specific to the petroleum industry.

2 Warranties are also given by a buyer in favour of a seller. These are generally not extensive and less industry-specific. The purpose of this chapter is to consider warranties given by a seller and relied on by a buyer. Furthermore, this chapter does not discuss vendor due diligence (the practice whereby a seller commissions a due diligence report and allows the successful bidder to rely on it).

3 The first three remedies are difficult to establish in law. Misrepresentation is the easiest claim to prove. However, SPAs often include a 'complete agreement' clause, preventing a party from relying on information other than warranties contained in the SPA.

4 In this chapter both possibilities are referred to as the target.

expected, the buyer will generally need to look to the express terms of the SPA for a remedy. Because of this non-interventionist approach, market practice has developed standard warranties and a due diligence process providing safeguards. The discussion below covers both.

The degree of protection sought varies between deals and depends on the parties' negotiating strength. The investigations undertaken, and warranties provided, will also be particular to the target. It is not possible to produce an exhaustive checklist of relevant subject areas. Instead, this chapter discusses selected issues common to the petroleum industry in the context of due diligence and warranties.

1.2 Share versus asset acquisitions

The discussion covers both share and asset transactions. Asset acquisitions in the petroleum industry take several different forms (including purchases, swaps and farm-ins). Where a buyer acquires its interest through an asset-level transaction the relevant warranty or due diligence issue arises directly. In a share purchase it is shares (rather than petroleum interests) which are being acquired and therefore the due diligence or warranty issue arises indirectly through the target company's ownership of the assets. The same analysis applies to each type of agreement.

1.3 What is due diligence?

Pre-acquisition due diligence is performed by a buyer and its advisers at the start of negotiations.[5] It is a process whereby a buyer investigates the books, records and agreements of a target and puts questions to management. In an upstream petroleum transaction, this also includes geological and geophysical data. The information prepared by the seller for the buyer's due diligence process is accessed by the buyer in a data room. In modern practice, this is more likely to be a secure website than a physical location although, for petroleum transactions, technical data is still often made available separately in hard copy.

By such investigations the buyer assesses the target, identifying risks, liabilities and notable issues, in particular for valuation purposes. Due diligence may result in the buyer deciding not to proceed with the transaction. If the buyer chooses to go ahead, due diligence findings influence both the purchase price and the buyer's negotiation of the SPA (including, in particular, indemnities and warranties). If a buyer cannot reflect the results of its due diligence in drafting the SPA (as a result, for example, of a competitive bidding process in which amendments are not permitted), the exercise will be of limited value.

Once the SPA becomes effective, contractual provisions will typically exclude a buyer's reliance on pre-contractual representations. Therefore, as a matter of practice, a seller often excludes claims for misrepresentation based on the contents of, or omissions from, a data room.[6] Occasionally a seller warrants the completeness of a data room. However, more usually, the buyer and its advisers merely form a view on

---

5 Due diligence is carried out by different types of professional: accountants, legal advisers, reservoir engineers, tax and risk consultants. Areas of investigation overlap and it is in both a client's and its advisers' interests to allocate and document responsibilities clearly.

6 See note 3. An example of a limited exception is given in note 17.

how carefully and completely the seller has assembled the data room and, if necessary, ask for further information and clarifications or seek protections in the SPA.

If the acquisition is financed by a commercial lender (which requires its own assessment and valuation process), then an adviser may be asked to address its report to both buyer and lender. As a result, each party may rely on the report and duplication of work is avoided. Other than this exception, an adviser will restrict the categories of person that may rely on its findings.

1.4 What is a warranty?

A warranty is a contractual statement of fact about the circumstances, conditions, status or qualities of the target or other matters indirectly connected with the target. It is an assurance given by seller to buyer. It provides a buyer with a snapshot of the target on one or multiple dates (typically at SPA signature and completion). Warranties are qualified by a seller's disclosures, which are set out in a separate disclosure letter.[7] The discussions accompanying the negotiation of, and disclosures against, warranties often improve a buyer's understanding of the target by identifying areas of concern for the seller.

As well as flushing out information, warranties allocate risk between buyer and seller. If a warranty given by the seller is incorrect, the buyer's remedy includes a claim for damages for the reduction in value of the target resulting from the breach. Damages will be assessed with the aim of putting the buyer in the position it would have been in if the warranty had been true. For this reason, warranty claims are often described as a method of purchase price adjustment, albeit one that is pursued through a dispute resolution mechanism with the accompanying costs, inconvenience, limitations of liability and uncertainties. The defences and limitations to which a warranty claim may be subject are described in this chapter.

Whether warranties are given at both signing and completion is a matter for negotiation. Where warranties are repeated, a seller will seek to limit these to matters within its control. The ability of the seller to update its disclosures for events occurring during this period is also negotiable. The parties will agree the buyer's remedies – for example, an SPA termination right – if a breach of warranty is asserted prior to completion.

Warranties commonly given in oil and gas M&A are discussed below. A seller of petroleum interests provides assurances on a number of issues also found in other industries. In most acquisitions, warranties and due diligence cover subjects such as due incorporation of seller and target companies, employment matters, insurance coverage, environmental compliance, accounting methodologies and absence of disputes. Despite their importance, these issues lack industry specificity and are not described below. Tax is also excluded from this chapter.[8]

---

7 In English law transactions, disclosures are contained in a separate document drafted as a letter from seller to buyer. Alternatively, disclosures may be included as a schedule to the SPA. Both methods achieve the same purpose.

8 Although it is clear from recent transactions that tax due diligence (in its widest sense – including the link between payment of tax and obtaining governmental consents) is an important area of buyer investigation. Cove Energy plc's takeover in 2012 and the sale of Ugandan petroleum assets between Tullow Oil and Heritage Oil in 2010 have created recent high-profile tax issues and disputes.

Geological and geophysical issues are not covered here for other reasons. Although a review of technical data will form an important part of a buyer's investigations, petroleum operations are inherently risky and, however carefully prepared, a range of outcomes attach to reliance on such data. As a result, geological and geophysical information does not lend itself to being covered by warranties. For example, the seller will not give assurances about reserve estimates. As well as technical uncertainties, the question of whether reserves will be commercially produced (and, if so, in what quantity) will also depend on future oil prices and technological innovations. Such factors, which influence whether a field continues to be economic, are outside the parties' control. For these reasons, a seller will not warrant the quality of technical data – but will instead encourage the buyer to satisfy itself on these issues during due diligence. In almost all M&A transactions, reservoir risk is assumed by the buyer.

1.5 Warranties versus indemnities

Due diligence influences which issues are elevated from the status of warranties to indemnities. As discussed, a warranty is a contractual assurance of a target's condition and circumstance on a particular date and breach gives rise to a claim for damages. An indemnity, on the other hand, is a reimbursement obligation designed to compensate the buyer for an identified potential future loss.

Indemnities are limited to matters where the circumstances giving rise to an adverse event (although not the final amount of potential loss)[9] are known and where it is agreed that these should not be the buyer's responsibility. These circumstances are sometimes discovered during due diligence and may include, for example, unresolved disputes, unquantified tax liabilities, expenses (eg, tax and employment claims) arising from intra-group reorganisations or environmental liabilities. Historically, the allocation of unrealised decommissioning liabilities between a buyer and seller's periods of ownership has also been dealt with by cross-indemnities given to and from the SPA parties.

The fact that these circumstances are known to the buyer at the time of the transaction may mean that any resulting loss is not suitable to recovery by way of warranty claim. By relying on an indemnity, the buyer is held harmless against adverse circumstances. This terminology ('to indemnify and hold harmless') is often used in contractual drafting. Tax liability incurred as a result of the receipt of indemnity payments will reduce amounts recovered. In keeping with the hold harmless principle, indemnity payments are often required to be made on an after-tax basis.

In contrast to the calculation of damages for breach of warranty (described earlier) the amount of an indemnity reimbursement obligation is calculated without reference to the value of the target. As well as this different method of assessing loss, indemnity protection is attractive to a buyer because it is not subject to defences and limitations which apply to warranty claims. For example, in relation to a warranty claim:

- the buyer has a duty to mitigate its loss;

9 If the amount of loss is certain then it could more easily be reflected by a reduction in the purchase price.

- the buyer's claim is limited to the extent that the circumstances giving rise to that claim have been properly disclosed (or, even if not properly disclosed, were otherwise known to the buyer);[10] and
- the buyer will be subject to contractual limitations on financial liability and time-bars on making claims.

Indemnities are used where the parties acknowledge that this basis of calculation of damages is inappropriate. Without these defences and limitations, indemnity claims often produce larger awards of damages than similar actions based on breach of warranty.

In summary, an indemnity provides a buyer with a standalone action to recover specific potential losses without having to prove their effect on the valuation of the target and without standard contractual defences and limitations. For these reasons, indemnities are described as producing 'dollar-for-dollar' recovery. In contrast, warranties are poorer in terms of amounts recovered – but richer in terms of breadth of issues covered.

1.6 Joint and several liability

Upstream oil and gas projects depend on the grant of a concession, licence, production sharing contract (PSC), risk service agreement or similar underlying permission to explore and produce. In the vast majority of cases this instrument is issued by a host government (HG).[11] A licence is often held by several co-licensees and, when this occurs, the proportion of the legal interest owned by each co-licensee is called a participating (or working) interest. A participating interest which is subject to a sale process is defined in the SPA as the transferred interest.

The terms of the licence are often issued in a form prescribed by the HG. Typically, the non-financial terms are subject to limited commercial negotiation. Despite the document's uniformity across a country's petroleum sector (and the lack of time that may have been spent on its negotiation), it is a key agreement and of particular interest to a buyer. It forms the cornerstone of the buyer's future contractual and regulatory relationship with the HG. It will also impose joint and several liability on a future buyer for the acts of co-licensees.

Oil and gas projects are often developed by two or more commercial companies. This may arise from several parties jointly bidding for the original licence award. Alternatively, it may result from a sole licensee diluting its participating interests during the term of the licence. A sole licensee may be incentivised to sell a part-interest in order to diversify risk and share the costs of exploration or development. Where a petroleum interest is held by more than one entity, the unincorporated joint venture thereby created is called a joint operating agreement (JOA). The JOA

10 The SPA may specify the criteria of what constitutes proper disclosure. The parties normally agree that, in order to qualify, disclosures must be 'fully and fairly' set out in the disclosure letter. Despite these provisions contained in the parties' agreement, a buyer's knowledge of relevant facts at the time of entering into an SPA may be a defence against a claim for breach of warranty; see *Eurocopy plc v Teesdale* [1992] BCLC 1067.

11 Although it is given different names and takes several forms, this instrument is referred to in this chapter as a licence.

party nominated to perform the work obligations required by the licence is known as the operator. It performs this role on the principle of no loss, no gain.

The question therefore arises: how does a licence allocate liability arising where there are multiple commercial parties acting as co-licensees? The near-universal answer is that the HG insists on the most favourable outcome for itself – namely, it imposes joint and several liability on co-licensees. Furthermore, no allowance is made for the fact that a co-licensee is a non-operator. Whether a co-licensee has an operating or non-operating interest will have no consequence on its obligations to the HG.[12] Joint and several liability allows the HG to enforce the licence in full against any of the co-licensees. Therefore, in conducting due diligence and drafting warranties, the creditworthiness, competence and compliance of non-selling co-licensees are relevant considerations. The buyer will want to extend some warranties to cover the activities of non-selling co-licensees. The extent to which a seller is willing to provide this comfort will be negotiated. In warranties where a seller is asked to provide assurances about the conduct of a co-licensee, this is typically qualified as being given to the "best of the seller's knowledge".

The remainder of this chapter describes due diligence and warranty issues specific to the petroleum industry. It divides these into title issues (and matters affecting title), changes in physical and legal interests, transfer issues, work performance issues and miscellaneous.

2. Title issues

2.1 Ratification of the licence

A number of jurisdictions require parliamentary ratification of each licence.[13] Relevant law may allow the competent minister to sign a licence but provides that the licence becomes valid and binding only after its ratification by parliament. Law may also require that the ratified licence be published in an official gazette. These ratification and publicity requirements form part of a country's anti-corruption measures. It is important in these jurisdictions to verify that the licence has received appropriate approval.

Whether or not ratification is required, it is also important to verify the authority of the signatory acting on behalf of the HG. The office-holder vested with the power to sign a licence varies between jurisdictions and the validity of a licence's execution is a question for local counsel. Typically, a president, prime minister, minister of energy or permanent secretary of the competent department has authority. In some jurisdictions, PSCs and risk service agreements are signed by the HG; in others, the power to enter into these documents is given to the state-owned national oil company.

This issue is particularly relevant in countries where, upon a change in political regime, an incoming government may challenge the legitimacy of its predecessor's awards. It is also an important consideration in jurisdictions where the power to award licences is disputed between federal and state governments.

---

12 The most high-profile recent example of non-operator liability for the acts of an operator is the Deepwater Horizon disaster.

2.2 Title to the transferred interest

The rights that a buyer acquires as a result of petroleum M&A arise to a significant extent from the assumption, assignment or novation of existing contractual rights. In an asset acquisition, the most important contractual right acquired is the participating interest in the licence. In a share acquisition, the licence is held by the target company and indirectly acquired by the buyer by its purchase of shares in the target. In either case it is vital that warranties cover the seller's or the target company's unencumbered title to the licence. Assurance on this issue is derived by different methods.

The licence, JOA and other key documents are often included within the defined term 'transferred interest documents'. It is important that the buyer receives copies of the transferred interest documents at an early stage. Having satisfied itself during due diligence of the obligations that will be assumed by the buyer by the future assignment of the transferred interest documents, the seller warrants in the SPA that the copies provided are accurate and that these documents represent the entirety of the licensee's obligations to the HG.

(a) Due diligence issues

Some countries maintain a register of petroleum licences with details of the names of licensees, coordinates of the licence area, date of award and duration.[14] Although a buyer will want to perform a search of any register, limited reliance should be placed on the results. Transfer of title in petroleum interests is not perfected through the agency of a registry in the same way as, for example, in some jurisdictions, real estate. As a consequence, it is unlikely that searches of a petroleum register provide a buyer with the same guarantees of ownership as a search of title using a sophisticated land registration system.

Therefore, in addition to investigating any register, the buyer will want to satisfy itself that it has reviewed documentation demonstrating a chain of title from the licensee granted the first licence award to the current seller. This forms a key element of due diligence.

(b) Warranties

Warranty example 1: The particulars relating to the Transferred Interest set out in schedule 1 are true and accurate in all [material] respects.[15]

Warranty example 2: The seller is a licensee of the Licence and the sole legal and beneficial owner of the Transferred Interest free of Encumbrances (other than Permitted Encumbrances) with the right (subject to the satisfaction of the conditions precedent) to sell, transfer and assign the Transferred Interest Documents to the buyer.

---

13 For example, Ghana and Sierra Leone.

14 A register of licence allocations is required by paragraph 3.9 of the Extractive Industries Transparency Initiative's Requirements.

15 This warranty example, and those that follow, are included for the purposes of illustrating the issues discussed and are not provided as recommended clauses. Bracketed language in the examples highlights wording which may be subject to negotiation between the parties.

'Transferred interest' is a defined term that will cross-reference schedule 1. This schedule sets out, in abstract, title issues such as details of the licence, JOA and the seller's participating interests in both. The seller warrants the accuracy of this summarised information (as shown in example 1).

In addition to verifying information, the seller warrants that it (in the case of an asset sale) or the target company (in the case of a share sale) is the legal and beneficial owner of the transferred interest and that this is held free of encumbrances. This concept is sometimes also expressed (outside the warranty provisions) in the operative clause requiring the seller to sell with "full title guarantee". This term (which, under English law, is taken from the Law of Property (Miscellaneous Provisions) Act 1994) implies that the seller has the right to dispose of its interests and that the seller will (at its own cost) take all reasonable steps to transfer title.

Title issues are so fundamental that relevant warranties are typically excluded from general limitation of liability provisions relating to time and financial caps included in favour of the seller. Alternatively, title warranties are made subject to separate limitations which are more generous to the buyer (eg, a financial limit on liability of 100% of the purchase price and a time cap of six years (or the maximum period allowed for claims under the appropriate Limitation Act)).

Both examples (above) are typically included. The second deals more directly with title. The statements about encumbrances, the right to transfer the transferred interest and reference to satisfaction of conditions precedent are discussed below.

(c) ***Joint operating agreement***

Warranty example: See above. Transferred Interest Documents will include the JOA.

A licence regulates the vertical relationship between HG and licensees. The JOA governs the joint venture arrangements among co-licensees. Although, strictly speaking, the JOA is not a title document, it is an agreement of vital importance. It allocates the co-licensees' assumption of joint and several liability, determines governance procedures for petroleum operations, allocates costs, grants entitlements over the lifting of petroleum and (in the event of breach) determines a forfeiture procedure. For these reasons, it is given the status of a transferred interest document and thereby is made subject to the same warranties as the licence (discussed above).

(d) ***Past breaches***

Warranty example: The seller has not committed any [material] breach of the Transferred Interest Documents [other than historical breaches which have been cured or waived] and the seller has not received any notice of any such breach and the seller is not aware that any of the other current or previous parties to any of the Transferred Interest Documents has committed any such breach.

A title warranty merely gives a snapshot of ownership issues on a certain date or dates. In addition to this, a buyer needs to be concerned with historic and ongoing events which may provide a justification for a HG to terminate the licence or for the JOA parties to forfeit a participating interest. Both documents typically include draconian provisions allowing termination or forfeiture for an extended event of default. As a result of the severe consequences of licence or JOA breach, the SPA includes a warranty stating that none exist. Since the buyer may also be jointly and severally liable for an ongoing breach by a non-selling party, this warranty extends (subject to a knowledge qualifier) to non-selling co-licensees.

(e) ***Transferred interest documents***

Warranty example 1: The Transferred Interest Documents, together with applicable laws, contain the entirety of the obligations of the seller to the government, and no other understanding or agreement exists between the seller and the government in relation to the subject matter of the Licence except as otherwise disclosed under this Agreement.[16]

Warranty example 2: True, complete and up to date copies of all Licensed Interest Documents have been provided to the buyer.

Although a seller will not usually warrant the completeness of the data room in its entirety,[17] an exception is made for transferred interest documents. A seller will warrant that it has provided complete and accurate copies of certain key documents (eg, the licence, JOA and work programmes) and that these are the only agreements governing the creation, existence and validity of the transferred interest. For evidential certainty, copies of the transferred interest documents may be annexed to the SPA or disclosure letter. The due diligence process allows a buyer to decide which documents should fall within this definition and, as a result, be included within the scope of this warranty.

2.3 Encumbrances

Warranty example: No mortgage, charge (whether fixed or floating), pledge, lien, encumbrance or other security or net profit or royalty interest or third-party rights has been created over the Transferred Interest other than those arising under the Transferred Interest Documents and the SPA and the seller is not a party to any agreement to give or create any of the same.

The question of whether a seller holds good title, and whether an encumbrance exists over an asset, are separate issues. A seller may correctly warrant that it has full legal and beneficial title to an asset that is encumbered in favour of a third party. Therefore, it is important that warranties cover both title issues and a statement of no encumbrances.

'Encumbrances' is included as a defined term in the SPA and will list those instruments (eg, charges, mortgages, liens) commonly covered by this term. In an oil and gas context, the definition may be widened to include options, pre-emptive rights, rights of first refusal and royalties over or attaching to the transferred interest.

---

16 This is adapted from the model form farm-out agreement (2004) of the Association of International Petroleum Negotiators (with some modifications to reflect the subject matter of this chapter).

17 Although this is the more common position, one warranty reviewed for the purpose of this chapter stated: "The Data Room Documents include all material agreements, material correspondence and other material documents and material data and material written information in the seller's possession (or in the possession of its Affiliates) relating to the Licence and the Seller has not intentionally omitted from the Due Diligence Documents anything which would reasonably likely to render any of the information discussed in them (when read as a whole) materially inaccurate."

Royalties are a common feature of the petroleum industry. These may be described in different ways: non-operating interest, net profit interest, overriding royalty interest, production payments or similar. They provide the royalty owner with a stream of income or petroleum production free and clear of operating and other costs. Often these are created to attach themselves permanently to a participating interest and to burden any future assignee. Encumbrance is therefore often defined to cover royalties.

'Permitted Encumbrances' (which is a definition used to qualify a statement of no encumbrances) typically include encumbrances created pursuant to the licence, JOA or SPA. For example, if a national oil company has a back-in right (ie, an option to acquire a participating interest from the licensees after a commercial discovery has been made) then this will fall within this definition as a permitted encumbrance created pursuant to the licence. As discussed in section 4, pre-emptive rights and rights of first refusal are also common features of licences and JOAs. The definition of permitted encumbrances needs to be wide enough to exclude these provisions from the 'no Encumbrances' warranty.

2.4 Development plans

The development plan represents an approval required after exploration and before production. It is the licensee's proposal to the HG about how and where a discovery will be exploited. The plan specifies the drilling programme, completion of wells and details what facilities and installations are required for the production, storage and transportation of petroleum. It provides details about the cost and timetable. The date of 'first oil' or gas is of particular concern to the HG. A buyer acquiring a transferred interest post-commercial discovery but pre-production will bear its participating share of the expenses set out in the development plan. Once approved by the HG, there will be a licence obligation to implement the plan in accordance with its terms. It is important, therefore, that a buyer acquiring a transferred interest at this stage has reviewed and is comfortable with any development plan previously proposed by existing licensees.

When a buyer is entering a project during this phase, the seller will warrant that it has provided the buyer with complete and accurate copies of all development plans – or otherwise warrant that none exist. A development plan which has been rejected by a HG indicates that different views exist about how a discovery should be exploited. A buyer will want to ensure, therefore, that this warranty is wide enough to cover both draft and final development plans.

3. Changes in physical and legal interests

3.1 Relinquishment

Warranty example: None of the rights under the Licence have been relinquished, surrendered, forfeited, re-determined or modified, in whole or in part.

A licence provides rights of exploration, development and production over a delimited contract area. This is defined by coordinates of longitude and latitude and a statement of the total amount of contract area (expressed as square kilometres) and is most commonly also demarcated on a map attached as a schedule to the licence. The size of contract area will reduce over time and it is important that the buyer understands the extent of the area over which it is acquiring an interest.

The contract area is, in most licences, subject to an obligation to relinquish to the HG a stipulated percentage of the original contract area at specified times. This is also known as surrender. Relinquishment commonly occurs at the start of the licence, often after the expiry of certain exploration phases. By the end of a licence term, the relinquishment requirements may have resulted in the contract area reducing to half of its original size. This compulsory reduction in contract area is intended to accelerate exploration (and ultimately, therefore, production) under the licence.

The licence often also allows voluntary partial relinquishment of contract area by the licensee, provided that this does not affect the fulfilment of its work obligations. Since the annual licence fee is calculated based on the size of the contract area, licensees are incentivised to relinquish areas over which they no longer have any exploration plans. HGs may then re-license these rights in future bid rounds.

Since it may be different from that stated on the face of the licence, a buyer must clarify during due diligence what contract area remains. A warranty (similar to the example above) will be given by the seller. Any relinquishments will be set out in the disclosure letter.

3.2 Exclusive operations

Warranty example: No sole risk or non-consent operations have been formally proposed or carried out by the seller or by any of the other parties to the Licence and the seller is not aware of any proposal to conduct such operations.

JOA parties, as a general principle, develop exploration and development opportunities collectively in accordance with their joint venture. The cohesion of the group benefits from an alignment of the parties' commercial objectives and an amicable and consensual decision to proceed with petroleum operations. If agreement between all parties is not possible then the JOA allows fewer than all parties to proceed without the participation of others. These provisions are known as sole risk (if a party proceeds without the majority) or non-consent (if a party opts out of a majority decision). Collectively, they are referred to as 'exclusive operations'.

Despite exclusive operations provisions being common in JOAs, they are rarely used. Exclusive operations are sometimes threatened but seldom formally invoked. The buyer will therefore have an expectation that the JOA is being administered with all parties participating in, and paying for, petroleum operations in accordance with their respective participating interests. If this is not the case, a buyer will find itself either excluded from a potential opportunity (where the transferred interest being acquired has no rights over a petroleum development) or paying for a higher proportion of costs than the corresponding transferred interest being acquired (where another JOA party is not participating). More particularly, where a seller has exercised sole risk, the buyer:

- will be required to bear a larger proportion of the costs and risks of the petroleum operations over which the seller has claimed sole risk (rather than an expectation that the buyer will be responsible for only the transferred interest percentage of costs and risks); and

- will acquire operations about which a majority of JOA parties have expressed reservations by their failure to support the project.

Where a seller has exercised non-consent, the buyer will have an expectation that it will benefit from discoveries and production of the JOA (whereas in fact, in order to participate, the buyer of a transferred interest subject to non-consent will need to buy back into the non-consent project at a penalty rate).

The example warranty (above) will flush out whether any JOA party (including the seller) has exercised the right to exclusive operations.

3.3 Unitisation

Warranty example 1: None of the petroleum reservoirs discovered in the contract area extend beyond the borders of the contract area.

Warranty example 2 (where a UUOA exists): No redetermination is in progress under the UUOA nor [so far as the seller is aware] is there any proposal to carry out any such redetermination [other than in accordance with the UUOA].

If relinquishment and exclusive operations can be viewed as a potential diminution of a contract area, unitisation may be considered the opposite. Unitisation enlarges the physical size of the parties' geographic interests but reduces legal interests in resulting production.

Most licences and petroleum laws contain regulations regarding unitisation. This is the compulsory joint collaboration and conduct of operations of petroleum reservoirs straddling contract areas held under separate licences. If a discovery is found to extend beyond the boundary of a contract area, arrangements requiring the joint development of a straddling field are usually mandatory and require separate JOA groups to enter into a unitisation and unit operating agreement (UUOA). If a reservoir also straddles an international boundary then governmental (as well as commercial) agreement is required as well.

The UUOA determines the division of equity interests between neighbouring JOA groups. This will be set in accordance with how much of the reservoir falls within each contract area. Each JOA party's interest in the unit development is diluted by a corresponding amount. Therefore, if a seller sells a 20% transferred interest in a licence subject to a UUOA and the JOA group to which the seller belongs has a 25% interest in the unitised block, the transferred interest will represent a 5% equity interest in the unitised block.

The first warranty example will flush out whether unitisation is relevant. If there is a straddling reservoir, the buyer must establish what UUOA is in place or envisaged. The manner in which unitisation is dealt with for the purposes of the transaction depends largely on the identity of the owner of the neighbouring licence. If it is a third party, any existing UUOA (and perhaps also operatorship of the unitised block) will be assigned to the buyer and the terms of the UUOA need to be reviewed as part of due diligence.

If the seller itself holds the neighbouring licence it may be that no UUOA is yet in place. In this case, execution of a UUOA may be included as a condition precedent to the transaction. In either case, the buyer needs to consider the qualities of the proposed operator of both the licence and any unitised block.

A determination of the appropriate equity split between neighbouring JOA parties can be difficult to establish and agree. A better understanding of the boundaries of the reservoir will emerge as production matures. Equity interests between neighbouring licensees are therefore sometimes not permanently fixed and may periodically be redetermined. If a UUOA is in place then a buyer will want to understand whether a redetermination of the equity interests of the unitised block is contemplated and, if so, when it is next due, what costs are likely to be incurred and whether redetermination is likely to be favourable to the JOA group the buyer is joining.

3.4 Boundary disputes

Where a border dispute exists, it needs to be disclosed against the warranty that no material litigation or disputes affect the licence. The following paragraphs of this section 3.4 are an extract from Chapter 1, "Territorial delimitation and hydrocarbon resources", of *Oil and Gas* (Globe Law and Business, 2009) by Mhairi Main Garcia. It is reproduced here with the permission of the author and publisher.

Throughout the world, numerous boundaries between states remain unresolved, including regions where oil and gas reserves are of prime importance. This does not necessarily equate to numerous territorial disputes, since the states involved may not have commenced the delimitation process. However, in areas where there are abundant hydrocarbons resources neighbouring or straddling an undefined or disputed boundary, oil and gas companies will need to make a full evaluation of the risks involved in advance of committing their resources and commercial reputations. Whilst it is not possible to predict with certainty how a boundary may be delimited or what the outcome of a dispute may be, various safeguards can be considered by oil and gas companies in order to mitigate the very real economic and commercial risks of operating in disputed waters.

(a) Due diligence

The first step for an oil and gas company being granted a concession or awarded licensing rights is to check the status of the contract area. Where a contract area lies within 200 nautical miles of a neighbouring state, this indicates that there is at least a potential for competing claims.

A state's right to grant rights over its hydrocarbon resources can only be exercised within its own boundaries. Therefore, if there is a determination that all or part of the contract area does not lie within the boundaries of the host state, this could lead to the concession/licence holder losing rights in so far as the rights do not lie in an area which is within the boundaries of the host state.

The ramifications are, however, broader than a mere loss of rights, since the neighbouring state which exercises sovereignty over an excluded contract area could demand that any activities be discontinued and/or impose penalties against a company which has been illegally operating in its territory. The fact that the activities were authorised by the host state will not protect a company from action by the neighbouring state in such circumstances. For this reason, it is not only necessary to examine the applicable laws of the host state, but where there is uncertainty over the jurisdiction of the contract area, the potentially applicable laws of any relevant neighbouring states should also be assessed.

Where there is a determination that all or part of the contract area does not lie within the boundaries of the host state, the company could also be in breach of its concession/licensing agreement with the host state, in the absence of provisions granting relief from targets and contractual obligations in such a scenario. It is thus critical that the status of the territory within which the contract area lies be established at the outset.

If the contract area belongs to the host state and this is confirmed by way of an undisputed treaty, judgment or arbitral award, then this should provide a degree of legal certainty and comfort going forward. However, if the contract falls within an area which has not been delimited and/or potentially neighbours or crosses a disputed boundary, this will necessitate a more detailed assessment of the risks and uncertainties involved as a result of the geographical scope of the contract area being potentially uncertain.

If there is a dispute between the host state and a neighbouring state with a competing claim over all or part of the territory constituting the contract area, an assessment must be made of the potential for settling the dispute, taking into account the political relations between the states concerned, the legal principles that may be applied (bearing in mind that whilst the International Court of Justice generally commences any delimitation by applying the equidistance line, the application of 'equitable solutions' may give rise to a number of possible outcomes) and the technical difficulties which may be involved in delimiting the boundary in question. If the matter has been referred to an arbitral tribunal, the International Court of Justice or other judicial body, this could indicate that it will take a long time to resolve the dispute; such disputes are generally protracted.

(b) Contractual safeguards

In addition to general legal and technical due diligence, oil and gas companies should to the extent possible include safeguards in the relevant contract, whether it is a concession agreement, PSC or licensing agreement. These safeguards should aim to protect the company against the adverse consequences of the contract area falling within a disputed area or of an unfavourable determination that all or part of the contract area does not lie within the boundaries of the host state. Although host state governments may be reluctant to include additional provisions to protect companies, where there is doubt as to the territorial scope of the contract area, companies should seek to negotiate safeguards such as the following:

- *If there is a territorial or boundary dispute which involves the contract area, there should be no breach of the contract by the company and the host state should not apply any penalties. This could be included as part of a force majeure or compensation event mechanism in the contract, or as a separate relief clause.*
- *If it is determined that all or part of the contract area does not lie within the*

boundaries of the host state, the contract should include an indemnity by the host state indemnifying the company for any losses due to such circumstances.

- *The company's obligations, in so far as they are affected or put at risk by a boundary determination, should be suspended until the matter is resolved. The contract should remain in full force until the boundary dispute is finally resolved.*

4. Transfer issues

4.1 Transfer restrictions

Oil and gas M&A needs to be structured to take account of consent and pre-emption rights in favour of existing parties. These occur at different levels. In addition to the completion mechanics discussed, several warranties need to be qualified by an assumption that consents or waivers to transfer restrictions will be granted (an example is given in section 2.2(b)(1)). These consents and waivers are included as conditions precedent to the SPA.

(a) Restrictions in favour of host governments

The licence nearly always requires HG consent to any direct or indirect sale, assignment or other transfer of interest in the licence. This is linked to a HG's policy (often expressed in the petroleum law and sometimes recited in the licence) that all licensees operating within the jurisdiction must be qualified and demonstrate technical and financial capabilities to conduct petroleum operations. HGs gain nothing by granting licences to parties without the technical competence or financial resources to exploit opportunities. HG consent is generally required whether the transaction is a direct assignment of a transferred interest in a licence or an indirect transfer (eg, a sale of shares in a licensee resulting in a change of corporate control).

The licence may also contain a right of first refusal granting the HG an option over the transferred interest on the same terms and conditions (including price) as negotiated between the commercial parties.

Frequently, the transaction requires both HG confirmation that the buyer satisfies the qualification requirements set out in the licence and a waiver by the HG of its right to participate in the transaction. The seller normally takes responsibility for obtaining these – and their delivery is a condition precedent to completion of the acquisition. The buyer must, through the due diligence process and with assistance from local counsel, become familiar with the required processes for obtaining consents or waiver so that appropriate conditions precedent can be included.

(b) Restrictions in favour of JOA parties

Similarly, the JOA nearly always includes one or more of pre-emption rights, rights of first refusal and change of control provisions in favour of non-selling JOA parties. Often this is a right for each non-selling party to participate in the transaction by acquisition of a proportion of the transferred interest representing its existing participating interest (in order that its equity is not diluted). Waivers of such rights are required from each JOA party for purposes of the transaction and these are also included as conditions precedent. The acquisition of each of the governmental and JOA consents and waivers will dictate the timetable for M&A completion.

4.2 Area of mutual interest agreements

This is an example of the buyer's desire to know that the seller has the right to freely dispose of its transferred interest. These types of agreement are common in the petroleum industry and may prohibit or restrict a seller's ability to dispose of its interests without first offering them to a third party (in this case, not necessarily an existing party to the JOA). If an area of mutual interest agreement does grant an option to a third party, then a waiver of the third party's rights is required before a transfer of the transferred interest can proceed.

5. Work performance issues

5.1 Work programme (minimum expenditure and work obligations)

Warranty example: All accrued obligations and liabilities imposed by the Licence, including work obligations arising from the Licence, have been duly fulfilled and discharged and there is no outstanding work obligation to be fulfilled under the Licence.

One criticism of old-fashioned concessions (granted in the early days of the petroleum industry) was that these agreements gave international oil companies (IOCs) too much control over the timing and extent of exploration activity. As a result, foreign companies accumulated exploration rights over large areas of a country without any requirement as to when or how these should be exploited.

This position has changed. Modern licences now require licensees to develop, rather than merely accumulate, the contract area. This is set out in licences as minimum work obligations, minimum expenditure obligations or both. A work obligation will specify the minimum amount (and type) of seismic studies that need to be undertaken and the number and depth of drilling operations (in each case, to be performed in accordance with good international petroleum practice). An expenditure obligation (as the name suggests) is a cruder assessment of the amount spent by a licensee during an exploration period.

Ministries have teams monitoring compliance with these obligations and governments are willing to terminate the licences of oil companies that are not in compliance with their work obligations. In other situations, some licences are drafted to expire automatically if the minimum work obligation has not been completed within the relevant exploration period. As well as requiring a warranty that the obligations have been fulfilled, buyers will want to satisfy themselves during due diligence that the work programme has been (or will be) complied with.

5.2 Local employment, training and content

It is common that PSCs require employment of local nationals and the establishment or sponsorship of higher education, training programmes and research projects in order to create expertise in the local petroleum industry. Similarly, a PSC often requires that operators give preference to local suppliers, producers, manufacturers and service providers. These obligations may be drafted as a statement of general principle or, alternatively, set out as a specific contractual obligation – for example, allowing imported goods only if using a local supplier results in an increase in costs in excess of a certain percentage. Such local employment, training and content requirements may be imposed by both the PSC and local law. Due diligence should identify PSC obligations in this area, the extent to which local content arrangements have been put in place, the competence and capacity of the domestic oilfield services industry to service the project and the future additional cost of compliance.

In addition to due diligence (which will reveal the counterparties with which the operator has contracted), the buyer derives comfort on this issue through the seller's warranties regarding its compliance with transferred interest documents (which will include the licence's local content obligations) and with applicable law. An example of the former warranty is given in section 2.2(d); the latter warranty is discussed below.

5.3 Compliance with laws

Warranty example: The seller has complied [in all material respects] with applicable laws, regulations and orders of government agencies in respect of the Licence.

The governing law of the licence will be the law of the host country. As such, the buyer's due diligence process requires not just a legal review of data room documents, but also an analysis of the local legal requirements imposed on the licensee. These will apply to the buyer after its acquisition of the transferred interest. It is essential that the buyer appoints local counsel to advise on the petroleum regime (statutory, regulatory or otherwise) and to verify the licensee's compliance with, for example, permits, land use, environmental compliance, labour law requirements, health and safety, and tax matters. These are examples of matters which are likely to be set out in general law (rather than as express terms of the licence). The seller should warrant that it has complied with both the terms of the licence and laws applicable to petroleum operations.

5.4 Bonus payments

Licences (particularly PSCs) often require the payment of bonuses to the HG. These may include signature bonuses (payable when the licence is signed), development bonuses (payable when the HG grants development consent) and production bonuses (payable when a certain level of production is reached). The licence is typically subject to termination by the HG if payment default lasts for more than a specified number of days. It is therefore important for a buyer to satisfy itself that all the relevant payments have been made to the HG.

5.5 Domestic supply obligations

Many licences and petroleum legal regimes in developing countries stipulate a domestic supply obligation requiring a certain percentage of production to be sold to the local consumers (often at prices lower than otherwise obtainable on international markets). This type of obligation applies, in particular, to natural gas production. If a domestic supply obligation is included in the licence and if it applies to the type of petroleum development being contemplated, a buyer must consider this obligation in the context of its review of the wider economic terms of the licence. If the project is in production, the buyer should also check that the supply obligation is being fulfilled.

5.6 Decommissioning

(a) *Abandonment of wells*

Warranty example: All wells which have been drilled in the contract area have been plugged and abandoned or suspended in accordance with good oilfield practice and with the terms of the Licence and applicable regulations.

The plugging or abandonment of wells is an obligation which may be applicable while a field is still producing and the warranty example (above) covers this type of ongoing (rather than end-of-life) decommissioning obligation.

(b) *Decommissioning end-of-life infrastructure*

For the acquisition of mature fields in certain jurisdictions, decommissioning is such an important issue that the proposed allocation of liability between buyer and seller may be significant enough to prevent the parties from reaching agreement. In other countries and for other types of asset, this potential liability may be less crucial. The regime for decommissioning liability varies between jurisdictions and due diligence and warranties in this area need to be adapted in accordance with local requirements. The level of protection required also depends on other factors, including:

- whether the transferred interest relates to exploration, development or production assets – the nearer the field is to cessation of production, the more immediate the decommissioning liability;
- whether the project is offshore or onshore – the complexity, and therefore cost, of decommissioning is higher for offshore infrastructure;
- whether offshore production is in shallow or deep water – the potential cost of decommissioning increases for infrastructure in deeper water;
- the age of infrastructure in place – modern equipment (in order to comply with recent international regulations in this area) is designed to allow removal at the end of its production life; and
- the weight and type of infrastructure in place – certain types of infrastructure (eg, floating production facilities) are easier to remove than others (eg, gravity-based concrete structures).

A buyer's first task, therefore, is to assess the age, location and type of physical assets being acquired. Its second task is to understand the local and international law governing decommissioning. Notwithstanding the applicable law in place, the buyer will also want to consider what will be best practice for the infrastructure to be decommissioned. This is an area where oil companies are concerned with both legal liability and reputational damage. Even if they are not applicable to the relevant jurisdiction, oil companies will look to the International Maritime Organisation and Convention for the Protection of the Marine Environment of the North-East Atlantic guidelines as representing best practice in this area.

A buyer will want to know whether a decommissioning programme has been prepared by the current licensee and, if so, whether this has been approved by the HG. A decommissioning programme serves a function similar to a development plan (see section 2.4), except for the reverse engineering of the project first proposed in that plan. Failure to comply with the decommissioning programme will be a breach of licence. Unless the licensees have other producing fields operating under the same licence, termination in these circumstances is a worthless remedy for a licence relating to a depleted field. Therefore, petroleum regimes will often impose criminal liability on both the oil company and its senior executives for non-compliance. Finally, modern petroleum laws require (and even if it is not required, good industry practice will sometimes expect) the parties to have put in place security or cost provisions to pay for the future cost of decommissioning.

Security or cost provisions can take several forms. In relation to due diligence, several matters need to be considered:

- Predicting future costs of decommissioning can be imprecise. A buyer needs to evaluate the licensees' cost estimates (set out in the decommissioning programme and often updated on an annual basis) and assess whether it believes that these are realistic. Estimates should typically include a contingency factor of up to 50% to reflect uncertainties relating to future costs. This contingency may reduce over time as decommissioning draws nearer and the range of cost estimates narrows.
- Have agreements been put in place with service providers for the removal of infrastructure? If so, are these priced with any certainty about future costs? If contracts do contain comfort on future cost, then this may reduce risks related to assuming decommissioning liabilities (and the buyer may feel comfortable with a lower contingency factor).
- Have the existing licensees put a decommissioning security agreement (a field DSA) in place and has the buyer reviewed this? What type of security will it require the buyer to post (eg, cash, parent company guarantee or letter of credit) for its share of decommissioning liability? Cash is the least preferred option for an oil company. Whether a company is allowed to provide a guarantee instead will depend on the credit rating of its parent company. If the buyer has a reserve-base lending facility in place which contemplates the lender issuing decommissioning letters of credit, does the bank's credit rating qualify under the criteria specified in the field DSA?
- The field DSA will contain a trigger date on which licensees are required to begin posting security for future decommissioning costs. This date is activated once a certain percentage of estimated reserves have been depleted. The buyer needs to consider what security has been provided by the seller (and other co-licensees) and whether this amount is in compliance with the terms of the field DSA.

The answer to these questions determines how the parties deal with decommissioning issues. If a field DSA exists, then it may be a JOA requirement that the buyer become a party to, and contribute towards, this mechanism and that the security previously provided by the seller remains in place. If no field DSA has been agreed, then the buyer and seller may enter into their own decommissioning security agreement (an SPA DSA) in order to allocate decommissioning liabilities in accordance with the date on which the buyer assumes the transferred interest.

This issue is dealt with in more detail in the chapter on decommissioning.

6. Miscellaneous issues

6.1 Locally incorporated company

Several jurisdictions have rules relating to the ownership of companies holding title to oil and gas assets. In some cases, the law requires a locally incorporated company but will not look further up the corporate chain and ultimate ownership can vest with a foreign company. In other cases, jurisdictions require that ultimate ownership lies with a domestic company owned by local nationals. Where these rules are in place, a party may be allowed to bid for a licence using a foreign company but with an obligation to transfer it to a local company after the licence has been awarded.

It is important that the due diligence process identifies relevant requirements and ensures that the seller (and its JOA partners) have complied with these and that the buyer (and its acquisition vehicle) will also meet these obligations.

6.2 Adequate financing

If the buyer remains on the licence after completion of the M&A transaction (eg, on a sale of part only of a participating interest or with a farm-out agreement), then after the M&A process the buyer and seller will have an ongoing joint venture relationship governed by the JOA. The post-acquisition ability of the seller to finance its share of cash calls will be a consideration for the buyer. To the extent that the buyer agrees to carry the future costs of the seller as part of the SPA consideration, concerns about the seller's creditworthiness may be reduced.

6.3 Performance guarantees

The licence commonly requires that the HG have recourse to a performance guarantee in relation to minimum work and expenditure obligations to be performed by the licensee. This is most usually provided in the form of a letter of credit from an international bank with a minimum credit rating, or otherwise in the form of a corporate guarantee provided by the licensee's parent company. The licence typically sets out a mechanism whereby the amount of this guarantee is reduced as obligations and expenditures are satisfied. The due diligence process should confirm that such guarantee of the seller's obligations was provided and remains in place, and also identify whether it has been called upon by the HG. The seller should warrant this information.

For purposes of the M&A transaction, the buyer's provision of a replacement guarantee to the HG is almost always a condition precedent to completion, and the licence or SPA commonly sets out in a schedule the required form of such guarantee.

6.4 Stabilisation

The buyer should consider during the due diligence process whether it will benefit from a stabilisation provision in the licence. Since the licensee must typically comply with all laws in force from time to time, it is at risk of a HG's future change of laws, regulations and tax regime. Stabilisation provisions attempt to prevent or limit this political risk. They provide that if there is a change of law that has a material adverse impact on the licensee, the parties will seek to restore and retain the original economics of the licence in order to prevent or limit this impact. While the protection offered by such stabilisation provisions is not a panacea to political risk, the buyer should consider whether this principle is included in the licence.

6.5 Sovereign immunity

Warranty example: The seller warrants that this SPA is being delivered as part of a commercial transaction and it waives sovereign immunity (whether characterised as state immunity, sovereign immunity, act of state or otherwise) that may exist now or in the future.

The buyer should consider, in its assessment of political risk associated with the transaction, whether the licence includes an express waiver of sovereign immunity or whether such waiver is implied under local law (eg, by virtue of the HG engaging, through the licence, in commercial activity). Although the enforceability of such a waiver needs to be further assessed, as a starting point it is important for the buyer to establish whether this principle is included in the relevant documents.

If the seller is itself a government-owned company, then a similar analysis (and, if applicable, waiver of immunity) should be included in the SPA. An example is given above.

6.6 Anti-bribery and corruption

Warranty example: The seller has not offered, paid, promised to pay, authorised the payment of, or transferred money or anything of value to any competent authority or any official, employee or agent of any competent authority to secure, in breach of applicable law, any improper advantage or benefit in relation to the matters contemplated by this agreement or the Transferred Interest.

Anti-bribery issues could have fallen into the category of issues that lack industry specificity and that are therefore outside the remit of this chapter. Anti-bribery laws with global reach have long been a feature of US practice. The recent enactment in the UK of the Bribery Act 2010 has renewed focus on corresponding UK law in this area. As a result of these (and similar) developments, corporate compliance has become an increasingly important due diligence item for all M&A transactions. The adverse consequences for a buyer acquiring a target that has engaged in corrupt activities may have reputational, as well as financial and criminal, consequences. This is an area of particular importance to the oil and gas industry and, for this reason, extensive warranties are often included. If there are concerns in this area, a buyer may also commission a report by an investigator into prior dealings on the licence.

6.7 Security issues

The due diligence process often identifies security issues in a contract area, for example local or national conflict, militancy, sabotage and theft. These concerns are particularly relevant for onshore operations – although piracy is relevant to offshore activities in certain waters.

These issues may have a tangible impact on petroleum operations, for example resulting in oil spills and shutting down key infrastructure. Given the potential impact of these issues on the valuation of the transaction, and on the conduct of the buyer's future licence obligations, the buyer should seek to obtain information about these issues from the seller. The buyer should also require that the seller retain and indemnify the buyer against all pre-completion liabilities in relation to security matters.

6.8 Related-party and multi-licence contracts

(a) Related party contracts

Warranty example: The [seller][operator] is not a party to any [contract][Material Contract] which has not been entered into on an arm's-length basis.

Related-party contracts between the operator and other companies affiliated with its corporate group are not uncommon in the petroleum industry. When entered into between an operator and its affiliate, they may be justified as producing operational efficiencies between the operator and its group company (compared with a similar arrangement with a commercial third-party supplier). However, when the affiliate company requires a profit element for the performance of its services, this may offend against the principle that the operator performs its duties on a no loss, no gain basis. For this reason, JOAs often include contracting procedures requiring the operator either to tender these service arrangements in accordance with good industry practice or to seek prior operating committee approval for related-party contracts to avoid conflicts of interests, or a combination of these safeguards.

Related-party contracts may be important in two respects. First, if these contracts are to continue after the sale of the transferred interest, it allows a seller to continue to profit from the project after it has disposed of its interest in the licence. The upside to these arrangements (the operational efficiencies between operator and its group company) may, however, no longer be relevant. Secondly, a seller affiliate may have no interest (or the same commercial motivation) in continuing to provide services after the transferred interest has been sold.

(b) Multi-licence contracts

Oil companies may also enter into multi-licence contracts whereby a contractor provides oilfield services to a group on an international or regional basis. Where a seller disposes of an interest in one contract area (but retains an interest in other contract areas, which necessitates keeping the service contract), the buyer needs to consider the likelihood that it can enter into a replacement contract with the same (or similar) service provider on comparable terms. This issue is likely to be more of a concern in developing and remoter oil-producing regions. In mature markets similar replacement services are likely to be readily available. Where there is a possibility that a buyer cannot enter into an alternative contract (or the cost of this will be higher), then this may affect the economics of the acquisition.

6.9 Cost recovery

We have seen that a licence is often jointly held by several licensees and, when this occurs, their legal interests are divided into participating interests. The JOA provides that each party bears its costs and expenses of petroleum operations corresponding with the interest that it takes from production. However, this general principle is often varied in two common situations. In these cases, the 'paying interest' and the participating interest may diverge. Where a party incurs a greater share of costs, these amounts may be later recovered from petroleum production. This is known as 'cost recovery'.

(a) Production sharing contracts

In PSCs, the petroleum produced is owned by the HG or its national oil company. Exploration activity is undertaken by the IOC at its own risk and initial cost. If petroleum is produced, then the first tranche of production (cost petroleum) is allocated to the reimbursement of the IOC's cost recoverable activities. These may include exploration, development and production costs.

Cost recovery is often capped during each accounting period (eg, 50% of production during a fiscal year). Sometimes different types of activity may be cost recoverable at different rates. For example, operating expenses may be recoverable in full in the accounting period in which they are incurred but historic exploration expenses may be recovered at a slower rate.

Amounts not recovered in one accounting period may be carried forward to the next. The cap therefore affects the speed and (because production may cease before costs have been fully recovered) certainty that an IOC will recover its costs.

After the IOC has received its cost recoverable expenses (or has otherwise reached the cap in any accounting period), 'profit petroleum' will thereafter be shared in accordance with the parties' agreed production sharing ratios.

Activities qualifying as cost recoverable are set out in a schedule and, in addition to the headline production sharing ratio and cost recovery percentage, will be an important consideration for a buyer. If the accounting principles exclude an activity from cost recovery, then this will be an expense which the IOC will have to assume.

For a buyer acquiring a transferred interest during the exploration phase, these are important financial terms. A buyer acquiring a transferred interest during production will want to review financial reports providing details on the extent of historic cost recovery by the seller and the amount that the buyer can expect to cost recover after it has acquired the transferred interest.

(b) Farm-out agreements

The carry arrangements found in farm-out agreements are, to a certain extent, similar to PSCs. However, these take place at a commercial (rather than governmental) level.

In a farm-out situation (which most commonly occurs at an exploration or pre-development phase), the farmee may carry the future exploration costs of the farmor and this type of acquisition structure therefore provides a form of financing of the farmee's future costs in return for an assignment of a transferred interest.

The carried financing may be recovered (if the project is successful) from production but at a rate that is capped on both an accounting period and aggregate basis. If the accounting period cap is exceeded, the surplus is carried forward and recoverable in the next accounting period.

If a buyer acquires a transferred interest which is currently carrying another party's participating interest, the terms of the carry will be important to the buyer's financial assessment. If a buyer acquires a transferred interest which is being carried, then it will want to understand what costs have been recovered to date and what remains to be recovered after the buyer acquires the transferred interest.

This chapter remains the same as published in the previous edition.

Dealing with material adverse changes in upstream acquisitions and divestitures

John C LaMaster
Akin Gump Strauss Hauer & Feld LLP

1. Introduction

In any acquisition of upstream oil and gas assets or companies that own upstream oil and gas assets, there will typically be a period of time between signing of the sale and purchase agreement (SPA) and completion of the sale and purchase. This is because it is a nearly universal requirement that the host government in the country where the upstream oil and gas assets are located have the right to approve the buyer.[1] In any transaction with deferred completion of this type, there is a risk that the target assets or target company may somehow deteriorate between signing and completion. This risk is often dealt with by means of a material adverse change (MAC) clause.

A MAC clause is a provision in an SPA that allows the buyer to terminate the transaction during the interim period between signing and completion if certain events occur that have a substantially adverse effect on the target assets or company. A MAC clause is therefore a means of allocating risk between a seller and a buyer.

As is discussed in this chapter, a MAC clause can take several forms, including a condition precedent or a warranty combined with a 'bring down' condition precedent. Whatever the form, a MAC clause typically gives the buyer an opportunity to terminate the SPA prior to completion if a MAC has occurred. At a minimum, where a MAC has occurred in a sale and purchase where the SPA includes a MAC clause, the buyer will have leverage to renegotiate more favourable commercial terms by threatening to terminate the SPA via the MAC clause.[2]

A MAC clause has three seemingly simple elements:

- There must be a change;
- It must be adverse; and
- The adverse change must be material.

These three elements, however, are typically heavily negotiated by the parties to the SPA. There is also case law interpreting elements of a MAC clause. As a result, MAC clauses have evolved over recent years from relatively simple boilerplate

1 Claude Duval *et al* (2009), *International Petroleum Exploration and Exploitation Agreements: Legal, Economic and Policy Aspects*, at 161; Lou R Kling and Eileen T Nugent, "Negotiated Acquisitions of Companies, Subsidiaries and Divisions", *Law Journal Press* 2005, §2.08[3].

2 Bryan Monson, "The Modern MAC: Allocating Deal Risk in the Post-IBP v. Tyson World", 88 *California Law Review* 769 at 803 (2015).

provisions into increasingly sophisticated and complicated provisions, often including exceptions and even exceptions to exceptions.[3]

This chapter examines how MAC clauses are interpreted and some of the issues that arise from those interpretations. It goes on to discuss some practical drafting techniques for MAC clauses in SPAs.

2. Interpreting MAC clauses

2.1 Lack of case law

There are few cases interpreting MAC clauses. There appear to be several reasons for this. First, many oil and gas SPAs provide for dispute resolution by arbitration rather than through the courts, which means that the resulting decision – absent appeal to the courts – will remain confidential. Second, disputes regarding MAC clauses are very fact specific and depend in large part on the contractual language of the MAC clause. This makes it difficult for buyers and sellers to predict the outcome of the dispute. Rather than incurring substantial expense and time in litigating an unpredictable dispute, it is more likely that parties will try to negotiate an acceptable resolution.[4] Third, the few cases that do exist – especially in the United States[5] – tend to be quite pro-seller, which may have a chilling effect on buyers seeking to enforce MAC clauses by litigation.

There is a difference in practice between the United States and England regarding MAC clauses. These clauses have been common in SPAs in US sales and purchases for many years, but it is only recently that the practice has transferred into private English sales and purchases. Partly as a result, there is more US case law than English case law regarding MAC clauses. Despite the overall dearth of case law, some generalities can be drawn with respect to interpreting MAC clauses under both US and English law.

2.2 Generalities in interpreting MAC clauses

(a) MAC clauses will be narrowly construed

Both the US[6] and English[7] courts have stated that MAC clauses should be narrowly construed. There are several policy reasons underlying this interpretation. First, public policy favours enforcement of signed deals, especially where the contracting parties are sophisticated entities represented by legal counsel. Second, courts are aware that buyers may use MAC clauses as a means to walk away from deals when they get cold feet or otherwise change their minds about the benefits of the

---

3 Robert T Miller, "Canceling the Deal: Two Models of Material Adverse Change Clauses in Business Combination Agreements", 31 *Cardozo Law Review* 99 at 105 (2009); Andrew C Elken, "Rethinking the Material Adverse Change Clause in Merger and Acquisition Agreements: Should the United States Consider the British Model?", 82 *Southern California Law Review*, 291 at 307 (2009).

4 "A Change for the Worse", *The National Law Review*, www.natlawreview.com/article/change-worse-material-adverse-effect-upstream-acquisitions.

5 See, for example, *IBP, Inc v Tyson Foods, Inc*, 789 A 2d 14 (Del Ch 2001).

6 See, for example, *IBP, Inc v Tyson Foods, Inc*, 789 A 2d 14 (Del Ch 2001).

7 See, for example, *Grupo Hotelero Urvasco SA v Carey Value Added SL* ([2013] EWHC 1039 (Comm)).

transaction.[8] Third, courts want to maximise economic efficiency by preventing the adverse economic effects that inevitably befall the target of a failed acquisition.[9] Fourth, a seller-friendly interpretation theoretically reduces transaction costs by avoiding the need to draft detailed MAC clauses with multiple exceptions and 'carve-outs' to protect the seller.[10] This last policy reason seems questionable, however, as in practice buyers and sellers often spend more time negotiating the carve-outs than the description of the MAC itself.[11]

(b) MAC clauses must be read in the context of the entire agreement

Courts in both the United States[12] and England[13] will consider and interpret MAC clauses in the context of the entire agreement. For example, in *Ipsos SA v Dentsu Aegis Network Ltd,*[14] the buyer claimed that a downward revision of an economic forecast constituted a MAC. The English court considered this in the context of the entire agreement and concluded that considering the revised forecast as a MAC would in substance give the buyer a warranty regarding the forecasts, which would be inconsistent with the express exclusion of warranties in the agreement. Similarly, in *Hexion Specialty Chemicals, Inc v Huntsman Corp,*[15] a Delaware court rejected a buyer's claim that decreased earnings projections constituted a MAC on the basis that such a conclusion would fall foul of the merger agreement's express disclaimer of representations or warranties regarding projections, forecasts or other estimates.

(c) The MAC event must be significant

Both the US[16] and English[17] courts have stated that the event triggering the MAC must be 'substantial' or 'significant'. The rationale, in the context of an SPA, is that in a transaction between a sophisticated seller and a sophisticated buyer, the parties will not have intended for the MAC clause to have set such a low standard for the buyer's termination right that the SPA would become, in effect, an option agreement in favour of the buyer. The requirement of materiality seems self-evident, but in practice it can become one of a buyer's greatest challenges in seeking to enforce a MAC clause.[18]

---

8 Bryan Monson, "The Modern MAC: Allocating Deal Risk in the Post-IBP v. Tyson World", 88 *California Law Review* 769 at 781 (2015), citing IBP, *Inc v Tyson Foods, Inc,* 789 A 2d 14 (Del Ch 2001) as a case involving buyer's remorse.

9 Adam B Chertok, "Rethinking the U.S. Approach to Material Adverse Change Clauses in Merger Agreements", 19 *U Miami Int'l and Comp. Law Review* 99 (2011) at 137.

10 Bryan Monson, "The Modern MAC: Allocating Deal Risk in the Post-IBP v. Tyson World", 88 *California Law Review* 769 at 800 (2015), citing *IBP, Inc v Tyson Foods, Inc,* 789 A 2d 14 (Del Ch 2001).

11 See sections 3.2 and 3.6.

12 See, for example, *Hexion Specialty Chemicals, Inc v Huntsman Corp,* 965 A 2d 715 (Del Ch 2008).

13 See, for example, *Ipsos SA v Dentsu Aegis Network Ltd* ([2015] EWHC 1171 (Comm)).

14 [2013] EWHC 1039 (Comm).

15 965 A 2d 715 (Del Ch 2008).

16 See, for example, *IBP, Inc v Tyson Foods, Inc,* 789 A 2d 14 (Del Ch 2001).

17 See, for example, *Grupo Hotelero Urvasco SA v Carey Value Added SL* ([2013] EWHC 1039 (Comm)).

18 Rafal Zakrzewski, "Material Adverse Change and Material Adverse Effect Provisions: Construction and Application", 5 *Law & Fin Mkt Rev* 344 at 348 (2011); Bryan Monson, "The Modern MAC: Allocating Deal Risk in the Post-IBP v. Tyson World", 88 *California Law Review* 769 at 797 (2015).

(d) ***The MAC event must not have been previously known***

Both the US[19] and English[20] courts have held that a party cannot trigger a MAC clause on the basis of facts or circumstances of which it was aware at the time it entered into the SPA. There appear to be two rationales for this requirement. First is the idea that, if the parties were concerned about existing known facts or circumstances, they would have dealt with them in a specific clause in the agreement, such as a warranty or an indemnity. If they failed to do so, it can be assumed that they agreed to enter into the agreement despite those facts or circumstances. Second, known events or circumstances do not constitute a 'change'. A MAC clause, therefore, must be intended to deal with unforeseen or unforeseeable events.

(e) ***The MAC event must be durationally significant***

Both the US[21] and English[22] courts have held that the MAC must generally be durationally significant – that is, not an event that is temporary or has only short-term consequences. For example, in *IBP, Inc v Tyson Foods, Inc*, Tyson tried to invoke a MAC clause on the basis that, among other things, IBP had restated its earnings during the interim period between signing and closing. The court held that: "A short-term hiccup in earnings should not suffice; rather the Material Adverse Effect should be material when viewed from the longer-term perspective of a reasonable acquiror."[23]

(f) ***The party seeking to invoke the MAC clause has the burden of proof***

Absent clear language to the contrary in the SPA,[24] in both the United States[25] and England,[26] the party seeking to invoke the MAC clause has the burden of proving that a MAC has occurred. For example, in *IBP, Inc v Tyson Foods, Inc*, the court held that the buyer which was attempting to invoke a MAC to terminate the transaction had the burden of proving that the MAC had occurred.[27] Similarly, in *Grupo Hotelero Urvasco SA v Carey Value Added SL*,[28] the court held that a lender which was seeking to cease lending under a finance document on the basis that the borrower had suffered a MAC had the burden of proving that the MAC had occurred.

3. Drafting MAC clauses

The generalities discussed above regarding how MAC clauses will be interpreted inform draftspersons about how MAC clauses ought to be drafted, whether

19 See, for example, *IBP, Inc v Tyson Foods, Inc*, 789 A 2d 14 (Del Ch 2001), where Tyson was deemed to have knowledge of the cyclical nature of the beef industry.

20 See, for example, *Grupo Hotelero Urvasco SA v Carey Value Added SL* ([2013] EWHC 1039 (Comm)).

21 See, for example, *IBP, Inc v Tyson Foods, Inc*, 789 A 2d 14 (Del Ch 2001); *Hexion Speciality Chemicals, Inc v Huntsman Corp*, 965 A 2d 715 (Del Ch 2008).

22 See, for example, *Grupo Hotelero Urvasco SA v Carey Value Added SL* ([2013] EWHC 1039 (Comm)).

23 *IBP, Inc v Tyson Foods, Inc*, 789 A 2d 14, at 68 (Del Ch 2001).

24 Bryan Monson, "The Modern MAC: Allocating Deal Risk in the Post-*IBP v Tyson* World", 88 *California Law Review* 769 at 798 (2015); Kenneth A Adams, "A Legal Usage Analysis of 'Material Adverse Change' Provisions", 10 *Fordham Journal of Corporate & Financial Law* 9 at 47 (2004).

25 See, for example, *IBP, Inc v Tyson Foods, Inc*, 789 A 2d 14, at 68 (Del Ch 2001).

26 See, for example, *Grupo Hotelero Urvasco SA v Carey Value Added SL* ([2013] EWHC 1039 (Comm)).

27 *IBP, Inc v Tyson Foods, Inc*, 789 A 2d 14, at 68 (Del Ch 2001).

28 [2013] EWHC 1039 (Comm).

representing a buyer or a seller. The following are some specific drafting points relevant to MAC clauses.

3.1 The form of a MAC clause – condition precedent or warranty

As explained above, the fundamental purpose of a MAC clause in an SPA is to give the buyer a termination right if, during the interim period between signing and completion, certain events occur that have a substantially adverse effect on the target assets or target company. This purpose can be achieved by drafting a MAC clause as:

- a condition precedent;
- a representation and warranty (or, more commonly in an English law SPA, just a warranty);
- a termination provision; and/or
- a default provision.

In upstream oil and gas SPAs, MAC clauses are most commonly drafted as a condition precedent or as a warranty coupled with a bring down condition precedent.

A MAC clause can be drafted as a standalone condition precedent to completion stating that there has been no MAC in the target assets or the target company between the date of signature of the SPA and the completion date. If the condition precedent is not satisfied by a specified longstop date, then the buyer will have the right to terminate the SPA for failure to satisfy the condition precedent. A simple standalone condition precedent could be formulated as follows:

The obligation of the Buyer to consummate the transactions to be performed by it in connection with the Completion is subject to satisfaction of the following conditions:...

([•]) there having been no Material Adverse Change during the interim period between the Signature Date and the Completion Date.

MAC provisions can be incorporated into warranties in one of two ways. First, an SPA can include a specific warranty from the seller that the target assets or the target company has not suffered a MAC between a specified date and completion. A simple example of a specific warranty of this type would be:

Since [date], no events or circumstances have occurred that constitute, individually or in the aggregate, a Material Adverse Change to [the Assets] [the Target Company].

Another example is as follows:

Since the date of the Balance Sheet, there has not been any material adverse change in the business, operations, properties, prospects, assets, or condition of any Acquired Company, and no event has occurred or circumstances exist that may result in such a material adverse change.[29]

Second, a MAC provision can be used as a qualifier to a seller's warranties so as to indicate the absence of any events or circumstances leading to a MAC. This can be done in in the negative or in the affirmative.[30] An example in the negative would be

29 *Model Stock Purchase Agreement with Commentary* (American Bar Association 1995), p81.
30 Kenneth A Adams, "A Legal Usage Analysis of 'Material Adverse Change' Provisions", 10 *Fordham Journal of Corporate & Financial Law* 9 at 11 (2004).

that the seller warrants that there is no litigation other than litigation that would not reasonably be expected to result in a MAC. An example in the affirmative would be a warranty that there are no defaults under any agreements, being a default that would reasonably be expected to result in a MAC.

In order for a MAC provision that is formulated as a seller's warranty to serve the intended purpose of giving the buyer a termination right if the warranty is not true, the warranty must be coupled with a bring down condition precedent. A bring down condition precedent is a condition precedent that all of the seller's warranties are true and correct at completion. An example of a bring down condition precedent is as follows:

> *All of the Sellers' representations and warranties in this Agreement (considered collectively), and each of these representations and warranties (considered individually), must have been accurate in all material respects as of the date of this Agreement, and must be accurate in all material respects as of the Closing Date as if made on the Closing Date, without giving effect to any supplement to the Disclosure Letter.*[31]

Alternatively, the warranty could be coupled with a termination provision or a default provision that allows the buyer to terminate the SPA if the warranty proves to be untrue. The MAC clause could even be drafted as a standalone termination provision or a standalone default provision. None of these structures, however, is as common in an oil and gas SPA as a standalone condition precedent or as a warranty coupled with a bring down condition precedent.

There are two important differences between structuring a MAC clause as a standalone condition precedent or as a warranty coupled with a bring down condition precedent. First, the buyer's remedies may be different under each structure. If a condition precedent is not satisfied by the specified longstop date, the buyer will have the right to terminate the SPA and walk away from the transaction. Conversely, if a warranty is untrue, the buyer will have the right to terminate the SPA and walk away from the transaction on the basis of the bring down condition precedent; but the buyer may also have a cause of action for damages for breach of warranty.[32] For example, if a natural disaster such as a hurricane, flood or earthquake damages the target assets, the seller may face unintended liability for something that was outside of its control. This possibility for the buyer to 'walk and sue' is the main reason why sellers typically prefer that MAC clauses be structured as a standalone condition precedent.[33]

Second, the two structures may cover different periods of time. Typically, a standalone condition precedent covers only the time period between the signature date of the SPA and completion. Conversely, a warranty regarding the absence of a MAC can be drafted to cover any period of time. For example, it is not uncommon for a warranty to state that there has been no MAC since the date of the most recent audited accounts of the target, which date will typically be prior to the signature date

---

31 *Model Stock Purchase Agreement with Commentary* (American Bar Association 1995), p158.

32 Kenneth A Adams, "A Legal Usage Analysis of 'Material Adverse Change' Provisions", 10 *Fordham Journal of Corporate & Financial Law* 9 at 12 (2004); *Model Stock Purchase Agreement with Commentary* (American Bar Association 1995), p165.

33 *Model Stock Purchase Agreement with Commentary* (American Bar Association 1995), p165.

of the SPA. This difference can have consequences. For example, assume that the target's business has improved between the date of its most recent audited accounts and the signature date of the SPA, but has deteriorated since the signature date of the SPA. If the MAC clause is structured as a standalone condition precedent that applies to the time period between the signature date of the SPA and completion, then the determination of whether there has been a MAC will focus only on the deterioration in the business since the signature date of the SPA. Alternatively, if the MAC clause is structured as a warranty coupled with a bring down condition precedent, then the determination of whether there has been a MAC will have to take into account the net effect of the improvement in the business between the date of the most recent audited accounts and the signature date of the SPA, and the deterioration in the business between the signature date and completion.[34]

3.2 Vague or specific MAC clause

When contemplating a MAC clause, draftspersons must consider whether to draft the description of what constitutes a MAC (as opposed to carve-outs of what does not constitute a MAC) in general terms or with specificity. Traditionally, descriptions of what constitutes a MAC have been written in general terms – some would say vaguely or ambiguously. From a seller's standpoint, generality may be viewed as preferable because it makes it more likely that the transaction will close or, if there is a dispute, that a court will not find a MAC. Given the pro-seller interpretations applied to MAC clauses by both US and English courts, as discussed above, this would seem to be a reasonable viewpoint. But traditionally, buyers also seem to prefer more general descriptions of what constitutes a MAC. This may be because buyers think they can use the resulting ambiguity to their advantage in arguing with the seller that a MAC has occurred and that the deal should be either renegotiated or terminated.[35]

The risks of deliberately general, vague or ambiguous descriptions of what constitutes a MAC is that the parties may have conflicting interpretations, which can lead to disputes and even to arbitration or litigation. It seems, however, that traditionally both sellers and buyers are willing to trade this risk for the savings realised upfront in lower transaction (drafting and negotiating) costs.[36]

The alternative approach is for the buyer to negotiate specific examples by way of inclusions or 'carve-ins' to the description of what constitutes a MAC, in order to ensure that those specific risks are catered for. This would seem to be an advisable approach, considering the reluctance of both the US and the English courts to find that a MAC has occurred. The downside to this approach is that a court may not consider a specific event or circumstance to constitute a MAC if it does not resemble the specific examples. This downside could possibly be addressed by making the specific examples illustrative rather than exhaustive – for example, by using an

34 *Model Stock Purchase Agreement with Commentary* (American Bar Association 1995), p164.

35 Adam B Chertok, "Rethinking the U.S. Approach to Material Adverse Change Clauses in Merger Agreements", 19 *U Miami Int'l and Comp Law Review* 99 (2011) at 109.

36 Adam B Chertok, "Rethinking the U.S. Approach to Material Adverse Change Clauses in Merger Agreements", 19 *U Miami Int'l and Comp Law Review* 99 (2011) at 111.

'including without limitation' proviso to the carve-ins. However, the concept of adding specific examples also goes against the idea that a MAC clause is intended to cover unforeseen and unforeseeable events or circumstances. As a result, if there are specific risks known to the parties, these are usually addressed in other clauses, such as warranties, covenants or indemnities.[37] For example, the non-occurrence of these specific risks could be included in a warranty which, combined with a bring down condition precedent, would give the buyer a termination right.

3.3 Defining 'material'

The concept of what is or is not 'material' is inherently imprecise and somewhat abstract, like the concept of what is or is not 'reasonable'. When deciding what is or is not material, courts tend to use a fact-specific, case-by-case analysis.[38] The resulting decisions do not provide much guidance to sellers and buyers as to what events or circumstances may constitute a MAC.

Parties to an SPA could attempt to define the concept of 'materiality', either objectively or subjectively. An objective definition of 'material' could be based, for example, on a quantitative benchmark. For example, the value of the target assets could be deemed to be materially affected if their value were reduced by a specified dollar or pound amount, or by a specified percentage of the purchase price. Similarly, the value of the target company could be deemed to be materially affected if it suffered a specified decline in earnings before interest, taxes, depreciation and amortisation. An example of a quantitative benchmark used to define 'material' was in *Great Lakes Chem Corp v Pharmacia Corp*, where the SPA defined a 'MAC' as "a negative effect or negative change on the operations, results of operations or condition (financial or otherwise) in an amount equal to $6,500,000 or more".[39]

Alternatively, the parties to an SPA could set a subjective standard. An example of a subjective standard would be the phrase: "in the reasonable opinion of the buyer there has been a Material Adverse Change." This approach would typically be resisted by a seller, as it appears to give wide discretion to a buyer. Further, it layers the vague concept of 'reasonableness' over the already vague concept of 'materiality'.

There are several difficulties in trying to define 'material'. As discussed above with respect to the inclusion of specific examples in the description of what constitutes a MAC, the downside of including a specific quantitative benchmark is that not every adverse event or circumstance may meet the same quantitative benchmark, and a court may not consider a specific event or circumstance to constitute a MAC if it does not meet that same benchmark. Further, not all events or circumstances may be easily measured against a quantitative benchmark (eg, a newly filed lawsuit whose outcome is uncertain). Also, a 'one size fits all' quantitative benchmark seemingly goes against the idea that a MAC clause is intended to cover

---

37 Kenneth A Adams, "A Legal Usage Analysis of 'Material Adverse Change' Provisions", 10 *Fordham Journal of Corporate & Financial Law* 9 at 43 (2004); Bryan Monson, "The Modern MAC: Allocating Deal Risk in the Post-*IBP v Tyson* World", 88 *California Law Review* 769 at 800 (2015).

38 Adam B Chertok, "Rethinking the US Approach to Material Adverse Change Clauses in Merger Agreements", 19 *U Miami Int'l and Comp Law Review* 99 (2011) at 121.

39 *Great Lakes Chem Corp v Pharmacia Corp*, 788 A 2d 544, 557 (Del Ch 2001).

unforeseen and unforeseeable events or circumstances. Lastly, introducing a quantitative benchmark to negotiations of an SPA will add time and cost to the negotiation process. Given these difficulties, it is perhaps unsurprising that most SPAs for oil and gas transactions do not attempt to define 'material'.

3.4 Forward-looking MAC clauses

It is often a subject of debate between sellers and buyers whether a MAC clause should be concerned only with events or circumstances that have already occurred, thereby causing a MAC, or whether a MAC clause should also be forward looking. Forward-looking elements can be included in a MAC clause in various ways. For example, the MAC clause could refer to the 'prospects' of the target company. Alternatively, the MAC clause could refer to events or circumstances that "would be reasonably likely to have a material adverse effect" on the target assets or the target company.

From a buyer's perspective, a forward-looking element is important, as the buyer is purchasing the target assets or target company for its future business opportunities. But from a seller's perspective, the inclusion of a forward-looking element can be troublesome, because it involves determining the probable future consequences of an event of circumstance, rather than determining just the actual consequences that have already occurred. This predictive element can be especially worrying where the seller has given a MAC clause in the form of a warranty, as that structure potentially opens up the seller to damages for future losses, even where the relevant event or circumstance has not yet actually caused a material adverse change.[40]

3.5 Not requiring a 'change'

It can be debated whether 'material adverse change' or 'material adverse effect' is the better formulation in an SPA. Arguably, "a change is easier to note than an effect is to measure".[41] Some SPAs use just one of the two terms, others use both terms and some use the terms interchangeably.

In either case, it is clear that some sort of 'change' is required. The *Concise Oxford English Dictionary*[42] defines 'change' as to "make or become different" or "the action of changing", and defines 'effect' as "a change which is a result or consequence of an action or other cause". So, in the context of an SPA, if an event or circumstance has a 'material adverse change' or a 'material adverse effect' on the target assets or the target company, this means that it has changed some aspect of the target assets or the target company.[43]

Of course, the parties to an SPA are free to draft the MAC clause so that it does not require a 'change'. For example, the MAC clause could include the "continuation of any events or circumstances". This formulation is more commonly seen in finance

40 Lou R Kling and Eileen T Nugent, "Negotiated Acquisitions of Companies, Subsidiaries and Divisions", *Law Journal Press* 2005, §11.04[9]; Rafal Zakrzewski, "Material Adverse Change and Material Adverse Effect Provisions: Construction and Application", 5 *Law & Fin Mkt Rev* 344 at 347 (2011).

41 "A Change for the Worse: Material Adverse Effect in Upstream Acquisitions", *The National Law Review*, www.natlawreview.com/article/change-worse-mateiral-adverse-effect-upstream-acquisitions.

42 *Concise Oxford English Dictionary* (12th ed 2011).

43 See also Kenneth A Adams, "A Legal Usage Analysis of 'Material Adverse Change' Provisions", 10 *Fordham Journal of Corporate & Financial Law* 9 at 43 (2004).

documents than in SPAs. An example is in the Loan Market Association Mandate Letter – Joint Arrangers – Underwritten,[44] which provides:

The obligations of each Mandated Lead Arranger, each Bookrunner and each Underwriter under the Mandate Documents are subject to the absence, in its opinion, of any event(s) or circumstance(s) (including any material adverse change or the continuation of any circumstance(s)) which, in its opinion, has (have) adversely affected or could adversely affect:...

3.6 Exceptions or carve-outs to MAC clauses

It is commonplace for the parties to an SPA to exclude certain exceptions or carve-outs from the definition of 'MAC', regardless of whether the MAC clause takes the form of a condition precedent or a warranty. The purpose of the carve-outs is to remove certain risks from the definition and thereby shift those risks from the seller back to the buyer. The carve-outs are therefore seller-friendly provisions.

The carve-outs tend to fall into several generic categories. Below are descriptions of the various categories, together with some examples that sometimes appear in SPAs for upstream oil and gas transactions. Note that some of the examples could fit into one or more of the general categories.

(a) Systemic risks

Perhaps the most usual and customary carve-outs are systemic or macro-economic risks that are deemed to be beyond the control of the seller. Examples of these types of carve-outs include:

- changes in conditions in the global economy generally or in global capital, credit or financial markets generally;
- changes in interest rates, financing costs or currency exchange rates; and
- changes in accounting standards or practices (eg, generally accepted accounting principles).

(b) Industry risks

In an SPA for an upstream oil and gas transaction, it is also usual and customary to carve out some risks that are specific to the oil and gas industry. Examples of these types of carve-outs include:

- changes in oil and gas commodity prices (including forecasted and future prices);
- any general economic trend affecting any aspect of the exploration, development, extraction, transportation, purchase, refining or sale of oil or gas (or any byproduct of oil or gas);
- a casualty loss, property loss, accident or other incident affecting the target assets or the target company that is covered by insurance (except for usual and customary deductibles);

44 [LMA.MandLet-underwritten.03 (November 2010)]; Rafal Zakrzewski, "Material Adverse Change and Material Adverse Effect Provisions: Construction and Application", 5 *Law & Fin Mkt Rev* 344 at 345 (2011).

- changes in the prospective resource or actual reserve potential of the [area of interest or the host country in general] that results from any oil and gas operations, where such operations shall include, but not be limited to, drilling, seismic acquisition, processing and/or interpretation of geoscientific or other technical data; and
- industry-wide strikes, work stoppages, slowdowns or similar acts of labour unrest.

(c) **Force majeure *risks***

Force majeure events are by definition beyond the control of the seller. Examples include:

- natural disasters such as hurricanes, floods or earthquakes; and
- war (whether or not declared), acts of terrorism, vandalism, sabotage or civil unrest, or any worsening of any such circumstances existing on the date of signing the SPA.

(d) ***Political risks***

Political risks are government-based risks, such as changes in law, governmental decisions, changes in governments themselves or even governmental instability. These risks are therefore different from the types of market, financial or physical risks described above. Political risks are often an issue for the oil and gas industry, which is active in many developing countries around the world, where political risks are typically perceived to be higher than in developed countries. Examples of political risks that may be included in carve-outs to the definition of 'MAC' in an SPA for an upstream oil and gas transaction include:

- changes in applicable law (including rules, regulations, codes, judgments, orders, decrees or rulings, or interpretations of any of the foregoing);
- changes in applicable taxes;
- country-wide strikes, work stoppages, slowdowns or similar acts of labour unrest;
- the imposition by the United Nations or another relevant government of any sanction, retribution or other penalty;
- a change of government; and
- any action required by law.

(e) ***Transaction-specific risks known to the parties***

The sale and purchase may present certain transaction-specific risks that are known to the parties. Depending on whether the buyer has factored these risks into its purchase price, the buyer may agree to include these as carve-outs. Some examples include the following:

- the effect of the negotiation, execution, announcement or pendency of the SPA or the transactions contemplated by the SPA on the target company's relationships – contractual or otherwise – with its customers, suppliers, vendors, lenders, joint venture partners or employees;
- any deterioration in the business, assets, prospects or financial condition of

the target assets or the target company resulting from circumstances or conditions existing on the date of signing of the SPA that were generally known publicly as of the date of signing of the SPA;

- loss of employees;
- compliance by the seller or the target company with the terms of the SPA;
- announcement of the transaction or the change of control of the target company as a result of the transaction;
- any failure to meet analysts' or internal earnings estimates;
- actions taken by the seller or the target company with the express written consent of the buyer; and
- any matter disclosed by the seller in the disclosure letter.

(f) ***Carve-outs to carve-outs***

Some of these carve-outs can be further qualified by a statement that the carve-outs do not apply if the target assets or the target company is disproportionately affected thereby, in which case the relevant event, occurrence, circumstance, development, change or fact can be a MAC rather than an exception to a MAC. These carve-outs to the carve-outs bring the described event or circumstance back into the definition of 'MAC' and thereby shift the risk from the buyer back to the seller. The following is a typical example:

> *changes in applicable law (including rules, regulations, codes, judgments, orders, decrees or rulings, or interpretations of any of the foregoing), except where the changes have a disproportionate adverse effect on the [Assets] [Target Company].*

4. Conclusion

MAC clauses are important provisions for the allocation of certain risks between sellers and buyers. It is therefore no surprise that MAC clauses can be some of the most controversial and heavily negotiated provisions in an SPA for upstream oil and gas assets or companies.

Environmental considerations in oil and gas M&A

Julie Vaughan
Herbert Smith Freehills

1. The context – managing risk in a harsh environment

Working offshore with oil and gas brings with it inherent operational risk of accident and incident, exacerbated by the difficulties of rescuing people in the event of a serious incident and of containing and cleaning up spills in a dynamic environment. Large spills of crude oil are liable to cause environmental damage not only to the marine environment, but also to the shoreline if they are carried towards land by wind and tides. This level of risk sets offshore operations apart from operating onshore. Images of the Piper Alpha conflagration in the UK North Sea and the billowing black clouds from the Deepwater Horizon disaster in the Gulf of Mexico burn long in the public memory. Such incidents cost operators and licence holders dear – not only in fines, compensation claims and the interruption of production, but also in damage to their reputations and by jeopardising their standing with national regulators and their commercial relationships where it is necessary to attribute the blame elsewhere.

Even in the absence of unplanned emergencies, saltwater, weather and wave action attack the fabric of offshore installations and exposed working parts and equipment, which must therefore be built and maintained to withstand these harsh conditions – in turn reducing the likelihood of accidents and spills, but also necessitating costly capital upgrades and loss of production during unplanned shutdowns for emergency maintenance. Licensing authorities expect operators to adopt good practice as a part of compliance with their production licences. In extreme cases, poor stewardship of facilities with regard to environmental and safety risk may jeopardise a licence operator's ability to continue in this function and at the same time accelerate the commencement of closure and decommissioning of an installation.

As a result, oil and gas operators deploy vast resources to manage operational risk of this nature and publicly commit to making the health, safety and security of workers and protection of the environment their number one priority. The challenge for purchasers of oil and gas operations is twofold. First, they must assess where the target's management stands with respect to its peers in managing this type of risk. Secondly, they must determine where to focus due diligence, so as to be alerted in a cost-efficient manner to serious problems that are likely to go to the value of the investment, affect the ability to continue to run operations at a profit and in legal compliance post-acquisition, or result in liability arising post-acquisition as a result of legacy issues for which the seller bears some responsibility.

Onshore operations bring their own challenges. Impacts from onshore spills are more likely to be noticed by the public and may cause nuisance or loss to third parties – for example, through appreciable noise or odour to local residents living in proximity to the oil and gas facility or blast damage to houses and local business in the event of a major explosion.

Regimes for onshore environmental damage also tend to be more developed than those protecting the marine environment, leading more readily to liability. However, the principles with regard to the focus of due diligence remain largely the same, with additional focus on the potential for liability to third parties and their ability, for example, to seek court orders to restrain impacts of the oil and gas operations on their enjoyment of their land. There is also the possibility of liability in relation to historic contamination of soil and groundwater from prior uses of the site or its surrounding area.

2. The due diligence strategy

The keys to conducting a successful due diligence exercise in this area are understanding:

- the complementary nature of legal and technical input, and having a multi-disciplinary team that communicates well and draws on each other's strengths;
- how the various layers and overlapping legal and licensing regimes fit together or overlap; and
- what the hallmarks of good environment, health and safety (EHS) management look like and how risk is managed in the industry.

Technical due diligence by consultants with experience of the upstream industry is essential. Wherever possible, this needs to be accompanied by a visit to offshore facilities in order to visually inspect the condition of the assets, as poor maintenance or housekeeping with regard to offshore safety may be evidence of an inadequate approach to EHS management and culture. Technical consultants should, for example, review the target's maintenance and repair records for evidence of underinvestment that may materialise in a growing backlog and repeated derogations given by management from the need to comply with the target's own internal policies. In the worst case, poor maintenance leads to assets that are no longer economic to operate and results in prolonged shutdowns, incidents and/or early cessation of operations.

Technical consultants should establish that the target has up-to-date systems in place that are being actively implemented for the verification of safety and environment-critical equipment that is necessary to control risks to people and the environment. Reports of internal operational audits (and/or regulatory inspections) may have been made available identifying shortcomings in complying with the target's internal standards, and these may also flag issues considered to breach legal requirements and the corrective measures needed to address the finding. Operators may be legally required to report spills of both oil and chemicals, as well as safety accidents and near-miss incidents that have occurred on board. Such reports should be examined for repeated events, particularly where these show recurrence of negative trends in the target's performance.

Legal due diligence is complementary to the technical diligence, focusing on:

- whether the target has the necessary environmental permits in place and is in compliance with them;
- actions taken by regulators indicating current or potential future enforcement action by regulators and the potential for material cost or business disruption to rectify non-compliance;
- the target's ability to continue in regulatory compliance when faced, for example, with imminent changes to permit limits or other conditions, or the introduction of new regulatory requirements;
- the liability consequences (if any) of failings identified by the technical diligence; and
- the existence or potential for claims by third parties arising from the operations.

A good understanding by the legal team of the technical findings is needed in order to suggest well-crafted contractual protections in the transaction documents.

3. Permits for oil and gas activities

The particular permitting requirements of each jurisdiction will vary, but some commonality of approach is driven by regional international agreements such as the Convention for the Protection of the Marine Environment of the North-East Atlantic, applicable to countries with a North Atlantic coastline, and the legislation of the European Union.

Using the United Kingdom as an example, discrete consents are required for, among other things:

- disposal of chemicals into the marine environment;
- disposal of oil into the marine environment (including in produced water exiting the well alongside hydrocarbons);
- flaring or release (venting) of gas into the atmosphere;
- combustion activities and handling of crude oil – which will regulate the entire installation, including associated activities;
- release of greenhouse gases into the atmosphere; and
- impacts on protected species and habitats.

However, this is far from the end of the story, as further environmental requirements may be contained within the consents given by the licensing authority at various operational stages, such as the commencement of drilling a well or the approval of a field development plan. These conditions are recommended by the relevant government department following its assessment of the environmental impacts of the activity based on the information submitted to it by the operator in an environmental impact assessment (in accordance with EU law). The conditions may include monitoring and reporting requirements enforceable by the relevant department's enforcement unit. Where the activities involve a likelihood of significant impacts to EU protected species or habitats, the government department is required to conduct an additional 'appropriate assessment' in order to verify that all the necessary mitigation measures are in place to avoid such impacts, failing which activities are prohibited unless they can be demonstrated to be of overriding national importance.

Such decisions by regulators in granting (or refusing) permits or other consents are often open to legal challenge on the basis that the necessary procedures have not been properly followed or key considerations ignored. This is likely to be a route available to claimants in countries that are party to the Aarhus Convention. For projects with controversial impacts on the environment (or public fear thereof), there may be a passionate lobby of environmental campaign groups and local objectors willing to bring a legal challenge to overturn the decision. Environmental non-governmental organisations typically have standing to bring such challenges and may be able to take advantage of protection against the need to pay the full amount of the losing party's court courts if their challenge proves unsuccessful. From a transactional perspective, therefore, it is important to ascertain whether key regulatory decisions are still within the timeframe when such a challenge can be brought. In the United Kingdom, the relevant period is three calendar months.

4. Environmental liability

Effective due diligence involves having a good understanding of the legal backdrop. The applicable environmental law will be that of the jurisdiction in which the relevant asset or project is located. However, the principal categories of loss that may be encountered as a result of environmental impacts are usually as follows.

4.1 Liability to remediate damage to the environment

This is typically imposed through legislation enforced by a relevant government department or environmental regulator. It may arise in respect of damage caused to wildlife and habitats, but also for degradation of water quality or (in the case of spills that beach on land) to soil and coastal waters. Legislation may also require action to avert damage that has not yet occurred, where damage is threatened as a result of the operator's activities.

Assessing the nature and level of harm and the steps required to effect a clean-up may be complex, involving the need for extensive technical investigation. It may not be possible to fully rectify the harm done to the environment or there may be a period of several years before this can be achieved. Some systems impose a scheme of compensatory liability in these circumstances, which may not necessarily take the form of a simple monetary payment, but may involve the operator making amends by undertaking works or funding enhancements of the protection of the environment in another location.

Due to the often untested nature of laws imposing liability for environmental damage to the marine environment, insurance cover may not be available. The European Union periodically considers making it mandatory for operators in its offshore waters to hold insurance for this type of loss, but has so far been unable to do so due to the lack of appetite among marine insurers to take on such risk.

4.2 Liability for breach of permit

Environmental permits are generally 'living' documents, subject to frequent variation and updating and full of specific conditions on how operations must be conducted to avoid undue environmental impacts – for example, by specifying limits on the level of pollutants which the operator is allowed to emit without being subject to regulatory enforcement action. The permit may be necessary for legal operation of the whole upstream facility or apply to particular activities or processes that form part of it. In some jurisdictions permits may expire and require renewal; but in others, such as the United Kingdom, most permits are not time limited.

Regulators typically have wide powers to suspend or prohibit continued operations in the event of a breach entailing serious risk to the environment or to revoke permits – for example, for persistent breach or inability to comply. Breach of permit conditions may also be a criminal offence under local law, with potential for fines or even custodial sentences for business managers or directors.

Regulatory oversight is usually by periodic inspections, announced or unannounced, which may be followed by a written record of the inspection and demands by the regulator for improvements to be made. Operators must also monitor emissions and submit regular reports. Permit conditions may impose heavy capital costs where plant or process upgrades are required by the regulator to improve environmental performance.

Permits tend to require that the regulator be notified of transgressions and of any changes that will materially affect the operation. The due diligence exercise will include checking for onerous permit conditions and whether and how permits can be transferred to a buyer purchasing assets, and local regulatory practice may differ as to the circumstances in which the regulator could object to a transfer to a new owner.

4.3 Liabilities to compensate third parties

These may involve, for example, personal injury, property damage or damage to fishing rights caused through contact with oil spills.

In common law jurisdictions, personal injury claims will usually take the form of an action in the tort of negligence, requiring the claimant to prove the existence of a duty of care, breach and loss. Regulators may also be able to bring claims in relation to money they have expended in remediating environmental damage caused by the operator.

Third-party claims may (if they result from sudden and accidental incidents) be covered by third-party liability insurance, subject to the exceptions and limitations of cover. However, injury resulting from gradual seepage of pollutants (typically onshore) is usually covered only under specialist environmental impairment liability cover.

A particular category of negligence claims will be claims from the operator's employees, for which some jurisdictions require employers to carry mandatory insurance. Alternatively, government compensation schemes may be available to claimants.

4.4 Workplace injuries

In addition to claims by employees for compensation for injuries or disease, operators will be required to comply with health and safety regulation for the protection of both their own employees and others in the workplace.

Upstream operations, as with any heavy industry, do result in accidents involving employees and contractor personnel. States are empowered under the Law of the Sea Convention (to which most are party) to extend their onshore environmental and safety regulation to oil and gas operations located in their continental shelf area. Offshore operators may therefore be subject to criminal prosecution for breaches of regulation in the same way as onshore operators. In jurisdictions such as the United Kingdom, the regime imposes strict liability, with no need to establish that the employer either knew about the existence of the breach in question or was negligent.

Non-compliance may occur not only where an accident has happened, but also where failings in the operator's management of safety lead to the potential for accidents to occur. In some jurisdictions, company directors and officers will be prosecuted in lieu of the company. In others (eg, the United Kingdom), company directors and officers may, where personally at fault, be prosecuted alongside the operating entity itself.

4.5 Lease/planning obligations

The operator may also be required to comply with conditions contained in development (or planning) consents or obligations contained in property documentation such as leases.

5. Climate change

At the macro level, the risks posed by climate change and governments' regulatory response to it loom over the more quantifiable environmental compliance and liability issues. Oil and gas producers (together with coal miners) are uniquely affected – the business being founded on fossil fuel extraction and consumption – and are thus a prime target of environmental campaigners calling for divestment of oil and gas company shares. Campaigns also take the form of activist shareholders tabling climate change-related resolutions at annual general meetings and increasingly bringing climate change litigation against major producers for failure to disclose risk or for harm caused. Litigation may feed on the emissions and climate change risk information disclosed to meet the increasing expectation of investors and the financial community, and in some cases mandatory disclosure requirements, such as the need for listed entities to disclose material risks to the stock markets.

At the domestic level, oil and gas producers are likely to be subject to compliance with climate change regulation in their home jurisdiction. This may, for example, take the form of a requirement to participate in a carbon trading scheme of the sort operated in various jurisdictions, including the European Union and now China. The philosophy behind such schemes is that participants are annually required to acquire and surrender allowances to match their greenhouse gas emissions. The amount of allowances made available for either free allocation or auction is less than the amount expected to be required, driving participants to make their processes more carbon efficient and forcing an overall reduction in emissions by all participants. However, some participants will be better placed to achieve efficiencies than others and will have surplus allowances to sell on a dedicated carbon marketplace. The trade in allowances ensures that efficiencies are made where it is most efficient economically to do so. To ensure that the scheme functions properly, strict rules must be in place with regard to the monitoring of emissions and submission of data to the scheme authorities, with penalties in force for breaking the requirements or failing to surrender allowances when due.

6. The interface with petroleum licences and joint venture agreements

Environmental law does not exist in a vacuum, but needs to be understood alongside EHS requirements imposed on licensees and operators through petroleum law and licensing regimes, and by contractual allocation in operating agreements.

6.1 Responsibilities

Oil and gas operations may involve a number of parties: licensees may choose to appoint either one of their own number as the licence operator or a third-party licence operator. The licence operator may subcontract day-to-day control of particular facilities to a third-party 'dutyholder', which may in turn employ contractors to undertake particular services. Drilling contractors may be brought in by the appointed well operator to drill wells, while mobile drill ships may be owned by yet another party. The overlapping responsibilities create a risk of difficulties in attributing environmental liability in the event of an incident.

In EU waters, the risk of accidents posing a serious risk to people or the environment is now managed by requiring operators of production facilities (and owners of non-production facilities such as drill ships and flotels) to prepare, submit to national authorities and comply with the measures set out in a major accident hazard report. This system is fairly closely based on the UK 'safety case' approach, whereby the competent authority must approve the contents of the safety case before operations commence and review it at least every five years or whenever a material change to operations is proposed. A scheme must also be in place for the independent inspection of safety and environmentally critical equipment. This regime was introduced by the 2013 Offshore Safety Directive for member states with an oil and gas industry. Successful renewal of an installation's safety case and the ability to comply with it on an ongoing basis are thus highly important, and due diligence should seek to work out whether there are any significant issues with either aspect.

The obligations under the directive are primarily directed at operators and hence their capabilities are recognised as being pivotal. Non-operator licensees, however, retain responsibility for ensuring that the operator is capable of performing its directive obligations. National authorities are required to remove operators which they have reason to believe are not up to the task. The default responsibility for conduct of operations in that scenario will rest with the licensees until a suitable replacement is found.

6.2 Liability under petroleum licences

The provisions of petroleum licences or concessions may place the onus on the licensees jointly and severally to ensure that assets are operated according to a particular standard of care that is drawn widely enough to include management of EHS risk. In the United Kingdom, the standard of care is to adopt 'good oilfield practice' and avoid harmful methods of working, without the licence provisions being prescriptive as to exactly what these entail. In the United States, a very different approach is taken, with compliance with industry (American Petroleum Institute) standards being required.

Licensees may be liable to indemnify the licensing authority against losses which the latter suffers in the event of an environmental incident. Thus, in the United Kingdom, the relevant government department can take charge of incident response in the event of an emergency and the licensing authority may incur costs as well as obligations to compensate third parties affected by its activities. It can then pass these back to licensees (jointly and severally) under the model clauses applicable to the petroleum licence.

6.3 Agreements among operators

One method for reducing the risk of claims for loss against oil and gas operators being unpaid in the event of major accidents resulting from offshore activities is a mutual fund or pooling arrangement. In recent years the European Union has given a great deal of thought to establishing a scheme among parties licensed to operate in its offshore waters, although this has not given rise to any concrete proposals as yet.

The European Commission showed great interest in a similar scheme in the United Kingdom known as OPOL. Operators of offshore oil and gas facilities are required by the UK licensing authority to have funds available to discharge liability for damages caused by pollution. Operators have therefore entered into the Offshore Pollution Liability Agreement: a voluntary agreement in relation to losses from pollution damage or clean-up costs caused to third parties as a direct result of oil spills from wells, pipelines and offshore installations such as platforms within a defined geographical area. Operators within that area can also become OPOL members.

Under the agreement,[1] operators agree with each other to meet claims made against them up to $250 million (with half of that sum per incident available for third-party compensation and half available for reimbursing regulator clean-up costs). Claimants do not have to establish that the operator was at fault. There are some exclusions from liability where damage is caused by *force majeure*, a government authority or a third party with intent. Notably, from the perspective of an acquisition that is undertaken after an oil spill incident, claimants have a period of one year to bring an OPOL claim. However, OPOL does not limit a claimant's rights to claim through the courts for losses which exceed the cap or which are not within scope (eg, indirect losses to the extent recoverable through the courts). Nor does OPOL restrict a claimant's right to seek redress (including against parties other

---

1 Version dated 21 June 2017.

than the operator, assuming that a valid claim exists) through the courts instead of proceeding under OPOL. If a claimant does choose to claim under OPOL, however, it will commit not to pursue that claim through the courts.

OPOL parties must also become a member of the OPOL Association and must maintain financial security in the form of insurance, self-insurance or other suitable means (which can include parent company guarantees or bonds) to meet their potential OPOL obligations. In the event of a default in a member meeting its OPOL obligations to pay out to a third party, the other members together guarantee to meet the claims.

7. Environmental liabilities and joint operating agreements

In any transaction involving multiple licensees, it will be important to understand the sharing of environmental risk through the joint operating agreement. Under the English regime, the person appointed by the co-licensees to operate the facility or facilities will be the party likely to incur any environmental liability at law, and this liability may be incurred regardless of the operator's intention or knowledge. Joint operating agreements then typically include an indemnity from the licensees according to their participating interest against the operator's losses, often subject to an exclusion where the operator was guilty of wilful default.

In the environmental context, there are two problems with this from the perspective of the licence operator:

- Indemnities may not be enforceable in respect of criminal fines where they would serve to protect the operator from the consequences of its own wrongdoing (in England, this is on public policy grounds); and
- The underlying law may in fact direct liability towards another party – thus, amendments made by the 2013 EU Offshore Safety Directive make licensees financially liable for environmental damage under the EU Environmental Liability Directive rather than the operator; and under international conventions, liability for third-party claims resulting from a ship is channelled to the shipowner (which may arguably, depending on its particular configuration, include a floating production storage and offloading unit).

8. Environmental liability of shareholders and directors

Private equity and overseas investors in oil and gas operating assets are frequently keen to understand the possibility of incurring liability as a shareholder with no direct control over operational matters. Equally, investors may be seeking to appoint one of more directors to the target's board after an acquisition and those individuals need to understand the potential liability risk for them in that capacity.

8.1 Shareholder liability

Investors which are new to the oil and gas industry will often be concerned about the potential to incur environmental liability in their role as a shareholder in an operator or licensee. Under English environmental law, liability usually rests with the person causing the breach or harm – often referred to as the 'polluter pays' principle. However, the principle itself has no binding force (in England at least), and it is the letter of the legislation that is important in each case. One of the main exceptions to application of this principle is that the owner or occupier of land that has been polluted by a person that can no longer be traced can be liable to remediate it where the contamination is causing or threatening to cause significant harm to the natural environment, property or people. So, for example, liability to remediate hydrocarbons spilled decades ago by now-defunct oil companies at onshore terminals or having escaped over many years through leaking pipelines may fall to be cleaned up by the current terminal operator or landowner if this poses a significant risk to the environment of a type prescribed in the legislation. As this is not so far an area covered by EU law, the legal position on soil contamination in each member state is different. The United States also has a stringent contaminated land regime, known as the Comprehensive Environmental Response, Compensation, and Liability Act (also known as Superfund).

Generally, then, where environmental harm results from operations of (or land occupied or owned by) a subsidiary company, the liability relating to that harm will rest with the subsidiary company, rather than a parent company or any shareholders. Corporate law principles of limited liability and separate legal personality apply in the usual way, such that the parent company will not usually be liable for that harm, outside of limited exceptions such as fraud.

However, if a parent company intervenes directly in its subsidiary's operations such that the parent could be said by its own actions to have caused harm, the parent can incur its own liability. In England, certain environmental legislation also expressly allows for one party that causes another to commit an offence (eg, a breach of an environmental permit or regulation) to be held liable itself. In practice, this is rarely, if ever, used by regulators bringing prosecutions. Pressure is sometimes brought to bear on parent companies in cases where inability to pursue the subsidiary (eg, where it is insolvent) means that contamination would otherwise have to be cleaned up by the regulator at public expense. A parent could also be vicariously liable for the actions of personnel seconded to a subsidiary or joint venture operation. Hence, it is important that secondees take instructions from the subsidiary or joint venture rather than their employer while on secondment.

In some jurisdictions, statutory regimes impose obligations on a parent company in respect of its entire group of companies. In the United Kingdom, for example, these are limited to the Carbon Reduction Commitment (effectively a tax on energy usage) and the Energy Savings Opportunities Scheme (a requirement to periodically audit to identify possible energy savings), as well as obligations on larger companies to report their greenhouse gas emissions in group annual financial statements.

8.2 Class action 'tourism'

In common law jurisdictions, the general position in relation to tortious liability applies in respect of loss or harm caused by environmental pollution, such as personal injury for people coming into contact with hazardous substances. The legal entity which caused the harm is usually the only party that can be successfully sued for compensation. However, an area of developing law (but targeting the extractive industry predominantly) is the potential for large groups of claimants organised by claimant law firms to sue parent companies in their home jurisdiction for harm alleged to have been caused by their separately incorporated subsidiaries operating in an overseas jurisdiction. The harm may include environmental degradation, personal injury and property damage claims, and/or allegations of economic loss through damage to livelihoods and/or disrespect of the claimants' human rights (eg, through being effectively forced out of the area to make way for the defendant's project without adequate compensation).

Claimants in these cases seek to use favourable court rules allowing group claims to be brought and allowing claimant lawyers to charge on a conditional (no win, no fee) basis, which may not be available to the claimants in the courts of their home jurisdiction. Claimants also benefit from the higher levels of damages awarded by the courts of the more developed jurisdictions. They are assisted by treaties which require courts in the parent's country of registration to accept jurisdiction when the parent is sued there, in effect ousting the ability of the parent to claim that those courts are not the appropriate forum to hear the case. This is despite the fact that the harm is alleged to have occurred overseas, from operations located overseas and to claimants who are overseas nationals.[2] In practice, widely drawn allegations and distance and language barriers contribute to making these extremely difficult, protracted and costly cases to defend. A number of such claims have been brought or threatened before the English High Court in recent years.

The leading English authority on when a duty of care exists is *Caparo Industries plc v Dickman*,[3] which set out that a duty of care will exist only if:

- the particular damage suffered was foreseeable;
- there is a relationship of proximity or neighbourhood between the parties; and
- the court considers it fair, just and reasonable in the circumstances to impose a duty of care on the parent company in relation to the claimant.

In *Chandler v Cape*[4] it was held that the following factors point towards the parent company owing a tortious duty of care in relation to the operations of a subsidiary:

- The businesses of the parent and subsidiary companies are in all relevant respects the same;
- The parent company has, or ought to have, superior knowledge of some relevant aspect of health and safety in the particular industry;
- The subsidiary's system of work is unsafe, as the parent company knew or ought to have known; and
- The parent company knew or ought to have foreseen that its subsidiary or its subsidiary's employees would rely on the parent company using its superior knowledge.

---

2 The Recast Brussels Regulation (1215/2012) provides that (subject to certain exceptions) persons should be sued in the EU member state in which they are domiciled. English companies are domiciled in the place of their registered office. Accordingly, provided that the English parent company's registered office is in England, the English court will have jurisdiction over any claim against it. It will not be open to either party to argue that the case should be determined by the courts of a different jurisdiction.

3 [1990] 2 AC 605.

Under these principles, a court will consider whether a parent company is better placed than the subsidiary to have prevented the tort complained of and, if so, whether it is fair and reasonable to infer that the subsidiary will rely upon the parent. Notably, case law has drawn a clear distinction between holding and operating companies. A holding company (where the parent company merely holds shares) will not owe a duty of care, as it is not operating the same type of business as the subsidiary.

Whether a parent company is to be viewed as a mere holding company will turn on the facts of each case. Notably, recent group actions in the English courts have seen claimants seeking to rely on group structure reporting systems and quotations from corporate group statements and policies to allege that an English domiciled parent company owed a duty of care to foreign nationals in respect of the actions of a foreign subsidiary. Only in one case, *Lungowe v Vedanta Resources plc*,[5] has leave to bring a claim been successful. In *Lungowe*, an action was brought against the English parent and its Zambian subsidiary in relation to tortious liability for events occurring and causing environmental pollution in Zambia, where the subsidiary conducted copper mining operations. The Supreme Court is due to hear an appeal against this decision.

In the most recent case heard by the Court of Appeal, *Okpabi v Royal Dutch Shell Plc*,[6] a claim that the parent company was liable in respect of environmental impacts of its subsidiary's operations was rejected (by the majority). The claimants had alleged that the parent controlled the subsidiary's operations through, among other things, issuing mandatory policies and imposing mandatory practices, imposing a system of supervision and financial control, and directing and overseeing the subsidiary's operations. In rejecting the claims, the court held that it is important to distinguish between a parent that:

- controls a subsidiary's material operations; and
- issues mandatory policies which apply throughout a group of companies.

High-level operating policies which accord with industry best practice and apply at a group level are unlikely to indicate the requisite degree of control over the subsidiary to found a duty of care. It is necessary to establish that the parent has taken control (or joint control) of the relevant operations in a much more direct and substantial way.

Provided that the tests set out above are satisfied, the ultimate parent company of the subsidiary – not just the immediate and/or any intervening parent company – can be liable in tort for the acts or omissions of the operating subsidiary. However, the degree of separation between the ultimate parent company and the subsidiary may be relevant when determining the existence of a duty of care.

4 [2012] 1 WLR 3111.
5 [2017] EWCA Civ 1528.
6 [2018] EWCA Civ 191.

9. Directors' and officers' liability

Another concern to investors is the potential exposure of individual directors and officers to environmental liability. It may be possible (as it is in the United Kingdom) to prosecute directors, officers and senior managers of companies alongside the company itself for breaches of environmental regulation where those individuals are personally at fault. This could include parent company nominees to the board or management positions. Corporate law rules on incurring liability as a shadow director can potentially result in environmental liability being incurred by a parent closely involved in directing the subsidiary's actions; hence, it is important to maintain the autonomy of the subsidiary's decision making on operational matters involving environmental risk.

10. Contractual protection for the buyer

As explained in earlier chapters, a buyer acquiring shares will inherit the target with all of its liabilities incurred since it was formed. However, the position may end up being little different in the case of an asset purchase, to the extent that this structure is chosen to achieve a particular aim, such as a tax saving, but the seller otherwise intends to transfer all the legal risk to the buyer.

10.1 Indemnities

In the case of offshore assets, sellers typically expect to receive a 'clean break' indemnity to enable them to divest any residual environmental liability that would otherwise remain with the seller in relation to its period of ownership. If the seller does not receive such an indemnity, it is unlikely to retain any exposure to environmental liability above and beyond its participating interest share, unless it has also acted as the operator of the asset – and then only to the extent that it loses the ability to claim indemnity under the joint operating agreement after completion.

Onshore, while the seller may request the same outright transfer of environmental risk in its opening gambit, buyers are more reluctant to absolve the seller from all responsibility associated with poor past management that has given rise to a legacy of contamination or perhaps exposure of workers to hazards such as asbestos fibres that may result in terminal disease in years to come after the transfer of ownership. Onshore, therefore, where environmental information disclosed by the seller or the buyer's own surveys shows evidence of significant contamination concerns, it is reasonable for the buyer to request that it rather than the seller be protected from a subsequent legal requirement to remediate; and perhaps also from any third-party claims arising from the impacts of the contamination. The latter might, for instance, come from neighbouring property owners or farmers, or result from health impacts to people as a result of coming into contact with contaminants either on the oil and gas site itself or in other locations to which contaminants may have travelled through the soil or been carried in ground or surface waters.

Environmental indemnities may be included within the main body or a schedule to the purchase agreement, or take the form of a standalone agreement or deed. They are typically subject to agreed financial caps on liability and a time limit on the period during which claims must be notified. There may also be a range of exclusions and limitations, such as precluding claims where the liability only results or is increased by a voluntary ground investigation conducted by the buyer, or where the buyer ceases to operate or chooses to redevelop the facility. The trigger that enables a claim under the indemnity to be brought will also be important – typically, this is the commencement of proceedings or the receipt of a notice from the regulator imposing liability. Boilerplate is likely to consider the effect of a change in law on the obligation to indemnify, the duty to mitigate and whether the indemnity stretches to consequential or economic losses arising.

Environmental indemnities may get very complex, especially where a reverse or counter-indemnity is included for the seller's liability. Sometimes the transfer of risk is not immediate as at completion of the sale, but is phased over time according to a sliding scale of diminishing risk borne by the seller and increasing risk borne by the purchaser. Different treatment may be applied for known and unknown risks, or for onsite and offsite contamination caused by the operation.

10.2 Warranties

Warranties in respect of compliance with environmental law, no claims or enforcement action, having all necessary permits and being in compliance with their conditions are standard fodder in most M&A transactions. Definitions of concepts such as 'environment' and 'hazardous substance' are also unlikely to prove very controversial. More specific warranties tailored to the particular business may also be given.

However, exceptions exist where warranty cover may be unavailable or subject to very low limits on the level of claims that may be made. These include sales by insolvency practitioners and by private equity sellers. Warranty and indemnity insurance is sometimes provided to fund damages for breach of warranties; but it tends to exclude most, if not all cover in relation to environmental pollution.

To protect the seller against warranties from other areas – such as the property or general litigation warranties – also being open to claims with an environmental basis, environmental warranties are often 'ring-fenced': that is, claims in respect of environmental matters (as defined in the sale and purchase agreement) can be brought only against the environmental warranties in a particular paragraph of the warranties schedule.

11. Transfers of permits and allowances

11.1 Permits

Since oil and gas assets need environmental permits in place in order to be legally operated, the seller will be keen to ensure that they are in force and held by the correct entity, and that the conditions they contain are not unusually onerous. Permit conditions may require, for example, that the operator undertake capital upgrade works. Permits can also be a source of uncertainty, due to pending further reports and studies that must be undertaken and submitted to the regulator for approval.

In the United Kingdom, most permits continue indefinitely until surrendered or revoked by the regulator. They will survive intact upon a change of ownership of the permit holder. In certain cases (eg, licences to disturb protected species), they may be issued to a named company representative and it will be important to check that that person is not leaving the business as a result of the change of control.

For asset purchases, however, the permits are likely to require transfer to the buyer upon completion of the sale and this may require the seller's cooperation. If transfer is not possible with effect from completion, the seller may agree that the buyer will operate the business for a short period, with the seller remaining the permit holder, but being indemnified for any resulting loss that it suffers in the interim period. This is not an ideal situation; and indeed for key operating permits, the buyer may insist on transfer of the permit as a condition to completion.

The process for effecting transfers is usually governed by legislation, but may also be set out in regulatory guidance. If no procedure is given and the local law does not, for example, provide that the permit 'runs with the land', the presumption will likely be that an application by the buyer for a new permit is necessary.

Likewise, lenders asked to finance development projects will most likely insist that the project has the necessary environmental permits in place before they will commit funds. Permits for complex or novel projects may take several months to issue, and buyers looking to acquire such a project should seek to understand as part of the diligence process the status of the application and any communications with the regulator regarding it.

11.2 Allowances

Where assets must be included in an emissions trading scheme, the buyer will likely want ownership of any associated emissions allowances held by the seller and these should therefore be included in the description of the assets transferring. Sometimes, rather than transferring the allowances, the same is achieved by changing the name of the registry account holder to the buyer, leaving the allowances in situ. Receiving allowances from the seller may not completely avoid the buyer having to buy additional allowances on the carbon markets to meet in full its obligations to surrender sufficient allowances to match the target's emissions, but it may help to alleviate the buyer's exposure to market price fluctuations. The buyer will want to make sure that it is getting good title to the allowances and that they are of a type that is accepted by the relevant scheme operator.

12. Conclusion

Environmental due diligence on oil and gas assets has many facets and is very much led by the nature and location of the facilities involved. The potential for environmental liability to arise cannot be determined in isolation without considering the actual circumstances and the interaction of the oil and gas business with its surroundings, local residents and campaign groups. Likewise, it is not always black and white whether an operator is in breach of a regulation or a permit condition; this may depend on the view taken by the regulator in light of best practice elsewhere within the industry. The upshot for purchasers is that it is not usually sufficient to consider the technical aspects without the liability and compliance position and *vice versa*. The two are interdependent and the lawyers should be put in touch early with the environmental consultants. Within the legal team, the best results are obtained by close collaboration between environmental lawyers and their counterparts in the areas of energy, real estate, planning and often insurance.

This is also an area of ever-changing regulatory requirements. It is often key to understanding the real risks for the business going forward to scan the horizon for upcoming developments with potentially material impacts. A team which is abreast of policy and legislative proposals as they are likely to apply within the industry should be able to provide invaluable insight to shape questions about how well placed the target is to achieve ongoing compliance with new requirements and at what cost to the business.

Decommissioning in an M&A context

Paula Kidd
Norman Wisely
CMS Cameron McKenna Nabarro Olswang LLP

1. Introduction

Decommissioning – and in particular, decommissioning security – has become a key factor in oil and gas M&A transactions in recent years. Working within a legal framework consisting of a combination of international and national law, a primary focus of governments is to ensure that decommissioning costs do not fall upon the taxpayer. Consequently, the burden of decommissioning oil and gas assets is placed firmly on the companies which have derived a benefit from those assets.

When selling interests in an upstream oil and gas asset, or shares in an oil and gas company owning upstream oil and gas assets, a seller will seek to ensure, to the fullest extent possible, that it is protected from liability for decommissioning such assets in the future. As a result, measures designed to provide the seller with such protection have been a prominent consideration in sale and purchase negotiations. However, as reserves deplete in more mature basins, in order to facilitate M&A activity, sellers may consider retaining decommissioning liability in respect of the assets being transferred.

This chapter explores the origins of decommissioning liabilities in respect of oil and gas assets (principally offshore), and the impact that these liabilities have on shaping transactions for the sale and purchase of such assets. It is written principally from a UK North Sea perspective, given the comparative maturity of assets and, consequently, the experience gained in this area.

2. International law

2.1 United Nations Convention on the Law of the Sea 1982

Many nations' obligations in relation to the decommissioning of offshore installations have their origins in the United Nations Convention on the Law of the Sea (UNCLOS) of 1982.[1] The convention entered into force in 1994. Article 60(3) includes the following provision:

> *Any installations or structures which are abandoned or disused shall be removed to ensure safety of navigation, taking into account any generally accepted international standards established in this regard by the competent international organisation. Such removal shall also have due regard to fishing, the protection of the marine environment*

* The publisher acknowledges Julie Jones, formerly of CMS, as author of this chapter in the previous edition.

1 See http://treaties.un.org/ for a list of countries that have ratified UNCLOS.

and the rights and duties of other States. Appropriate publicity shall be given to the depth, position and dimensions of any installations or structures not entirely removed.

The 'competent international organisation' for this purpose is the International Maritime Organisation (IMO), which in 1989 adopted its Guidelines and Standards setting out the minimum global standards for the removal of offshore installations. These Guidelines and Standards are not legally binding, as the IMO Assembly made only a recommendation for member governments to take them into account when making decisions concerning decommissioning or abandonment of disused facilities. The IMO Guidelines entitled coastal states to determine that installations could be left wholly or partially in place if they would not cause unjustifiable interference with other uses of the sea and if, where they did not project above the water surface, there was an unobstructed water column of at least 55 metres. The IMO Guidelines also provided that no installation should be placed on any continental shelf or in any exclusive economic zone after 1 January 1998, unless its design and construction allowed entire removal on abandonment.

Many countries' obligations in respect of decommissioning offshore infrastructure are reflected in the more detailed and restrictive requirements of the London Convention on the Prevention of Marine Pollution by Dumping of Wastes and Other Matter 1972, as amended by its 1996 Protocol (London Convention), and the Convention for the Protection of Marine Environment of the North-East Atlantic (OSPAR Convention).

2.2 The London Convention, the OSPAR Convention and Decision 98/3

The London Convention prohibits all dumping with the exception of wastes and other matter included in Annex I to the 1996 Protocol (the so-called 'reverse list'). Annex I includes, for example, "vessels and platforms" and "bulky items primarily comprising iron, steel and concrete". However, a special permit is required before the dumping takes place and its grant must accord with the provisions of Annex II to the 1996 Protocol, which is entitled "Assessment of Wastes or Other Matter that May Be Considered for Dumping". Moreover, due to the convention's adoption of both the 'polluter pays' principle and the precautionary principle, anyone proposing to dump a structure is required to demonstrate that there were no more environmentally friendly options available and that all relevant preventive measures to avoid any harm to the marine environment are being taken.

The OSPAR Convention replaces two earlier conventions covering marine and land pollution sources and was agreed in Paris in 1992. The OSPAR Convention has been signed and ratified by all of the contracting parties to the original Oslo or Paris Conventions (Belgium, Denmark, the European Community, Finland, France, Germany, Iceland, Ireland, the Netherlands, Norway, Portugal, Spain, Sweden and the United Kingdom), and by Luxembourg and Switzerland. It entered into force on 25 March 1998. The OSPAR Convention deals with many aspects of pollution affecting the "maritime area",[2] but the primary focus for those contemplating the decommissioning of offshore installations is OSPAR Decision 98/3.

In July 1998, in the aftermath of the Brent Spar incident,[3] there was considerable

2 As defined in Article 1 of the OSPAR Convention.

political pressure to tighten the rules governing the disposal of offshore installations. The OSPAR Commission developed a new regime for the decommissioning of disused offshore installations, which is set out in OSPAR Decision 98/3. Under the terms of OSPAR Decision 98/3, which entered into force on 9 February 1999, there is a general prohibition on the dumping and leaving wholly or partly in place of offshore installations. However, this general rule is subject to certain exceptions.

OSPAR Decision 98/3 recognises that there may be difficulty in removing the "footings" of large steel jackets weighing more than 10,000 tonnes, concrete installations and some others in "exceptional and unforeseen circumstances". As a result, there is a facility for derogation from the main rule for such installations on a case-by-case basis. The presumption is that all installations will be removed entirely and exceptions to that rule will be granted only if the assessment and consultation procedure, which forms part of OSPAR Decision 98/3, shows that there are significant reasons why an alternative disposal option is preferable to reuse or recycling or final disposal on land. The decision provides for review by the OSPAR Commission at five-yearly intervals to consider, in light of experience and technical developments, whether the derogations from the general ban on dumping continue to be appropriate. The next consultation is due in 2018.

3. National law

The decommissioning regime in most oil and gas jurisdictions attempts to reallocate the burden of compliance with international law from the host government to the oil companies. Even countries which are not parties to the conventions described above tend to have environmental and/or petroleum-specific laws and regulations concerning decommissioning, which may be expanded upon in the terms of the licence or form of production sharing contract (PSC) (or services contract) awarded to oil companies.

In order to prevent the financial burden of decommissioning oil and gas assets from falling on the taxpayer, many regimes allow the government to make some or all of the following persons liable for decommissioning oil and gas infrastructure:

- present licensees/parties to a PSC/services contract/joint operating agreement (JOA);
- parties to other relevant agreements allowing entities to enjoy the benefit of production of petroleum – these would include, for example, those entitled to a royalty or other interest in the production;
- owners of relevant infrastructure;
- parties previously in the above three categories which have transferred their interest;[4] and
- associated/affiliated entities of any of the above.

---

3 The Brent Spar (or 'Brent E') was a North Sea oil storage and tanker loading buoy situated in the Brent oilfield operated by Shell UK. In 1995 Shell applied for disposal of the Brent Spar in deep Atlantic waters at North Feni Ridge. The UK government supported the application, which sparked a worldwide campaign by Greenpeace against this plan. Eventually, Shell abandoned its plans to dispose of the Brent Spar at sea and later announced its decision to reuse much of the main structure in the construction of new harbour facilities near Stavanger, Norway.

4 This can be on a joint and several basis, as in the United Kingdom, or in order of the most recent exit from the relevant asset, as in Norway.

The purpose of imposing decommissioning liabilities on the above categories of persons is to cast the net widely so as to avoid the host government having to pay for decommissioning costs in a default scenario.

In many jurisdictions, there are no regulatory requirements to set aside funds for the costs of future decommissioning and no 'sinking funds'.[5] If such provision or funds are not in place, there is a greater risk of default when the time comes to pay for the costs of decommissioning. This has an impact on sellers of assets or shares in oil and gas companies. They will fall within one of the last two categories of persons listed above and could continue to be liable at law for the costs of decommissioning notwithstanding their exit from an asset.

4. Impact on sellers

The result of the above on sellers is that in relevant regimes, notwithstanding the sale of their interest in an asset to a third party or the sale of shares in a party to the licence/PSC, depending on the jurisdiction in question, they might either be:

- contingently liable for decommissioning costs in the event of a default by the purchaser or parties which were more recently 'involved' in the relevant asset than the seller; or
- jointly and severally liable with the purchaser (and any other licensees/parties to the PSC/JOA) for decommissioning costs.

As such, when entering into sale and purchase arrangements with a buyer, sellers are likely to seek to protect themselves from this liability in various ways.

4.1 Decommissioning security in a sale and purchase scenario

(a) Indemnities

It is the common desire of most sellers to achieve a clean exit from an asset such that they have no residual liabilities or, to the extent that they may otherwise have residual liabilities at law, to seek full protection from the buyer in respect of such liabilities. It is therefore common practice in sale and purchase agreements (SPAs) for the buyer to indemnify the seller against any liability connected to the decommissioning of the assets being purchased. This is also true in share purchase agreements for exploration and production companies, where the seller may have such a liability by virtue of its affiliate relationship with the entity to be sold, notwithstanding that following such a sale it would cease to be an affiliate. In each case the indemnity will operate as a promise by the buyer to reimburse the seller in the event that the seller is made liable at law for carrying out or contributing to the costs of decommissioning.

Given the extent of potential liability, most sellers are unwilling to accept an indemnity only from the buyer in respect of this risk, given that an indemnity is only as good as the future financial capability of the party providing it. Instead, sellers will often seek specific security in respect of this potential liability from the buyer in the

5 A sinking fund in the context of decommissioning is a fund established by a company to accumulate sufficient funds to finance future decommissioning of a particular asset.

form of a parent company guarantee or, more typically, an annual renewable letter of credit.

The provisions relating to this security requirement will be contained in detail either in the SPA itself or in a separate decommissioning security agreement (DSA).

Where the assets involved are more mature, there is likely to be a need to move away from a clean break structure, with the seller retaining certain liability for decommissioning.[6] Here, given the economics of mature assets with significant decommissioning costs, the seller will be faced with a choice of retaining the asset until end of field life or seeking to divest to receive cash and defer its decommissioning expenditure via the buyer being better able to extend field life. This trend has recently emerged in the United Kingdom, where there is also a regulatory requirement to "maximise economic recovery" from the UK Continental Shelf[7] (UKCS), whereby companies may in some cases be encouraged by the regulator to divest of assets in order to maximise production from the UKCS. The buyer will expect the seller to grant an indemnity in respect of any retained liability and will likely require one of the forms of security referred to above.

(b) Decommissioning security agreements and provisions for decommissioning security within an SPA

In addition to the concern of many sellers in relation to default by a buyer and the potential decommissioning liability to which the sellers may be exposed, co-venturers under a licence, PSC, JOA or service contract will also be concerned about default by their partners, as they may be potentially jointly and severally liable for the full cost of decommissioning if those licensees or PSC, JOA or service contract parties default.

DSAs are contractual arrangements – typically between seller and buyer (SPA DSAs) or between co-venturers under the licence, PSC, JOA or service contract (field DSAs) – under which security is provided by the owner(s) of the relevant interest(s) in the asset in respect of their share of the estimated future costs of decommissioning the asset. Some DSAs may involve the state as a party.

DSAs provide for security to be given annually, based on an estimate of decommissioning costs prepared by the operator under a field DSA or by the security provider (ie, the buyer) under an SPA DSA. As the provider is estimating the level of security it will provide under these latter types of DSA, they tend to include requirements for more regular independent scrutiny by an expert than a field DSA, where the operator may be viewed as more neutral due to the fact that it both gives and receives security. The usual formula is to take estimated decommissioning costs multiplied by a contingency (the risk factor) (since decommissioning cost estimates are notoriously inexact), discounted to get a net present value. This risk factor can vary, but may be up to 50% on top of the estimated costs. Security is then given for the relevant participating interest share of those costs.

In the case of field DSAs, it is usual to deduct the net present value of the relevant

---

6 Potential alternative mechanisms are discussed in section 4.1(e) below.

7 The principal objective is the "objective of maximising the economic recovery of UK petroleum" as set out in Section 9A of the Petroleum Act 1998.

party's share of remaining reserves and other income from the field from the cost estimate, on the basis that if such party defaults in its obligations under the DSA, its partners will be able to claim its share of reserves and use the proceeds to pay for its share of decommissioning under the default provisions within the JOA (backed as appropriate, depending on the jurisdiction, with a charge over those assets). The reserve value is not typically deducted in the case of SPA DSAs, since the seller is generally unable to benefit from any remaining reserves in event of a default, but the seller may be persuaded to agree a lower risk factor.

If the party seeking security is unhappy with the calculation, then there is usually a provision for disputes to be referred to an expert for resolution. There may also be a requirement for regular independent reviews by an expert, even in the absence of a dispute. The calculation is reviewed annually to take account of changes in the value of the reserves and in the estimate of decommissioning costs. There may also be a requirement for a review during the year if there is a significant shift in the estimate of costs or, more likely, reserves.

Security may be provided in a variety of forms, including cash or an on-demand bond from a bank or insurance company, with the most common forms being a guarantee from a parent or affiliate of the company providing security or a letter of credit from a bank. Cash is rarely used in practice, as often it is not tax efficient and ties up funds which could be used for investment. However, it may be the only option for certain classes of buyer, such as investment fund special purpose vehicles, which are often unable to access letter of credit facilities and do not have parent companies or other affiliates capable of granting guarantees on their behalf.[8] It is important where security is to be renewed on an annual basis that the new security is provided well in advance of the old security expiring. If the relevant party fails to provide such new security, this allows time for the old security to be enforced.

It would be more unusual for any charge over assets (either the assets which are the subject of security or other assets within the seller's group) to constitute security under a DSA (other than, in effect, in a field DSA, to the extent of any default or forfeiture provisions in the relevant JOA). The reasons for this are principally from a seller's or security holder's perspective and stem from the potential difficulties associated with creating valid and enforceable security over petroleum reserves in several jurisdictions (including the existence of prior/forfeiture rights of co-venturers under a JOA or PSC in the event of default), and the delay or uncertainty in enforceability of charges versus on-demand instruments. The effect on a buyer's ability to borrow funds from third parties in creating prior charges for decommissioning security purposes means that buyers are also often resistant to giving any security over assets or shares of their group.

It is invariably a requirement that any bank providing a letter of credit or bond, or any affiliate providing a guarantee, must be credit rated to a minimum prescribed level. The UK Industry Model Form DSA[9] suggests a rating of AA-/Aa3, while the UK

8 A recent trend in the North Sea is for midstream infrastructure to be acquired by investment fund special purpose vehicles.

9 Available on the Oil & Gas UK website at www.oilandgasuk.co.uk.

government's guidance suggests that a rating of AA/Aa2 will be required. However, following the financial crisis, far fewer banks and companies meet these criteria and there is considerable pressure to adopt lower thresholds. Further, some licensees' parent companies are not credit rated and the relevant licensee may therefore seek to negotiate a market capitalisation or other financial worth test in order to be able to provide a parent company guarantee instead of a letter of credit.

The bank will charge a fee for providing the letter of credit and will increasingly ask for collateral security from the entity requesting it, depending on its credit rating, or deduct the amount of the security from that company's borrowing base. Inevitably, therefore, the provision of decommissioning security has a major impact on the ability of purchasers – particularly new, smaller investors – to invest in assets; this issue has become a major hurdle to successful asset transfers in recent years.

From a buyer's perspective, having to provide a large letter of credit can make a transaction uneconomic. As such, in many transactions, notwithstanding the seller's desire to achieve the 'clean break' described above, there needs to be a balancing of risk between buyer and seller in order to make transactions workable. Ideally, from a seller's perspective, it will enter into an SPA DSA with the buyer, with provision for security to be provided immediately thereunder (on completion of the sale and purchase).

The most contentious issues when negotiating DSAs are usually the commercial issues of the ratings of the entities providing letters of credit and guarantees and the risk factor to be applied to decommissioning costs.

Historically, decommissioning costs have often been calculated without allowance for the tax relief which it is anticipated will be granted by the government when the costs are incurred. This was a result of a lack of confidence on the part of those seeking the security that such relief would in fact be available to them when decommissioning costs were incurred, which would possibly be many years into the future, when tax laws may have changed.[10]

Security may be provided for many years while the field continues to produce. Each year as the reserves fall, the amount of the security will tend to increase until, by the time of cessation of production, it is at least as much as the anticipated cost of decommissioning, usually with a significant contingency built in. Provided that the company which is giving the security remains solvent and carries out its decommissioning obligations, the letter of credit or guarantee is never 'called' (ie, enforced). Once decommissioning has been completed, the obligation to provide

10 However, in the United Kingdom, the government introduced 'decommissioning relief deeds' in 2013, being contracts between the government and those potentially liable for the costs of decommissioning oil and gas facilities, under which the government guarantees the present rate of tax relief. On the whole, this has resulted in decommissioning costs being calculated on a 'post-tax' basis, thereby freeing up capital which can then be reinvested in the UK North Sea. For more information see the Finance Act 2013, which is the enabling legislation authorising the UK government to enter into the decommissioning relief deeds. See also the UK government's consultation paper on this issue: *Decommissioning Relief Deeds: Increasing tax certainty for oil and gas investment in the UK Continental Shelf*, issued on 9 July 2012. In Norway, a seller's decommissioning liability is limited to the after-tax value by law; whereas in the Netherlands, tax relief for decommissioning expenditure is not given as a matter of law on the basis that a large part of the decommissioning cost for an asset will be met by the government as a result of it being a state party to all licences.

security will cease and the final letter of credit or guarantee will simply expire and/or be returned to the entity which provided the security and will not be replaced.

On the other hand, if a company that has provided security falls into financial difficulty or for any other reason is in breach of its obligations under the DSA (eg, if the provider of its guarantee or letter of credit ceases to meet the specified criteria and it is unable to provide replacement security in the time specified), then the letter of credit or guarantee will be called, even if this occurs before the decommissioning work has begun. If security is called, the bank or affiliate in question will be required to pay out cash under the letter of credit or guarantee, usually to a trustee on behalf of the beneficiaries (ie, the seller or the other licensees, PSC, JOA or contract parties). In this situation, the funds are held by the operator or trustee separate from the assets of the defaulting licensee and invested in a low-risk manner (in either cash or gilt-edged securities) until the time of decommissioning. The discount rate used in the calculation of the security is intended to ensure that in such a situation the funds held by the trustee grow over the remaining life of the field such that they are sufficient to meet the estimated costs of decommissioning at the time it is expected to occur. The monies could be held for a considerable period if the failure occurs early in the life of a field.

If a party that is a beneficiary of security is obliged by the government to carry out decommissioning, then it will be able to claim reimbursement of the costs of that decommissioning activity from the trustee (provided that there are sufficient trust funds to cover the costs incurred by the beneficiary).[11] Further, if the party in default has recovered and can fulfil its decommissioning obligations, then, upon providing adequate security to the trustee, it will be reimbursed out of the trust fund in respect of any letter of credit or guarantee which has been called.

Security is usually provided until decommissioning is complete and then for a further 12 months at a much reduced level in case of additional work requirements being imposed by the state. After the expiry of such period, any remaining monies in the trust or any uncalled security will be returned to the party that provided the security. Residual obligations in relation to decommissioned assets may remain, particularly if assets have not been fully removed from the seabed, but these obligations are felt to be too remote and liability too unquantifiable to justify security.

If a party sells its interest in the field, then a field DSA will usually provide for the return of its security once its assignee has put substitute security in place.

Some regimes, such as that in the United Kingdom, ensure that funds set aside as financial security for decommissioning are available for that purpose in the event of insolvency by excluding the application of insolvency laws to those funds. This means that it should be very difficult for any creditors of an insolvent licensee to claim, for the benefit of the general creditors of the relevant party, funds set aside for

---

11 In the UK Industry Model Form DSA, where security is provided on a 'post-tax' basis, a party which has incurred decommissioning costs as a result of another's default will be entitled to claim reimbursement only for the 'post-tax' portion from the trust fund, with the balance to be recovered by the paying party through a claim for tax relief. Given that there will be a delay of, on average, eight or nine months to receive the tax relief, the UK Industry Model Form DSA allows for a financing fee to be recovered by a paying party.

decommissioning. In any event, it is important in many jurisdictions that the entity holding the security is independent from the parties, as if security is held by the operator, licensee or seller, there is a risk that in case of the insolvency of such entity, the security may be lost via amalgamation with the security holder's own funds.

(c) *Impact of field DSA on sale and purchase*

The provision of security can cause difficulties for a buyer as it may (depending on the JOA and any field DSA in place) be required to post security to the seller and may also be required to post security to its new co-venturers in respect of future decommissioning costs under a field DSA or the JOA. As such, the buyer could potentially be required to post security twice in respect of the same liability.

One solution is for the JOA co-venturers, the seller and, in some cases, any other historic asset owners (that may require or be entitled to security) to enter into one decommissioning security agreement whereby security can be posted by the buyer for the benefit of all beneficiaries.[12] This is provided for in the UK Industry Model Form DSA, which allows for 'second-tier participants'[13] to be party to the deed and allows them to exercise the benefit of security granted by each of the co-venturers.

From a seller's perspective, the advantages and disadvantages of accepting the benefit of an existing field DSA versus bilateral security from the buyer are as follows:

- Commonly in field DSAs, security is not required to be provided until a trigger date, normally calculated with reference to a point in time where the net remaining revenues attributable to a field multiplied by a factor are equal to the net cost of decommissioning. It may be that on completion of a transaction, if the trigger date has not been reached, the seller will enjoy only a contractual right against the buyer to put security in place in the future rather than any security itself. In this situation, if the participants are insolvent and unable to put up security at a future date, the seller is exposed. The concept of a trigger date is therefore rare in a bilateral security arrangement, since the seller will look to be provided with full security (or as close as it can realistically achieve) at the outset.
- The seller may also be uncomfortable with the formulaic calculation of security costs in the field DSA, in that these would commonly allow for deduction of net revenue from the net cost of security. This is on the basis that in a field DSA, if there is a default by a co-venturer, some of the other parties may be entitled to take the defaulting co-venturer's share of future net revenue through the JOA or PSC default or forfeiture provisions, thus mitigating their liability for decommissioning costs. This will not apply to a person which is not a party to the JOA or PSC, with the result that such person may be made liable for decommissioning the field infrastructure, but will not be entitled to any remaining net revenues.
- In achieving second-tier participant status, a seller will be entitled not just to

---

12 See, for example, J Aldersey-Williams, "The Decommissioning Cost Provision Deed: Facilitating Asset Transfers on the UKCS", IELR 2008, 5, 169–177.

13 Namely, those entities which are parties to the DSA as beneficiaries, but which no longer hold an interest in the asset (eg, the seller)

security provided by a buyer, but also to security from any other field participants. This may in effect give it more security than it would otherwise enjoy, since commonly buyers will only ever provide bilateral security to the extent of the percentage of interest acquired from the seller, theoretically leaving the seller exposed to decommissioning security liability in the event of insolvency of the co-venturers.

The principal issue with the above is that if there is no existing field DSA in place, significant time is required to negotiate one and this may significantly delay deal completion. The co-venturers whose consent is required to allow completion of the transaction to take place will enjoy a significant amount of leverage in any such negotiation. Such co-venturers may not be inclined to enter into a true field DSA and provide any security at all, meaning that the DSA resulting from the negotiation can be a fusion of an SPA/field DSA where only the purchaser is required to provide security for the benefit of both the co-venturers and the seller. In this situation, the buyer can proceed to complete the transaction, but is placed in the awkward position of providing security to its partners with no requirement for them to do likewise in return.

(d) Hybrid bilateral DSAs

Due to the seller's reluctance to accept the position under a field DSA, or where there is no field DSA in place, the seller may request bilateral security from the buyer. However, in order to avoid double security, there may be provision for this bilateral security to be reduced by the amount of any field security in place, such that only the difference between the field DSA security and that required by the seller is provided.

Crafting what is required for the bilateral security to be so reduced is therefore critical. Ideally, the seller would want direct access to the field DSA security as a party thereto (and not necessarily just as a third-party beneficiary) in order to allow the offset (since a third-party beneficiary which is not a party to the field DSA may not be entitled to receive the information necessary to calculate the offset and will have no rights to prevent future amendments to the DSA).

A less risk-averse seller may even be prepared to accept an offset without having direct rights to benefit from any security under the field DSA, on the basis that it may be comfortable in the knowledge that security is being provided in connection with decommissioning, albeit to someone else. This approach is rarer, as the seller will not enjoy any access to the security in a default scenario and may therefore be exposed where the recipient of the security is insolvent or otherwise does not carry out the decommissioning required.

(e) Alternatives to SPA DSA and/or seller becoming a beneficiary to a field DSA including seller retention of liabilities

It is not unknown for the estimated costs of decommissioning to affect the base economics of a sale and purchase. An example is where the seller pays the buyer to take off its hands older assets with little remaining field life on the basis that the buyer will also be responsible for decommissioning costs – the parties may regard the value as negative on the basis that they might consider that the value of remaining production in the field is outweighed by the remaining decommissioning costs.

Different mechanisms can be used to allow a buyer to acquire the interest in the remaining production in a field in such circumstances. These options are not mutually exclusive and elements of any of them may be adopted by the seller and buyer during negotiations. At the core of many of these mechanisms is a retention of decommissioning liability by the seller to some extent driven by the desire of the seller:

- to obtain a cash consideration which it can use in its other business elsewhere; and
- to push back the decommissioning date, with the seller anticipating that the buyer will be able to extend field life through greater investment and drilling or exploration work in relation to the asset.

The only alternative to a sale in such cases might be for the seller to retain the asset until end of field life. It may be that, given the maturity of the assets, the consideration is nominal. Despite this, there is benefit to a seller in the 'time value of money' that is gained by delaying its decommissioning spend. There is also a hope that by extending the life of the field, the decommissioning industry will be more developed at the time the decommissioning takes place, resulting in cost savings from the application of new technology and greater economies of scale. Similarly, it will be in the buyer's interest to extend field life and receive revenues from ongoing production, knowing that it will not be responsible for costs of decommissioning the existing infrastructure at end of field life. This type of arrangement has found favour relatively recently in a number of transactions in the North Sea. A key issue, however, is that in most cases some form of consent is required by other co-venturers to achieve this, which adds to deal completion risk.

Mechanism 1 – sale of the asset with an obligation on the seller to take back the asset at the end of production: The seller may retain the liability to decommission the existing infrastructure, but sell the asset to the buyer for a limited period. A retransfer SPA or lease will be necessary, detailing the terms upon which the seller will take back the assets for decommissioning at end of field life. The retransfer SPA is normally signed at the same time as the first SPA, but will not become effective until notice of hand-back is issued by the buyer at a future date.

It is important from the seller's perspective that it receives protection in the form of indemnities or warranties that it will acquire and be responsible for only those assets it transferred to the buyer and no other liabilities. As such, it will seek wide indemnification in the retransfer SPA against any additional decommissioning liabilities, environmental liabilities, personnel or contract liabilities in particular. The buyer may be nervous giving such protections at this time in respect of a future state of affairs over which it may not have full control and negotiation is often necessary in this regard.

The other important agreement in this structure is what is often known as the 'interim agreement' or 'intervening period agreement'. In effect, this document will regulate the relationship of the buyer and the seller in the interim period, from the date of transfer to the buyer until hand-back and decommissioning.

The seller will want certain controls over the activities carried out by the buyer during the interim period. For example, the buyer will often wish to upgrade or modify the existing infrastructure in some manner, but the seller will not want to take on this extra decommissioning liability and liaison will be necessary to allocate such liability to the buyer. Indeed, often the seller will seek decommissioning liability security from the buyer in this regard. Part of the value the buyer sees in the assets may be through using the facilities as a hub for third-party transportation of production, allowing it to receive tariff or operating cost share in this regard. The seller will want to ensure that such third-party arrangements are terminable on hand-back and decommissioning of the asset. The seller will therefore seek to impose controls of this nature on the buyer in order to police and control at an early stage any potential liabilities that it may suffer on hand-back.

On the occurrence of any default by the buyer under this interim agreement, the seller will have the right to require a hand-back and proceed to decommissioning. Similarly, the buyer may itself elect to cease production if not economic and hand back the asset. In both cases, if hand-back happens earlier than the parties expect, this is disadvantageous for the seller, since it will have factored into its sale economics the fact that field life would be extended by a certain period and that it would therefore postpone decommissioning costs. The seller may insist on a liquidated damages payment in an early hand-back scenario. Again, this will be the subject of negotiation.

In addition, the seller may need to retain a small interest in the field and/or a licence interest in the interim or intervening period in order to protect its tax position in respect of decommissioning, whereby it can effectively obtain credit for decommissioning costs spent against production profits and tax paid.

One aspect of the above structures is the transfer and retransfer of title to the assets, which in certain circumstances may expose the seller to too great a risk if the buyer were to become insolvent in the period between the initial sale and the retransfer. In these circumstances, the buyer's insolvency practitioners are unlikely to be required to comply with the terms of the transaction documents and instead will follow their duty to maximise the return for the creditors of the buyer. Where this risk is considered to be material, an alternative structure would be to lease the physical assets to the buyer and have a renunciation of the lease at the time of retransfer. This results in the buyer having access to the property to enable further economic benefit to be gained from the assets while the title remains with the seller and therefore greater certainty of retransfer exists in the event of the buyer's insolvency.

Mechanism 2 – retention of decommissioning liability and monetary obligation: The retransfer mechanism noted above will be difficult to utilise if the seller is not the operator or if the sale relates to anything less than the full 100% interest in the asset, given likely JOA/PSC consent requirements on the part of co-venturers. As an alternative, the seller may agree to retain liability *vis-à-vis* the buyer[14] for all or some of its financial share of decommissioning without the transfer back to it of the asset as envisaged in Mechanism 1. The simplest way, mechanically speaking, for this to operate is for the seller to retain liability for full decommissioning of the asset. In order to reduce the day-to-day administrative burden of the asset, the seller may cease to be a party to the PSC or JOA upon completion of the transfer of the interest to the buyer, but as a result the seller will have no direct visibility or control over decommissioning activities or costs. The appropriate balance will need to be negotiated between the seller and buyer, but ultimately will require the approval of the co-venturers to the PSC or JOA in respect of access to and control over decommissioning spend, and the terms of the required DSA. An alternative might be for the seller to seek to amend the JOA or PSC to allow the seller to remain a party and have certain rights and obligations as regards decommissioning only. Each option represents completion risk to the deal between the seller and buyer.

Given that the buyer will not be financially responsible for decommissioning the asset as a result, it follows that it will be unwilling to provide security under any field DSA and accordingly the seller will be expected to provide the necessary security in respect of the interest to be sold. This will require some amendments to the field DSA (if already in place) or add complication to any new field DSA that may be required in connection with the transaction at the very least in order to enable an unaffiliated non-licensee to provide security. A variation on a seller assuming full responsibility for decommissioning is for the seller to split liability with the buyer. Options to do so include the following:

- The seller could retain liability for the decommissioning up to a monetary cap – for example, based on the estimated decommissioning cost at the date of sale.
- The seller could retain decommissioning liability for facilities existing at the date of sale with the buyer liable for any 'new' property. Careful distinction between 'existing' and 'new' property will be required – for example, to determine whether repairs or replacement constitute 'existing' or 'new' property and to allocate common decommissioning costs incurred across various facilities in an equitable manner; or
- A percentage apportionment of final decommissioning costs (capped or uncapped) between seller and buyer could be agreed.

This may or may not be set out in an amended JOA/PSC to reflect such a split, or instead dealt with in a back-to-back arrangement between buyer and seller only. A split of decommissioning liability (whether monetary or 'facilities' based as above) between the seller and buyer will again require amendment to a field DSA and approval of the co-venturers, unless the seller or buyer is willing to assume all such liability *vis-à-vis* the co-venturers. In such case any sub-allocation of such liabilities will be addressed in a back-to-back arrangement between the buyer and seller only.

To the extent that the buyer assumes any liability for decommissioning, unless

14 Liability at law as discussed earlier in this chapter will remain applicable to both parties.

the buyer will be providing security for that element under a field DSA, the seller will want to seek bilateral security from the buyer for that share. Where possible, the seller will want this to be on the same terms as any field DSA. However, depending on the identity of the buyer, any security it is able to provide is likely to be weaker than that under a field DSA. It will be for the seller to decide the level of buyer credit risk that it is willing to accept.

A further variation may be required if the buyer is willing to assume some or all liability for decommissioning, but is unable to provide security in an acceptable form to the existing co-venturers.[15] In this scenario, the seller may agree to provide security on behalf of the buyer for all or some of the buyer's liability under a field DSA and accept the buyer's weaker credit under back-to-back security. Again, it will be for the seller to decide the level of buyer credit risk that it is willing to accept.

Mechanism 3 – negative consideration: Where the seller remains keen to achieve a clean break from the assets to be sold, it could agree negative consideration with the buyer (ie, the seller would pay the buyer to take the assets). Although this achieves the clean break, the 'time value of money' benefit is lost, with the seller effectively paying for decommissioning in advance. The tax implications of such a structure would also require careful consideration in the relevant jurisdiction.

Mechanism 4 – sinking fund: Where the buyer is willing to take on some or all decommissioning liability in respect of the assets being acquired, but is unable to provide security in one of the more usual formats, a sinking fund may be utilised. This is a commercial arrangement whereby funds are paid into a trust out of field profits allowing the fund to build up over time. This arrangement requires the seller to take increased risk until the fund fully builds up – likely over a number of years.[16] As a result, it is unlikely to be acceptable to co-venturers as a form of security in a field DSA (unless there is no existing field DSA in place and it can be negotiated as part of a new field DSA), and is more likely to be seen as a bilateral background form of security between seller and buyer. An alternative hybrid option would be for a trust fund to build up under a field DSA with the seller providing excess security until fully funded.

5. Conclusion

With the estimated costs of decommissioning ageing oil and gas infrastructure rising, any prudent seller will spend a considerable amount of time determining what protection, by way of decommissioning security or otherwise, it will require in striking a balance between the benefit of disposing of the asset and any potential future decommissioning liability to which it may be exposed. The issues and potential solutions highlighted in this chapter indicate that the parties to every oil

15 As discussed earlier in this chapter, even if it is willing to assume decommissioning costs, having to provide a large letter of credit can make a transaction uneconomic for a buyer and many will be unable to provide another form of security from a AA-/Aa3 rated bank or affiliate.

16 Here the fund build-up would typically be at a slower rate than that envisaged through cash provision under a field DSA.

and gas M&A transaction will likely find this balance through their own bespoke arrangements aimed at addressing the concerns of both seller and buyer in order to come to a solution acceptable to both parties. With the increase in the number of smaller, independent companies keen to invest in oil and gas assets, the added element of co-venturer involvement in DSA negotiations is becoming more frequent, with the result that the balancing act proves more difficult to achieve.

Competition law issues in oil and gas M&A

Paul Culliford
Andrew Hockley
Bryan Cave Leighton Paisner LLP

1. Introduction

Parties involved in mergers, acquisitions and joint ventures should have competition law issues at the forefront of their minds from the start of the process. It is not just 'merger control' (ie, the review of M&A transactions by competition agencies globally) and potential merger notifications that are relevant – competition law issues can arise from as early as initial exploratory discussions and due diligence. These issues often arise globally, even when the transaction in question has limited geographic reach.

Given the need for competitors to work together to share costs and risks in the oil and gas sector (eg, through joint venturing), the significant market power accruing to national oil companies and other market participants, and the importance of access to essential monopoly infrastructure such as liquefied natural gas (LNG) terminals and pipelines, substantive competition considerations may often arise. Even where a transaction does not raise potential substantive competition concerns, it is important not to slip up on process points associated with the competition review process.

This chapter provides an overview of the key areas where competition law issues can arise throughout the M&A process, together with associated practical considerations. The chapter also briefly addresses foreign direct investment regimes, which are often administered in parallel with competition regulation and which provide some national governments with the power to review and potentially limit foreign investment in exploration rights and other domestic energy assets.

2. Pre-merger considerations

From as early as initial discussions and due diligence, merger parties should have competition issues at the forefront of their minds. Issues around the sharing of potentially competitively sensitive information, competition risks in the deal itself and premature completion before obtaining merger clearance (so-called 'gun jumping') are all important considerations.

2.1 Information sharing and gun jumping

Until the point that a transaction closes, the parties remain independent businesses and the general rules of competition law apply to each of them. This leads to two separate but related considerations:

- If the transaction requires mandatory and suspensory merger notifications (meaning that the parties cannot complete the transaction until clearance is received) in one or more jurisdictions, the parties cannot take any steps to implement the transaction before clearance is received. If such steps are taken, the parties risk fines for prematurely implementing the transaction – often referred to as 'gun jumping'.

- Regardless of the merger control situation, the merger parties remain independent companies up until completion. Therefore, to the extent that the parties are competitors, extra care needs to be taken in relation to the sharing of information that could be seen as competitively sensitive during the period of negotiation and up until completion.

To avoid any allegations of gun jumping, the parties should not begin integrating their businesses prior to clearance being received. This does not simply mean formal completion of the transaction, but could include steps towards completion such as the integration of particular teams and systems, the purchaser being able to veto contracts that the target enters into and the parties presenting a joint offering to the market – for example, either jointly pitching for potential supply contracts or agreeing that only one party will do so. As a rule of thumb, any steps that go beyond what is necessary to ensure that the merged entity can be operational from 'day one' after completion, or to protect the material value of the investment during the review period, should not occur prior to clearance being received. In recent years, competition agencies globally have been increasing their enforcement of procedural merger control rules, meaning that merger parties should be careful to ensure compliance with any standstill obligations that they face.

The level of risk should always be assessed at the outset – if the merger parties are close competitors, a greater level of care is required than in cases where the parties have limited or no competitive overlap. Merger parties should therefore work with their advisers to tailor the most appropriate procedures to balance the level of risk with their commercial aims. In the case of competing merger parties, potential safeguards could range from the redaction of competitively sensitive information (eg, pricing and customer names) from documents disclosed to the use of 'clean teams' during the due diligence phase, where any competitively sensitive information that is crucial to assessing the transaction is shared only with a limited group. Further, the merger parties should continue to assess business opportunities independently of one another and not present a coordinated or joint face to the market until the transaction has closed.

2.2 Competition law risks – due diligence

Competition law liability does not attach only to shares. Liability for breaches of competition law can also attach to a business that is sold by way of asset sale. Further, the seller of a business by way of shares will not necessarily be absolved of liability for any breaches of competition law during its period of ownership – it will generally be considered jointly and severally liable for any breaches that occurred while it controlled that business. In Europe, it is presumed that a parent exercises control over a wholly owned subsidiary.[1] Competition law investigations can be time

1 *Akzo Nobel NV v Commission*, Case C-97/08, 10 September 2009.

consuming and costly, and can result in significant fines for a business (eg, the European Commission can impose fines of up to 10% of group worldwide turnover) and extremely costly 'follow-on' private damages actions. It is therefore important to assess during the due diligence phase whether the target carries any competition law risk – either by way of ongoing investigations or litigation or in its wider business operations.

It is common for an initial due diligence request to include questions about whether the target is or has been subject to competition law investigations or fines. Given the increasing importance of private enforcement of competition law globally, standard questions relating to ongoing or threatened litigation will also be important to competition law risk (eg, in the case of customers affected by illegal conduct suing to recover damages).

Whether any relevant investigations or litigation disclosed will inform the extent of further review. However, in some instances – particularly in the case of large potentially 'dominant' targets or in areas where there have been previous cases of breaches of competition laws – it may also be prudent to carry out a broader review of the business. For example, this could include analysis of existing contractual relationships for potential issues and examination of other potential risk areas, such as trade associations.

In transactions with a European Union (EU) nexus, it is also important to consider whether the target may have been the recipient of illegal state aid (ie, unauthorised public subsidy or support which may later need to be repaid).

2.3 Care in what is said and written

During merger control reviews, competition agencies request (and in most cases the parties are required to provide) various internal documents (especially those presented/exchanged at a senior level within the merger parties) relating to the parties' rationale for the transaction and their views on market dynamics. Such internal documents are invaluable to the competition agency, in that they assist it in understanding the market and the reasons for the transaction without the added gloss of advocacy that is included in the merger filing. As such, in preparing such internal documents, parties should be careful to avoid any comments that they do not want reviewed by competition agencies – while, from a commercial and marketing perspective, it might make sense for merger parties to 'talk down' competitors and 'talk up' their own strengths, such comments can hinder a merger investigation. At best, these sorts of comments can give a competition agency pause for thought as it carries out its review. At worst, they can push the agency towards finding competition issues with the transaction.

It is important to remember that internal documents do not necessarily just include formal reports or presentations. Simple emails and meeting minutes may also be caught. From as early as possible in the deal process, therefore, those involved in negotiations and internal considerations should be careful that what is put in writing is an accurate reflection of the true competition dynamics. In the case of more formal presentations and reports, it may be good practice to have internal or external counsel review the content for material that may later be troublesome.

3. Merger control

'Merger control' refers to the review of mergers and acquisitions by competition agencies to ensure that they will not significantly lessen competition. This is the most significant aspect of competition law to be considered during the M&A process. Merger control issues can have a profound impact on a transaction and if merger filings are needed, a condition precedent will likely be required in the transaction documentation and there may be an impact on the overall transaction timetable. In the simplest of cases, merger control can simply mean a slight delay in the timing of the transaction. In other cases, merger control can make or break a deal.

Merger control exists in well over 100 jurisdictions globally and a single transaction can require notification in multiple jurisdictions – even when it does not have a specific nexus to that jurisdiction. For these reasons, it is crucial that the parties to the transaction consider merger control early in the deal process. Failure to notify a transaction that meets the notification thresholds can attract significant fines.

It may be possible to structure a transaction to avoid merger control obligations – this may be important, for example, in a competitive bid context. However, in many cases there are benefits in obtaining merger clearance. Once a transaction is cleared by competition agencies, it is deemed to be compliant with competition law. This has clear benefits in many cases – for example, in relation joint operating agreements which may involve joint selling of natural gas production, where without merger clearance the parties may be open to scrutiny under general antitrust laws.

3.1 Types of merger control regime

While merger control regimes across the globe all have the same general aim – that is, ensuring that mergers do not substantially lessen competition – they take many different forms. Most regimes are mandatory – meaning that if the relevant thresholds are satisfied, the parties are obliged to notify the agencies of the transaction. This is the case in most significant jurisdictions, such as the United States, the EU (and most of its member states), China and Brazil. By contrast, other jurisdictions operate voluntary regimes under which there is no obligation to notify, but if the parties choose not to do so, they run the risk of the competition agency 'calling in' the transaction for examination. These voluntary regimes exist in countries such as the United Kingdom, Singapore, Australia and New Zealand.

In addition to the question of whether a merger notification is mandatory or voluntary, most regimes are 'suspensory', meaning that until clearance is granted, the parties cannot complete their deal, although derogations are often available in certain circumstances such as public takeover bids or insolvency. However, a limited number of regimes (eg, the UK regime) are non-suspensory, meaning that the parties can in certain circumstances complete their transaction prior to obtaining clearance.[2]

---

2 Voluntary regimes such as the UK regime can be complex (eg, the agencies may have the power to intervene post-completion and unwind a deal), and therefore contractual provisions dealing with notification options and transaction conditionality may benefit from specialist local advice.

3.2 Types of transaction

A broad range of transactions can be captured by merger control rules, with different merger control regimes often having differing definitions of what constitutes a merger for their purposes. For this reason, the transaction structure can have important competition law consequences. Indeed, in many instances, the analysis of the transaction structure under competition law can drive the commercial discussions and what is ultimately agreed.

This section considers some typical transaction structures that are seen in the oil and gas context, and the potential merger control issues that could be raised globally.

(a) Share acquisitions

Clearly, outright acquisitions of the voting share capital of an operating company will amount to a relevant merger in most jurisdictions. Further, absent any special control rights held by other shareholders, acquisitions of the majority of the voting capital in such a company will most likely be a relevant merger in most jurisdictions.

However, merger parties should not simply assume that any acquisition of less than 50% of the voting capital in an operating company is not a relevant merger. In many jurisdictions, certain minority acquisitions can be notifiable and parties should be careful to consider whether a minority acquisition could raise merger control issues. Examples include the following:

- Control: In many key jurisdictions, such as the EU (and the majority of its member states) and China, an acquisition will qualify as a merger if the acquirer gains control of the target. In the EU, 'control' is defined as "decisive influence"[3] and can arise in situations other than simple majority ownership. For example, in the case of a listed company with widely spread passive shareholdings, the acquisition of a minority stake may give the acquirer the ability to pass resolutions at shareholder meetings, thereby giving it *de facto* control. Similarly, the contractual ability to veto key business decisions (such as through reserved matters relating to senior appointments or significant investments) may also give control. Control can be held either individually or jointly (eg, when the agreement of more than one shareholder is required to pass key resolutions).
- Bright-line tests: Some jurisdictions operate with a 'bright-line' test. For example, in Germany and Austria, the acquisition of 25% or more of the share capital in a company can constitute a merger, regardless of the actual 'control' rights attached to those shares. In South Korea, the threshold is even lower with, acquisitions of just 20% of the voting capital being potentially notifiable.

(b) Asset acquisitions

Generally speaking, merger control does not distinguish between share and asset acquisitions and the principles outlined in the previous section will apply equally to the acquisition of a business by way of asset rather than share acquisition.

---

3 Council Regulation (EC) No 139/2004 of 20 January 2004 on the control of concentrations between undertakings (EU Merger Regulation), Article 3(2).

However, not all acquisitions of either shares or assets will constitute relevant mergers. This raises the question of whether the package of assets being acquired is sufficient to constitute a business for merger control purposes. In the EU and many of its member states, for example, only an acquisition of an "undertaking or part of an undertaking" – that is, a "business with a market presence to which a market turnover can be clearly attributed"[4] – will amount to a relevant merger. In the case of asset acquisitions, the acquirer should consider carefully whether the package of assets being acquired is enough to constitute an undertaking. This will be a matter of degree that depends on the assets being acquired and their ability to access the market. Relevant considerations could include whether the package includes the requisite intellectual property, personnel and contracts to carry on as a standalone business post-acquisition. However, the inclusion of contracts and a customer base is not always needed, so long as the assets being acquired form the basis of a market presence.[5]

The acquisition of exploration rights or licences is a useful example. For example, pure exploration rights without anything further may not amount to the acquisition of an 'undertaking' requiring notification, as there is no market presence to which turnover can be attributed. By contrast, the acquisition of a package of assets including exploration rights but also production assets and third-party offtake agreements will potentially be enough.

Other jurisdictions apply similar, but potentially wider tests. For example, in the United Kingdom, the acquisition of an 'enterprise' is caught; while in Germany, an acquisition of substantial parts of an undertaking can be caught, meaning that an asset package that does not constitute an 'undertaking' for EU purposes may nevertheless amount to a notifiable transaction in Germany.

(c) Joint ventures

The establishment of a joint venture, be it a greenfield joint venture or a joint venture to acquire an existing business, also often raises merger control issues. While the treatment of acquisitions is similar globally, the treatment of joint ventures varies significantly across different merger control regimes and parties to joint venture arrangements will need to carefully consider the differing rules across different jurisdictions. Further, even if a joint venture does not amount to a 'merger' that requires notification, it may still raise issues under the 'anti-competitive agreement' provisions (eg, Article 101 of the Treaty on the Functioning of European Union or Section 1 of the Sherman Act in the United States) in competition laws globally.

Given the potential for antitrust scrutiny, there may be benefits to the parties to structuring a joint venture such that it can obtain merger clearance. For example, the joint sale of gas from a joint development can raise antitrust concerns (as the joint venture participants have effectively agreed not to compete). However, if the parties

4 Commission Consolidated Jurisdictional Notice under Council Regulation (EC) No 139/2004 on the control of concentrations between undertakings (Consolidated Jurisdictional Notice), Paragraph 24.

5 See, for example, Case Comp/M.6360 – Nynas/Shell/Harburg Refinery, 2 September 2013, where a package of refining and manufacturing assets that did not include customer contracts or customer lists was held to amount to part of an undertaking.

structure such a joint venture as a 'merger' in the relevant jurisdictions, they may be able to obtain 'once and for all' clearance, thereby avoiding subsequent antitrust scrutiny.

The EU position: The EU merger control regime contains specific provisions relating to joint ventures, meaning that it makes sense to consider EU joint ventures separately. In particular, the establishment of a greenfield joint venture will only amount to a relevant merger for EU merger control purposes if:

- the parties establishing that joint venture have 'joint control' over the joint venture; and
- the joint venture performs "on a lasting basis all the functions of an autonomous economic entity."[6] This requirement is generally referred to as 'full functionality'.

The 'joint control' question is usually relatively straightforward. Clearly, in a typical 50/50 joint venture absent any specific control rights, the joint venture parties will have joint control – both will need to agree on key resolutions to pass them. However, a minority shareholder in a joint venture can also be seen as having joint control if, for example, it has a veto right over key decisions such as approving the budget and business plan or appointing senior management. Subsequent changes in the control structure of a joint venture can also trigger a 'fresh' merger – for example, in 1996 the European Commission cleared the establishment of the 'In Salah' gas joint venture in Algeria by BP and Sonatrach, which had joint control over the new business.[7] Subsequently, BP sold half of its share in the joint venture to Statoil, which meant that Statoil became a new joint controlling shareholder in the joint venture. This separate acquisition was cleared in 2003.[8]

The 'full functionality' requirement essentially asks whether, rather than simply being a vehicle to serve its parents, the joint venture is operating autonomously as an independent entity on the market. This can be a nuanced question, but relevant factors to consider include:

- whether the joint venture has sufficient resources (eg, staff, facilities and finance) to operate independently of its parents;
- whether its activities are beyond a specific function of the parents;
- whether it has sale and purchase relations with its parents; and
- whether it operates on a lasting basis rather than for a short duration.[9]

Joint acquisitions of assets (eg, a gas field) that are not yet in production and that cannot access the market, or entry into a joint operating agreement,[10] are unlikely to meet the full functionality criterion.[11] By contrast, a joint venture to independently

6 EU Merger Regulation, Article 3(4).

7 Case No IV/M.672 – *BP/Sonatrach*, 12 February 1996.

8 Case Comp/M.3230 – *Statoil/BP/Sonatrach/In Salah JV*, 19 December 2003.

9 Consolidated Jurisdictional Notice, Paragraphs 91 to 109.

10 However, if a joint operating agreement gives the joint venture the autonomy to determine the commercial sale of offtakes on the market, it may have the requisite level of full functionality. See, for example, Case Comp/M.5740 – *Gazprom/A2A/JV*, 16 June 2010.

11 See, for example, Case Comp/M.6910 – *Gazprom/Wintershall/Target Companies*, 3 December 2013, Paragraph 10.

produce LNG and sell it to third parties is likely to have the required element of full functionality.[12]

The joint control and full functionality requirements must both be met for a notifiable merger to arise. If, for example, a minority joint venture partner does not have any strategic vetoes over the newly formed joint venture, no notifiable merger arises. Similarly, if there is joint control but the joint venture is not full function (eg, if it produces oil or gas for the parents to sell on their own account), there will likely be no notifiable merger. However, in this respect, changes in the status of the joint venture down the track can give rise to a filing obligation. For example, in 2002 BP, Chevron, Eni, Sonangol and Total established a joint venture for the production of LNG in Angola. When initially established, the LNG was intended to be supplied only to the parents, meaning that it was not a full function joint venture. However, subsequently the parents decided to extend the joint venture's activities to marketing of LNG to third parties. This meant that the joint venture had gained full functionality and was now notifiable. Accordingly, the parties applied for, and the European Commission granted, clearance in 2012.[13]

The structure of the EU merger regime means that in many instances a joint venture (either greenfield or existing) that has limited or no actual or potential sales or presence in the EU can require notification simply due to the fact that the joint venture parents meet the EU thresholds. For example, a joint acquisition by BP, Shell and a subsidiary of Lufthansa of a low value local 'into-plane' software business operating at a single airport in Germany was notifiable to the European Commission on the basis of the parents' turnover.[14] Similarly, an acquisition of a natural gas gathering and processing business active solely in Texas and New Mexico was notified to the European Commission on the basis of the parents' turnover.[15]

Global considerations: As noted, the treatment of joint ventures varies significantly between countries. While some jurisdictions have specific provisions for treatment of joint ventures, joint ventures might be notifiable in other countries only if they fit into a more general definition of what constitutes a merger. Some considerations in the establishment of joint ventures globally therefore include the following:

- Control rights: As in the EU, some jurisdictions require an element of joint control for a joint venture to amount to a merger. A notable example is China, where the competition agency's guidance states that newly formed joint ventures will amount to mergers if at least two undertakings jointly control the new business.[16]
- Ownership percentages: By contrast, some jurisdictions do not require any form of joint control but rather (as in the case of other acquisitions) state bright-line ownership percentages where notifications may arise. Countries such as South Korea (as noted above) operate such systems.

---

12 See, for example, Case Comp/M.6477 – *BP/Chevron/Eni/Sonangol/Total/JV*, 16 May 2012, Paragraph 8.
13 Case Comp/M.6477 – *BP/Chevron/Eni/Sonangol/Total/JV*, 16 May 2012.
14 Case Comp/M.5182 – *Shell/BP/AFS/Globefuel*, 11 July 2008.
15 Case Comp/M.8800 – *Goldman Sachs/Riverstone Investment Group/Lucid Energy Group II*, 7 February 2018.
16 Ministry of Commerce Merger Control Guidelines.

- Full functionality: The full functionality requirement principally arises in the EU and many of its member states. However, full functionality is also a requirement in a number of other countries worldwide, such as Albania, Serbia and Singapore (although Singapore operates a voluntary notification regime).
- Existing businesses and greenfield joint ventures: Not all merger control regimes will capture the establishment of a greenfield joint venture, meaning that only joint acquisitions of existing businesses will be captured. For example, in India, only the acquisition of an 'enterprise' constitutes a merger, meaning that greenfield joint ventures are unlikely to be captured.[17]

(d) Other agreements

In certain circumstances, something less than a sale of shares or assets, or the establishment of a joint venture, can amount to a merger. For example, agreements such as loans and licences could raise merger control issues in one or more jurisdictions if they include provisions that, in effect, give some form of control over a business or assets.

In some instances, certain restrictions or agreements that are related to a merger may also require consideration under competition laws. In this regard, restrictions that are directly related and ancillary to the merger should be distinguished from other agreements that, while related to the business of the merged company or joint venture, are not directly related to the merger itself.

It is common for transaction documentation to contain certain provisions that are directly related to the merger, such as non-compete obligations or transitional supply or offtake agreements. In some jurisdictions, a clearance decision will be deemed to cover such ancillary restraints too. For example, a clearance decision from the European Commission is deemed to cover "restrictions directly related and necessary to the implementation of the transaction".[18] In this regard, merger parties are generally required to 'self-assess' whether restraints meet this criteria, unless they present genuinely novel issues in which case the parties can request that the European Commission directly address them.[19]

Transitional supply agreements are particularly relevant in the oil and gas sector and the European Commission recognises that there can be disruptions to sources of supply as the result of a merger. As long as they meet specified criteria, the Commission will view such transitional supply agreements as ancillary to a merger, but they "must be limited to a period necessary for the replacement of the relationship of dependency by autonomy on the market".[20] In the case of supply agreements, the Commission generally sees a period of five years as justifiable as ancillary.[21] That said, in exceptional circumstances the Commission might see a

---

17 Competition Act 2002 (India), Section 5.
18 EU Merger Regulation, Articles 6(1)(b), 8(1) and 8(2).
19 See Commission Notice on restrictions directly related and necessary to concentration, 5 March 2005.
20 See Commission Notice on restrictions directly related and necessary to concentration, 5 March 2005, Paragraph 33.
21 See Commission Notice on restrictions directly related and necessary to concentration, 5 March 2005, Paragraph 33.

longer period as justified. For example (under a previous regime where the Commission expressly approved ancillary restraints in its merger decisions), the Commission approved supply agreements of more than five years in circumstances where it could take a considerable time (potentially longer than five years) to identify an alternative source of supply[22] and when there were no alternative and viable sources of supply.[23]

Generally speaking, the Commission will not see exclusive supply agreements, agreements for unlimited quantities or preferred supplier/purchaser arrangements as ancillary.[24]

If a provision cannot be cleared as ancillary, this does not mean it automatically breaches competition law – it simply means that it may require a more detailed analysis of its impact on competition. Further, in many other jurisdictions, such as China and South Korea, a merger decision will not cover ancillary restraints, meaning that parties should separately consider whether substantive competition issues are raised by such provisions.

In other circumstances, agreements might have a relationship with the merger but in fact be separate agreements. For example, joint venture parties engaged in the exploration of a new gas field might seek to enter into a number of supply agreements with third parties before making their final investment decision. The provisions of such supply agreements will be subject to competition law more generally and the parties should consider whether they raise any issues. Particular care should be taken with parties that could potentially be seen as dominant, when entering into long-term supply agreements and when entering into agreements with actual or potential competitors. Another area that has attracted antitrust attention previously is profit sharing and diversion clauses in supply agreements and parties should ensure that such clauses are fashioned in a way that minimises their competition law risk.[25]

3.3 Types of thresholds and voluntary jurisdictions

The simple fact that a transaction is a qualifying merger in one or more jurisdictions does not necessarily mean it needs to be notified. A transaction will be notifiable in jurisdictions with mandatory merger control only if it meets the jurisdictional thresholds. Most commonly, jurisdictional thresholds will be based on the worldwide and local turnovers of the merger parties. However, other jurisdictions have thresholds based on other factors such as market shares, asset values and transaction values.

In addition to mandatory filings, it will sometimes be necessary to consider whether voluntary filings should be made in some jurisdictions. This will generally require an assessment of the potential competition issues raised by the transaction

---

22 See Case IV/M.612 – *RWE-DEA/Augusta (II)*, 27 July 1995 where a seven-year supply agreement was considered to be ancillary.

23 See Case COMP/M.2269 – *Sasol/Condea*, 30 January 2001.

24 See Commission Notice on restrictions directly related and necessary to concentration, 5 March 2005, Paragraph 34.

25 See, for example, European Commission press release relating to clauses in Algerian LNG contracts, 11 July 2007, http://europa.eu/rapid/press-release_IP-07-1074_en.htm.

and the risk of the competition agency 'calling in' the transaction after the parties have closed. Some voluntary jurisdictions, such as the United Kingdom, also operate jurisdictional thresholds that determine whether the competition agency can review a merger. However, other voluntary jurisdictions such as Australia and New Zealand do not have any such threshold, meaning that any merger is potentially reviewable.

3.4 The multi-jurisdictional merger control review

As noted, a single transaction can trigger merger filings in multiple jurisdictions globally. Therefore, the parties to a transaction may need to consider the application of merger control in various jurisdictions globally. For each relevant jurisdiction this requires an assessment of:

- whether the transaction is a qualifying merger for the purposes of that jurisdiction's merger control regime; and
- whether the transaction meets the jurisdictional thresholds in that jurisdiction.

The scope of the exercise needs to be determined before commencing the review. A useful starting point in this regard is generally to obtain a breakdown of revenue for each of the parties to the transaction for the most recent financial year. This will allow the initial review to focus on the jurisdictions where the parties have actual sales and in many cases will allow various countries to be excluded on the basis of thresholds not being met and/or the transaction not being a qualifying merger.

While a review of jurisdictions where the parties have turnover is a useful first step, this will not always be the end of the exercise. Various other factors may influence whether further review is required, including the following:

- The EU operates a so-called 'one-stop shop' for merger control. This means that if a transaction is notifiable to the European Commission, it does not need to be separately notified in any member states. However, if the transaction is not notifiable it is necessary to consider the application of merger control in each EU member state.
- Most thresholds are based on turnover of the merger parties in the most recently completed financial year. However, some jurisdictions also have thresholds based on, for example, market shares, asset values or transaction values. Given the 'lumpy' nature of supply and demand (particularly in the oil and gas industry), even if a business did not have any turnover in a particular jurisdiction in its last completed financial year, it may be necessary to consider its market share on the basis of a longer period of time or whether it has assets 'on the ground' in that particular country.
- In some cases – particularly borderline cases or cases where there is no local nexus, but thresholds are nevertheless met – the parties may decide to take a view as to whether to notify in that jurisdiction. This will ultimately be a judgement call based on the risk profiles of the companies involved and the parties may benefit from input from local counsel.

The parties should also consider with whom the responsibility for notifying the merger lies. In the majority of jurisdictions, the acquirer or acquirers (or the joint venture partners in the case of a new joint venture) are responsible for the notification. However, this is not always the case. In some jurisdictions – notably the United States, Brazil and Germany – the responsibility lies with the seller or target and the acquirer. While in practice the notification will usually still be made by the acquirer on behalf of all parties (except in the United States, where both parties must make separate filings), the fact that responsibility falls on all parties in those jurisdictions clearly enhances the incentive for the seller to get it right when carrying out the merger control review.

3.5 Mechanics of merger filings

In the vast majority of jurisdictions, merger filings require the parties to fill in a form that sets out a narrative description of the merger and the competitive impact of the transaction, including information such as:

- a description of the transaction and businesses of the parties;
- the rationale for the merger;
- the potential horizontal (ie, competitive) or vertical (ie, upstream and downstream) relationships between the parties;
- the relevant markets affected by the transaction; and
- the reasons why the transaction will not have a significant negative impact on competition.

In many jurisdictions, a streamlined filing form is available for cases that raise no significant competition issues (eg, if there is no or limited overlap between the parties or no local nexus). A notable exception to the 'narrative' filing is the United States, where the filing obligation largely requires the provision of existing documents to the competition agencies.

Merger parties also need to consider important timing and coordination issues when preparing merger filings. Clearly, the overall timeline for clearance in simple cases will be much quicker than in cases where issues arise, but the procedure can largely be split into three distinct periods:

- Filing preparation: The preparation of a filing can be a significant task, particularly where there are many markets affected. At EU level, simplified 'no-issues' filings can sometimes be prepared in a matter of weeks, but more complicated filings can take many months to prepare. The need to work these into the deal timetable emphasises the need to consider merger control early in the process.
- Pre-notification: In most jurisdictions, it is standard practice to provide a draft filing to the competition agency prior to formal filing. The parties can then work with the agency to ensure the filing contains all the information it requires before formal filing occurs. For simple cases, pre-notification can be a matter of days, but for more complicated cases it can extend for several months. While it is not clear at which point the first engagement with the European Commission was, Halliburton announced its proposed takeover of Baker Hughes in November 2014, but did not have its notification accepted as complete until November 2015 (an initial filing was rejected by the

Commission as incomplete in July 2015). This suggests a lengthy pre-notification period lasting for in excess of six months.

- Formal review: Once the formal filing is made and accepted as complete by the competition agency, it will be subject to statutory deadlines after which the agencies must make a decision. Most regimes have an initial Phase 1 review period, after which the competition agency will either clear the merger or refer it to a more in-depth Phase 2 review. The formal periods differ between jurisdictions, but by way of example, in the EU the initial Phase One period is 25 working days and the Phase Two period is 90 working days, although these periods can be and often are extended for various reasons, including if remedies are submitted or by agreement of the parties.

The potential for multiple filings to be required, along with the differing time periods for each filing, means that it is important for the merger parties to coordinate all filings. As well as coordinating on timing, it is important to coordinate on content. Competition agencies generally coordinate with one another when reviewing the same merger. Therefore, it is important to ensure that filings globally portray a consistent message to each competition agency.

3.6 Substantive assessment

The multi-jurisdictional merger control assessment is purely a question of which competition agencies have jurisdiction to review a transaction. It does not deal with the question of the substantive assessment of that transaction – that is, whether it actually raises competition law concerns.

The substantive assessment of any given transaction is heavily fact dependent – the vast majority of notified cases will raise no competition issues, while others may raise significant concerns. In the context of this chapter, therefore, it is possible to provide only a high-level overview of the approach that competition agencies globally tend to take when assessing mergers and the potential theories of harm that could be raised.

As an initial step, competition agencies tend to define a 'relevant market', which represents the sphere of competition in which the merger parties operate. The market as defined helps to guide the analysis of the transaction and helps to inform the competition agency as to where the merger parties' key competitive constraints come from. Generally, there are two key elements to market definition:

- Product market: The product market represents the precise line of business and level of the supply chain impacted. For example, in the oil and gas context, product markets could range from upstream exploration for oil and gas[26] to downstream activities such as refining.[27]
- Geographic market: The geographic market represents the geographic scope of competition associated with the product market and can be anything from narrow local markets to worldwide markets. For example, upstream activities

26 The European Commission has defined "the exploration of crude oil and natural gas" as a product market – see, for example, Case COMP/M.5629 – *Normeston/MOL/MET JV*, 11 December 2009.

27 The European Commission has defined a number of separate product markets for different fuel and non-fuel products – see, for example, Case COMP/M.4934 – *Kazmunaigaz/Rompetrol*, 19 November 2007.

such as exploration and production of oil and gas are often considered to take place on a worldwide basis,[28] whereas downstream activities such as refining can be regional,[29] national or even narrower (eg, retail supply of petrol may be defined on a very narrow local basis).

Once a competition agency has defined the relevant market or markets, it will generally consider the application of a number of theories of harm to the merger. Generally, these can be split into 'horizontal' and 'vertical' theories of harm.

Horizontal concerns potentially arise when the merger parties are active at the same level of the market, meaning that the merger reduces the competitive pressure that they place on one another with the potential for higher prices and lower quality. Whether this loss of competition is enough to cause a significant competition issue will depend on a number of factors, such as the market shares of the merger parties, the closeness of competition between them, the competitive constraint provided by third parties and the potential for new entry into the market.

Vertical theories of harm arise when the merger parties are active upstream and downstream of one another, such that the merger leads to new vertical integration in the market. In assessing vertical theories of harm, competition agencies consider whether the transaction could lead to either input foreclosure, such that competing businesses lose access to a key input from the newly vertically integrated company; or customer foreclosure, such that the merger removes a potential customer for other competition businesses. In the oil and gas context, vertical issues may arise in the case of essential facilities, such as the acquisition of pipeline networks or LNG terminals by downstream users of those facilities.

3.7 Potential outcomes

Following the competition agencies' substantive review, the vast majority of transactions are cleared unconditionally. However, cases that do raise competition concerns may require the parties to provide some form of remedy to allay those concerns. In very rare cases, where no such remedy that satisfies both the merger parties and the competition agency can be found, a transaction may be blocked.

What, if any, remedy is appropriate in any given case will be heavily fact dependent. Potential remedies vary and can be categorised as either structural or behavioural. Structural remedies generally involve the divestment of a whole business in order to maintain an independent competitor on the market. Behavioural remedies, by comparison, tend to involve a promise to do or not to do something – for example, a promise to supply downstream competitors with inputs. As a general rule, competition agencies prefer the cleanness of structural remedies, which ensures that an independent competitor remains on the market without any need for ongoing monitoring.

Generally speaking, there is no obligation to offer remedies and it will be a

---

28 The European Commission has defined the exploration market as worldwide in scope – see, for example, Case COMP/M.5629 – *Normeston/MOL/MET JV*, 11 December 2009.

29 The European Commission has defined the market for crude oil refining to be EEA-wide – see, for example, Case COMP/M.4934 – *Kazmunaigaz/Rompetrol*, 19 November 2007.

business decision for the parties as to whether the remedies that would be required to clear the transaction meet their commercial objectives. For this reason, in some instances transactions have been abandoned because the remedies required to clear the deal meant that the transaction was no longer consistent with the merger parties' objectives. A notable recent example in this context was Halliburton's proposed acquisition of Baker Hughes, which was abandoned after the parties could not agree appropriate remedies with both EU and US competition agencies.

3.8 Treatment of state-owned companies

The prevalence of state-owned national oil companies means that the treatment of state-owned enterprises under merger control warrants special mention. In particular, the involvement of state-owned companies in transactions can raise questions as to whether a merger actually arises, how turnover is calculated and how the substantive competition impact of a merger is assessed.

In most cases, the question of whether a relevant merger arises should be straightforward – if only one merger party is a state-owned entity, it is clear that independent undertakings are being merged. However, the question is more difficult if both the acquirer and the target are enterprises owned by the same state – is this a merger of independent enterprises or simply an internal restructuring by the state? At the EU level, the key question is whether, prior to the transaction, the acquirer and target were both independent economic units with the power to make their own decisions on the market.[30] For example, in 1998 the European Commission considered the merger of Neste and IVO, which were both active in the oil and energy sectors.[31] Both companies were majority owned by the Finnish state. However, although both companies were owned by the Finnish state, the Commission took the view that each was able to act independently on the market and there was no indication that their conduct had been coordinated previously. Therefore, for EU purposes, this was a merger of independent companies.

A similar question arises in relation to the calculation of group turnover for a state-owned enterprise – does the turnover of just the business in question need to be taken into account for thresholds or do all state-owned enterprises need to be aggregated? As with the question of whether a merger itself actually arises, the key question in the European Union is whether the enterprise in question is an economic unit with an independent power of decision.[32] If it is, then only its own turnover needs to be taken into account. However, if the state coordinates the businesses of a number of enterprises, then it may be necessary to aggregate their turnover in assessing thresholds. This question also has an impact on the substantive assessment of the transaction – if several state-owned enterprises are considered as one single economic unit, their market positions will generally need to be aggregated to assess the competitive impact of the transaction. That is, they may be looked at as a single entity in the substantive competition analysis.

---

30 Consolidated Jurisdictional Notice, Paragraph 52.
31 Case IV/M.931 – *Neste/IVO*, 2 June 1998.
32 EU Merger Regulation, Recital 22.

Rosneft's acquisition of TNK-BP is a useful illustration of these points.[33] Rosneft was 75% owned by the Russian state and active in the exploration of crude oil and natural gas. The Russian state owned a number of other enterprises active in the oil and gas sector, namely Gazprom, Zarubezhneft and Transneft. The Commission's investigation suggested that the Russian state had significant powers to involve itself in Rosneft's commercial behaviour, including through the voting of its shares and the appointment of board members who were required by law to vote in accordance with the instructions of the Russian government. While the Commission did not reach a final view, it considered that these factors "strongly suggested" that Rosneft could not be deemed to have an independent power of decision from the Russian state. Given that Rosneft would have met the turnover thresholds regardless of whether its turnover was aggregated with other state-owned companies, the commission did not reach a final view on the correct turnover group. However, for its 'worst-case' substantive analysis of the transaction, the Commission considered Rosneft, Gazprom, Zarubezhneft and Transneft to be a single economic unit, meaning that their market positions were combined.

4. Transaction documentation

The outcome of both the due diligence risk review and the merger control assessment has an important bearing on the transaction documentation that is ultimately agreed. While in many cases commercial considerations and bargaining power as between the parties will dictate the exact extent of what is ultimately agreed, some of the key provisions that may be included or attract attention from a competition law perspective are set out below.

4.1 Merger control

The requirement for merger control clearance has the most important bearing on the transaction documentation from a competition perspective – if the result of the merger control review is that one or more mandatory and suspensive competition filings are required, it will be important to include a condition precedent to ensure that closing cannot take place until clearance is received. The precise scope of that condition precedent, as well as the extent of other competition clauses, will depend on a number of factors such as the time at which the merger control review is completed (eg, was the agreement executed prior to the merger control review being finalised?), the extent to which the transaction raises substantive competition issues rather than a technical 'no-issues' filing, and the relative bargaining power of the parties.

Set out below are the key categories of clause relating to merger control that may be included.

(a) Conditions precedent

The most important inclusion in any agreement will be an appropriate condition precedent, ensuring that the transaction cannot close until all relevant merger clearances are obtained. Such conditions precedent can take many forms and the precise wording that is adopted will be highly deal specific. For example, if the full

33 Case COMP/M.6801 – *Rosneft/TNK-BP*, 8 March 2013.

merger control review has not been completed before the agreement is concluded, the condition may simply specify that the transaction cannot complete until all relevant clearances are received or waived – for example:

The agreement to purchase the [Shares/Assets] is conditional on …

such written consents, orders, clearances, authorisations or exemptions as may be necessary in order for Completion to occur [in terms satisfactory to the Buyer].

In cases where the list of required filings is known prior to signing, the parties may decide to list the requisite filings. Parties should also be careful to adopt the appropriate language for the relevant jurisdictions. For example, in the United States, a transaction can close once the waiting period under the Hart-Scott-Rodino Antitrust Improvements Act has expired, whereas in most other jurisdictions the competition agency must issue a formal clearance decision before closing can occur.

If the parties make voluntary non-suspensive notifications, such as in the United Kingdom, they will need to decide between themselves whether the transaction will be conditional on clearance or whether they are happy to close the deal and either:

- notify later, thereby taking the risk of the competition agency imposing remedies, including potentially to unwind the transaction; or
- not notify at all.

(b) Cooperation clauses

In most jurisdictions, a merger filing will be prepared and submitted by the purchaser. However, in preparing the filing and dealing with the competition agencies, the purchaser will usually require input and assistance from the target or seller. To this end, it is common for the parties to include a clause under which the parties agree to cooperate in relation to dealings with the competition agencies. Again, how far this clause needs to go will depend on the extent of potential competition issues present. Variations of these clauses may be required for different transaction structures or jurisdictions. For example, in the case of a joint venture, the joint venture parties will generally make a joint notification and will need to cooperate in doing so.

(c) Break fees

In transactions that raise substantive competition concerns and where there is no guarantee of obtaining clearance, the parties may like to consider a break fee, under which the purchaser is required to pay the target or seller a fee in the event that the transaction is abandoned due to competition law concerns. Depending on the value of the transaction, such fees can be significant. For example, when Halliburton and Baker Hughes called off their $35 billion merger in 2016 due to competition concerns in both the United States and the EU, Baker Hughes was required to pay Halliburton a $3.5 billion break fee.[34] These fees will clearly incentivise the purchaser to push as hard as possible to get the transaction through the antitrust agencies.

34 "Halliburton and Baker Hughes Announce Termination of Merger Agreement", Halliburton press release, 1 May 2016, www.halliburton.com/public/news/pubsdata/press_release/2016/halliburton-baker-hughes-terminate-merger.html.

(d) ***'Hell or high water' clauses***

In some instances, particularly where the seller or target has significant bargaining power, the parties may include a so-called 'hell or high water' clause, under which the purchaser is required to take all steps necessary to obtain clearance, including submitting remedies to the relevant competition agencies. A 'lighter' version of such clauses could see the purchaser being obliged to submit remedies (eg, divestments of businesses) up to a certain value.

(e) ***Long-stop date***

Transactions will generally have a 'long-stop' date for a number of reasons. Merger control obligations can, in some circumstances, hinder the ability of the parties to satisfy all conditions precedent prior to the long-stop date, so the parties may wish to consider including an ability for the long-stop date to be extended if merger clearance is not received in time.

(f) ***Provision for post-completion filings***

As well as the clauses listed above, a number of other clauses may need to be considered depending on where filings are made. For example, if any post-completion filings will be made and competition issues are foreseen, the parties may like to provide for what happens if the agency raises concerns post-closing.

4.2 Warranties and indemnities

As discussed earlier in this chapter, it is prudent for the due diligence process to include a review of competition law risks – in respect of either ongoing competition law investigations or potential competition law business risks. Again, the extent of what comes to light during due diligence and the relative bargaining power of the parties will inform precisely what level of warranties and indemnities are included.

4.3 Other provisions

As set out further above, other provisions in the transaction or associated documents may raise competition issues in themselves. For example, restraints of trade can raise concerns depending on their scope and duration. In certain circumstances they may be ancillary to a merger, while in others more detailed competition advice should be sought.[35]

Notably, ongoing relationships between a divested target and a seller, such as supply and offtake arrangements, may benefit from competition law review. While in some instances they may be justified as ancillary to the merger,[36] in others cases they may require a more detailed review of their impact on competition.

5. Foreign direct investment protection

It is not just competition law issues that may require pre-merger clearance. Merger

35 See Commission Notice on restrictions directly related and necessary to concentration, 5 March 2005, Paragraphs 18 to 26.

36 See Commission Notice on restrictions directly related and necessary to concentration, 5 March 2005, Paragraphs 32 to 35.

parties should also be alert to the foreign direct investment regimes that are in place or developing in various countries globally and therefore consider whether non-competition filings may also be required. Broadly speaking, these regimes are intended to control foreign ownership of critical national infrastructure and/or the broader national interests of the country in question, such as national security.

One of the most significant such regimes is that in the United States, where the Committee on Foreign Investment in the United States (CFIUS) can review the national security implications of foreign investments into the United States. Clearly, oil and gas will be important to US national security and CFIUS can be expected to carefully consider some international acquisitions into US oil and gas companies, as it did when it imposed conditions on Chinese state-owned company CNOOC's takeover of Canadian oil and gas company Nexen Inc in 2013.[37]

In the EU, the merger regime does not itself allow non-competition issues to be taken into account. However, Article 21 of the EU Merger Regulation allows member states to take appropriate measures to protect their own national interests, with public security, media plurality and prudential rules specifically noted as legitimate interests. Separately, the European Commission has recently proposed a regime that allows member states to implement mechanisms to review foreign investments, including on the basis of public order or national security. If member states elect to implement such a regime, the proposal provides a framework for doing so and also allows the Commission to issue an opinion to member states on certain transactions, which must be taken into account.[38] At the time of writing, this regime is working its way through the EU's legislative process and it remains to be seen when and in what form it will be implemented. While this is a long way off the CFIUS regime, this represents the first EU-wide step towards a wider foreign direct investment regime.

At the time of writing, the United Kingdom is considering its foreign direct investment regime for after it leaves the EU. Other jurisdictions with foreign direct investment regimes (which may include political control over oil and gas acquisitions) include Russia, Germany, Canada, Australia and New Zealand.

37 Although CFIUS does not publish decisions, this case was widely reported on by the press. For example, see www.reuters.com/article/us-nexen-cnooc/cnooc-nexen-deal-wins-u-s-approval-its-last-hurdle-idUSBRE91B0SU20130212.

38 European Commission proposal for a regulation establishing a framework for review of foreign direct investments into the European Union, 2017.

About the authors

Robert Aulsebrook
Partner, Akin Gump Strauss Hauer & Feld
raulsebrook@akingump.com

Robert Aulsebrook is head of international finance and a partner at Akin Gump Strauss Hauer & Feld in London. He advises clients on a wide variety of cross-border lending, debt capital markets and derivatives transactions, with particular experience in energy-related financings in emerging markets.

He has advised many clients on financing acquisitions of upstream and downstream oil and gas assets in various jurisdictions around the world. He recently advised the sponsor on the construction of a gas-processing plant in Uzbekistan and previously advised on the development of oil and gas fields in the Caspian Sea off the coast of Azerbaijan.

Fluent in Russian, he has worked in the Russian market for more than 25 years. He is a solicitor of the Senior Courts of England and Wales and an attorney qualified in New York. He received his BA *magna cum laude* from Vanderbilt University and his JD *cum laude* from Georgetown University.

Paul Bannister
Director, acquisitions and divestitures, GMP FirstEnergy
ppbannister@gmpfirstenergy.com

Paul Bannister joined FirstEnergy in early 2010 and has been involved in a range of M&A and acquisition and divestiture (A&D) transactions in the upstream oil and gas sector across multiple jurisdictions. Prior to this, Mr Bannister spent a decade gaining technical and commercial experience at both Schlumberger and Expro North Sea. During this period, Mr Bannister held a number of different roles and was based in a variety of locations across Europe, Africa and the Middle East, the most recent of which entailed management of an internal business unit providing data consulting and technical support to reservoir engineering and flow assurance projects. Mr Bannister attained a first-class honours degree in environmental chemistry and an MSc in petroleum engineering from Heriot Watt University. He is a member of the Society of Petroleum Engineers (SPE) and the European Petroleum Negotiators Group (EPNG).

Mary Bartle
Senior associate, Clifford Chance LLP
mary.bartle@cliffordchance.com

Mary Bartle is a senior associate in the M&A corporate group of Clifford Chance in London. She holds a BA in international relations and a JD in law. Prior to joining Clifford Chance, she spent several years advising on an array of corporate transactions in Vancouver, with a practice focused in particular on mergers and acquisitions involving listed natural resources companies.

In London, she regularly advises listed companies in a variety of sectors, with a focus on M&A transactions governed by the UK City Code on Takeovers and Mergers. She has also advised on private M&A transactions and investments, including in the alternative energy sector.

Mark Beeley
Partner, Orrick, Herrington & Sutcliffe (UK) LLP
mbeeley@orrick.com

International dispute resolution partner Mark Beeley primarily focuses on disputes arising in the energy sector (he is described by *Chambers & Partners UK 2018* as "an excellent litigator" who knows "oil and gas inside out"). He regularly acts in disputes involving production sharing contracts, joint operating agreements, and farm-in/out agreements, as well as litigating matters under investment agreements/treaties. In addition, he has significant experience with construction, insurance, shareholder and white-collar/civil fraud matters as part of a broader commercial practice.

He has sat as an arbitrator (including as chair) in multiple cases, but primarily practises as counsel and advocate both in arbitrations and in English and Dubai International Financial Centre court proceedings (as well as supervising proceedings in other jurisdictions).

Recognised and ranked by *Chambers & Partners* (since 2012) and the *Legal 500* (since 2009) for his international arbitration practice, Mr Beeley has also been recognised as a foreign expert in disputes in both the United Arab Emirates and India by *Chambers*.

Paul Culliford
Associate, Bryan Cave Leighton Paisner LLP
Paul.Culliford@blplaw.com

Paul Culliford is a New Zealand-qualified associate based in Bryan Cave Leighton Paisner's Brussels office since Spring 2015, where he specialises in antitrust and competition law. He has experience in all aspects of competition law, including merger control, restrictive practices, investigations and general compliance. Mr Culliford has advised clients active in all areas of the oil and gas industry, from exploration to retail, on mergers and acquisitions and competition law more generally.

Jubilee Easo
Legal director, Eversheds Sutherland
JubileeEaso@eversheds-sutherland.com

Jubilee Easo is a legal director at Eversheds Sutherland. She is an experienced international oil and gas lawyer, having advised state oil and gas entities, international oil and gas companies and financial institutions on a wide range of upstream and downstream acquisitions and developments, LNG development projects and offshore LNG projects. Jubilee has worked for leading law firms in London as well as in-house with oil and gas developers. In 2015, Jubilee was recognised in *The Lawyer* Hot 100 for her work in the energy sector. She was also recognised as a London Rising Star by Super Lawyers in 2013.

Marc Hammerson
Partner, Akin Gump Strauss Hauer & Feld LLP
mhammerson@akingump.com

Marc Hammerson is a solicitor and partner at Akin Gump Strauss Hauer & Feld LLP in London. He is an experienced upstream energy lawyer specialising in both M&A and project development. He has worked in private practice and in-house, and was based in the Far East in the early 2000s. Mr Hammerson has degrees in law from Manchester University and the London School of Economics, and is a member of the Association of International Petroleum Negotiators.

Andrew Hockley
Partner, head of Antitrust and Competition,
Bryan Cave Leighton Paisner LLP
andrew.hockley@bclplaw.com

Andrew Hockley is the head of the Antitrust and Competition group at Bryan Cave Leighton Paisner LLP. He has extensive experience in advising on merger control and other antitrust and regulatory issues in the oil and gas sector. Prior to joining the firm as a partner in 2010, he was competition counsel at BP plc in London, responsible for advising all areas of the business on competition law and regulatory matters.

Mr Hockley holds postgraduate qualifications in competition law and economics from Kings College London. He is an English-qualified solicitor and a former member of the Brussels Bar, and contributes actively to numerous competition and regulatory law publications, organisations and events. He is recognised as one of the United Kingdom's leading competition lawyers by *Global Competition Review Who's Who 2018* and as a leading individual (Tier 1) by *Legal 500 UK 2018*.

Joanna Kay
Of counsel, Orrick, Herrington & Sutcliffe (UK) LLP
jkay@orrick.com

Joanna Kay, of counsel in the London office of Orrick, Herrington & Sutcliffe, works in the firm's oil and gas practice and advises on domestic and international transactions, including country entry, mergers and acquisitions, joint ventures, LNG project developments and sales contracts. Prior to joining Orrick, she was an in-house lawyer in a FTSE 100 exploration and production company based in London, where she focused on upstream asset work and frontier exploration opportunities in a number of different jurisdictions. She is a committee member of the UK Energy Lawyers Group and has contributed to a number of leading oil and gas market publications.

Paula Kidd
Senior associate, CMS Cameron McKenna Nabarro Olswang LLP
Paula.Kidd@cms-cmno.com

Paula Kidd is a senior associate who specialises in oil and gas law, particularly in relation to mergers and acquisitions in the United Kingdom.

Ms Kidd has extensive experience in oil and gas law in M&A transactions, upstream projects and the industry more generally. She has been involved in a number of transactions which, due to recent trends in the United Kingdom, have involved retention of decommissioning liability structures.

Ms Kidd is also noted for her expertise in decommissioning security arrangements, having assisted in updating the Oil & Gas UK Industry Standard Joint Operating Agreement in 2013 to reflect decommissioning tax relief. She has experience of both field-wide and bilateral arrangements, and has been involved in advising on a number of bespoke arrangements.

John C LaMaster
Partner, Akin Gump Strauss Hauer & Feld LLP
jlamaster@akingump.com

John C LaMaster has over 30 years of experience in virtually all areas of the oil and gas industry, including upstream, midstream and downstream, throughout Europe, Africa, Russia and the former Soviet Union, the Middle East and the United States. Mr LaMaster is highly rated by various publications, including being one of only six lawyers rated Band 1 in Energy & Natural Resources: Oil & Gas in the 2017 edition of *Chambers & Partners*. Mr LaMaster is a frequent author on oil and gas subjects, including co-editing *Oil & Gas in Africa – A Legal and Commercial Analysis of the Upstream Industry* (2015) and *Oil and Gas Sale and Purchase Agreements* (2017), and contributing chapters to both of those books and several others. He holds a BA in economics and business administration from Vanderbilt University and a JD with honours from the Paul M Herbert Law Centre at Louisiana State University.

David Lewis
Partner, Clifford Chance LLP
david.lewis@cliffordchance.com

David Lewis has been a partner in the London office of Clifford Chance since 2003. He specialises in mergers and acquisitions and equity capital market transactions, with a primary focus on the oil and gas sector. Mr Lewis studied land economy and law at Downing College Cambridge.

David has advised on numerous M&A projects in both upstream and downstream. His recent experience includes advising Trans European Oil and Gas on its investment in IGas; Salamander Energy on its strategic review and the subsequent sale of a significant interest in one of its most material assets, which was then cancelled in favour of a competitive takeover process which was ultimately won by Ophir Energy; Gunvor in respect of its investments in PA Resources and its proposed acquisition of Chevron South Africa; Glencore on its takeover of Caracal Energy; and Dominion Petroleum on its takeover by Ophir Energy.

Mark W Llamas
Managing director, acquisitions and divestitures, GMP FirstEnergy
mwllamas@gmpfirstenergy.com

Mark Llamas joined FirstEnergy in November 2009 following 10 years of M&A and A&D advisory experience with Tristone Capital and Waterous & Co, where he was managing director of their respective London operations. Mr Llamas has managed projects across the globe including corporate M&A projects, production and development asset transactions, strategic alternative processes and exploration farm-outs. Previously, Mr Llamas gained 13 years of technical experience with Shell, where he held a variety of geological and geophysical roles in both exploration and development teams, and later as the lead geoscientist at a 3D visualisation centre located within Imperial College, London University serving both academia and the oil and gas industry. Mr Llamas holds an honours degree in geology and biology and an MSc in sedimentology, both from the University of London. He is a member of the Petroleum Exploration Society of Great Britain and serves as a member of the steering committee of the EPNG.

Christopher R K Moore
Managing director, Moyes & Co, Inc
cmoore@moyesco.com

Chris Moore is a managing director with upstream commercial advisers Moyes & Co, Inc. He provides a wide range of consulting services on technical, financial and economic issues, particularly fair market valuations and expert witness testimony. His experience in economic analysis includes many of the world's fiscal regimes.

Mr Moore read natural sciences at the University of Cambridge. He joined BP as a geologist in 1975 and later joined Tricentrol. He subsequently joined ARCO in London and then at its international headquarters in Plano, Texas, where he held a variety of technical, commercial and management positions before joining Moyes & Co.

Mr Moore is a fellow of the Geological Society and a member of the SPE, the American Association of Petroleum Geologists and the Association of International Petroleum Negotiators. He teaches at the University of Texas, where he is an adjunct professor in the School of Law, and at the University of Texas at Dallas.

Caroline-Lucy Moran
Counsel, Akin Gump Strauss Hauer & Feld LLP
cmoran@akingump.com

Caroline-Lucy Moran practises as counsel in the cross-border transactions department of Akin Gump Strauss Hauer & Feld LLP in London. She specialises in international mergers and acquisitions, joint ventures and project development, with a focus on upstream and downstream oil and gas and power sectors.

Ms Moran was named an "Associate to watch" in the 2018, 2017 and 2016 editions of *Chambers & Partners UK* and won the Rising Star: Corporate award at the Euromoney/IFLR Women in Business Law Awards 2016.

Ms Moran has worked on transactions throughout Europe, Asia, the Middle East and

Africa while based in London, Milan and Singapore. She has worked in-house on secondment at one of the world's largest investment firms and also at one of the largest energy corporations.

Ms Moran graduated from the University of Oxford in 2006 and was admitted as a solicitor of the senior courts of England and Wales in 2010.

Maarten Overmars
Associate, Latham & Watkins
maarten.overmars@lw.com

Maarten Overmars is an associate in the corporate department of Latham & Watkins LLP in London. He holds a degree in corporate law and has specialised in private equity transactions while based in London and Amsterdam, with a particular focus on investments by private equity sponsors in the oil and gas industry. In addition, he also advises frequently on stock options and other forms of share-based compensation, including international aspects of stock-based incentivisation and tax-efficient management incentives for private equity-sponsored companies. He is admitted to the Bar in both England and Wales and the Netherlands.

Alexander Reid
Partner, HFW
alexander.reid@hfw.com

Alexander Reid is a partner in the energy and resources department of HFW. He has significant experience advising clients on a range of cross-border corporate and commercial transactions, including share and asset acquisitions and disposals, restructurings, joint ventures, commercial contracts and projects, with a particular focus on the energy and resources, transport and technology sectors. His experience in the energy sector covers a variety of upstream sale and purchase agreements, project development and oilfield services contracts, joint ventures and downstream agreements. He is qualified in England and Wales, and – having previously practised in London, Paris, Shanghai and Stockholm – is currently based in the Middle East.

Chris Searle
Partner, BDO LLP
Chris.Searle@bdo.co.uk

Chris Searle is a partner in the corporate finance department of BDO LLP in London, where he specialises in transaction services work involving due diligence on acquisitions and reporting accountant work on initial public offerings (IPOs) and subsequent transactions. He has specialised in this type of work for 30 years, during which time he has worked on over 100 IPOs. In undertaking such work, he has worked with companies of all sizes in a wide range of sectors.

Mr Searle chairs the Technical Committee of the Corporate Finance Faculty of the Institute of Chartered Accountants in England and Wales and is a member of the faculty's executive board.

Tamer A Soliman
Partner, Mayer Brown LLP
tsoliman@mayerbrown.com

Tamer Soliman is a partner in Mayer Brown's Washington DC and Dubai offices, global head of the firm's export control and sanctions practice, and a member of the international trade practice. He advises corporate and government clients on a wide range of international trade issues governing cross-border investments, joint ventures and sales, manufacturing and the development of emerging technologies.

His practice focuses on export control, sanctions and related national security restrictions on trade. Mr Soliman has handled complex export control and sanctions regulatory issues and enforcement proceedings spanning multiple jurisdictions. He advises clients in a wide range of industries, including aerospace and defence, sovereign wealth and investment funds, private equity, internet technology and logistics.

Mr Soliman is known for handling cutting-edge issues involving application of export comtrol and sanctions laws to both US and non-US entities, and has successfully advised boards, audit committees and companies in high-stakes investigations and enforcement actions.

Simon Tysoe
Partner, Latham & Watkins
simon.tysoe@lw.com

Simon Tysoe is a corporate partner and co-head of Latham & Watkins' global oil and gas industry group. He specialises in mergers and acquisitions and joint ventures in the energy sector, with a particular emphasis on advising private equity investors looking to invest into the industry. He has advised on private equity investments in the United States, Latin America, Africa and Europe. He has been consistently ranked in the legal directories as being among the leading oil and gas lawyers in the United Kingdom.

Julie Vaughan
Senior associate, Herbert Smith Freehills LLP
julie.vaughan@hsf.com

Julie Vaughan leads Herbert Smith Freehills' environmental advice in London and has been a practising lawyer for 24 years. Her environmental experience spans a broad range of regulatory regimes as well as health and safety regulation, and often involves her in significant oil and gas M&A transactions. She has considerable UK Continental Shelf offshore upstream experience, as well as in-depth involvement in onshore shale gas exploration and refineries, having also spent time seconded in-house to oil and gas client legal teams. She has a master's degree in international and European environmental and natural resources law from University College London, and is individually ranked in the leading legal directories.

Norman Wisely
Partner, CMS Cameron McKenna Nabarro Olswang LLP
Norman.Wisely@cms-cmno.com

Norman Wisely is a partner who specialises in all areas of oil and gas law, in particular oil and gas M&A work. Mr Wisely has extensive experience in advising clients on oil and gas matters in the United Kingdom and internationally, including leading numerous acquisitions and disposals of UK Continental Shelf and international offshore and onshore oil and gas assets, oil and gas-related share transactions, transportation and infrastructure projects, decommissioning and decommissioning security, licensing, production sharing and joint venture matters, product sales arrangements and all matters relevant to the exploration, production and sale of hydrocarbons.

Mr Wisely's predominant focus is on UK matters and given the recent trends in that market, his recent experience has included consideration of alternative M&A structures involving retention of decommissioning structures.

David Ziyambi
Senior associate, Latham & Watkins
david.ziyambi@lw.com

David Ziyambi is an associate in the London office of Latham & Watkins and a member of the firm's finance department and Africa practice. Mr Ziyambi's practice focuses on project finance, investment-grade real estate and leveraged finance. He holds a law degree from the University of Cambridge.

David's particular area of focus is on African financings in the project finance space and across the oil and gas value chain. He has advised on over $10 billion of financings in Nigeria's oil and gas sector alone.

Index

About Globe Law and Business

Globe Law and Business was established in 2005 as an imprint of Globe Business Media Group. We set out to create law books which are sufficiently high level to be of real use to the experienced professional, yet still accessible and easy to navigate. Most of our authors are drawn from Magic Circle and other top commercial firms, both in the UK and internationally.

In Autumn 2015, we had an exciting turn in our history when Globe Law and Business was bought by a management team which includes my colleague Jim Smith and me, Sian O'Neill.

We love books, and our hardback titles are carefully produced, with the utmost attention paid to the editorial, design and production processes. We hope this results in high-quality titles which are easy to read, and a pleasure to own.

Our customers and authors are of paramount importance – we are committed to devoting time and attention to each book as well as everyone involved in the publishing process.

We'd very much like to hear from you with your thoughts on our titles or ideas for improving what we offer. Please do feel free to email me on sian@globelawandbusiness.com with your views.

Sian O'Neill
Managing director
Globe Law and Business

www.globelawandbusiness.com

www.ingramcontent.com/pod-product-compliance
Ingram Content Group UK Ltd.
Pitfield, Milton Keynes, MK11 3LW, UK
UKHW062251150926
8656IPUK00007B/43

9 781787 421486